THE

Wealth
Inequality
READER

Edited by Dollars & Sense
and United for a Fair Economy

Preface by Jesse Jackson Jr.

DOLLARS & SENSE — ECONOMIC AFFAIRS BUREAU
CAMBRIDGE, MASSACHUSETTS

THE WEALTH INEQUALITY READER

Edited by Chuck Collins, Amy Gluckman, Meizhu Lui, Betsy Leondar-Wright, Amy Offner, Adria Scharf.

"Women's Property Property Rights Around the Globe" map. Reproduced from *The Penguin Atlas of Women in the World* by Joni Seager (Penguin, 2003). Copyright © Myriad Editions. www.MyriadEditions.com.

"How Wealth Defines Power," Kevin Phillips. Reprinted with permission from *The American Prospect*, Volume 14, Number 5: May 1, 2003. The American Prospect, 11 Beacon Street, Suite 1120, Boston, MA 02108. All rights reserved.

"The Tax-Cut Con," Paul Krugman. Copyright 2003, Paul Krugman. Reprinted by permission from *The New York Times Magazine*.

"Is Maximizing Returns to Shareholders a Legitimate Mandate?" Marjorie Kelly. Reprinted with permission from *Business Ethics*.

Tulsa photo reprinted with permission from the Tulsa Historical Society.

Photo by Ellen Shub. Copyright © 2004 by Ellen Shub. All other rights reserved.

Photo by Jim West. Copyright © 2004 by Jim West/jimwestphoto.com. All rights reserved.

ISBN: 1-878585-45-2

Published by:

Dollars & Sense
Economic Affairs Bureau
740 Cambridge Street
Cambridge, MA 02141
617-876-2434
dollars@dollarsandsense.org

United for a Fair Economy
37 Temple Place, 2nd Floor
Boston, MA 02111
617-423-2148
info@faireconomy.org

Cover and section illustrations: Doug Beekman
Production: Sheila Walsh
Manufactured by Capital City Press
Printed in the United States

Contents

Preface

BY JESSE JACKSON JR.

Wealth does matter.

It's the difference between being a tenant and a homeowner, a sharecropper and a shareholder.

It's the difference between buying a soda, wearing sneakers, or eating a hamburger—and owning Coca-Cola, Nike, or McDonalds.

It's what divides consumers standing in check-out lines from stakeholders who have a voice in the future of the economy.

As *The Wealth Inequality Reader* chronicles, our country's disparities of wealth and power are now at their greatest point since the 1920s. The richest 1% of the population now owns almost 35% of all the private wealth in America, more than the bottom 90% of the population combined.

The racial wealth divide is even more dramatic, underscoring how the legacy of discrimination in lending practices, business ownership, and employment has thwarted wealth-building opportunities for people of color. In 2001, the typical black household had a net worth of just $19,000, including home equity, compared with $121,000 for whites. Blacks had 16% of the median wealth of whites, up from 5% in 1989. This is progress, but at this rate it will take until 2099 to reach parity in median wealth.

The growth in wealth inequality is the result of two and a half decades of government policies tilted in favor of large asset owners at the expense of wage earners. Tax policy, trade policy, monetary policy, government regulations, and other rules have reflected this pro-investor bias. Under President George W. Bush, pro-rich policies have gotten worse, as Congress and the president funnel tax giveaways to their wealthy friends and donors.

It hasn't always been like this. Throughout U.S. history, our government has helped expand the wealth and security of many of its citizens. For example, after the Civil War, the government gave millions of acres of land to homesteaders. Then, in the two decades after World War II, massive government scholarships for higher education, and subsidies for small business development and affordable housing, greatly expanded the white middle class. These scholarships and subsidies, plus federally insured low-interest mortgages to homebuyers, enabled millions to get on board the wealth-building train. Unfortunately, discrimination in federal policies left red, brown, and black people standing at the train station during both historical periods.

We must work to overcome the perpetuation of wealth inequality. The accumulated advantages and disadvantages of wealth inequality are like sediment. The opportunities for those with wealth build up, layer upon layer, from the previous generation's wealth, education, and opportunity. And the accumulated disadvantages of having no wealth and savings deepen the hole of discrimination, poverty, debt, and blocked opportunity.

Inclusion is the key to economic growth. If people have adequate incomes and access to capital, they can buy homes and increase their stake in society. Instead of redlining low-income communities, let's green-line America and make the grass grow in scorched areas.

We know from research that the wealth of a child's parents has an enormous influence on his or her economic prospects. Only a bold approach to wealth building will dramatically reduce the number of "asset-less" households and create wealth-building opportunities for all those who have been left out.

Our challenge is to level the playing field, expand the marketplace, embrace the assurances of the American dream, and allow all to realize life, liberty, and the pursuit of happiness.

Jesse Jackson Jr. represents the 2nd Congressional District of Illinois in the U.S. House of Representatives. He is the author of A More Perfect Union: Advancing New American Rights *(Welcome Rain Publishers, 2001).*

Introduction

The United States entered the new millennium with the most unequal distribution of wealth since the eve of the Great Depression. This sorry fact forms the kernel of *The Wealth Inequality Reader*. The authors here—sociologists, economists, activists—analyze the issue of wealth inequality through multiple entry points and a range of disciplines.

Most discussions of inequality focus on income, not wealth, in part for the simple reason that data on income are more readily available. But wealth has its own dynamic, and its distribution has unique causes and consequences. More than income, wealth both tells of the past and foretells the future. A family's wealth today reflects the asset-building opportunities open not only to this generation, but to parents, grandparents, and great-grandparents. Likewise, parents use their wealth to position their children for future economic success in countless ways—moving into an excellent school district or giving an adult child money for a down payment, for example—that are out of reach for those who may earn a middle-class income but have few assets.

Given the country's severe and growing wealth gap, asset-building as a solution to poverty has recently come into vogue (although its chief policy incarnation, a matched savings plan known as an Individual Development Account, has yet to become more than a minor pilot program). This approach is in line with the individualistic ethos that reigns in U.S. politics. This volume describes IDAs plus a range of other policies than can help individuals accumulate assets. But more important, several of the authors here argue that the wealth gap cannot be addressed unless our shared public assets, which after all form the foundation of individual wealth, are expanded and redistributed.

1

Section I documents the worsening landscape of wealth inequality. Here are just a few items:

- In just 10 years, from 1992 to 2002, the average net worth of the wealthiest 400 Americans more than doubled in real terms, from $937 million to $2.15 billion.
- Between 1995 and 2001, white families saw their median net worth rise by 37% to $120,900, while families of color saw it fall by 7% to $17,100.
- Households headed by single men are far better off (median net worth $46,990) than households headed by single women (median net worth $27,850).
- In several East Asian countries, the richest 10 families control 30% or more of the country's total market capitalization; in Indonesia and the Philippines, the top 10 families control around 70%.

Although systematic data are scarce for many other parts of the world, the trend in the United States is clear: wealth is becoming more and more concentrated. The recent bear market in stocks trimmed a bit off the share of total wealth owned by the top 1% of American households between 1998 and 2001. (Of course, if and when the bubble in many regional housing markets bursts, plenty of average Americans whose home is their single largest asset will likewise see their net worth tumble.) But there is every reason to believe that wealth concentration will continue to grow, given the current direction of so many of the political-economic vectors that shape wealth distribution.

Why is the wealth gap in the United States widening now? It's not hard to see (and Section II fills in the details). For nearly 30 years following World War II, both the state and organized labor acted as counterweights to the power of corporations. Building on the legacy of the New Deal years, a range of government policies and a relatively stable business-labor compact moderated the excesses of the market, and as a result, a broad swath of Americans shared, at least to a degree, in the prosperity of the time.

But since the mid-1970s, determined efforts by conservatives and corporations have succeeded in dismantling parts of the New Deal legacy and crushing the labor movement. These efforts have both contributed to and benefited from the country's history of race discrimination. Playing "the race card" has been a key piece of the GOP's strategy for enlisting low- and moderate-income white voters against their own economic interests; meantime, conservative economic policies worsen the racial wealth gap, an artifact of centuries of slavery and post-slavery discrimination.

The consequences of the growing wealth gap are dissected in Section III. As we noted, inequality is usually conceptualized in terms of income. But wealth inequality matters at least as much as, if not more than, income inequality. For one thing, incomes are volatile, subject to the vicissitudes of the domestic business cycle and deepening global competition. In contrast, assets like a home, land, or savings offer a more stable form of security and allow families to survive financial setbacks without seeing their standard of living permanently undermined. Ownership and control of assets may be particularly important for members of historically disadvantaged groups; for example, a study in India has shown that women who own land or a house in their own names are, other things being equal, far less likely to be victims of domestic violence.

Furthermore, wealth inequality is self-reinforcing and worsens over time absent proactive efforts at redistribution. Wealth allows parents to give their children a wide range of advantages that position them to build even greater wealth as adults.

Extreme concentrations of wealth hurt not only those far down the economic ladder. Concentrated wealth distorts democracy, by giving a small elite both the motive and the means to buy the policies they want from contribution-hungry politicians. Concentrated wealth bites the hand that feeds it, too: evidence suggests that extreme wealth inequality actually undermines economic growth. And concentrated wealth spawns a culture of excessive consumption that subverts all of the nonmaterial values people find difficult enough to sustain in a modern capitalist economy.

While the picture up to this point may seem dismal, we need only look back to find cause for optimism. Throughout U.S. history, periods of excessive wealth polarization have been followed by mass movements for economic reform. The Gilded Age was followed by populism and progressivism; the 1929 crash was followed by poor people's movements and the New Deal. These movements for change succeeded, however unevenly, in moving the country's capitalist economy to a new equilibrium in which working people and the middle class had access to a larger morsel of the ownership pie than they otherwise would have (although, to be clear, wealth has never been divided near equitably, even in the country's most egalitarian eras).

Likewise, today, a movement to restructure the economy and reorient government policies so that wealth will be more widely shared is beginning to grow. "Movements" might be a more appropriate term: countless activists, scholars, unions, politicians (a few), and even businesspeople (a few) are engaging this issue from many angles. Sections IV and V sketch out some of these potential solutions, from the nuts and bolts of specific asset-building programs to visionary proposals for institutionalizing an overall more equitable distribution of wealth—for example, by collecting rents and fees from private interests who use common assets like the sky and the airwaves, then paying those revenues out to all.

For those who believe that two human beings can vary so widely in merit—however merit is defined—that one of them deserves to possess billions of dollars and a surfeit of mansions and jets while the other deserves to sleep on a sewer grate, the authors here will have little to say. But for anyone who is convinced that inherent in any definition of a just society are some limits to the unequal distribution of wealth, this volume provides a roadmap through—and, we hope, beyond—the current political economy of wealth.

SECTION I

Wealth Inequality by the Numbers

N ot since the Gilded Age has this country seen such a yawning gap between the very rich and those with little wealth. Global wealth disparities are even larger. The following pages capture this polarization with facts and figures on the distribution of wealth in the United States and, to the extent possible, worldwide.

The Wealth Pie

The wealthiest 1% of households owns almost a third of the nation's household wealth. The next tier, those in the 95th through 98th percentiles, claims another 25%. While the top 5% holds well over half of the wealth pie, the bottom 50% makes do with the crumbs—holding a meager 2.8% of total net worth.

Source: Arthur B. Kennickell, "A Rolling Tide."

BOTTOM 50%
2.8%

TOP 1%
32.7%

NEXT 40%
27.4%

NEXT 5%
12.1%

NEXT 4%
25.0%

ILLUSTRATIONS IN THIS SECTION BY NICK THORKELSON

What Is Wealth?

A family's wealth, or net worth, is defined as the sum of its assets minus its debts. In other words, wealth is "what you own" minus "what you owe." *Assets* are all resources that a household holds in store—the bank of reserves a family has available to invest in its members and their futures. Many assets grow in value and generate interest income. Just as important, asset wealth provides a cushion, protecting families from the vicissitudes of the business cycle, as wealth assets may be drawn down during periods of crisis (a job loss, for example). *Financial assets* include savings, bonds, certificates of deposit, stocks, mutual fund investments, retirement pensions, and the like. *Nonfinancial assets* may include homes, other real estate, vehicles, ownership in a privately held business, and all sorts of other property—from rare baseball card collections to jewelry or hobby equipment. *Debts* are liabilities—credit card balances, mortgages, and other loans—that are owed.

One way to think about wealth, as distinct from income, is to picture it as a pool of resources—much like a pond. Income, by contrast, is more like a stream or a river that flows. Most adults receive an income stream of paychecks, entitlement payments like Social Security, child support, or pensions. This cash flow is normally spent on housing, health care, food, clothing, consumer goods, entertainment, and miscellaneous expenses. If any trickle of income remains, it is set aside as savings—becoming wealth. People with large "ponds" of wealth typically receive streams of income in the form of interest, dividends, or rent from those assets. The very wealthy have "lakes" of assets that spring substantial rivers of income.

Looking at information about wealth can tell us a lot about people's lives, and it can tell us things that income statistics fail to reveal. The bottom quartile of

Different researchers use slightly different definitions of wealth. For example, some exclude those retirement pensions that an individual cannot currently access, while others include the estimated present value of pensions. And some scholars consider automobiles a form of wealth, whereas others exclude the value of automobiles from their calculations.

Data on wealth is far scarcer than data on income. The primary source of information on private wealth in the United States is the Federal Reserve's triennial Survey of Consumer Finances, which collects household-level data on assets, liabilities, income, use of financial services, and other household financial behavior.

U.S. families has a mean net worth of $0—an average family in the bottom quartile carries a debt burden equal to all of its assets combined. From this, we can surmise that such a family most likely does not own a home, or if they do, all of its value has been mortgaged or its market value has declined. If such a family owns any asset, it is probably a car that they had to borrow money to purchase. By contrast, a family in the second or third wealth quartile is likely to own a home as its largest asset. Families in the top quartile probably own not just one or more homes, but also stocks and other financial assets.

While private wealth is an important source of security in our society, *social wealth* can reduce and even eliminate the need for substantial individual or household wealth. For instance, an adequate social safety net that includes income support and health care would reduce the need for individual savings to ensure basic economic security.   —*Chuck Collins and Adria Scharf*

The Super-Rich

Over a 30-year period beginning in 1970, the richest 1% (as ranked by income) accrued a mounting share of the nation's private wealth. Throughout the 1990s, the top percentile held a larger concentration of total household wealth than at any time since the 1920s. Its wealth share declined somewhat during the 2001 recession, thanks to falling corporate share prices, but remained above 33%.

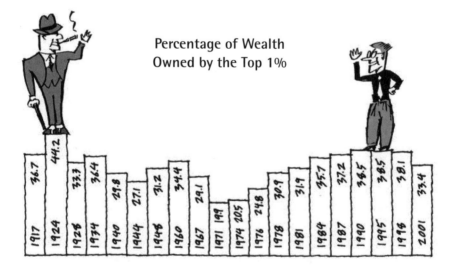

Percentage of Wealth
Owned by the Top 1%

Sources: Edward N. Wolff, *Top Heavy* (for 1917-1989); Wolff, "Recent Trends" (for 1992-1998); Wolff, "Changes in Household Wealth" (for 2001).

The past decade has been kind to the super-rich. Since 1992, the average wealth held by the nation's wealthiest 400 people more than doubled, rising from $937 million to a whopping $2.15 billion. Within the top 400, the highest ranked saw the largest gains.

The Wealthiest 400 People in the United States

Wealth by Rank and Average Wealth (in millions of 2001 dollars), 1992-2002

Wealth by Rank in the *Forbes* 400	1992	1995	1999	2000	2001	2002
1st	$7,746	$17,002	$89,716	$64,318	$54,000	$42,361
10th	$4,303	$4,940	$17,943	$17,356	$17,500	$11,723
50th	$1,537	$2,068	$4,222	$4,798	$3,900	$3,152
100th	$984	$1,034	$2,533	$2,654	$2,000	$1,773
400th	$326	$391	$660	$740	$600	$542
Avg. Wealth	$937	$1,025	$2,731	$3,057	$2,366	$2,148
Number of billionaires	92	107	278	301	266	205

Source: Arthur B. Kennickell, "A Rolling Tide." Calculated from the *Forbes* 400 and the Survey of Consumer Finances.

Households with Net Worth Equal to or Exceeding $10 Million

The number of households with $10 million or more has grown more than five fold since 1983 (from 66,500 to 338,400).

Source: Edward N. Wolff, "Changes in Household Wealth."

The Wealthless

The 1980s and 1990s were supposed to be economic good times, but the share of Americans with no wealth at all was larger in 2001 than it had been in 1983. The late-1990s economy gave a small boost to those at the bottom, but it didn't make up for the losses of the previous 15 years. The result: even after the 1990s—the most fabulous decade of economic growth in recent U.S. history—over a quarter of American households had less than $5,000 in assets.

Households with Little or No Net Worth, 1983–2001

	Percentage of Households with Zero or Negative Net Worth*	Percentage of Households with Net Worth Less Than $5,000*
1983	15.5%	25.4%
1989	17.9%	27.6%
1992	18.0%	27.2%
1995	18.5%	27.8%
1998	18.0%	27.2%
2001	17.6%	26.6%

* Constant 1995 dollars. Excluding the value of automobiles.

Source: Edward N. Wolff, "Changes in Household Wealth." Studies of wealth ownership define wealth differently. Because Wolff subtracts the value of automobiles, his figures show a higher percentage of the population with little or no wealth than studies that include cars as wealth.

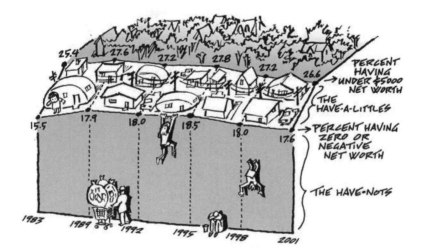

Class Mobility

LIKE PARENT, LIKE CHILD

In the United States, a sure way to secure a high income is to be born to parents with high incomes. Only 7.3% of children born to parents with incomes in the top 20% grow up to have incomes in the bottom 20%, no matter how lazy or incompetent they might be. Likewise, just 6.3% of children with parents in the bottom income quintile earn incomes in the top 20% as adults. So much for the myth of meritocracy.

If anything, these figures actually overstate the degree of income mobility in the United States. This is because it takes much more significant increases in income to enter the top quintile from the others than it takes to move up one, two, or even three quintiles from the bottom. In 1991, for example, the mean household income of the lowest quintile was $9,192 (2001 dollars), compared to $22,969 for the second quintile (a difference of $13,777). By contrast, the mean household income of the top quintile was $111,536, compared to $58,163 for the next highest quintile (a difference of $53,373—a much larger distance to travel). Although a large percentage of children born to parents in the bottom 20% move up a few quintiles as adults, their mobility is less striking than the *lack* of mobility into the top quintile.

Figures on mobility by wealth don't exist, but if they did, they'd probably paint an even bleaker picture.

Chance of Child Attaining Income Level as Adult, by Parental Income

Parents' Income Quintile	Child's Income Quintile as Adult		
	Top 20%	*Middle 20%*	*Bottom 20%*
Top 20%	37.3%	18.4%	7.3%
Middle 20%	17.3%	25.0%	15.3%
Bottom 20%	6.3%	16.5%	42.3%

Source: Thomas Hertz, "Rags, Riches and Race."

Note: These figures are based on total family income for black and white participants in the Panel Study of Income Dynamics who were born between 1942 and 1972, observed as children in their households of origin, and later as adults (26 or older) in their own households.

The Owning Class

While upwards of 90% of people in the United States make their living by work-ing for a wage or salary, a small number gain their incomes from the ownership of property. These large-scale property owners may have jobs (usually high-paying ones), but they do not *have* to work for a living. They own businesses, which yield profits; stocks, which yield dividends; real estate, which yields rent; and money, which yields interest. Unlike the houses and cars that are most Americans' primary assets, these forms of wealth typically accumulate income; they also give their owners, in varying ways and degrees, some control over the nation's economy.

Some of the 90% also own these kinds of property: a triple-decker or a small stock portfolio, perhaps. But ownership of income-accumulating property is even more highly concentrated than ownership of wealth overall. The income from such property is considerable—nearly $3 trillion in the United States in 2003, or over one-quarter of gross national income (even by the most conservative esti-mate). This is the tribute the owning class extracts each year from society's to-tal production.

Profits and other private property income have ranged between one-fourth and one-third of U.S. national income over the last 45 years. This variation may not seem like much, but when the private-property share of national income de-

Private Property Income (profits, interest, rent, etc., before taxes) as a Percentage of National Income, 1959-2003

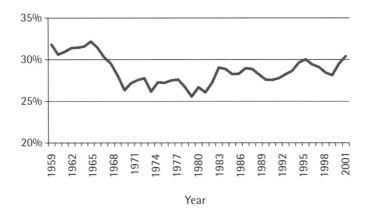

Year

Source: U.S. Dept. of Commerce, Bureau of Economic Analysis, National Income and Product Accounts, Table 1.10 Gross Domestic Income by Type of Income. Percentages equal "Net operating surplus, private enterprises" divided by the sum of itself and "Compensation of employees, paid."

clined sharply in the mid-1960s, as a result of high employment and rising worker militancy, U.S. capitalism went into crisis. The "recovery" beginning in the early 1980s coincided with property ownership garnering an increasing share of national income, as attacks on unions and social welfare programs eroded workers' bargaining power. In short, capitalism "functions" as long as the owning class can take a satisfactory cut of the national income.

THE STOCK OWNERSHIP PIE

If the distribution of wealth overall in the United States is very skewed, the distribution of financial assets such as stocks and bonds is far more so. A home is the single largest asset for most American families who have any wealth at all; most other kinds of assets are heavily concentrated in the hands of the wealthiest few percent of families. The chart shows the distribution of the nation's publicly traded stock that is directly held—in other words, outside of a managed account such as a mutual fund. The richest 1% of families owns over half of all directly held stock; the bottom 50% owns one-half of one percent. Assets not directly held—those in IRAs, 401(k)s, mutual funds, and similar accounts—are more equally distributed—among the wealthier half of the population. But the bottom 50% owns almost none of those assets either: only 0.9% of the value of mutual funds and 3.3% of the value of retirement accounts such as 401(k)s.

Share of Stock Owned, by Wealth Class (2001)

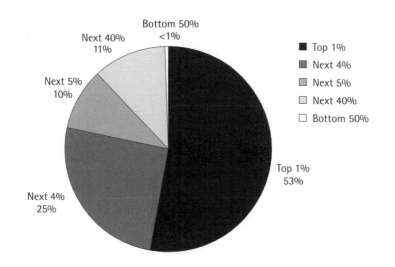

Source: Kennickell, "A Rolling Tide."

The Racial Wealth Gap

The United States has a racial wealth gap that far exceeds its racial income gap. This wealth gap persists even during periods of economic growth. In the 1990s boom, the wealth of families of color (nonwhite and Latino) actually *fell*. This intransigent wealth gap is the product of a long history of discrimination in the United States, and is perpetuated by family inheritance patterns that pass accumulated advantages and disadvantages from one generation to the next. The median net worth of families of color is just a fraction of white families', and racial wealth disparities are found across all categories of asset ownership.

Wealth vs. Income by Race, 1995–2001

		1995	1998	2001	$ change	% change
Median Net Worth	Families of color	$18,300	$17,900	$17,100	– $1,200	– 7%
	White families	$88,500	$103,400	$120,900	$32,400	37%
Median Income	Families of color	$23,000	$25,400	$25,700	$2,700	12%
	White families	$38,200	$41,100	$45,200	$7,100	18%

Source: Ana M. Aizcorbe, Arthur B. Kennickell, and Kevin B. Moore, "Recent Changes in U.S. Family Finances." Also see "African Americans Have Less Wealth and More Debt than White Americans," <www.faireconomy.org>.

The Racial Wealth Gap in 2001 (in 2000 dollars)

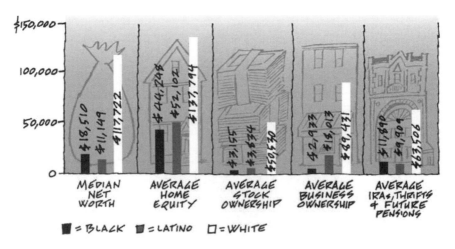

Source: 2001 Survey of Consumer Finances, analyzed by Bárbara Robles, LBJ School of Public Affairs at the University of Texas-Austin.

Women's Wealth

THE PENSION GAP

Pension wealth is the present value of expected future pension benefits, whether from a traditional defined-benefit plan or from a 401(k) or other defined-contribution plan. Today, a sharp gender gap characterizes the pension wealth of workers nearing retirement: men's median pension wealth is 76% higher than women's in this group. The gap reflects the labor-market experiences of these women: discrimination in hiring and promotions, lower wages, shorter job tenure.

As women enter the labor force in larger numbers, and as the income gap between women and men declines, the pension wealth gap will no doubt shrink. Just as the pension gap becomes less important, though, retirees of both genders are facing a different challenge: widespread cutbacks in private pension benefits and the replacement of defined-benefit plans with defined-contribution plans that shift the financial risks of saving for retirement from employers to employees. In other words, while pension security may become more equal by gender, it is deteriorating for everyone!

Median Pension Wealth on the Current Job

Full-Time Workers
Ages 51–61 (1992)

Source:
Richard W. Johnson, Usha Sambamoorthi, and Stephen Crystal, "Gender Differences in Pension Wealth." Data from the Health and Retirement Study, Wave 1 (1998).

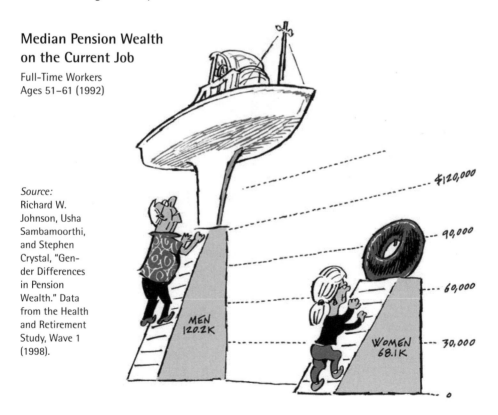

MEN
120.2K

WOMEN
68.1K

$120,000

90,000

60,000

30,000

0

WOMEN AND WEALTH IN THE UNITED STATES

Women own less wealth than men, but the gender wealth gap may be shrinking. So suggest the most recent data on wealth ownership in the United States. Virtually all data on asset ownership is by household and does not distinguish among people living in the household. So, the only gender comparison that typically can be made is between single women and single men.

According to the most recent Survey of Consumer Finances, there is still a dramatic gap overall between the net worth of households headed by single females and those headed by single males: the median net worth of the latter is 69% higher. Data on young baby boomers—those born between 1957 and 1964—from the National Longitudinal Survey of Youth, however, show a much smaller gap between these two groups. As young adults born after 1964 have relatively little wealth at all, this snapshot of the young boomers does suggest a promising trend.

Median Net Worth and Financial Assets of All Households (2001)

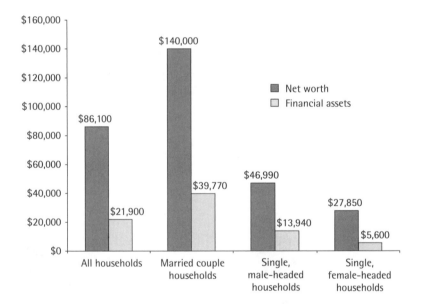

Source: Jeanne M. Hogarth and Chris E. Anguelov, "Descriptive Statistics on Levels of Net Worth." Data from 2001 Survey of Consumer Finances.

Median Net Worth of Young Baby Boomers (2000)

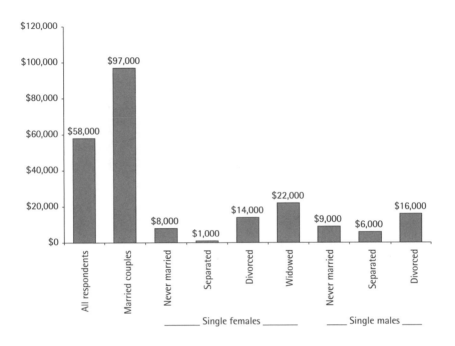

Source: Lisa A. Keister and Alexis Yamokoski, "Single Females and Wealth." Data from the National Longitudinal Survey of Youth, 1979 Cohort. The sample contained too few widowers to include.

GENDER AND PROPERTY RIGHTS

Around the world, as the map on pages 18–19 shows, women continue to face discriminatory laws and customs that restrict their rights to own and inherit property, whether land, houses, or financial assets. In the United States, a woman's right to own and control property was intially defined by the common law doctrines of *couverture* and *jure uxoris*: a woman's legal identity—and hence her right to own and control property—was "suspended" upon marriage. In the second half of 19th century, state statutes began giving married women property rights, but custom continued to limit those rights well into the 20th century. Likewise, many countries in the global South have passed laws or constitutional provisions giving women equal rights to own and control property, but customary practices continue to restrict the exercise of these rights.

Women's Property Rights Around the Globe

Source: Reproduced from *The Penguin Atlas of Women in the World* by Joni Seager (Penguin, 2003). Copyright © Myriad Editions / www.MyriadEditions.com

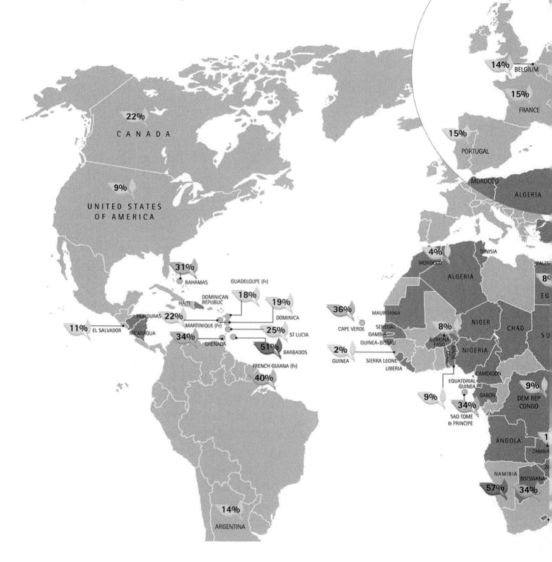

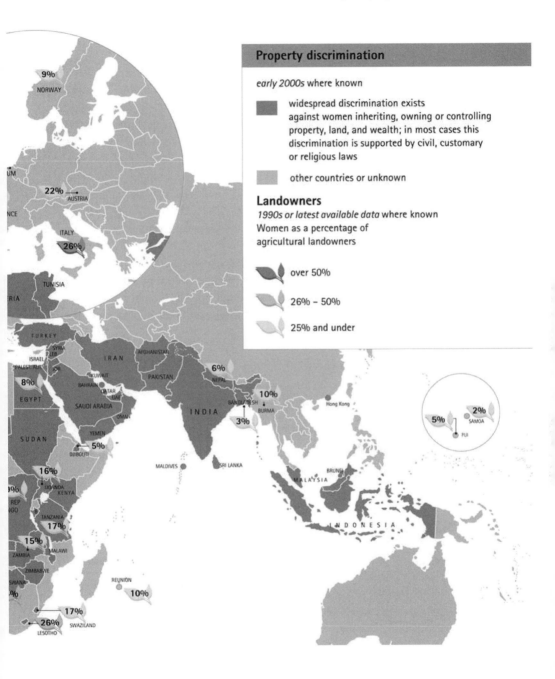

Property discrimination

early 2000s where known

widespread discrimination exists against women inheriting, owning or controlling property, land, and wealth; in most cases this discrimination is supported by civil, customary or religious laws

other countries or unknown

Landowners
1990s or latest available data where known
Women as a percentage of
agricultural landowners

over 50%

26% – 50%

25% and under

World Wide Wealth

Data on wealth ownership and its distribution are scarce compared to data on income. This is particularly true on an international scale: only a handful of countries systematically collect information on individual or household wealth holdings. In the absence of such data, two World Bank economists have estimated the per capita wealth in different world regions using national-level data. They derive total wealth by adding the monetary values of a nation's natural resources (for example, oil, timber, and cropland), its produced assets (for example, goods and factories), and its "human resources" (the wealth inhering in people's projected lifetime productivity, computed as a function of GNP with some adjustments). The authors acknowledge that these are rough, preliminary estimates.

Poor countries tend to have lower per-capita natural resource wealth than rich countries. But it's notable that the natural resource gap is much smaller than the gap in the other components of wealth (the Middle East excepted). This suggests that a country's natural endowments are less important than how it deploys them and how the international rules governing trade and financial transactions shape its economy.

Per Capita Wealth by World Region (1994)

	Total Wealth	Human Resources	Produced Assets	Natural Capital
North America	$326,000	$249,000	$62,000	$16,000
Pacific OECD (Australia, New Zealand, Japan, Korea)	302,000	205,000	90,000	8,000
Western Europe	237,000	177,000	55,000	6,000
Middle East	150,000	65,000	27,000	58,000
South America	95,000	70,000	16,000	9,000
North Africa	55,000	38,000	14,000	3,000
Central America	52,000	41,000	8,000	3,000
Caribbean	48,000	33,000	10,000	5,000
East Asia	47,000	36,000	7,000	4,000
East and Southern Africa	30,000	20,000	7,000	3,000
West Africa	22,000	13,000	4,000	5,000
South Asia	22,000	14,000	4,000	4,000

Note: West Africa does not include Nigeria or Algeria because of data quality issues.

Source: John A. Dixon and Kirk Hamilton, "Expanding the Measure of Wealth."

CONCENTRATED CORPORATE OWNERSHIP IN EAST ASIA

In several East Asian countries, vast wealth—in particular, the ownership of publicly held corporations—is concentrated in the hands of just a few families: the Suhartos in Indonesia and the Ayalas in the Philippines, for example. The figure shows the results of an analysis of the ownership of almost 3,000 companies as of December 1996. Notably, Japan stands out for its far lower concentration of ownership than the other countries studied—a result in part of land reform and related policies implemented by the Allied occupying forces following World War II.

The authors, economists at the World Bank and the Chinese University of Hong Kong, also discovered that greater wealth concentration was correlated with more dysfunctional legal and regulatory systems. This, in turn, may have contributed to the late-1990s East Asian financial crisis. "In some East Asian economies," they conclude, "successful legal and regulatory reform may require changes in ownership structures and concentration of wealth."

Share of Total Market Capitalization Controlled by the Wealthiest Families

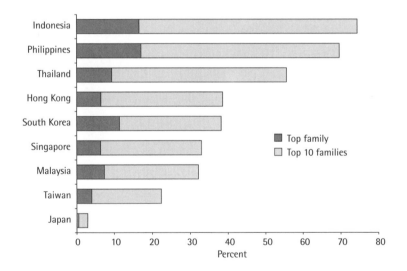

Source: Stijn Claessens, Simeon Djankov, and Larry H. P. Lang, "Who Controls East Asian Corporations."

SECTION II

The Causes of Inequality

Capitalist economies are characterized by an almost inexorable tendency toward ever-increasing levels of inequality. Government intervention in the form of regulation, taxation, and redistribution may partially counterbalance that tendency, but in recent decades, the U.S. political system has shifted in the opposite direction, to rig the economic game in favor of corporations and the very rich, at the cost of everyone else. Here are the seven recent government rule changes that have most exacerbated the wealth and income divide.

The Visible Hand

Seven Government Actions
That Have Worsened Inequality

BY CHUCK COLLINS

A primary reason that U.S. wealth inequality has accelerated in the last two decades is that power has shifted in our democracy. Corporations, investors, and campaign donors have gained power while main street business, wage earners, and voters have lost power. As political influence has shifted, the rules governing the economy have changed to benefit asset-owners and large corporations at the expense of wage-earners.

These rule changes—the visible hand of government—have worsened the wealth and income divide, putting a heavy thumb on the scale in favor of the rich and powerful. Rules governing taxes, trade, wages, spending priorities, and monetary policy have all changed, and in each case, the government has acted on behalf of corporations and the rich to rig who wins and who loses in the economy.

Of course, the U.S. economy has always been governed by rules that created inequality, from regulations protecting private property, to labor laws stacked against workers, to state taxes that fall disproportionately on the poor. Government actions can either mitigate or exacerbate inequality, and in recent years, hundreds of deliberate public policy choices have made it much worse. Here are seven nominations for the public policy hall of shame.

1. THE PLUMMETING MINIMUM WAGE

Decent wages are a prerequisite for individual wealth accumulation: workers cannot save money when their wages barely pay for basic necessities. Today, even when they earn a decent wage, most Americans are not able to save much of anything. And it's much worse for those at the bottom. The U.S. minimum wage has plummeted in value over the last 35 years, and today leaves families below the federal poverty line.

Over 2.1 million workers earn today's minimum wage of $5.15 per hour. In 1968, the minimum wage of $1.60—or $7.07 in today's dollars—was 86% of the amount needed to bring a family of four to the federal poverty line. But today the minimum wage is only 61% of that benchmark. A full-time worker earning today's minimum wage has an annual income of just $10,712. And Congress has not raised the minimum wage since 1996.

It didn't have to be this way. While the minimum wage has been falling, worker productivity has skyrocketed, reducing costs for employers and increasing their profits. If worker wages overall had shared in the productivity gains since the late 1970s, they would be 33% higher in real terms than they are today.

2. TAXING WAGES, NOT WEALTH

Over the last 30 years, the federal government has shifted the tax burden off wealth and onto wages. Since 1980, the payroll tax rate—the main tax on work income—has jumped 25%. In the same period, top tax rates on investment income fell by 31% and taxes on large inheritances have been cut by 79%. This shift means that a person who derives millions of dollars solely in dividend income from investments now pays a marginal tax rate of just 15%, down from 28% in 1997. Compare that with a schoolteacher earning an adjusted gross income of $28,400. The teacher pays a payroll tax rate of 15.3% plus a marginal income tax rate of 28% for a total marginal rate of over 43%!

One policy exacerbating this shift was the 1997 Tax Reform Act, signed into law by President Clinton, which reduced capital gains tax rates from 28% to 20%. The 1997 capital gains provision was wrapped in pretty packaging, including expanded child and education credits for the middle class, and it didn't get much attention. But it was a centerpiece of the right-wing tax program. The 2003 Bush tax cut further reduced the capital gains rate to 15% and cut taxes on dividend income, delivering windfalls for the wealthy.

At the same time that the tax burden has been shifted from wealth to wages, the sheer size of recent tax cuts threatens the social programs many wage-earners depend on. The 2001 and 2003 federal tax cuts, which the Bush administration's 2005 budget proposes to make permanent, guarantee further cuts to social spending. The 2001 tax cut was the largest income tax rollback in two decades, and the 2003 cut reduced dividend and capital gains taxes while accelerating the 2001 rate cut for the top income brackets. These tax cuts, which mainly benefit the rich, will cost at least $824.1 billion between 2001 and 2010; if extended, they will cost $5.9 trillion over the next 75 years, according to William G. Gale and Peter R. Orszag of the Brookings Institution. Revenue losses of this magnitude can be sustained only by cutting social programs.

3. STACKING LABOR LAWS AGAINST WORKERS

Collective action is the most effective means that workers have to win a larger share of the economic pie. But U.S. workers face repressive labor laws that make many forms of collective action difficult or even illegal.

Workers who want to organize a union in the United States must overcome obstacles unheard of in Canada and Western Europe. Canadian workers simply need to present signatures showing that a majority of workers wish to form a union. But in the United States, the 1935 National Labor Relations Act, which governs union organizing in most sectors of the economy, requires workers to complete a lengthy election process during which employers can run intimidating anti-union campaigns. Employers force workers to attend meetings, individually and in groups, in which supervisors spread misinformation about unions. They routinely challenge election bids on frivolous grounds, delaying elections and vote-counting for months and years. And employers illegally fire worker organizers in 25% of unionization drives. Workers who seek reinstatement after being illegally fired face years of hearings before the National Labor Relations Board.

Workers who win union representation face other legal obstacles. When protesting their employer, for instance, they cannot conduct "secondary boycotts," or protests targeting firms that do business with their employer. Moreover, U.S. labor law makes it very difficult for workers to strike. Employers can permanently replace workers who strike for "economic" reasons—like wanting higher wages. The 1947 Taft-Hartley Act banned "sympathy strikes" in which workers striking at one employer could be joined by those at other companies and in other sectors of the economy. Taft-Hartley also gave the president the right to end strikes by executive order.

Unions and legal scholars have proposed labor law reforms for decades, but have been thwarted by both Democrats and Republicans in Congress. Union certification procedures have not changed even as employers' anti-union campaigns have grown more virulent. Congress has taken no action on proposals to ban strikebreakers and permanent replacements, or to lift restrictions on secondary boycotts. The legislative record on workers' substantive demands has also been dismal. Congress and state legislatures could have passed laws to raise workplace standards, require minimum benefits, and limit the use of contract or temporary labor. Instead, Congress has passed laws to reclassify jobs in ways that disqualify workers from receiving overtime pay, reducing the paychecks and clout of millions of workers.

4. SHREDDING THE SAFETY NET

The U.S. safety net has historically been much thinner than those in other industrialized nations. Yet, over the last 20 years, state and federal governments have slashed public programs that historically worked to narrow economic inequalities. Cuts in social spending increase Americans' reliance on unequal personal income and savings, and guarantee a growing divide between rich and poor.

In 1996, President Clinton and a Republican Congress ended "welfare as we knew it" by abolishing Aid to Families with Dependent Children (AFDC) and replacing it with Temporary Assistance to Needy Families (TANF). Unlike AFDC, a federal entitlement that provided a guaranteed minimum benefit, TANF includes strict work requirements, a five-year lifetime limit on assistance, and sanctions that can push people off the rolls. TANF is administered by the states with little federal oversight, allowing for inequities in benefit provisions.

Federal Pell grants, created in 1972 to provide aid to working-class college students, are much less generous than they used to be. Whereas the maximum Pell grant in 1975–76 covered 84% of the average cost of attending a four-year public institution, today it covers just 39% of that cost.

In 2004, the Department of Housing and Urban Development (HUD) changed the formulas it uses to finance the Section 8 housing voucher program. Section 8 vouchers help 2 million poor, elderly, and disabled Americans pay their rent and were originally lauded by conservatives as a market-based alternative to public housing. The new HUD formulas mean that the state housing authorities that administer the vouchers received $183 million less than they expected, even though Congress had already appropriated the funds. The new policy wasn't announced until April 23, 2004, but

HUD made it effective retroactive to January 1, meaning that local housing authorities have to make up for funds they had already spent. In order to fill the budget gap, housing agencies across the country are being forced to take harmful steps including prohibiting eligible new families from receiving vouchers, reducing the maximum rent that a voucher will cover, and withdrawing newly issued vouchers from families that are still looking for an apartment. The Bush administration's proposed 2005 budget includes $1 billion in cuts for Section 8 housing vouchers, or 5.5% of the program's total funding.

5. LETTING EXECUTIVE PAY SKYROCKET

In 1992, President Clinton was elected calling for reform of executive compensation laws. At the time, corporations deducted the entire value of their bloated CEO pay packages as a tax-reducing business expense. Some salary expense is obviously a business expense, but corporations were using these excessive pay packages to shrink their tax liabilities on paper while bestowing largess on a privileged few. Clinton proposed limiting the "tax deductibility of excessive compensation" to $1 million. This still would have allowed corporations to take tremendous tax deductions, but it would have been a step in the right direction.

However, the final bill that passed was amended to exempt pay packages where compensation was judged to be "performance based." As a result, corporate boards today simply pass resolutions stating that their executive compensation pay packages are "performance based," and circumvent the law's intent. Apparently, it doesn't matter if that performance was abysmal. Safeway CEO Steven Burd cashed out $13 million in stock options in 2003 even as the company lost $169.8 million in net revenue. Imagine if a law with teeth had been in place during the late 1990s, when average executive compensation grew to more than 500 times average worker pay.

6. CHANGING THE RULES ON INVESTMENT AND TRADING

The recent stock market and accounting scandals have had a crushing effect on small stockholders and pension plans but put billions into the pockets of insider investors in America's largest corporations. The scandals were made possible by rule changes and "reforms" that took the few remaining teeth out of the regulatory process. In 1999, Congress repealed the 1933 Glass-Steagall Act, a banking law that prohibited mergers between banks, insurance companies, and securities trading firms. The New Deal-era law was designed to guard against the conflicts of interest that had led to a series of corporate abuses in the 1920s. The finance, insurance, and real estate sectors spent $200 million in campaign contributions, according to the Center for Responsive Politics, to remove this reform. Glass-Steagall was replaced by the Financial Modernization Act, which created a new kind of corporation—the financial holding company—that could bring together any number of these formerly separate financial institutions in a single corporation.

By removing the barriers between banks and securities firms, Congress ushered in a new wave of speculative mega-mergers. Firms such as Citigroup, J.P. Morgan Chase and others took advantage of the new rules by forming mega-conglomerates that financed Enron and other disasters.

Repealing Glass-Steagall also exposed small investors to new risks. Glass-Steagall had required banks to maintain a firewall between investment bankers (who facilitate deals between banks and corporations) and brokers (who buy and sell securities for investors). Eliminating this firewall gave brokers incentives to lie to investors about the quality of securities in order to promote deals that the bankers were pushing. In one case uncovered by New York State Attorney General Eliot Spitzer, Citigroup CEO Sandy Weill was on AT&T's board of directors when he sent an e-mail to Citigroup analyst Jack Grubman asking him to upgrade AT&T's investment rating as a personal favor. Grubman upped the company's rating just before Citigroup secured a deal to manage the AT&T wireless division's initial public offering. Soon after the IPO, Grubman downgraded AT&T's stock, and the price plummeted. Citigroup reaped over $40 million in fees from managing the IPO, while investors were duped out of millions more.

In 2000, Congress passed the Commodity Futures Modernization Act to deregulate derivative investments, which are highly speculative investment vehicles. Sen. Phil Gramm (R-Texas) attached the act to an omnibus bill immediately after the 2000 Supreme Court decision in favor of Bush's selection. The bill included the infamous "Enron exclusion" that exempted Enron's online energy-trading floor from public oversight, creating the conditions in which Enron was able to manipulate California's electricity market. This law also exempted over-the-counter derivatives from regulation, helping to pave the way for the 2001 Wall Street fiascos. It specifically included an exception for the trading of energy derivatives, a provision strongly supported by Gramm, whose wife Wendy had deregulated energy swaps in 1993 as chairman of the Commodity Futures Trading Commission and then joined Enron's board of directors. These changes helped produce the corporate meltdowns that looted employees and investors alike, fueling wealth inequality.

Finally, thanks to a little-known 1995 rule change, shareholders and pensioners who saw their wealth vanish in the post-1990s corporate debacles found that they had little recourse against corporate malfeasance. This was because the 1995 Private Securities Litigation Reform Act had raised hurdles for investors attempting to file securities-fraud lawsuits in federal court. Investors fleeced by companies like WorldCom have been thwarted in their efforts to recoup their loses.

7. LETTING CORPORATE ACCOUNTING GO WILD

For years, shady corporate accounting left workers' savings and pensions dangerously exposed. The SEC and Congress failed to enact meaningful safeguards, and small investors were left holding the bag when disaster finally struck. Throughout the 1990s, the Financial Accounting Standards Board (FASB) and Securities and Exchange (SEC) Chairman Arthur Leavitt considered a number of reforms to make accounting more transparent and reduce opportunities for corporate manipulation. Leavitt proposed several reforms, including one which would have required companies to treat stock options as expenses. The SEC also proposed a rule requiring auditors to be independent of the companies they audited, as many were not. For instance, a number of accounting firms conducting corporate audits also maintained lucrative consulting contracts with the same firms. Knowing that they might lose consulting revenue if their audits weren't rosy enough, accounting firms had strong incentives to cook the books.

These proposals weathered an onslaught of industry and political attacks during the 1990s. Legislators led by Sen. Joseph Leiberman (D-Conn.), representing Connecticut's insurance industry, intervened to stop the SEC from implementing rules requiring auditor independence. When President Bush came into office, he appointed Harvey Pitt, the former chief lobbyist for the accounting industry, to replace Leavitt—a way of preventing further reforms. Rule changes were thwarted until corporate fraud scandals created a tremendous public backlash. Even then, Congress enacted only modest reforms such as the Sarbanes-Oxley Public Company Accounting and Investor Protection Act of 2002. While this law mandated some restrictions on certain non-auditing services that auditors can provide for their clients, it left in place the cozy auditor-client relationships that encouraged auditors to approve the shady accounting practices of Enron and WorldCom. In the end, even these weak reforms came too late to protect the millions of working Americans who saw their pensions and savings vanish, nor did it insure that similar scandals would be prevented from happening in the future.

Today, economic inequality in the United States is more extreme than at any time since the 1920s. Left to its own devices, the underlying tendency of the U.S. private sector is toward ever-increasing levels of inequality. This tendency must be counteracted by the visible hand of progressive government policies. But the rule changes and policy choices described here have taken the country in exactly the wrong direction. It doesn't have to be that way. We could have public policy that restores the lost purchasing power of the minimum wage; insists that the rich pay their fair share in taxes by blocking the repeal of the estate tax and reinstituting the lost progressivity of the income tax; patches the holes in the social safety net by returning non-defense discretionary spending to its level at the beginning of the Reagan administration (5.2% of GDP); enforces labor laws that oversee an orderly process of helping workers gain a voice in their work life; and reregulates financial markets and large corporations as opposed to celebrating corporate recklessness. These measures would go a long way toward counteracting the two-decade trend of widening inequality of the U.S. economy.

Wealth doesn't just reside in individual bank accounts, but in public pro-
grams that take care of people when they are elderly or fall on hard times.
During the 1930s and 1960s, new public initiatives began providing Ameri-
cans with greatly expanded social wealth. Whereas Americans had previously
depended on unequal private resources to finance their retirement and health
care, and to support themselves during periods of unemployment, programs
like Social Security, Medicare, Medicaid, and unemployment insurance cre-
ated a safety net available to all.

Today, however, federal tax cuts are threatening to bankrupt these pro-
grams. Paul Krugman explains that the 2001–2003 tax cuts can only be
sustained by shredding the federal safety net. And that's exactly the point.
Krugman notes that conservatives have always opposed initiatives that
promote social, rather than individual, wealth, and he argues that they
pushed through the recent tax cuts precisely to starve these programs out of
existence.

The Tax-Cut Con

BY PAUL KRUGMAN

Bruce Tinsley's comic strip, "Mallard Fillmore," is, he says, "for the average person out there: the forgotten American taxpayer who's sick
of the liberal media." In June 2003, that forgotten taxpayer made an
appearance in the strip, attacking his TV set with a baseball bat and
yelling: "I can't afford to send my kids to college, or even take 'em out of
their substandard public school, because the federal, state and local governments take more than 50% of my income in taxes. And then the guy on the
news asks with a straight face whether or not we can 'afford' tax cuts."

Nobody likes paying taxes, and no doubt some Americans are as angry
about their taxes as Tinsley's imaginary character. But most Americans also
care a lot about the things taxes pay for.

All politicians say they're for public education; almost all of them also say
they support a strong national defense, maintaining Social Security and, if
anything, expanding the coverage of Medicare. When the "guy on the news"

asks whether we can afford a tax cut, he's asking whether, after yet another tax cut goes through, there will be enough money to pay for those things. And the answer is no.

But it's very difficult to get that answer across in modern American politics, which has been dominated for 25 years by a crusade against taxes.

I don't use the word "crusade" lightly. The advocates of tax cuts are relentless, even fanatical. An indication of the movement's fervor—and of its political power—came during the Iraq war. War is expensive and is almost always accompanied by tax increases. But not in 2003. "Nothing is more important in the face of a war," declared Tom DeLay, the House majority leader, "than cutting taxes." And sure enough, taxes were cut, not just in a time of war but also in the face of record budget deficits.

A result of the tax-cut crusade is that there is now a fundamental mismatch between the benefits Americans expect to receive from the government and the revenues government collect. This mismatch is already having profound effects at the state and local levels: teachers and policemen are being laid off and children are being denied health insurance. The federal government can mask its problems for a while by running huge budget deficits, but it, too, will eventually have to decide whether to cut services or raise taxes. And we are not talking about minor policy adjustments. If taxes stay as low as they are now, government as we know it cannot be maintained. In particular, Social Security will have to become far less generous; Medicare will no longer be able to guarantee comprehensive medical care to older Americans; Medicaid will no longer provide basic medical care to the poor.

How did we reach this point? What are the origins of the antitax crusade? And where is it taking us?

SUPPLY-SIDERS, STARVE-THE-BEASTERS, AND LUCKY DUCKIES

It is often hard to pin down what antitax crusaders are trying to achieve. The reason is not, or not only, that they are disingenuous about their motives—though as we will see, disingenuity has become a hallmark of the movement in recent years. Rather, the fuzziness comes from the fact that today's antitax movement moves back and forth between two doctrines. Both doctrines favor the same thing: big tax cuts for people with high incomes. But they favor it for different reasons.

One of those doctrines has become famous under the name "supply-side economics." It's the view that the government can cut taxes without severe cuts in public spending. The other doctrine is often referred to as "starving the beast," a phrase coined by David Stockman, Ronald Reagan's budget director. It's the view that taxes should be cut precisely in order to force severe cuts in public spending. Supply-side economics is the friendly, attractive face of the tax-cut movement. But starve-the-beast is where the power lies.

The starting point of supply-side economics is an assertion that no economist would dispute: taxes reduce the incentive to work, save and invest. A businessman who knows that 70 cents of every extra dollar he makes will go to the IRS is less willing to make the effort to earn that extra dollar than if he knows that the IRS will take only 35 cents. So reducing tax rates will, other things being the same, spur the economy.

This much isn't controversial. But the government must pay its bills. So the standard view of economists is that if you want to reduce the burden of taxes, you must explain what government programs you want to cut as part of the deal. There's no free lunch.

What the supply-siders argued, however, was that there was a free lunch. Cutting marginal rates, they insisted, would lead to such a large increase in gross domestic product that it wouldn't be necessary to come up with offsetting spending cuts. What supply-side economists say, in other words, is, "Don't worry, be happy and cut taxes." And when they say cut taxes, they mean taxes on the affluent: reducing the top marginal rate means that the biggest tax cuts go to people in the highest tax brackets.

The other camp in the tax-cut crusade actually welcomes the revenue losses from tax cuts. Its most visible spokesman today is Grover Norquist, president of Americans for Tax Reform, who once told National Public Radio: "I don't want to abolish government. I simply want to reduce it to the size where I can drag it into the bathroom and drown it in the bathtub." And the way to get it down to that size is to starve it of revenue. "The goal is reducing the size and scope of government by draining its lifeblood," Norquist told *U.S. News & World Report.*

What does "reducing the size and scope of government" mean? Tax-cut proponents are usually vague about the details. But the Heritage Foundation, ideological headquarters for the movement, has made it pretty clear. Edwin Feulner, the foundation's president, uses "New Deal" and "Great Society" as terms of abuse, implying that he and his organization want to do away with the institutions Franklin Roosevelt and Lyndon Johnson created. That means Social Security, Medicare, Medicaid—most of what gives citizens of the United States a safety net against economic misfortune.

The starve-the-beast doctrine is now firmly within the conservative mainstream. George W. Bush himself seemed to endorse the doctrine as the budget surplus evaporated: in August 2001 he called the disappearing surplus "incredibly positive news" because it would put Congress in a "fiscal straitjacket."

Like supply-siders, starve-the-beasters favor tax cuts mainly for people with high incomes. That is partly because, like supply-siders, they emphasize the incentive effects of cutting the top marginal rate; they just don't believe that those incentive effects are big enough that tax cuts pay for themselves. But they have another reason for cutting taxes mainly on the rich, which has become known as the "lucky ducky" argument.

Here's how the argument runs: to starve the beast, you must not only deny funds to the government; you must make voters hate the government. There's a danger that working-class families might see government as their friend: because their incomes are low, they don't pay much in taxes, while they benefit from public spending. So in starving the beast, you must take care not to cut taxes on these "lucky duckies." (Yes, that's what the *Wall Street Journal* called them in a famous editorial.) In fact, if possible, you must raise taxes on working-class Americans in order, as the *Journal* said, to get their "blood boiling with tax rage."

So the tax-cut crusade has two faces. Smiling supply-siders say that tax cuts are all gain, no pain; scowling starve-the-beasters believe that inflicting pain is not just necessary but also desirable. Is the alliance between these two groups a marriage of convenience? Not exactly. It would be more accurate to say that the starve-the-beasters hired the supply-siders—indeed, created them—because they found their naive optimism useful.

A look at who the supply-siders are and how they came to prominence tells the story. The supply-side movement likes to present itself as a school of economic thought like Keynesianism or monetarism—that is, as a set of scholarly ideas that made their way, as such ideas do, into political discussion. But the reality is quite different. Supply-side economics was a political doctrine from Day 1; it emerged in the pages of political magazines, not professional economics journals.

That is not to deny that many professional economists favor tax cuts. But they almost always turn out to be starve-the-beasters, not supply-siders. And they often secretly—or sometimes not so secretly—hold supply-siders in contempt. N. Gregory Mankiw, now chairman of George W. Bush's Council of Economic Advisers, is definitely a friend to tax cuts; but in the first edition of his economic-principles textbook, he described Ronald Reagan's supply-side advisers as "charlatans and cranks."

It is not that the professionals refuse to consider supply-side ideas; rather, they have looked at them and found them wanting. A conspicuous example came earlier this year when the Congressional Budget Office tried to evaluate the growth effects of the Bush administration's proposed tax cuts. The budget office's new head, Douglas Holtz-Eakin, is a conservative economist who was handpicked for his job by the administration. But his conclusion was that unless the revenue losses from the proposed tax cuts were offset by spending cuts, the resulting deficits would be a drag on growth, quite likely to outweigh any supply-side effects.

But if the professionals regard the supply-siders with disdain, who employs these people? The answer is that since the 1970s almost all of the prominent supply-siders have been aides to conservative politicians, writers at conservative publications like National Review, fellows at conservative policy centers like Heritage or economists at private companies with strong Republican connections. Loosely speaking, that is, supply-siders work for the vast right-wing conspiracy. What gives supply-side economics influence is its connection with a powerful network of institutions that want to shrink the government and see tax cuts as a way to achieve that goal.

Supply-side economics is a feel-good cover story for a political movement with a much harder-nosed agenda.

A PLANNED CRISIS

Right now, much of the public discussion of the Bush tax cuts focuses on their short-run impact. Critics say that the 2.7 million jobs lost since March 2001 prove that the administration's policies have failed, while the administration says that things would have been even worse without the tax cuts and that a solid recovery is just around the corner.

But this is the wrong debate. Even in the short run, the right question to ask isn't whether the tax cuts were better than nothing; they probably were. The right question is whether some other economic-stimulus plan could have achieved better results at a lower budget cost. And it is hard to deny that, on a jobs-per-dollar basis, the Bush tax cuts have been extremely ineffective. According to the Congressional Budget Office, half of this year's $400 billion budget deficit is due to Bush tax cuts. Now $200 billion is a lot of money; it is equivalent to the salaries of four million average workers. Even the administration doesn't claim its policies have created four million jobs. Surely some other policy—aid to state and local governments, tax breaks for the poor and middle class rather than the rich, maybe even WPA-style public works—would have been more successful at getting the country back to work.

Meanwhile, the tax cuts are designed to remain in place even after the economy has recovered. Where will they leave us?

Here's the basic fact: partly, though not entirely, as a result of the tax cuts of the last three years, the government of the United States faces a fundamental fiscal shortfall. That is, the revenue it collects falls well short of the sums it needs to pay for existing programs. Even the U.S. government must, eventually, pay its bills, so something will have to give.

The numbers tell the tale. This year and next, the federal government will run budget deficits of more than $400 billion. Deficits may fall a bit, at least as a share of gross domestic product, when the economy recovers. But the relief will be modest and temporary. As Peter Fisher, undersecretary of the treasury for domestic finance, puts it, the federal government is "a gigantic insurance company with a sideline business in defense and homeland security." And about a decade from now, this insurance company's policyholders will begin making a lot of claims. As the baby boomers retire, spending on Social Security benefits and Medicare will steadily rise, as will spending on Medicaid (because of rising medical costs). Eventually, unless there are sharp cuts in benefits, these three programs alone will consume a larger share of GDP than the federal government currently collects in taxes.

Alan Auerbach, William Gale and Peter Orszag, fiscal experts at the Brookings Institution, have estimated the size of the "fiscal gap"—the increase in revenues or reduction in spending that would be needed to make the nation's finances sustainable in the long run. If you define the long run as 75 years, this gap turns out to be 4.5% of GDP. Or to put it another way, the gap is equal to 30% of what the federal government spends on all domestic programs. Of that gap, about 60% is the result of the Bush tax cuts. We would have faced a serious fiscal problem even if those tax cuts had never happened. But we face a much nastier problem now that they are in place.

And more broadly, the tax-cut crusade will make it very hard for any future politicians to raise taxes.

So how will this gap be closed? The crucial point is that it cannot be closed without either fundamentally redefining the role of government or sharply raising taxes.

Politicians will, of course, promise to eliminate wasteful spending. But take out Social Security, Medicare, defense, Medicaid, government pensions, homeland security, interest on the public debt and veterans' benefits—none of them what people who complain about waste usually have in mind—and you are left with spending equal to about 3% of gross domestic product. And most of that goes for courts, highways, education and other useful things. Any savings from elimination of waste and fraud will amount to little more than a rounding-off error.

So let's put a few things back on the table. Let's assume that interest on the public debt will be paid, that spending on defense and homeland security will not be compromised and that the regular operations of government will continue to be financed. What we are left with, then, are the New

Deal and Great Society programs: Social Security, Medicare, Medicaid and unemployment insurance. And to close the fiscal gap, spending on these programs would have to be cut by around 40%.

It's impossible to know how such spending cuts might unfold, but cuts of that magnitude would require drastic changes in the system. It goes almost without saying that the age at which Americans become eligible for retirement benefits would rise, that Social Security payments would fall sharply compared with average incomes, that Medicare patients would be forced to pay much more of their expenses out of pocket—or do without. And that would be only a start.

All this sounds politically impossible. In fact, politicians of both parties have been scrambling to expand, not reduce, Medicare benefits by adding prescription drug coverage. It's hard to imagine a situation under which the entitlement programs would be rolled back sufficiently to close the fiscal gap.

Yet closing the fiscal gap by raising taxes would mean rolling back all of the Bush tax cuts, and then some. And that also sounds politically impossible.

For the time being, there is a third alternative: borrow the difference between what we insist on spending and what we're willing to collect in taxes. That works as long as lenders believe that someday, somehow, we're going to get our fiscal act together. But this can't go on indefinitely.

Eventually—I think within a decade, though not everyone agrees—the bond market will tell us that we have to make a choice.

In short, everything is going according to plan.

For the looming fiscal crisis doesn't represent a defeat for the leaders of the tax-cut crusade or a miscalculation on their part. Some supporters of President Bush may have really believed that his tax cuts were consistent with his promises to protect Social Security and expand Medicare; some people may still believe that the wondrous supply-side effects of tax cuts will make the budget deficit disappear. But for starve-the-beast tax-cutters, the coming crunch is exactly what they had in mind.

WHAT KIND OF COUNTRY?

The astonishing political success of the antitax crusade has, more or less deliberately, set the United States up for a fiscal crisis. How we respond to that crisis will determine what kind of country we become.

If Grover Norquist is right—and he has been right about a lot—the coming crisis will allow conservatives to move the nation a long way back toward the kind of limited government we had before Franklin Roosevelt. Lack of revenue, he says, will make it possible for conservative politicians—in the name of fiscal necessity—to dismantle immensely popular government programs that would otherwise have been untouchable.

In Norquist's vision, America a couple of decades from now will be a place in which elderly people make up a disproportionate share of the poor, as they did before Social Security. It will also be a country in which even middle-class elderly Americans are, in many cases, unable to afford expensive medical procedures or prescription drugs and in which poor Americans generally go without even basic health care. And it may well be a place in which only those who can afford expensive private schools can give their children a decent education.

But that's a choice, not a necessity. The tax-cut crusade has created a situation in which something must give. But what gives—whether we decide that the New Deal and the Great Society must go or that taxes aren't such a bad thing after all—is up to us. The American people must decide what kind of a country we want to be.

Excerpted from the New York Times Magazine, *September 14, 2003*

Taxation is arguably the single most important means we have to mitigate capitalism's tendency to concentrate wealth. But recent tax changes have seriously weakened this effect. Michelle Sheehan shows just how much money the rich got out of the 2001–2003 tax cuts, and lists the social needs that the lost tax revenue could have met.

Tax Breaks for the Rich

Or Public Programs for Everyone?

BY MICHELLE SHEEHAN

Who is benefiting from the massive 2001 and 2003 tax cuts? Not the working families President Bush talked about when he pushed the cuts, but the wealthy. The 2001 tax cut was the largest income tax rollback in two decades; it lowered tax rates on the top four income brackets and gave small advance refunds to those less well-off. The 2003 tax cut—the third largest in U.S. history—slashed dividend and capital gains taxes, and accelerated the 2001 rate cut for the top income brackets. Finally, the 2001 estate tax cut reduced the top tax rate each year, meaning that the top 2% of taxpayers will pay progressively fewer taxes on wealth that they leave to heirs.

The figures on the next page represent just a sliver of what the rich will get from the 2001–2003 cuts. The largest tax breaks, and those most geared toward the wealthy, were designed to kick in later. According to Citizens for Tax Justice, the cumulative costs of the 2001–2003 tax cuts will be $824.1 billion in 2010. If the cuts are made permanent beyond 2010, as Bush's 2005 budget proposes, they will cost $5.9 trillion over the next 75 years, and could force massive cuts to already strapped social welfare programs. The right-hand column of the table shows some of the things that the 2001–2003 tax cuts could have paid for in 2004.

TAX CUTS VS. SOCIAL PROGRAMS

2001–2003 Tax Cuts	Cost of Tax Cuts in 2004	Cost in Social Programs*
Estate tax break for top 1%	$7 billion	Provide Section 8 housing subsidies for 1 million families
Dividends and capital gains tax cut for top 1%	$15 billion	Insure 11 million children under Medicaid (2000)
Benefits to top 1% from cuts in corporate taxes	$25 billion	Fund 2 million Americorps members
Personal income tax cut for top 1% (excluding dividends and capital gains)	$32 billion	Bridge "No Child Left Behind" budget gap
Total tax cuts for top 1%	$79 billion	Bridge the Head Start funding gap 18 times over
Dividends and capital gains tax cut for top 5%	$20 billion	Clean up 143 Superfund "megasites"
Benefits to top 5% from cuts in corporate taxes	$36 billion	Fund Amtrak 20 times over (FY 2005)
Total dividends and capital gains tax cut	$28 billion	Provide WIC nutrition subsidies to 47 million parents and children
Total corporate tax cut	$61 billion	Build 871,000 new units of affordable housing
Total tax cut on personal income (excluding dividends and capital gains)	$169 billion	Pay salary and benefits for 3.1 million elementary school teachers (2001)
TOTAL TAX CUTS IN 2004	$266 billion	Pay four years' tuition at public universities for 13 million students *or* more than half of all Social Security benefits

* Numbers for 2003 unless otherwise noted.

Sources: Tax cuts: Citizens for Tax Justice <www.ctj.org>. *Social spending figures:* Center for Budget and Policy Priorities <www.cbpp.org>; Center for Medicare and Medicaid Services <www.cms.hhs.gov>; Americorps <www.americorps.org>; National Education Association <www.nea.org/esea>; U.S. Department of Health and Human Services, Administration for Children and Families <www.acf.hhs.gov> and United Way <national.unitedway.org>; *Environmental Health Perspectives,* March 2003 <ehp.niehs.nih.gov>; Amtrak <www.amtrak.com>; USDA Food and Nutrition Service <www.fns.usda.gov>; National Priorities Project <www.nationalpriorities.org>; Bureau of Labor Statistics, Occupational Employment Statistics <www.bls.gov/oes>; Social Security 2004 Trustees Report <www.ssa.gov>; College Board <www.collegeboard.com>.

African Americans and other minorities hold far less wealth than whites. But why should the wealth gap be so large, greater even than the racial income gap? It turns out that government has played a central role. Throughout U.S. history, countless specific laws, policies, rules, and court decisions have made it more difficult for nonwhites to build wealth, and transferred wealth they did own to whites. Activist Meizhu Lui spells out the story.

Doubly Divided

The Racial Wealth Gap

BY MEIZHU LUI

Race—constructed from a European vantage point—has always been a basis on which U.S. society metes out access to wealth and power. Both in times when the overall wealth gap has grown and in times when a rising tide has managed to lift both rich and poor boats, a pernicious wealth gap between whites and nonwhite minorities has persisted.

Let's cut the cake by race. If you lined up all African-American families by the amount of assets they owned minus their debts and then looked at the family in the middle, that median family in 2001 had a net worth of $10,700 (excluding the value of automobiles). Line up all whites, and *that* median family had a net worth of $106,400, almost 10 times more. Less than half of African-American families own their own homes, while three out of four white families do. Latinos are even less wealthy: the median Latino family in 2001 had only $3,000 in assets, and less than half own their own homes.

We do not know how much Native Americans have in assets because so little data has been collected, but their poverty rate is 26% compared to 8% for whites, even though more than half own their own homes. Nor is much information collected about Asian Americans. What we do know is that their poverty rate is 13%, and that 60% of Asian Americans own their own homes, compared to 77% of whites.

Almost 40 years after the passage of the 20th century's major civil rights legislation, huge wealth disparities persist. However, the myth that the playing field was leveled by those laws is widespread. For anyone who accepts the myth, it follows that if families of color are not on an economic par with whites today, the problem must lie with *them*.

But the racial wealth gap has nothing to do with individual behaviors or cultural deficits. Throughout U.S. history, deliberate government policies transferred wealth from nonwhites to whites—essentially, affirmative action for whites. The specific mechanisms of the transfer have varied, as have the processes by which people have been put into racial categories in the first place. But a brief review of American history, viewed through the lens of wealth, reveals a consistent pattern of race-based obstacles that have prevented Native Americans, African Americans, Latinos, and Asians from building wealth at all comparable to whites.

NATIVE AMERICANS: IN THE U.S. GOVERNMENT WE "TRUST"?

When European settlers came to what would become the United States, Indian tribes in general did not consider land to be a source of individual wealth. It was a resource to be worshipped, treasured, and used to preserve all forms of life. Unfortunately for them, that concept of common ownership and the way of life they had built around it would clash mightily with the idea that parcels of land should be owned by individuals and used to generate private profit.

After the American Revolution, the official position of the new U.S. government was that Indian tribes had the same status as foreign nations and that good relations with them should be maintained. However, as European immigration increased and westward expansion continued, the settlers increasingly coveted Indian land. The federal government pressured Native Americans to sign one treaty after another giving over land: In the United States' first century, over 400 Indian treaties were signed. Indians were forcibly removed, first from the south and then from the west, sometimes into reservations.

Eventually, the Indians' last large territory, the Great Plains, was essentially handed over to whites. In one of the clearest instances of land expropriation, the 1862 Homestead Act transferred a vast amount of land from Indian tribes to white homesteaders by giving any white family 160 acres of land for free if they would farm it for five years. Of course, this massive land transfer was not accomplished without violence. General William Tecumseh Sherman, of Civil War fame, wrote: "The more [Indians] we can kill this year, the less will have to be killed the next year, for the more I see of these Indians, the more convinced I am that they all have to be killed or be maintained as a species of paupers." (Ironically, the Homestead Act is often cited as a model government program that supported asset-building.)

Out of the many treaties came the legal concept of the U.S. government's "trust responsibility" for the Native nations, similar to the relationship of a legal guardian to a child. In exchange for land, the government was to provide for the needs of the Native peoples. Money from the sale of land or natural resources was to be placed in a trust fund and managed in the best interests of the Indian tribes. The government's mismanagement of Indian assets was pervasive; yet, by law, Indian tribes could not fire the designated manager and hire a better or more honest one.

The Dawes Act of 1887 was designed to pressure Indians to assimilate into white culture: to adopt a sedentary life style and end their tradition of collective land ownership. The law broke up reservation land into individual plots and forced Indians to attempt to farm "western" style; "surplus" land was sold to whites. Under this scheme, millions more acres were transferred from Native Americans to whites.

After 1953, the U.S. government terminated the trust status of the tribes. While the stated purpose was to free Indians from government control, the new policy exacted a price: the loss of tribally held land that was still the basis of some tribes' existence. This blow reduced the remaining self-sufficient tribes to poverty and broke up tribal governments.

Thus, over a 200-year period, U.S. government policies transferred Native Americans' wealth—primarily land and natural resources—into the pockets of white individuals. This expropriation of vast tracts played a foundational role in the creation of the U.S. economy. Only in recent years, through the effective use of lawsuits to resurrect tribal rights assigned under the old treaties, have some tribes succeeded in building substantial pools of wealth, primarily from gaming businesses. This newfound casino wealth, though, cannot make up for the decimation of Native peoples or the destruction of traditional Native economies. Native Americans on average continue to suffer disproportionate poverty.

AFRICAN AMERICANS: SLAVES DON'T OWN, THEY ARE OWNED

From the earliest years of European settlement until the 1860s, African Americans were assets to be tallied in the financial records of their owners. They could be bought and sold, they created more wealth for their owners in the form of children, they had no rights even over their own bodies, and they worked without receiving any wages. Slaves and their labor became the basis of wealth creation for plantation owners, people who owned and operated slave ships, and companies that insured them. This was the most fundamental of wealth divides in American history.

At the end of the Civil War, there was an opportunity to create a new starting line. In the first few years, the Freedmen's Bureau and the occupying Union army actually began to distribute land to newly freed slaves: the famous "40 acres and a mule," a modest enough way to begin. But the Freedmen's Bureau was disbanded after only seven years, and the overwhelming majority of land that freed slaves had been allotted was returned to its former white owners. Unable to get a foothold as self-employed farmers, African Americans were forced to accept sharecropping arrangements. While sharecroppers kept some part of the fruits of their labor as in-kind income, the system kept them perpetually in debt and unable to accumulate any assets.

In 1883, the Supreme Court overturned the Civil Rights Act of 1875, which had given blacks the right to protect themselves and their property. By 1900, the Southern states had passed laws that kept African Americans separate and unequal, at the bottom of the economy. They began migrating to the North and West in search of opportunity.

Amazingly, some African-American families did prosper as farmers and businesspeople in the early 20th century. Some African-American communities thrived, even establishing their own banks to build savings and investment within the community. However, there was particular resentment against successful African Americans, and they were often targets of the vigilante violence common in this period. State and local governments helped vigilantes destroy their homes, run them out of town, and lynch those "uppity" enough to resist, and the federal government turned a blind eye. Sometimes entire black communities were targeted. For example, the African-American business district in north Tulsa, known as the "Black Wall Street" for its size and success, was torched on the night of June 21, 1921 by white rioters, who destroyed as many as 600 black-owned businesses.

The Depression wiped out black progress, which did not resume at all until the New Deal period. Even then, African Americans were often barred from the new asset-building programs that benefited whites. Under Social Security, workers paid into the system and were guaranteed money in retirement. However, domestic and agricultural work—two of the most significant black occupations—were excluded from the program. Unemployment insurance and the minimum wage didn't apply to domestic workers or farm workers either. Other programs were also tilted toward white people. The Home Owners' Loan Corporation was created in 1933 to help homeowners avoid foreclosure, but not a single loan went to a black homeowner.

Following World War II, a number of new programs provided a ladder into the middle class—for whites. The GI Bill of Rights and low-interest

TULSA HISTORICAL SOCIETY

Thirty-five blocks in Greenwood, a prosperous African–American business district in Tulsa, were destroyed by white rioters on June 1, 1921.

home mortgages provided tax-funded support for higher education and for homeownership, two keys to family wealth building. The GI Bill provided little benefit to black veterans, however, because a recipient had to be accepted into a college—and many colleges did not accept African-American students. Likewise, housing discrimination meant that homeownership opportunities were greater for white families; subsidized mortgages were often simply denied for home purchases in black neighborhoods.

In *The Cost of Being African American*, sociologist Thomas Shapiro shows how, because of this history, even black families whose incomes are equal to whites' generally have unequal economic standing. Whites are more likely to have parents who benefited from the land grants of the Homestead Act, who have Social Security or retirement benefits, or who own their own homes. With their far greater average assets, whites can transfer advantage from parents to children in the form of college tuition payments, down payments on homes, or simply self-sufficient parents who do not need their children to support them in old age.

These are the invisible underpinnings of the black-white wealth gap: wealth legally but inhumanely created from the unpaid labor of blacks, the use of violence—often backed up by government power—to stop black wealth-creating activities, tax-funded asset building programs closed to blacks even as they, too, paid taxes. The playing field is not level today. For example, recent studies demonstrate that blatant race discrimination in hiring persists. But even if the playing field were level, the black/white wealth gap would still be with us.

LATINOS: IN THE UNITED STATES' BACK YARD

At the time of the American Revolution, Spain, not England, was the largest colonial landowner on the American continents. Unlike the English, the Spanish intermarried widely with the indigenous populations. In the 20th century, their descendents came to be identified as a distinct, nonwhite group. (In the 1800's, Mexicans were generally considered white.) Today, Latinos come from many countries with varied histories, but the relationship of Mexicans to the United States is the longest, and people of Mexican descent are still the largest Latino group in the United States (67% in 2002).

Mexico won its independence from Spain in 1821. Three years later, the Monroe Doctrine promised the newly independent nations of Latin America "protection" from interference by European powers. However, this doctrine allowed the United States itself to intervene in the affairs of the entire hemisphere. Ever since, this paternalistic relationship (reminiscent of the "trust" relationship with Native tribes) has meant U.S. political and economic dominance in Mexico and Central and South America, causing the "push and pull" of the people of those countries into and out of the United States.

Mexicans and Anglos fought together to free Texas from Mexican rule, creating the Lone Star Republic of Texas, which was then annexed to the United States in 1845. Three years later, the United States went to war against Mexico to gain more territory and continue fulfilling its "manifest destiny"—its God-given right—to expand "from sea to shining sea." Mexico lost the war and was forced to accept the 1848 Treaty of Guadalupe Hidalgo, which gave the United States half of Mexico's land. While individual Mexican landowners were at first assured that they would maintain ownership, the United States did not keep that promise, and the treaty ushered in a huge transfer of land from Mexicans to Anglos. For the first time in these areas, racial categories were used to determine who could obtain land. The English language was also used to establish Anglo dominance; legal papers in English proving land ownership were required, and many Spanish speakers suffered as a result.

In the twentieth century, government policy continued to reinforce a wealth gap between Mexicans and whites. The first U.S.-Mexico border patrol was set up in 1924, and deportations of Mexicans became commonplace. Like African Americans, Latino workers were disproportionately represented in the occupations not covered by the Social Security Act. During World

War II, when U.S. farms needed more agricultural workers, the federal government established the Bracero program, under which Mexican workers were brought into the United States to work for subminimum wages and few benefits, then kicked out when their labor was no longer needed. Even today, Mexicans continue to be used as "guest"—or really, reserve—workers to create profits for U.S. agribusiness.

The North American Free Trade Agreement, along with the proposed Central American Free Trade Agreement and Free Trade Agreement of the Americas, is the newest incarnation of the Monroe Doctrine. Trade and immigration policies are still being used to maintain U.S. control over the resources in its "back yard," and at the same time to deny those it is "protecting" the enjoyment of the benefits to be found in papa's "front yard."

ASIAN AMERICANS: PERPETUAL FOREIGNERS

The first Asian immigrants, the Chinese, came to the United States at the same time and for the same reason as the Irish: to escape economic distress at home and take advantage of economic opportunity in America. Like European immigrants, the Chinese came voluntarily, paying their own passage, ready and willing to seize the opportunity to build economic success in a new land. Chinese and Irish immigrants arrived in large numbers in the same decade, but their economic trajectories later diverged.

The major reason is race. While the Irish, caricatured as apes in early cartoons, were soon able to become citizens, the Naturalization Act of 1790 limited eligibility for citizenship to "whites." Asians did not know if they were white or not—but they wanted to be! The rights and benefits of "whiteness" were obvious. Other Americans didn't know whether or not they were white, either. Lawsuits filed first by Chinese, then by Japanese, Indian (South Asian), and Filipino immigrants all claimed that they should be granted "white" status. The outcomes were confusing; for example, South Asians, classified as Caucasian, were at first deemed white. Then, in later cases, courts decided that while they were Caucasian, they were not white.

A series of laws limited the right of Asians to create wealth. Chinese immigrants were drawn into the Gold Rush; the Foreign Miners Tax, however, was designed to push them out of the mining industry. The tax provided 25% of California's annual state budget in the 1860s, but the government jobs and services the tax underwrote went exclusively to whites—one of the first tax-based racial transfers of wealth. And with the passage of the Chinese Exclusion Acts in 1882, the Chinese became the first nationality to be denied the right to join this immigrant nation; the numbers of Chinese-American citizens thus remained small until the 1960s.

The next wave of Asians came from Japan. Excellent farmers, the Japanese bought land and created successful businesses. Resentment led to the passage of the 1924 Alien Land Act, which prohibited noncitizens from owning land. Japanese Americans then found other ways to create wealth, including nurseries and the cut flower business. In 1941, they had $140 million of business wealth.

World War II would change all that. In 1942, the Roosevelt administration forced Japanese Americans, foreign-born and citizen alike, to relocate to internment camps in the inland Western states. They had a week to dispose of their assets. Most had to sell their homes and businesses to whites at fire sale prices—an enormous transfer of wealth. In 1988, a successful suit for reparations gave the survivors of the camps $20,000 each, a mere fraction of the wealth that was lost.

Today, Asians are the group that as a whole has moved closest to economic parity with whites. (There are major variations in status between different Asian nationalities, however, and grouping them masks serious problems facing some groups.) While Asian immigrants have high poverty rates, American-born Asians have moved into professional positions, and the median income of Asians is now higher than that of whites. However, glass ceilings still persist, and as Wen Ho Lee, the Chinese-American nuclear scientist who was falsely accused of espionage in 2002, found out, Asians are still defined by race and branded as perpetual foreigners.

The divergent histories of the Irish and the Chinese in the United States illustrate the powerful role of race in the long-term accumulation of wealth. Irish-Americans faced plenty of discrimination in the labor market: consider the "No Irish Need Apply" signs that were once common in Boston storefronts. But they never faced legal prohibitions on asset ownership and citizenship as Chinese immigrants did, or the expropriation of property as the Japanese did. Today, people of Irish ancestry have attained widespread material prosperity and access to political power, and some of the wealthiest and most powerful men in business and politics are of Irish descent. Meantime, the wealth and power of the Chinese are still marginal.

*　*　*　*　*

Throughout history, federal policies—from constructing racial categories, to erecting barriers to asset building by nonwhites, to overseeing transfers of wealth from nonwhites to whites—have created the basis for the current racial wealth divide. If the gap is to be closed, government policies will have to play an important role.

It's long past time to close the gap.

The myth of the "self-made man" denies society's role in private wealth accumulation. This individualistic narrative of success, which buttresses the whole range of wealth-concentrating tax and economic policies, must be challenged. Here, several wealthy indivduals discuss the social roots of their personal fortunes.

"I Didn't Do It Alone"

BY CHUCK COLLINS

"Self-made men, indeed! Why don't you tell me of the self-laid egg?"
—19th century athlete Francis Leiber

An interesting thing happened during the political battle to preserve the federal estate tax. Thousands of multimillionaires and billionaires signed a petition, sponsored by the Boston-based advocacy group Responsible Wealth, in support of taxing large inherited estates. The fact that wealthy people would endorse the tax was news in itself.

Some commentators argued that the "billionaire backlash," as *Newsweek* called it, was rooted in unselfishness or class betrayal. But for many of the individuals who signed the petition, it was a matter of simple accounting: "We owe something back to the society that created opportunities for us."

The notion that the rich have an obligation to pay society back is a radical departure from the individualistic, antigovernment ethos that prevails among the most well off. Many view government and society as irrelevant to their good fortune—or worse, as a hindrance—and attribute their prosperity to their own character, values, and performance.

A 2004 report "I Didn't Do It Alone," published by United for a Fair Economy, takes on the "great man" theory of wealth creation, presenting interviews with several wealthy individuals who credit government, public infrastructure, and historical timing, in addition to their own moxie, creativity, and hard work, in their personal financial achievements.

- Amy Domini, founder and president of Domini Social Equity Fund, believes she owes her success in part to basic government-provided public infrastructure. "Getting my message out over the public airwaves has allowed me to be far more successful than if I had been born in another time and place," she said in a recent interview. "The mail runs on time, allowing me to communicate with existing and potential shareholders, and the rise of the publicly financed Internet has lowered the costs of these communications still further. I can fly safely—and most often conveniently—throughout the country, sharing my ideas and gaining new clients, again thanks to a publicly supported air travel system."

- Billionaire investor Warren Buffett observes that his investment and forecasting skills have been "disproportionately" and idiosyncratically rewarded by the U.S. marketplace. As he explained in a public television interview: "I do think that when you're treated enormously well by this market system, where in effect the market system showers the ability to buy goods and services on you because of some peculiar talent...I think society has a big claim on that." He speculates that if he were to attempt to do business in another country, one without a clear system of property laws or functioning market mechanisms, he "would still be struggling 30 years later."

- New York-based software designer Martin Rothenberg argues, "[My] wealth is not only a product of my own hard work, but resulted from a strong economy and lots of public investment in others and me." He credits a public New York City technical school for his early education, and the GI Bill and government-backed student loans for funding his university degree. Later, government investment directly supported the lab research that eventually led to his establishing a company that he recently sold for $30 million.

- Venture capitalist Jim Sherblom was the chief financial officer of biotech wonder company Genzyme when it went public in 1986. He estimates that the stock market, a socially financed and government-regulated institution, created 30% to 50% of the value of the company. The stock market's value and liquidity depend enormously on societal institutions that regulate market transactions, ensure transparency, and enforce fair transactions—maintaining public trust. If there is any doubt about this, just consider how the accounting scandals of 2001 depressed the value of dozens of publicly traded technology and telecommunications companies. When the Enron and WorldCom scandals broke, hundreds of billions of dollars in wealth vanished overnight. Cook the books, shake the public trust, and, in the absence of adequate oversight and enforcement, watch the wealth disappear.

Our society needs a new narrative of success, one that recognizes that societal forces are important in fostering wealth creation. This is no small challenge, for the American self-made success narrative is deeply rooted.

The mythology would not be such a problem if it were a matter of simple personal self-delusion. But many who hold power in U.S. society buy into this creed of individual achievement, with serious political consequences. It's a short distance from "I made this money myself" and "it's all mine" to "government has no business taking any part of it." If one really believes that "I did it all myself," then one probably sees any taxation as a form of larceny.

On the other hand, wider recognition of the social roots of wealth should strengthen public understanding of the need to pay taxes and invest in public goods and services.

Perhaps the myth-makers understand what is at stake here. If society's role in wealth creation is far larger than the myth of the self-made man acknowledges, then society has a claim upon these great fortunes—and an obligation to level the playing field.

The United States' growing wealth gap reflects the fact that, for about three decades now, government policies have channeled the gains from the country's expanding economy and increasing productivity more and more toward a small elite. How did policies that disadvantage the majority of Americans ever get adopted in the first place? United for a Fair Economy's Chuck Collins dissects one explanation: the right built public-policy advocacy organizations designed to bring about long-term shifts in public opinion, and then gave them the resources to do it.

The Right-Wing Idea Machine

Moving an Economic Agenda

BY CHUCK COLLINS

For decades, right-wing conservatives have advanced an economic agenda that has worsened America's wealth divide: tax cuts for the rich, weaker labor rights, privatization of public services, corporate-driven global trade agreements, and the rest of the familiar litany. What is striking is that a small number of conservative foundations and nonprofit policy organizations have promoted—and with great success—a public policy agenda that runs counter to the interests of the vast majority of Americans. Those who support moving the United States away from a wealth-gap agenda and toward a wealth-broadening agenda can learn a great deal from how it was done. The lessons for progressive forces are clear: think big, get the message right, fund movement-building, dig in for the long term, and build power.

"DEATH TAX" DECEPTION

The battle over the federal estate tax, the United States' only tax on accumulated wealth, offers a telling case study. Today, over 60% of Americans support abolishing this tax. How do you convince the majority of Americans that it is in their interest to abolish a tax that only multimillionaires and billionaires pay?

The short answer is that the right-wing infrastructure, which has been so effective in the battle of ideas over three decades, was fully deployed to shift public opinion and get the tax repealed.

In March 2001, a new group, "Disabled Americans for Death Tax Relief," placed a full-page ad in newspapers around the country. The ad claimed that there are "2.5 million disabled people who are family members of million-

RIGHT-WING ECONOMIC POLICY ADVOCACY: THE TOP FIVE

The **Heritage Foundation** was founded in 1973 by beer magnate Joseph Coors and new right institution-builder Paul Weyrich. Heritage is the grand dame of conservative think tanks, with an annual budget over $50 million and more than 200 employees. It came to prominence with the 1980 election of Ronald Reagan, whose policy agenda it played a significant role in shaping. Heritage not only conducts research, but, as any journalist can testify, also has a sophisticated capacity to package and disseminate its ideology. For example, the foundation issues daily briefs, via fax broadcast and email, on a variety of policy issues. Among the conservative donors who also serve on Heritage's board are banking scion Richard Mellon Scaife, beer magnate Joseph Coors, and Jay van Andel, the founder of Amway and a major funder of initiatives to privatize education.

Americans for Tax Reform was founded by conservative activist Grover Norquist in the mid-1980s, based inside the Reagan White House as an in-house operation to build support for the 1986 tax reform bill. It is now an independent organization that is propelled by Norquist's strong movement-building orientation. Its policy focus is on federal and state tax cuts. The group's financial backing comes largely from corporations in the tobacco, gambling, and alcohol industries. Americans for Tax Reform has links to hundreds of local anti-tax committees and organizations.

The **Cato Institute** was founded in 1977 by libertarian businessmen Charles Koch and Edward Crane. It has an annual budget of over $17 million and a staff of 90, plus more than 75 adjunct scholars and research fellows. With its libertarian orientation, Cato sometimes clashes with other conservative advocacy groups, and has campaigned with progressive groups on issues like civil liberties and corporate welfare.

aires." It argued that the estate tax deprives these people of the inheritance they need: "Some of us who would receive this wealth are in wheelchairs. Some are deaf and blind. Some are on respirators. Others require medication or nursing services. In order to live a full life, these Americans may require medical help, nursing and living assistance far beyond that which is covered by medical insurance." Claiming her group had attracted 1,000 members in

But as a major advocate of shrinking the federal government and privatizing public services such as Social Security, Cato is solidly in the aid-the-rich camp on key economic issues. The organization's funding comes from the usual conservative foundations and a large number of corporations including Philip Morris, Viacom International, and Chase Manhattan Bank.

Citizens for a Sound Economy was founded in 1984 by multimillionaire Libertarian Party vice-presidential candidate David Koch. Its primary focus is on free markets and limited government, but the group also works to oppose environmental and corporate regulation. CSE functions as a field operation for the conservative economic movement, claiming 280,000 members and chapters in 23 states. The bulk of the group's financial support comes from corporations that want to advance specific policy agendas, which has gained it a reputation as a corporate shill. For instance, in 1998 CSE received over $700,000 in contributions from the Florida sugar industry, which was fighting federal efforts to restore the Everglades at the time.

The Club for Growth was founded in 1999 by Stephen Moore, the former director of fiscal policy at the Cato Institute. It functions as a sort of EMILY's list for economic conservatives, bundling donations from wealthy Wall Street financiers and executives. The organization also runs a 527 committee that runs issue ads (527 committees are groups permitted to use unlimited soft-money contributions for political activities but not to directly support a candidate) and a traditional Political Action Committee to contribute to candidates. It works to maintain ideological discipline within the Republican party, running far-right candidates against moderate Republicans who stray from its anti-tax and limited government orthodoxy. In April 2004, a Club for Growth-backed challenger was narrowly defeated in his bid to unseat longtime incumbent Senator Arlen Specter (R-Pa.).

just two weeks, Erin O'Leary, the group's photogenic leader, held a Capitol Hill press conference, followed by appearances on "Hardball" with Chris Matthews, the "O'Reilly Factor," and "Special Report" with Brit Hume.

Groups claiming to represent other alleged victims of the estate tax—for example, African-American, Hispanic, and women small business owners—sprang up as well, generating plenty of press.

Small farmers were another group of alleged victims. Time and again, repeal backers claimed the estate tax was costing many working farmers their farms. When Congress passed legislation to repeal the tax in 2000, it delivered the bill to the White House on a tractor to symbolize the pain they claim the tax causes farmers.

Repeal backers like to describe their movement as "grassroots," a mad-as-hell uprising by all of the ordinary Americans the estate tax supposedly injures. Peek behind the curtain, though, and you find a well-funded public relations, lobbying, media, and research apparatus led by sophisticated operatives, many with deep connections to the Republican Party. The "Disabled Americans" group was the creation of conservative communications maven Craig Shirley, whose public relations firm represents the National Rifle Association, the Heritage Foundation, and the Republican National Committee. It's impossible to evaluate the 1,000-members claim (a query to the group went unanswered), but O'Leary's is the only name that appears anywhere on the group's website.

The pro-repeal American Farm Bureau Foundation, when challenged, could not produce one actual example of a farm that was lost because of the estate tax, according to the *New York Times*. The group sent an urgent memo to its affiliates in 2001, stating "it is crucial for us to be able to provide Congress with examples of farmers and ranchers who have lost farms ... due to the death tax," but even this plea produced no real farm-loss stories. Other front groups advertising themselves as grassroots supporters of estate tax repeal included the Small Business Survival Coalition, United Seniors Association, and Americans for Job Security. All of these groups have articulated a single, carefully-crafted message; for example, they always called the estate tax a "death tax," a moniker that Republican pollster Frank Luntz urged repeal backers to use as a rhetorical centerpiece of the repeal campaign.

BEHIND THE CURTAIN

If the campaign to repeal the estate tax was not a genuine outpouring of grassroots concern, then where did it come from? In the early 1990s, a group including the heirs to the Mars and Gallo family fortunes embarked on a long-term effort to eliminate the tax. They enlisted the help of Patricia Soldano, an Orange County, Calif., advisor to wealthy families. She formed a lobbying organization called the Policy and Taxation Group to provide an "outlet" for wealthy families "interested in communicating their concerns to members of Congress." Soldano channeled funds to congressional backers of repeal and hired the powerful lobbying firm Patton Boggs.

By the mid-1990s, Soldano's outfit and other early pro-repeal groups had joined together with a veritable industry of think tanks, lobbying firms, and interest groups in Washington, D.C., to form a powerful "death tax elimination" lobby.

Conservative think tanks, including the Heritage Foundation and the libertarian National Center for Policy Analysis, produced policy backgrounders criticizing the estate tax, and generated the requisite op-eds and TV appearances as well. The antigovernment group Citizens for a Sound Economy encouraged its members to lobby their senators and representatives against the tax.

Other groups involved in the anti-estate tax crusade include the private campaign organization Club for Growth; the political arm of the libertarian Cato Institute; the American Conservative Union; Grover Norquist's Americans for Tax Reform; and the 60 Plus Association, a self-styled conservative alternative to the American Association of Retired Persons. At the center of the lobbying effort is the National Federation of Independent Businesses (NFIB), a business trade association and one of the most influential organizations in Washington.

The combined efforts of these groups succeeded in getting estate tax repeal included in the 2001 Bush tax cut. What would have seemed unthinkable a decade earlier is now a fact of public policy.

WHO PAID THE PIPER?

It takes money to whip up "grassroots" political organizations where none exist, to place full-page newspaper ads, to conduct research, and to lobby. But the funding that underwrites right-wing public policy advocacy is largely hidden. Corporations are an important source of funds, but they don't have to disclose the bulk of their philanthropic giving.

The strategic role of conservative grantmaking foundations is more visible, though, thanks to research by the National Committee for Responsive Philanthropy. The committee's 2004 report, "Axis of Ideology: Conservative Foundations and Public Policy," discloses that right-wing foundations like the David H. Koch Charitable Trust, the Linde and Harry Bradley Foundation, the Carthage Foundation (one of the Scaife Foundations), the John M. Olin Foundation, and the Claude R. Lamb Charitable Trust don't have the net worth or grantmaking dollars of the giants such as the Ford Foundation, which are all centrist or liberal; however, they spend their money in a more focused way. For example, these foundations specifically support public policy advocacy, directing over a fifth of their resources to it. Their advocacy includes Social Security privatization, free-trade agreements, tax cuts, corporate deregulation and weakening of labor laws. Liberal and centrist foundations tend to shy away from policy advocacy, focusing their funding instead on provision of basic services.

Right-wing nonprofits and the foundations that fund them are networked in a way that centralizes their efforts and leverages their resources. The 20 largest right-wing foundations donated over 80% of the $250 million that conservative foundations allocated to public policy advocacy between 1999 and 2001. And 20 nonprofit organizations—key groups that set the conservative agenda through research and market and lobby for that agenda—received over half of these allocations.

Conservative foundations are also strategic about *how* they fund the groups they fund. While liberal foundations tend to fund "projects," the leading-edge conservative foundations fund movement infrastructure. While liberal foundations rarely provide multiyear support that would enable grantees to build up permanent capacity, conservative foundations often provide long-term general support, in some cases over decades. While only 27% of grants from liberal and centrist foundations are for general operating support, almost 80% of conservative foundation grants are of this kind.

Progressive infrastructure is outgunned on almost every front. But there are efforts underway to change this. The National Committee on Responsive Philanthropy has stimulated discussion within the funding community about applying some of the lessons of right-wing grantmaking. Some liberal funders, recognizing the need for a message-oriented progressive think tank, ponied up $10 million in 2003 to launch the Center for American Progress.

Today, conservatives are harvesting the fruits of several decades of investment in shaping public attitudes and promoting right-wing ideas and policies. Ideas that were once considered marginal, such as privatizing Social Security, providing vouchers for private education, and eliminating the progressive income tax, are now at the center of policy debates. If progressive forces can build and fund an equally effective infrastructure, the wealth-broadening agenda will have a fighting chance.

Like nobility in feudal times, shareholders claim wealth they do little to create. Marjorie Kelly questions our assumptions about the rights of the corporate stockholder, and asks why employees, by contrast, have no claim on corporate wealth, no voting rights, and no say in corporate governance.

A Legitimate Mandate?

Maximizing Returns to Shareholders

BY MARJORIE KELLY

Where does wealth come from? More precisely, where does the wealth of major public corporations come from? Who creates it?

To judge by the current arrangement in corporate America, one might suppose capital creates wealth—which is odd, because a pile of capital sitting there creates nothing. Yet capital-providers (stockholders) lay claim to most wealth that public corporations generate. They also claim the more fundamental right to have corporations managed on their behalf.

Corporations are believed to exist for one purpose alone: to maximize returns to shareholders. This principle is reinforced by CEOs, the *Wall Street Journal*, business schools, and the courts. It is the law of the land—much as the divine right of kings was once the law of the land. Indeed, "maximizing returns to shareholders" is universally accepted as a kind of divine, unchallengeable mandate.

It is not in the least controversial. Though it should be.

What do shareholders contribute to justify the extraordinary allegiance they receive? They take risk, we're told. They put their money on the line, so corporations might grow and prosper.

Let's test the truth of this with a little quiz:

Stockholders fund major public corporations—*True or False*?

False. Or, actually, a tiny bit true—but for the most part, massively false.

What's intriguing is that we speak as though it were entirely true: "I have invested in AT&T," we say—imagining AT&T as a steward of our money, with a fiduciary responsibility to take care of it.

In fact, "investing" dollars don't go to AT&T but to other speculators. Equity "investments" reach a public corporation only when new common stock is sold—which for major corporations is a rare event. Among the Dow Jones Industrials, only a handful have sold any new common stock in 30 years. Many have sold none in 50 years.

The stock market works like a used car market, as accounting professor Ralph Estes observes in *Tyranny of the Bottom Line*. When you buy a 1989 Ford Escort, the money doesn't go to Ford. It goes to the previous owner. Ford gets the buyer's money only when it sells a new car.

Similarly, companies get stockholders' money only when they sell new common stock—which mature companies rarely do. According to figures from the Federal Reserve and the Securities and Exchange Commission, about 99% of the stock out there is "used stock." That is, 99 out of 100 "invested" dollars are trading in the purely speculative market, and never reach corporations.

Public corporations do have the ability to sell new stock. And they do need capital (funds beyond revenue) to operate—for inventory, expansion, and so forth. But they get very little of this capital from stockholders.

In 1993, for example, corporations needed $555 billion in capital. According to the Federal Reserve, sales of common stock contributed 4% of that. I used this fact in a pull-quote for a magazine article once, and the designer changed it to 40%, assuming it was a typo. It's not.

Well, yes, critics will say—that's recently. But stockholders did fund corporations in the past. Again, only a tiny bit true. Take the steel industry. An accounting study by Eldon Hendriksen examined capital expenditures in that industry from 1900 to 1953, and found that issues of common stock provided only 5% of capital. That was over the entire first half of the 20th century, when industry was growing by leaps and bounds.

So, what do stockholders contribute, to justify the extraordinary allegiance they receive? Very little. And that's my point.

Equity capital is provided by stockholders when a company goes public, and in occasional secondary offerings later. But in the life of most major companies today, issuance of common stock represents a distant, long-ago source of funds, and a minor one at that. What's odd is that it entitles holders to extract most of the corporation's wealth, forever.

Equity investors essentially install a pipeline, and dictate that the corporation's sole purpose is to funnel wealth into it. The pipeline is never to be tampered with—and no one else is to be granted significant access (except executives, whose function is to keep it flowing).

The truth is, the commotion on Wall Street is not about funding corporations. It's about extracting from them.

The productive risk in building businesses is borne by entrepreneurs and their initial venture investors, who do contribute real investing dollars, to create real wealth. Those who buy stock at sixth or seventh hand, or 1,000th hand, also take a risk—but it is a risk speculators take among themselves, trying to outwit one another like gamblers.

It has little to do with corporations, except this: Public companies are required to provide new chips for the gaming table, into infinity.

It's odd. And it's connected to a second oddity—that we believe stockholders are the corporation. When we say "a corporation did well," we mean its shareholders did well. The company's local community might be devastated by plant closings, its groundwater contaminated with pollutants. Employees might be shouldering a crushing workload, doing without raises for years on end. Still we will say, "the corporation did well."

One does not see rising employee income as a measure of corporate success. Indeed, gains to employees are losses to the corporation. And this betrays an unconscious bias: that employees are not really part of the corporation. They have no claim on wealth they create, no say in governance, and no vote for the board of directors. They're not citizens of corporate society, but subjects. Investors, on the other hand, may never set foot inside "their" companies, may not know where they're located or what they produce. Yet corporations exist to enrich investors alone. In the corporate society, only those who own stock can vote—like America until the mid-1800s, when only those who owned land could vote. Employees are disenfranchised.

We think of this as the natural law of the free market. It's more accurately the result of the existing corporate governance structure, which violates free-market principles. In a free market, everyone scrambles to get what they can, and they keep what they earn. In the construct of the corporation, one group gets what another earns.

The oddity of it all is veiled by the incantation of a single, magical word: "ownership." Because we say stockholders "own" corporations, they are permitted to contribute very little, and take quite a lot.

What an extraordinary word. One is tempted to recall [Greek poet] Lycophron's comment, during an early Athenian slave uprising against the aristocracy. "The splendour of noble birth is imaginary," he said, "and its prerogatives are based upon a mere word."

"The feminization of poverty," "the gender gap"—these terms have helped put women's economic status onto the agenda in both rich and poor countries. We know that in the United States, the racial wealth gap outpaces the racial income gap in both magnitude and, very likely, effects. Is the same true for gender? Here, Dollars & Sense co-editor Amy Gluckman reviews what we know about women and wealth ownership, in the United States and globally.

Women and Wealth

A Primer

BY AMY GLUCKMAN

Put "wealth" and "women" into the same sentence, and contradictory images jump to mind: from Cleopatra, Marie Antoinette ("let them eat cake"), or Oprah to an anonymous Asian, Latin American, or African woman lugging buckets or bales along a rugged path. Each of these images bears some truth: women's relationship with wealth is not a simple one. Women have, historically, held every possible juxtaposition with wealth and property. They have been property themselves, essentially sold in marriage, and in some instances inherited upon a husband's death by his brother or other male relative. They have almost universally faced restricted rights to own, control, and inherit property compared to men. Yet women have also been fabulously wealthy, and in not insignificant numbers—sometimes benefiting from family-owned wealth, occasionally wealthy in their own right. Today, according to a recent report in *Datamonitor*, more than half of Britain's millionaires are women.

Furthermore, women's access to wealth is always conditioned by race, ethnicity, class, and all of the other parameters that shape the distribution of wealth in any society. Her gender is never the sole factor that shapes a woman's acquisition or use of property.

Marriage in particular has acted as a double-edged sword for women. On one hand, marriage typically gives a woman access to a man's income and wealth, affording her a higher standard of living than most social orders would have allowed her to achieve on her own. On the other hand, women have widely lost rights to own, control, and inherit wealth when they married. And when divorced or widowed, women have sometimes lost the access that marriage afforded them to their husbands' property without gaining any renewed rights to the property of their natal families.

Discriminatory laws and customs in many parts of the world have broken down, although it's sobering to remember how recent this change has been. In the United States, the first state to enact a comprehensive law removing restrictions on property ownership by married women was New York, in 1848. (Mississippi passed a limited statute in 1839. In a clear illustration of the complicated nexus of race, class, and gender that always shapes wealth ownership, the Mississippi law was primarily focused on giving married women the right to own slaves; the law was likely intended to offer plantation owners a way to avoid having their slaves seized to pay the husband's debts.) Other states were still passing similar laws up to 1900, and discrimination on the basis of sex and marital status in granting credit was made illegal at the federal level only in 1974. And of course, custom and economic institutions continued to discriminate against women in the ownership and control of property, access to credit in their own names, and related matters long after laws had been changed.

Around the world, many countries have only recently granted women—or married women in particular—property rights. A 2000 U.N. report lists Bolivia, the Dominican Republic, Eritrea, Malaysia, Nepal, Uganda, Tanzania, and Zimbabwe among countries that have recently passed laws recognizing women's ownership of land, for example. Many countries still lack statutes giving women an express right to own land or other wealth in their own names (see the map on pages 18–19).

FREE BUT NOT EQUAL

Even with the right to own wealth, women have not necessarily had the means to accumulate any. Among the factors key to building assets are income, education, and inheritance—and, of course, in each of these, women face obstacles, whether customary or legal.

In the rich countries, women today have largely the same educational attainment as men—up to, but not including, the highest levels. In the United States, for example, more girls than boys graduate from high school, and more women than men are enrolled in bachelor's degree programs. But there are still far more men than women who hold advanced degrees, especially in lucrative fields such as engineering, business, law, and medicine.

Women workers remain concentrated in female-dominated occupations that continue to pay less than male-dominated occupations requiring the same degree of skill, preparation, and responsibility. This is a key reason for the persistent gender pay gap. The median income of U.S. men working full-time, year-round was $38,275 in 2001; the equivalent figure for women was $29,215, or only 76% of men's pay.

Women in the global South continue to face far larger education and income gaps, although with great variation among countries. For example, Yemen, Pakistan, and Niger all have female-male adult literacy ratios under 60%, while Jordan, Sri Lanka, and Cameroon all have ratios of 95% or above. Income data disaggregated by sex is not available for many countries, according the most recent U.N. Human Development Report. But the report's rough estimates show a substantial gender gap in income in every country. And in many developing countries, women continue to hold only limited rights to inherit property.

Plenty of factors account for women's lack of wealth accumulation across the globe, but working too little is certainly not one of them. Women work longer hours every day than men in most countries, according to time-use studies assembled by the United Nations. The unequal work burden is most pronounced in rural areas, where women typically work 20% more minutes a day than men. Environmental problems in many countries have exacerbated women's work burden; a Population Reference Bureau report notes that "Given the variety of women's daily interactions with the environment to meet household needs, they are often most keenly affected by its degradation. In the Sudan, deforestation in the last decade has led to a quadrupling of women's time spent gathering fuelwood. Because girls are often responsible for collecting water and fuelwood, water scarcity and deforestation also contribute to higher school dropout rates for girls."

WOMEN'S WEALTH HOLDINGS: WHAT WE KNOW

Today's wealth distribution reflects the accumulation of assets over years, even generations. So it will take time before the uneven but dramatic changes in women's status over the past few decades will show up in the wealth statistics. Given that, what is the distribution of wealth by gender today?

The first thing to note is that we really don't know what it is, for a number of reasons. First, data on personal wealth are scarce. Most countries do not systematically collect data on wealth ownership. Among the few countries that do are the United States, Sweden, Germany, and Britain.

Where data *are* regularly collected, the unit is typically the household, not the individual. Thus the assets of most married couples are assigned to both wife and husband equally in wealth surveys, obscuring any differences in the two spouses' authority to manage or benefit from those assets or to retain them if the marriage ends. This leaves gender comparisons possible only between unmarried men and unmarried women, a minority of the adult population.

In many countries, property ownership is governed by customary or informal rules rather than legal title. The term "ownership" itself is a simplification; ownership is really a bundle of rights that don't necessarily reside in the same person. In statutory systems and particularly in customary systems, women may have limited ownership rights; for example, a woman may have the right to use a piece of property but not to transfer or bequeath it. This limits the value of any simple, quantitative snapshot of wealth distribution by gender. Instead, a complex qualitative portrait is necessary.

Given all of these limitations, what *do* we know?

In the United States, the significant gap is between married and unmarried people. Married-couple households have median net worth far more than two times that of households headed by unmarried adults (see "Women and Wealth in the United States," page 16). However, there is also a gender gap between unmarried men and unmarried women. The median net worth of single female-headed households in 2001 was $28,000; of single male-headed households, $47,000. And this gap has to be viewed in relation to the greater financial responsibilities of single women: a greater portion of single-female headed households include children under 18. There is also a vast wealth gap between white women and women of color: the median net worth of households headed by single white women was $56,590 in 2001; of households headed by single African-American women, $5,700; and of households headed by single Hispanic women, $3,900.

The young baby-boomer cohort, looked at separately, shows nearly no wealth gap between unmarried men and women (see page 17). This suggests that women are catching up—at least in a rich country like the United States. This is not surprising, as women are moving toward parity with men in several of the factors correlated with higher net worth, such as education and income. However, the income gap has long been smaller between young women and men than between older women and men, at least in part because the workforce participation of women—who typically bear greater parenting responsibilities than men—becomes more uneven over time. As the young boomers age, how much the wealth gap is really shrinking will become more clear.

For the global South, systematic personal wealth data simply do not exist. But it's possible to assess some of the factors that are shaping the distribution of wealth by gender in poor and middle-income nations. The transition to formal systems of property ownership has had complex effects in many poor, predominantly rural countries. In theory, holding legal title to land can benefit small farmers—many of whom around the world are women. With a legal title, a farmer can use the land as collateral and thereby gain access to credit; she can also more confidently invest in improvements. However, in the process of formalizing land titles, governments have often taken land that was customarily under a woman's control and given the title to it to a man. Likewise, land reform programs have often bypassed women. Women were "left out of the agrarian reforms of the 1960s and 1970s" in Latin America, according to a U.N. report, because household heads, to whom land titles were given, were simply assumed to be men. Women do 60% to 80% of the agricultural labor throughout the developing world, but are not nearly as likely to be actual landowners: the percentage of agricultural landowners who are women ranges from 3% in Bangladesh to 57% in Namibia, and their average holdings are smaller than men's.

Lacking formal title to land, women have very limited access to agricultural credit. The same is true outside of agriculture: of the 300 million low-income self-employed women in the global South, hardly any have access to credit (aside from moneylenders, who typically charge exorbitant interest rates that can range up to 100% a month). Microcredit programs have sprung up in many countries and are making a dent in this problem, but just a dent. Although it's now worth some $2.5 billion, the microcredit sector reaches only an estimated 3% of those across the global South (both women and men) who could benefit from it.

Liberalization and structural adjustment policies pressed on third world governments have been hard on women's economic status. Consider the case of Mexico where, following the introduction of economic liberalization in the mid-1980s, growth has been slow for everyone. But women have suffered disproportionately. With the opening of lots of export-oriented *maquiladoras*, women's share of industrial jobs grew. But women's industrial wages fell from 80% of men's in 1984 to 57% of men's in 1992. At the same time, the bland term "structural adjustment" means, in practice, often-huge cutbacks in public services such as health care, education, and aid to the poor. Women (and children) are typically more dependent on these programs than men, and so suffer more when they are cut.

WHAT IS WEALTH GOOD FOR?

Does it matter if women have less wealth and less capacity to acquire and control assets than men? Most adult women across the globe are married, and for most married women, these forms of gender-specific discrimination do not prevent them from enjoying a family standard of living underwritten by their husbands' income and wealth. But a woman's ability to own property in her own name turns out to be more important than it might appear. Women with property are less vulnerable to all of life's vicissitudes. Owning property can protect women affected by HIV/AIDS from destitution, for example; the International Center for Research on Women is currently documenting this association.

And asset ownership changes the balance of power between women and men. In a study of 500 urban and rural women in Kerala, India, Pradeep Panda of the Centre for Development Studies, Trivandrum, and Bina Agarwal of the Institute of Economic Growth, Delhi, found that women who are wealthless are considerably more vulnerable to domestic violence than women who own property. The study's remarkable results are worth quoting at length:

> The study's findings did bear out the fact that ownership of immovable property by women is associated with a dramatically lower incidence of both physical and psychological harassment, as well as long-term and current violence. For example, as many as 49% of the women who owned neither land nor house suffered long-term physical violence, compared with 18% and 10% respectively of those who owned either land or a house, and 7% of those who owned both.
>
> The effect of property ownership on psychological violence is even more dramatic. While 84% of property-less women suffered abuse, the figure was much lower (16%) for women who owned both land and a house.
>
> The ownership of property also offers women the option of leaving an abusive environment—of the 179 women experiencing long-term physical violence, 43 left home. The percentage of women leaving home was much higher among the propertied (71%) than among those without property (19%). Moreover, of the women who left home, although 24 returned, 88% of the returning women were property-less. Few propertied women returned.
>
> So, not only are propertied women less likely to experience marital violence, they are also able to escape further violence. Hence, property ownership serves both as a deterrent and as an exit option for abused women.
>
> Interestingly, while a fair proportion of women (propertied and property-less) faced dowry demands, only 3% of propertied women faced dowry-related beatings by their in-laws and husbands, compared to 44% of property-less women. This suggests another form in which the ownership of personal property lessens the incidence of domestic crimes against women.

The protective impact of house or land ownership on reducing a woman's risk of violence emerged as significant even after such factors as household economic status, a woman's age, duration of marriage, childlessness, educational and employment levels of both husband and wife, spousal gaps in education or employment, the husband's alcohol consumption, childhood exposure to violence and social support from parents and neighbours were controlled.

In contrast to a woman's property ownership status, there seems to be no clear relationship between risk of violence and employment status, except if the woman has a regular job. This reduces the risk only of long-term physical violence. Employment does not offer the same protection to women as does property ownership. ... Land access enhances a woman's livelihood options and gives her a sense of empowerment.

It has long been a shibboleth in the U.S. women's movement that all women can face domestic violence regardless of their economic circumstances. But owning and controlling some wealth surely offers women in rich countries the same kinds of protection the Kerala study revealed: a stronger position in the marital power dynamic, and the ability to exit. And owning some property no doubt underwrites a woman's ability to struggle against patriarchal institutions in other ways too, at least on an individual level, and to achieve her own potential. Virginia Woolf wrote a century ago that a woman who wanted to create needed a modest (unearned) income and a room of her own; Woolf's vision is no less true today.

But today most women around the world still don't have the modest unearned income or the room of their own—and not only because of their gender. What then would a progressive feminist agenda around wealth look like? Of course, it would address all of the remaining customs, statutes, and institutional barriers that limit women's economic rights relative to men's. But it would also seek to reorient all economic institutions toward the provision of social forms of wealth and the deconcentration of private wealth. Only a dual agenda like this can offer any hope—for achieving either gender equity *or* a decent standard of living—to a majority of the world's women.

A society's system of property rights underlies its distribution of wealth. It sets the rules that determine how ownership is defined, what benefits accrue to those defined as owners, and at what cost to the larger social good.

Property

Who Has a Right to What and Why?

BY ARTHUR MACEWAN

In 1948, siblings Joseph and Agnes Waschak purchased a home in Taylor, Pennsylvania, in the midst of coal mining country. Within a few years, hydrogen sulfide fumes and other gases from the nearby mines and mine waste turned the Waschaks' white house black and stained all the internal fixtures yellowish-brown or black. The Waschaks filed suit for damages. According to evidence presented in the subsequent court case, the Waschaks and other area residents who were forced to breathe the gases "suffered from headaches, throat irritation, inability to sleep, coughing, light-headedness, nausea and stomach ailments."

Eric Freyfogle describes the *Waschak v. Moffat* case in his book *The Land We Share: Private Property and the Common Good* as an illustration of how changing concepts of property relate to the preservation of the natural environment. Eventually, the case worked its way up to the Pennsylvania Supreme Court. *Waschak v. Moffat* was not simply an instance of citizens challenging property owners, but of one set of property owners positioned against another. On one side were the Waschaks and others who claimed that the actions of the coal companies constituted a nuisance that prevented them from fully using their property; on the other side were the coal companies who wanted to use their mines as they saw fit. The court had to decide not *whether* property rights would prevail, but *which* set of property rights had priority.

In 1954, the court ruled that a nuisance existed only when the actions involved were intentional or the result of negligence. The coal companies, the court maintained, intended no harm and were not negligent because they were following standard practices in the mining industry. The Waschaks lost.

Four decades later, concepts of property rights and priorities had changed, as illustrated by a 1998 case in Iowa, *Borman v. Board of Supervisors*, also described by Freyfogle. In this case, the landowning plaintiffs wanted to prevent another landowner from developing a "Confined Animal Feeding Operation" (CAFO) that would involve thousands of animals generating large amounts of waste, odors, and other damage to the surrounding properties. Again, the dispute was between the conflicting rights of two sets of property owners.

The Iowa Supreme Court ruled in favor of the plaintiffs, agreeing that the nuisance that would be created by the CAFO would be an illegitimate interference with their property rights. The court did not deny that its ruling limited the property rights of the CAFO planners, but it gave priority to the rights of the plaintiffs. Moreover, the court ruled that the CAFO planners were not due any compensation by the state, even though it was preventing them from using their land as they chose and thereby reducing the value of that property.

What changed between 1954 and 1998? Many things were different, of course, including the fact that the earlier case was in one state and the later case in another. But the most important difference was that society's views on environmental issues had changed, evolving along with the development of a broad social movement to protect the environment. As a result, concepts regarding property rights changed. What had earlier been seen as legitimate action by a property owner was, by the end of century, viewed as an illegitimate degradation of the environment.

Property rights, it turns out, are not fixed. They change. They are a product of society and of social decisions. As society changes, so too do property rights. And the changes in property rights are contested, subject to political power and social struggle.

WHY DO WE PROTECT PRIVATE PROPERTY?

Although we often take property rights for granted, as though they are based on some absolute standard, in reality they are both changing and ambiguous. Moreover, many widely accepted ideas about property rights start to fall apart when we ask: Why do we protect private property?

For example, suppose a family has a deed on a particular field. Why do we as a society say that another family cannot come along, take part of that field, and sow and reap their own crops? Does it make any difference if the family with the deed has never used the field for any productive purpose, but has simply let it sit idle?

Or, for another example, suppose a pharmaceutical company develops a new antibiotic. Why do we allow that company the right to take out a patent and then prevent other firms or individuals from producing and selling that same antibiotic? Does it make any difference if the antibiotic is one that would save the lives of many people were it more readily available—that is, available at a lower price than the company charges?

Or, for still another example, what if a man owns a large house in the suburbs, an extensive apartment in the city, a ski lodge in the mountains, a beach house at the shore, two or three other homes at convenient sites, three yachts, a jet plane, and seven cars? Why do we prevent a poor man who has nothing—no home, no car, and certainly no yacht or jet plane—from occupying one of these many homes?

Perhaps the most common argument in favor of our protection of private property is the claim: We protect private property because it works to do so. That is, secure property rights are viewed as a basis for a stable and prosperous society. If people do not know that their accumulated wealth—held in the form of cash, land, houses, or factories—will be protected by society, they will see little point in trying to accumulate. According to the argument, if the pharmaceutical company cannot be assured of the profit from its patent, it will have no incentive to finance the research that leads to the drug's development. And if the state did not protect people's wealth, society could be in a continual state of instability and conflict.

As a defense of private property rights, however, this it-works-to-do-so argument is incomplete, as the *Waschak* and *Borman* cases illustrate, because it does not tell us what to do when property rights come into conflict with one another. This defense of property rights is also flawed because it is too vague, failing to provide a sufficiently clear statement of what things can legitimately be held as private property. Can air or water or people be held as private property? Can a patent be held forever?

What's more, the argument puts defenders of property rights in a precarious position because it implicitly concedes that private property rights exist in order to serve the larger good of society. If we determine that the larger good of society dictates a change in property rights—new restrictions on the use of property, for example—then the it-works-to-do-so argument provides no defense.

In many instances, property owners have claimed that environmental regulations infringe on their property rights. Property owners who are prevented from establishing a CAFO as in the Borman case, from filling wet-lands, from building along fragile coast lines, or from destroying the habi-tat of an endangered species argue that government regulation is, in effect, taking away their property because it is reducing the value of that property. And they demand payment for this "taking." Such a claim loses its ideo-logical and legal force, however, in a world where property rights change, where they are a creation of society, and where the larger good of society is the ultimate justification for protecting private property.

While questions about property rights are surrounded by ideology, le-gal complications, and arguments about the larger good of society, at the core of these questions lie fundamental disputes about the distribution of wealth. Who gets to use a field, the extent of a pharmaceutical company's patent rights, the preservation of a rich man's houses—each of these exam-ples illustrates a conflict over the distribution of wealth as much as it illus-trates a complication of how we define and protect property rights. Prop-erty rights are the rules of the game by which society's wealth gets divided up, and how we shape those rules is very much connected to how we define the larger good of society.

PATENTS VERSUS LIFE

The relationship between property rights and the larger good of society has come to a head in recent years in the dispute over patent rights and AIDS drugs. It has become increasingly apparent that, when it comes to protect-ing the property rights of the pharmaceutical companies that hold patents on these life-saving drugs, it-*doesn't*-work-to-do-so.

In low-income countries, multinational pharmaceutical companies have attempted to enforce their patents on life-saving AIDS drugs and prevent the provision of these drugs at affordable prices. The matter has been especially important in several African countries where governments, ignoring the com-panies' patents, have taken steps to allow local production or importation of low-cost generic forms of the drugs. Large pharmaceutical corporations such as Glaxo, Merck, and Roche have fought back, and their resistance has received extensive support from the U.S. government. In 1998, for example, the South African government of Nelson Mandela passed a law allowing local firms to produce low-cost versions of the AIDS drugs on which U.S. pharmaceutical firms hold patents. The Clinton administration responded on behalf of the firms, accusing the South Africans of "unfair trade practic-es" and threatening the country with trade sanctions if it implemented the law. The drug companies have since backed off, seeking compromises that would allow access to the drugs in particular cases but that would avoid precedents undermining their property rights in the patents.

The conflict between patent rights and the availability of AIDS drugs, however, has continued and spread. In Thailand, for example, the Government Pharmaceutical Organization (GPO) sought permission from the country's Commerce Department to produce a drug, didanosine, for which Bristol-Myers Squibb holds the patent. In spite of the fact that the locally produced drug would allow treatment of close to a million HIV-positive people in Thailand who would otherwise be unable to afford the didanosine, the permission was rejected because the Thai Commerce Department feared trade retaliation from the United States. Instead, the GPO was only allowed to produce a form of the drug that has greater side effects. Early in 2004, however, Bristol-Myers Squibb ceded the issue. Fearing public outcry and damaging precedents in the courts, the company surrendered in Thailand its exclusive patent rights to manufacture and sell the drug.

These conflicts have not been confined to the particular case of AIDS drugs, but have also been major issues in World Trade Organization (WTO) negotiations on the international extension of patent rights in general. Popular pressure and government actions in several low-income regions of the world have forced compromises from the companies and at the WTO.

But the dispute is far from over, and it is not just about formal issues of property rights and patents. At its core, it is a dispute over whether medical advances will be directed toward the larger good of society or toward greater profits for the pharmaceutical companies and their shareholders. It is a dispute over the distribution of wealth and income.

"FREE THE MOUSE!"

Patents and, similarly, copyrights are a form of property (known as "intellectual property") that is quite clearly a creation of society, and the way society handles patents and copyrights does a great deal to shape the distribution of wealth and income. Acting through the state (the Department of Commerce in the United States), society gives the creator of a new product exclusive rights—in effect, monopoly control—to make, use, or sell the item, based on the general rationale that doing so will encourage the creation of more products (machines, books, music, pharmaceuticals, etc.).

The general rationale for these property rights, however, does not tell us very much about their nature. How long should patents and copyrights last? What can and what cannot be patented? What, exactly, constitutes an infringement of the copyright holder's property rights? And what if the rationale is wrong in the first place? What if patent and copyright protections are not necessary to promote creative activity? The answer to each of these questions is contested terrain, changing time and again as a consequence of larger political and social changes.

Beyond the issue of AIDS drugs, there are several other patent or copyright-related conflicts that illustrate how these rights change through conflict and the exercise of political power. One case is the Napster phenomenon, where people have shared music files over the Internet and generated outcry and lawsuits from music companies. This battle over property rights, inconceivable a generation ago, is now the subject of intense conflict in the courts.

An especially interesting case where rights have been altered by the effective use of political power has been the Mickey Mouse matter. In 1998, Congress passed the Sonny Bono Copyright Term Extension Act, extending copyright protection 20 years beyond what existing regulations provided for. One of the prime beneficiaries of—and one of the strongest lobbyists for—this act was the Disney company; the act assures Disney's control over Mickey Mouse until 2023—and Pluto, Goofy, and Donald Duck until 2025, 2027, and 2029, respectively.

Not surprisingly, the Copyright Extension Act aroused opposition, campaigning under the banner "Free the Mouse!" Along with popular efforts, the act was challenged in the courts. While the challenge had particular legal nuances, it was based on the seemingly reasonable argument that the Copyright Extension Act, which protects creative activity retroactively, could have no impact now on the efforts of authors and composers who created their works in the first half of the 20th century. The Supreme Court, apparently deciding that its view of the law trumped this reasonable argument, upheld the act. Congress and the Court provided a valuable handout to Disney and other firms, but it is hard to see how a 20-year extension of copyright protection will have any significant impact on creative efforts now or in the future.

"COULD YOU PATENT THE SUN?"

Indeed, in a recent paper issued by the Federal Reserve Bank of Minneapolis, economists Michele Boldrin and David K. Levine suggest that the government's granting of protection through patents and copyrights may not be necessary to encourage innovation. When government does grant these protections, it is granting a form of monopoly. Boldrin and Levine argue that when "new ideas are built on old ideas," the monopoly position embodied in patents and copyrights may stifle rather than encourage creativity. Microsoft, a firm that has prospered by building new ideas on old ideas and then protecting itself with patents and copyrights, provides a good example, for it is also a firm that has attempted to control new innovations and limit the options of competitors who might bring further advances. (Microsoft, dependent as it is on microprocessors developed in federal research programs and on the government-sponsored emergence of the Internet, is also a good example of the way property is often brought into being by public, government actions and then appropriated by private interests. But that is another story.)

Boldrin and Levine also point out that historically there have been many periods of thriving innovation in the absence of patents and copyrights. The economic historian David Landes relates how medieval Europe was "one of the most inventive societies that history has known." Landes describes, as examples, the development of the water wheel (by the early 11th century), eyeglasses (by the early 14th century), and the mechanical clock (by the late 13th century). Also, first invented by the Chinese in the ninth century, printing rapidly developed in Europe by the middle of the 15th century with the important addition of movable type. Yet the first patent statute was not enacted until 1474, in Venice, and the system of patents spread widely only with the rise of the Industrial Revolution. (There had been earlier ad hoc patents granted by state authorities, but these had limited force.)

Even in the current era, experience calls into question the necessity of patents and copyrights to spur innovations. The tremendous expansion of creativity on the Internet and the associated advances of open-access software, in spite of Microsoft's best efforts to limit potential competitors, illustrate the point.

The most famous inventor in U.S. history, Benjamin Franklin, declined to obtain patents for his various devices, offering the following principle in his autobiography: "That as we enjoy great Advantages from the Inventions of Others, we should be glad of an Opportunity to serve others by any Invention of ours, and this we should do freely and generously." Probably the most outstanding example of successful research and scientific advance without the motivation of patents and consequent financial rewards is the development of the polio vaccine. Jonas Salk, the principal creator of the polio vaccine, like Franklin, did not seek patents for his invention, one that has saved and improved countless lives around the world. Salk was once asked who would control the new drug. He replied: "Well, the people, I would say. There is no patent. Could you patent the sun?"

*   *   *   *   *

It turns out, then, that there is no simple answer to the question: "Why do we protect private property?" because the meaning of private property rights is not fixed but is a continually changing product of social transformation, social conflict, and political power. The courts are often the venue in which property rights are defined, but, as illustrated by the Pennsylvania and Iowa cases, the definitions provided by the courts change along with society.

The scourge of AIDS combined with the advent of the current wave of globalization have established a new arena for conflict over patent laws governing pharmaceuticals, and an international social movement has arisen to contest property laws in this area. The advances of information technology have likewise generated a new round of legal changes, and the interests, demands, and actions of a vast array of music listeners will be a major factor affecting those changes. With the emergence of the environmental movement and widespread concern for the protection of the natural environment, traditional views of how owners can use their land are coming into question. When society begins to question property rights, it is also questioning the distribution of wealth and income, and it is questioning the distribution of power.

Few realms of property rights can be taken for granted for very long. Whether we are talking about property in the most tangible form as land or property in the intangible form of patents and copyrights, the substance of property rights—who has a right to what and why—is continually changing.

The Consequences of Inequality

Progressives who decry economic inequality just don't know how the economy works—or so say conservative pundits. According to those on the right, inequality fuels economic growth. But as Chris Tilly explains, exactly the opposite is true. In fact, equality boosts economic growth, while inequality puts on the brakes.

Geese, Golden Eggs, and Traps

Why Inequality Is Bad for the Economy

BY CHRIS TILLY

Whenever progressives propose ways to redistribute wealth from the rich to those with low and moderate incomes, conservative politicians and economists accuse them of trying to kill the goose that lays the golden egg. The advocates of unfettered capitalism proclaim that inequality is good for the economy because it promotes economic growth. Unequal incomes, they say, provide the incentives necessary to guide productive economic decisions by businesses and individuals. Try to reduce inequality, and you'll sap growth. Furthermore, the conservatives argue, growth actually promotes equality by boosting the have-nots more than the haves. So instead of fiddling with who gets how much, the best way to help those at the bottom is to pump up growth.

But these conservative prescriptions are absolutely, dangerously wrong. Instead of the goose-killer, equality turns out to be the goose. Inequality stifles growth; equality gooses it up. Moreover, economic expansion does *not* necessarily promote equality—instead, it is the types of jobs and the rules of the economic game that matter most.

INEQUALITY: GOOSE OR GOOSE-KILLER?

The conservative argument may be wrong, but it's straightforward. Inequality is good for the economy, conservatives say, because it provides the right incentives for innovation and economic growth. First of all, people will only have the motivation to work hard, innovate, and invest wisely if the economic system rewards them for good economic choices and penalizes bad ones. Robin Hood-style policies that collect from the wealthy and help those who are worse off violate this principle. They reduce the payoff to smart decisions and lessen the sting of dumb ones. The result: people and companies are bound to make less efficient decisions. "We must allow [individuals] to fail, as well as succeed, and we must replace the nanny state with a regime of self-reliance and self-respect," writes conservative lawyer Stephen Kinsella in *The Freeman: Ideas on Liberty* (not clear how the free woman fits in). To prove their point, conservatives point to the former state socialist countries, whose economies had become stagnant and inefficient by the time they fell at the end of the 1980s.

If you don't buy this incentive story, there's always the well-worn trickle-down theory. To grow, the economy needs productive investments: new offices, factories, computers, and machines. To finance such investments takes a pool of savings. The rich save a larger fraction of their incomes than those less well-off. So to spur growth, give more to the well-heeled (or at least take less away from them in the form of taxes), and give less to the down-and-out. The rich will save their money and then invest it, promoting growth that's good for everyone.

Unfortunately for trickle-down, the brilliant economist John Maynard Keynes debunked the theory in his *General Theory of Employment, Interest, and Money* in 1936. Keynes, whose precepts guided liberal U.S. economic policy from the 1940s through the 1970s, agreed that investments must be financed out of savings. But he showed that most often it's changes in investment that drive savings, rather than the other way around. When businesses are optimistic about the future and invest in building and retooling, the economy booms, all of us make more money, and we put some of it in banks, 401(k)s, stocks, and so on. That is, saving grows to match investment. When companies are glum, the process runs in reverse, and savings shrink to equal investment. This leads to the "paradox of thrift": if people try to save too much, businesses will see less consumer spending, will invest less, and total savings will end up diminishing rather than growing as the economy spirals downward. A number of Keynes's followers added the next logical step: shifting money from the high-saving rich to the high-spending rest of us, and not the other way around, will spur investment and growth.

Of the two conservative arguments in favor of inequality, the incentive argument is a little weightier. Keynes himself agreed that people needed financial consequences to steer their actions, but questioned whether the differences in payoffs needed to be so huge. Certainly state socialist countries' attempts to replace material incentives with moral exhortation have often fallen short. In 1970, the Cuban government launched the *Gran Zafra* (Great Harvest), an attempt to reap 10 million tons of sugar cane with (strongly encouraged) volunteer labor. Originally inspired by Che Guevara's ideal of the New Socialist Man (not clear how the New Socialist Woman fit in), the effort ended with Fidel Castro tearfully apologizing to the Cuban people in a nationally broadcast speech for letting wishful thinking guide economic policy.

But before conceding this point to the conservatives, let's look at the evidence about the connection between equality and growth. Economists William Easterly of New York University and Gary Fields of Cornell University have recently summarized this evidence:

- Countries, and regions within countries, with more equal incomes grow faster. (These growth figures do not include environmental destruction or improvement. If they knocked off points for environmental destruction and added points for environmental improvement, the correlation between equality and growth would be even stronger, since desperation drives poor people to adopt environmentally destructive practices such as rapid deforestation.)
- Countries with more equally distributed land grow faster.
- Somewhat disturbingly, more ethnically homogeneous countries and regions grow faster—presumably because there are fewer ethnically based inequalities.

In addition, more worker rights are associated with higher rates of economic growth, according to Josh Bivens and Christian Weller, economists at two Washington think tanks, the Economic Policy Institute and the Center for American Progress.

These patterns recommend a second look at the incentive question. In fact, more equality can actually *strengthen* incentives and opportunities to produce.

EQUALITY AS THE GOOSE

Equality can boost growth in several ways. Perhaps the simplest is that study after study has shown that farmland is more productive when cultivated in small plots. So organizations promoting more equal distribution of land, like Brazil's Landless Workers' Movement, are not just helping the landless poor—they're contributing to agricultural productivity!

Another reason for the link between equality and growth is what Easterly calls "match effects," which have been highlighted in research by Stanford's Paul Roemer and others in recent years. One example of a match effect is the fact that well-educated people are most productive when working with others who have lots of schooling. Likewise, people working with computers are more productive when many others have computers (so that, for example, e-mail communication is widespread, and know-how about computer repair and software is easy to come by). In very unequal societies, highly educated, computer-using elites are surrounded by majorities with little education and no computer access, dragging down their productivity. This decreases young people's incentive to get more education and businesses' incentive to invest in computers, since the payoff will be smaller.

Match effects can even matter at the level of a metropolitan area. Urban economist Larry Ledebur looked at income and employment growth in 85 U.S. cities and their neighboring suburbs. He found that where the income gap between those in the suburbs and those in the city was largest, income and job growth was slower for everyone.

"Pressure effects" also help explain why equality sparks growth. Policies that close off the low-road strategy of exploiting poor and working people create pressure effects, driving economic elites to search for investment opportunities that pay off by boosting productivity rather than squeezing the have-nots harder. For example, where workers have more rights, they will place greater demands on businesses. Business owners will respond by trying to increase productivity, both to remain profitable even after paying higher wages, and to find ways to produce with fewer workers. The CIO union drives in U.S. mass production industries in the 1930s and 1940s provide much of the explanation for the superb productivity growth of the 1950s and 1960s. (The absence of pressure effects may help explain why many past and present state socialist countries have seen slow growth, since they tend to offer numerous protections for workers but no right to organize independent unions.) Similarly, if a government buys out large land-holdings in order to break them up, wealthy families who simply kept their fortunes tied up in land for generations will look for new, productive investments. Industrialization in Asian "tigers" South Korea and Taiwan took off in the 1950s on the wings of funds freed up in exactly this way.

INEQUALITY, CONFLICT, AND GROWTH

Inequality hinders growth in another important way: it fuels social conflict. Stark inequality in countries such as Bolivia and Haiti has led to chronic conflict that hobbles economic growth. Moreover, inequality ties up resources in unproductive uses such as paying for large numbers of police and security guards—attempts to prevent individuals from redistributing resources through theft.

Ethnic variety is connected to slower growth because, on the average, more ethnically diverse countries are also more likely to be ethnically divided. In other words, the problem isn't ethnic variety itself, but racism and ethnic conflict that can exist among diverse populations. In nations like Guatemala, Congo, and Nigeria, ethnic strife has crippled growth—a problem alien to ethnically uniform Japan and South Korea. The reasons are similar to some of the reasons that large class divides hurt growth. Where ethnic divisions (which can take tribal, language, religious, racial, or regional forms) loom large, dominant ethnic groups seek to use government power to better themselves at the expense of other groups, rather than making broad-based investments in education and infrastructure. This can involve keeping down the underdogs—slower growth in the U.S. South for much of the country's history was linked to the Southern system of white supremacy. Or it can involve seizing the surplus of ethnic groups perceived as better off—in the extreme, Nazi Germany's expropriation and genocide of the Jews, who often held professional and commercial jobs.

Of course, the solution to such divisions is not "ethnic cleansing" so that each country has only one ethnic group—in addition to being morally abhorrent, this is simply impossible in a world with 191 countries and 5,000 ethnic groups. Rather, the solution is to diminish ethnic inequalities. Once the 1964 Civil Rights Act forced the South to drop racist laws, the New South's economic growth spurt began. Easterly reports that in countries with strong rule of law, professional bureaucracies, protection of contracts, and freedom from expropriation—all rules that make it harder for one ethnic group to economically oppress another—ethnic diversity has *no* negative impact on growth.

If more equality leads to faster growth so everybody benefits, why do the rich typically resist redistribution? Looking at the ways that equity seeds growth helps us understand why. The importance of pressure effects tells us that the wealthy often don't think about more productive ways to invest or reorganize their businesses until they are forced to. But also, if a country becomes very unequal, it can get stuck in an "inequality trap." Any redistribution involves a tradeoff for the rich. They lose by giving up part of their wealth, but they gain a share in increased economic growth. The bigger the disparity between the rich and the rest, the more the rich have to lose, and the less likely that the equal share of boosted growth they'll get will make up for their loss. Once the gap goes beyond a certain point, the wealthy have a strong incentive to restrict democracy, and to block spending on education which might lead the poor to challenge economic injustice—making reform that much harder.

DOES ECONOMIC GROWTH REDUCE INEQUALITY?

If inequality isn't actually good for the economy, what about the second part of the conservatives' argument—that growth itself promotes equality? According to the conservatives, those who care about equality should simply pursue growth and wait for equality to follow.

"A rising tide lifts all boats," President John F. Kennedy famously declared. But he said nothing about which boats will rise fastest when the economic tide comes in. Growth does typically reduce poverty, according to studies reviewed by economist Gary Fields, though some "boats"—especially families with strong barriers to participating in the labor force—stay "stuck in the mud." But inequality can increase at the same time that poverty falls, if the rich gain even faster than the poor do. True, sustained periods of low unemployment, like that in the late 1990s United States, do tend to raise wages at the bottom even faster than salaries at the top. But growth after the recessions of 1991 and 2001 began with years of "jobless recoveries"— growth with inequality.

For decades the prevailing view about growth and inequality within countries was that expressed by Simon Kuznets in his 1955 presidential address to the American Economic Association. Kuznets argued that as countries grew, inequality would first increase, then decrease. The reason is that people will gradually move from the low-income agricultural sector to higher-income industrial jobs—with inequality peaking when the workforce is equally divided between low- and high-income sectors. For mature industrial economies, Kuznets's proposition counsels focusing on growth, assuming that it will bring equity. In developing countries, it calls for enduring current inequality for the sake of future equity and prosperity.

But economic growth doesn't automatically fuel equality. In 1998, economists Klaus Deininger and Lyn Squire traced inequality and growth over time in 48 countries. Five followed the Kuznets pattern, four followed the reverse pattern (decreasing inequality followed by an increase), and the rest showed no systematic pattern. In the United States, for example:

- incomes became more equal during the 1930s through 1940s New Deal period (a time that included economic decline followed by growth)
- from the 1950s through the 1970s, income gaps lessened during booms and expanded during slumps
- from the late 1970s forward, income inequality worsened fairly consistently, whether the economy was stagnating or growing.

The reasons are not hard to guess. The New Deal introduced widespread unionization, a minimum wage, social security, unemployment insurance, and welfare. Since the late 1970s, unions have declined, the inflation-adjusted value of the minimum wage has fallen, and the social safety net has been shredded. In the United States, as elsewhere, growth only promotes equality if policies and institutions to support equity are in place.

TRAPPED?

Let's revisit the idea of an inequality trap. The notion is that as the gap between the rich and everybody else grows wider, the wealthy become more willing to give up overall growth in return for the larger share they're getting for themselves. The "haves" back policies to control the "have-nots," instead of devoting social resources to educating the poor so they'll be more productive.

Sound familiar? It should. After two decades of widening inequality, the last few years have brought us massive tax cuts that primarily benefit the wealthiest, at the expense of investment in infrastructure and the education, child care, and income supports that would help raise less well-off kids to be productive adults. Federal and state governments have cranked up expenditures on prisons, police, and "homeland security," and Republican campaign organizations have devoted major resources to keeping blacks and the poor away from the polls. If the economic patterns of the past are any indication, we're going to pay for these policies in slower growth and stagnation unless we can find our way out of this inequality trap.

The 1990s saw concentrated wealth encroach into politics to an unprecedented degree—resulting in policy changes that produced crises in the accounting, telecom, and banking industries, and led to the Wall Street decline of 2001. Kevin Phillips puts today's plutocracy into historical perspective.

How Wealth Defines Power
The Politics of the New Gilded Age

BY KEVIN PHILLIPS

O f all the great deceptions that come to surround a gathering stock-market boom—from blather about the obsolescence of the business cycle to editorial claptrap about the United States turning into a republic of shareholders—one of the most pernicious has been the failure to recognize the character of the money culture it creates.

The pages of American history tell different stories about enormous wealth. Sometimes it has coexisted reasonably well with democracy, as in the days of Andrew Jackson or during the two decades after World War II. But the reverse has been true of the record concentrations of wealth that have grown up around the three most important financial boom periods: the post-Civil War Gilded Age, the Roaring Twenties, and the just-concluded bull market of the 1980s and '90s.

In a nutshell, these unusual wealth surges have bred unusual corruption. The moral degradation, in fact, has been multiple—financial corruption, political corruption, and philosophic or ideological corruption. Each has reinforced the others. When money is king, politicians get bought on a truly grand scale and philosophy bows to avarice. The genesis is much the same each time. All three booms have involved at least one decade—sometimes several—of hot new technology, surging stock markets, innovative finance, and the sense that the United States has transcended old limitations and rules. Money has fed on itself, creating a cult of railroad barons, automobile kings, hotshot CEOs, and financial masters of the universe. As the boom swells, so does the culture's preoccupation with money—and the competitive urge to ever more willingly cut corners. Human nature just can't resist. The ethical low usually becomes clear after the bull-market peak.

To get a fix on the corruption, it's necessary to begin with a portrait of the unusual wealth-creation dynamics involved. Each of these three periods saw a particularly lucrative convergence of economic forces. First, powerful new technology—railroads, steel, and oil in the Gilded Age; automobiles, radio, motion pictures, aviation, and household appliances in the 1920s; and personal computers, telecommunications, biotechnology, networking, and the Internet in the 1980s and '90s—energized the economy and captured the national imagination.

The second factor was financial innovation—new dimensions of banking, ballooning stock-market volume, innovations from ticker tapes, and investment trusts to computer programs and derivatives. There was also a cockiness each time about the United States having achieved a new level of sophisticated financial regulation—represented in the 1990s by the magic of Alan Greenspan—that would ensure against any calamity.

In all three periods, elements of the technology mania combined with new financial and speculative opportunities to create speculative excesses in bonds, stocks, or both. And each time a speculative bubble burst—in 1893, 1929, and 2000—the weakness in stocks and bonds spread into the real economy. But the wealth created was still notable, even after some or much of it was lost in the downturn.

The Gilded Age after the Civil War—it was 1873 when Mark Twain coined the term—lifted the American economy to not only new heights of success and industrialization, but also of economic polarization, and it introduced the nation to new lows of corruption. When the Civil War broke out in 1861, the largest fortune in the country was in the $15 million range, but by 1876, Commodore Vanderbilt had $100 million, and by the turn of the century both John D. Rockefeller (oil) and Andrew Carnegie (steel) were worth $300 million to $400 million. There had been maybe 300 U.S. millionaires in 1860, but by 1900 there were 4,000 to 5,000. And because there was little change in the value of a dollar between 1860 and 1900, the gains were real and not the product of inflation.

The financial corruption was lethal. Stocks and bonds were manipulated and watered down to such an extent that, after the Panic of 1893, thousands of banks and companies controlling one-third of the nation's railroad system were among the tens of thousands that failed. As for the political corruption of the Gilded Age, the U.S. Senate, then chosen by state legislatures rather than elected by the people, is even more emblematic than the Tweed Ring, Whiskey Ring, or Indian Ring. Millionaires frequently bought themselves Senate seats, and when one honest but naive member proposed legislation to unseat senators who had done so, Sen. Weldon B. Heyburn (R-Idaho) replied, in all seriousness, "We might lose a quorum here, waiting for the courts to act." Meanwhile, the philosophic corruption of the era produced a cult of markets and laissez faire, social Darwinism and survival of the fittest.

The 1920s made their greatest mark in financial corruption: Ponzi and his scheme, banks that peddled junk bonds and stocks, Samuel Insull and his pyramided utility holding companies, and New York Stock Exchange President Richard Whitney, who finally went to jail in 1938. The political side was highlighted by the Teapot Dome scandal and corrupt big-city machines owned by bootleggers and gangsters. The Dow Jones industrial average climbed 500% between 1921 and 1929, and the number of millionaires roughly quintupled to between 30,000 and 35,000 before collapsing in 1929 along with stock prices and the Indian summer of laissez faire.

Which brings us to the 1980s and 1990s and the corruption during those boom-crazed, wealth-fetishizing decades—behavior that was not just a matter of a few bad apples. As financial historians and economists such as Charles Kindleberger have pointed out, financial and political corruption seem to be an inevitable consequence of the psychologies and politics unleashed as a long bull market feeds a culture of money and greed.

The wealth and feeding pattern of the 1980s and '90s can be described in one word: unprecedented. The percentage increase in the Dow Jones industrial average between 1982 and 1999 was greater than the increase between 1921 and 1929, and the buildup in the largest American fortunes can be seen in the annual list of the *Forbes* 400 richest Americans. In 1982, looking at the richest 30 individuals and families, No. 30 had $500 million and No. 1, the du Pont family, had $8.6 billion; by 1999, after a 1,200% rise in the Dow, No. 30 had a fortune of $7 billion and No. 1, Bill Gates of Microsoft, had $85 billion.

Another set of numbers make clear just how rapacious America's top corporate echelon was. At its most intense, this was the mentality that gave us Enron, WorldCom and the like. In 1981 the 10 highest-compensated executives in the United States had an average annual compensation of $3.45 million; in 1988 the average compensation for this group had climbed to $19.3 million; in 2000 it had soared to $154 million.

Very little of this incredible gain at the top of the U.S. wealth-and-income structure trickled down. The top 1% of Americans did not do nearly as well as the top one-tenth of 1%, but their fortunes soared in comparison with the middle class. In the autumn of 2001, when the Senate was Democratic and the House Republican, the Congressional Budget Office published data showing changes in household after-tax income adjusted for inflation.

Income in After-Tax 1997 Dollars

	1979	1987	1997
Average Household in Lowest Quintile	$9,300	$8,800	$8,700
Average Household in Middle Quintile	$31,700	$32,000	$33,200
Average Household in Top 1%	$256,400	$421,500	$644,300

Source: Congressional Budget Office.

From the 1980s on, the enormous economic opportunities and benefits being concentrated at the top (and spreading down into the upper quintile) through tax cuts; bank, currency, and savings-and-loan bailouts; deregulation; mergers; leveraged buyouts; and a bull market in stocks had the predictable effects. Financial corruption ballooned, exemplified by the looting of savings-and-loan associations, the proliferation of insider-trading scandals, and the criminal machinations of junk-bond king Michael Milken. On the philosophic front, conservative think tanks promoted laissez faire and theorized about markets replacing politics. With so much at stake in policy-making and regulation, the rich stepped up their political involvement, and more and more money poured into congressional elections.

After a pause at the beginning of the 1990s, the boom, the technology mania, and the stock-market bubble continued to expand until they burst in 2000. After the crash, a mass of financial corruption and dirty laundry spilled out of the closet, tainting Enron, Citicorp, Merrill Lynch, Bell South, and dozens of others. The warping of ideas and thinking had in many ways resurrected the Gilded Age taste for survival of the fittest (this time globally), glorification of the rich, and deification of markets.

But my purpose here is to emphasize how the concentration and momentum of wealth spilled over, just as they had before, from economic self-interest and buccaneering into the corruption of politics. Money flowed into elections and into the many pockets of well-tailored politicians. If the corruption was not as obvious as in the buying of the U.S. Senate circa 1900, it was even greater in overall scale. Consider these highlights (or lowlights):

- **The presidential "money primary."** In the 1999–2000 election cycle, big donors in both parties were able for the first time to flood the system with enough money to anoint chosen candidates—Republican George W. Bush, Democrat Al Gore—scare off most rivals, and avoid a drawn-out primary contest on either side.

- **The buying of the national parties.** Soft-dollar contributions rose from very little in the early 1980s to some $495 million in the 1999–2000 cycle, more or less enabling wealthy individuals, corporations, and interests to rent the loyalties of both parties.

- **The rising cost of open seats.** Since the 1979–1980 election cycle, the cost of running for open House and Senate seats has roughly quintupled, ensuring that a candidate must either have money of his or her own or accept the conditions and fealty that come with large-scale fundraising.

- **The selling of representatives and senators.** Over the years, politicians have tailored more and more pockets into which money can be stuffed, including campaign war chests, leadership political action committees, personal foundations, allied think tanks and high-paying jobs for spouses, to say nothing of future job opportunities for themselves.

- **The ascendancy of the top 1%.** Not surprisingly, the dominance of money in politics has cemented the dominance of those who have it to give. In the 1999–2000 cycle, the 15,000 top campaign donors (of $10,000 and more) gave more than 40% of the total contributions greater than $1,000. Similarly, about 40% of the donors giving at least $200 were in the top 1% of Americans by income. This goes a long way toward explaining why Congress has voted for top-bracket income-tax cuts and for eliminating the federal inheritance or estate tax, which applies only to the top 1.6% of estates.

- **The purchase of key economic policies.** Since the mid-1990s, the ability of rich individuals and free-spending industries to buy victory on critical issues has been particularly evident in three congressional decisions: the 1995 legislation to shield accounting firms from liability for inaccurate corporate reporting (and the subsequent defeat of efforts to curb accounting industry conflicts of interest); the 1996 Telecommunications Act; and the 1999 legislation repealing the Glass-Steagall Act, a law that for 65 years had prohibited banks from being in the insurance or securities business. Money won each time. The accounting industry flooded Congress with money and marshaled allies to threaten the Securities and Exchange Commission's budget. Sen. John McCain (R-Ariz.), chairman of the Senate Committee on Commerce, called the Telecommunications

Act, in which broadcasters got $70 billion worth of free spectrum, "one of the greatest rip-offs since Teapot Dome." In 1999 the finance, insurance and real-estate sector was able to repeal Glass-Steagall in part because it was spending more on lobbying (more than $200 million in 1998) than any other economic sector. It had also become the biggest campaign giver in national politics, up from $109 million in 1991–1992 to a walloping $297 million in 1999–2000.

Alas, the changes won by the accounting, telecommunications, and banking industries—all of them promoting either something for nothing, lowered standards of responsibility, or corner-cutting—only exacerbated the collapse of ethics and responsible behavior. Not surprisingly, each of these industries would be front and center in the excesses and abuses that came to light in 2002 and 2003.

The bottom line, to use that phrase beloved by businessmen, is simply this: As the top 1% of Americans made so much money with the help of the political favoritisms of the 1980s and 1990s, they plowed even more money back into politics to secure and extend that favoritism—and they are still reaping the benefits. Meanwhile, of course, corrupted thinking is pushing the argument that giving a check to a candidate amounts to protected political speech under the First Amendment of the U.S. Constitution. It is amazing—literally amazing—how few opponents of these developments understand their larger historical context and symbolism.

For most Americans, a home is their single largest asset. For others, home-ownership seems increasingly out of reach, and, of course, thousands have no place to lay their heads at all. A place to live is one of the most funda-mental human needs, but in a society characterized by vast and growing pools of private wealth, it's also a lucrative investment; speculation in real estate markets is pushing many families out of decent housing. Activist Betsy Leondar-Wright recounts her direct experience of the issue.

Housing Blues

BY BETSY LEONDAR-WRIGHT

In 1996, the Seaborn family bought a four-bedroom condo down the street from me in an up-and-coming Boston neighborhood. They paid $150,000. The Seaborns' daughters were best friends with a girl across the street whose family, the Cranes, rented a two-bedroom apartment. The Cranes were beloved members of the community—hosts of picnics and tag sales—and wanted to stay in the neighborhood. They began looking for a house or condo; if they could find something under $250,000, they could swing it. But the neighborhood was gentrifying rapidly, and the Cranes faced getting priced out of the area.

Then, in 2002, Mr. Seaborn got a job in another state with far lower hous-ing costs. Several neighbors suggested that the Seaborns sell their condo to the Cranes. At $250,000, they would have made $100,000 profit in just six years. Instead, they put their condo on the market and sold it for $350,000. They've since moved, to a home on four acres with a pool. In the meantime, the Cranes had another baby, so they now live four people to a two-bed-room apartment. Their rent went up again; soon, they may not be able to stay in the neighborhood even as renters.

Usually we don't see the faces of both the people who make a windfall selling their homes in an overheated housing market and the people who are squeezed out of decent housing, but in this case both the Seaborns and the Cranes (whose names have been changed) were my friends. Watching these two families negotiate their housing choices, I became acutely aware of a "housing divide" that is widening in tandem with the United States' growing wealth gap.

DOWN THE HOUSING LADDER

Over the past 25 years, corporate actions and government policies have put trillions of additional dollars into the hands of the wealthiest Americans. When the rich get an additional surge of wealth, from a stock-market bubble—or a tax break—the new wealth moves in part into speculative investments. Prices for certain commodities—art, gold, and race horses, for example—start to rise.

Most Americans don't care whether race horses become more expensive. But when those dollars flow into real estate, investors' profits trickle down as housing hardship for everyone else. Investors and real estate developers buy and sell residential properties in rapid succession, for a higher price each time; soon they are out of reach for moderate-income homebuyers. As prices rise on rental properties, new owners have to jack up the rents just to cover the mortgage.

In those housing markets that see a steep run-up in prices, a process unfolds along these lines: Newly minted millionaires buy the biggest suburban houses, sometimes tearing down an existing house (or two!) to build a mansion. Professional two-career families who would have lived in those houses can afford only medium-sized suburban houses instead. Young professionals who would have moved to the suburbs instead stay in their urban starter homes for longer, or can't find a starter home and stay in the nicest rental housing. The working families who would have bought starter homes or rented nice apartments instead live in small, dingy rental housing. The working poor families who would have lived in small, dingy apartments instead live in substandard, dilapidated apartments or public housing. And the very poor people who would have lived in substandard or public housing become homeless.

Little or no research has been done to assess or quantify the effect of growing concentrations of wealth on housing markets, according to economists Lance Freeman and Bill Rohe. But this process is readily visible in cities around the country. I saw it firsthand in Boston in the mid-1980s, and again in the late 1990s. I was a community organizer in Jamaica Plain in 1986 when *Forbes Magazine* featured the neighborhood as having the fastest-rising property values in the nation. Flush with the Reagan tax cut, many investors made millions rapidly trading in Boston property. The average length of time new buyers held a Boston residential property was less than a year, according to the neighborhood group City Life/Vida Urbana.

Rents and purchase prices soared. Single-room occupancy units and tenements were turned into condominiums, until no very low-rent units remained. Suddenly there were homeless people on the streets who weren't mentally ill or addicted, just poor. The long-time residents, a mix in which working-class Latino families and low-budget white bohemians predominated, lost their homes in droves, and the neighborhood became whiter and much more affluent.

Only the tireless efforts of community groups kept a few affordable apartments in place. City Life/Vida Urbana developed affordable units itself as well as organizing a militant Eviction Free Zone campaign. A coalition put together a "Campaign of Conscience for Housing Justice": Landlords signed a pledge to keep rents reasonable, for example, promising to base rent increases on their actual costs, not overall market trends. Through tenant organizing, mediation, and negotiation, these groups prevented thousands of evictions and other displacements. Still, countless families found themselves sliding down the housing ladder.

What happened to housing in Boston and elsewhere highlights the difference between speculative and productive investments. If supply and demand worked the way the economics textbooks claim, the heightened demand for reasonably priced homes in Boston should have sparked a building boom, with every vacant lot filled in with modest condos, and new Levittowns springing up in the outer suburbs. In fact, developers built almost no new housing except for high-end luxury homes, and that increased supply did not trickle down into lower (or even stable) prices for non-luxury housing. The smart money avoided the risks of new construction and went instead into what seemed like a sure thing: buying and selling existing properties at ever higher prices.

REAL ESTATE ETHICS?

The Seaborns are good people. They were not speculating in real estate, merely selling their primary residence at the price the market offered them. Like most people, they saw no ethical problem in their choice, even if it contributed to making housing unaffordable for someone else. That's the norm for property owners in our society.

Most people bristle at the idea of incorporating any values into their property decisions. With pensions becoming less common, selling a home at an appreciated price has become the most reliable way to retire. But when property values rise rapidly, homeowners profit from the "social appreciation," that is, the price increase in excess of inflation plus the value of any property improvements.

Individual property owners can take steps to keep housing affordable. The Massachusetts-based Equity Trust, an advocacy organization that promotes alternative forms of ownership and investment, ran a program in which homeowners pledged to put some or all of the social appreciation from selling their homes into a pool invested in permanently affordable housing. My partner and I have made such a pledge. Our down payment and equity payments, plus the overall inflation rate, plus any improvements we make on our condo: that's a fair price. Any more and we're hurting someone else's chance to live in decent housing. If our home was affordable for a pair of 40-year-olds with masters degrees when we bought it, it should be affordable for a pair of 40-year-olds with masters degrees when we sell it— not only to people with trust funds. We will take some social appreciation profit only if not doing so would jeopardize our ability to meet our basic needs for food, shelter, and health care. But if, like millions of Americans, we aren't forced to relocate to a more expensive area, but can retire to a less expensive home, then we'll donate the social appreciation to an affordable housing group.

Working toward a fairer economy means taking into consideration all the people affected by personal financial decisions, even real estate decisions. Unless such individual practices are adopted by a significant cross-section of the population, though, they cannot fix a housing market distorted by the speculative investments that concentrated wealth makes possible. Only significant public investment in affordable housing can do that.

The racial wealth gap in America is persistent and large. It's like a fossil, the enduring imprint of policies and practices that closed off myriad avenues of asset-building to African Americans and other people of color throughout U.S. history. But it's also the consequence of an economic system that continues to discriminate today. For all of the attention to white-collar and high-tech jobs going overseas, the more typical laid-off U.S. worker today is a black manufacturing worker. Without steady employment, black workers cannot hope to buy a home, save for retirement, or otherwise build assets; without assets, periods of unemployment pose a severe burden—a vicious circle.

Black Job Loss Déjà Vu

BY BETSY LEONDAR-WRIGHT

In July 2003, Mary Clark saw a notice posted by the time-clock at the Pillowtex plant where she worked: the plant was closing down at the end of the month. The company would be laying off 4,000 workers. "They acted like we was nobody," she said; Pillowtex even canceled the workers' accrued vacation days. Clark had worked at the textile plant in Eden, North Carolina, for 11 years, inspecting, tagging, and bagging comforters. By 2003, she was earning more than $10 an hour.

Clark's unemployment benefits don't cover her bills. Because Pillowtex had sent her and her coworkers home frequently for lack of work in the final year, her unemployment checks are low, based on that last year's reduced earnings. She lost her health coverage, and now she needs dental work that she cannot afford.

It's happening again.

In the 1970s, a wave of plant closings hit African Americans hard. Two generations after the "Great Migration," when millions of black people had left the South to take factory jobs in Northern and Midwestern cities, the U.S. economy began to deindustrialize and many of those jobs disappeared—in some cases shifting to the low-wage, nonunion South.

The recession of 2001—and the historically inadequate "recovery" since— has again brought about a catastrophic loss of jobs, especially in manufacturing, and once again African Americans have lost out disproportionately. Jobs that moved to the South during the earlier era of deindustrialization are now leaving the country entirely or simply disappearing in the wake of technological change and rising productivity.

Media coverage of today's unemployment crisis often showcases white men who have lost high-paying industrial or information-technology jobs. But Mary Clark is actually a more typical victim. Recent job losses have hit black workers harder than white workers: black unemployment rose twice as fast as white unemployment in this last recession. Once again, African Americans are getting harder hit. Once again, they face a downturn with fewer of the resources and assets that tide families over during hard times. And once again, bearing a disproportionate share of job losses will make it more difficult for them to build wealth and economic security.

LAST HIRED, FIRST FIRED

The tight labor market of the late 1990s was very beneficial for African Americans. The black unemployment rate fell from 18% in the 1981–82 recession, to around 13% in the early 1990s, to below 7% in 1999 and 2000, the lowest black unemployment rate on record. But the 2001 recession (and the job-loss recovery since then) has robbed African Americans of much of those gains.

"The last recession has had a severe and disproportionate impact on African Americans and minority communities," according to Marc H. Morial, president of the National Urban League. In its January 2004 report on black unemployment, the Urban League found that the double-digit unemployment rates in the 14 months from late 2002 through 2003 were the worst labor market for African Americans in 20 years.

The 2001 recession was hard on African American workers both in relation to earlier recessions and in relation to white workers. Unemployment for adult black workers rose by 2.9 percentage points in the recession of the early 1980s, but by 3.5 in the 2001 recession. White unemployment, in contrast, rose by only 1.4 percentage points in the early-1980s recession and by 1.7 in the recent downturn. The median income of black families fell 3% from 2001 to 2003, while white families lost just 1.7%. Today, black unemployment has remained above 10% for over three years.

Official unemployment figures, of course, greatly understate the actual number of adults without jobs. The definition doesn't include discouraged people who have stopped looking for work, underemployed part-timers, students, or those in prison or other institutions. In New York City, scarcely half of African-American men between 16 and 65 had jobs in 2003, ac-

ELLEN SHUB

Local 7 ironworker Stephen Henry protests at a fundraiser for George W. Bush at Boston's Park Plaza Hotel, 2004.

cording to the Bureau of Labor Statistics' employment-to-population ratios for the city. The BLS ratios, which include discouraged workers and others the official unemployment statistics leave out, were 51.8% for black men, 57.1% for black women, 75.7% for white men, and 65.7% for Latino men. The figure for black men was the lowest on record (since 1979).

Manufacturing job losses in particular have hit black workers harder than white workers. In 2000, there were 2 million African Americans working in factory jobs. Blacks comprised 10.1% of all manufacturing workers, about the same as the black share of the overall workforce. Then 300,000 of those

WHERE IS THE NORTH OF TODAY?
BY ATTIENO DAVIS

Ellen Williams was 16 years old when she left Butler County, Georgia, one of the innumerable backwoods Georgia counties with Jim Crow and "Negroes Need Not Apply," no indoor plumbing, and one-room school-houses. When she arrived in Boston in 1946, she thought she'd died and gone to heaven. Though she'd left her family behind, her dream of accessing just a bit of the pie seemed realizable at last.

Momma never quite achieved her dream, but she did have a job for 41 years, a job that helped stabilize our lives. When she retired in the early 1990s, that job provided her a pension she lives on today, back in her beloved Georgia. My mother worked for Raytheon and was a member of the International Brotherhood of Electrical Workers. She never had a car until the early '70s, but she said she never thought of herself as poor, because she had a good job, which gave her a sense of hope.

I understood as a girl that the job was the key to my family's security. Momma could pay our rent, buy groceries, pay the insurance man, and take my sister and me to the doctor. Raytheon was a cornerstone in my family's life.

Momma made sure that her family members in the South did okay, regularly sending money home to help out. Our three-bedroom apartment was a temporary home to at least three other extended family members who fled the economically depressed South in the 1960s. Two of them also managed to get jobs at Raytheon.

It was a struggle for women working in the plants. Promotions weren't as forthcoming, especially if you were Black. Momma said the combined issue of race and gender was a problem even in the union.

jobs, or 15%, disappeared. White workers lost 1.7 million factory jobs, but that was just 10% of the number they held before the recession. By the end of 2003, the share of all factory jobs held by African Americans had fallen to 9.6%. "Half a percentage point may not sound like much, but to lose that much in such an important sector over a relatively short period, that is going to be hard to recover," Jared Bernstein of the Economic Policy Institute, a progressive economics think tank, told the *New York Times*. Latino workers increased their share of manufacturing jobs in 2002 and 2003 slightly, though their unemployment rate overall rose.

But she was a card-carrying member of IBEW, and she supported the union for the job security and cushion of wealth—however modest—it gave her. She said, "The union was my key. We had health care, vacation, pension, and the union protected my rights." With the union's support, she took community college courses and broke ground to become one of Raytheon's first women inspectors.

None of my daughters and nieces have worked in manufacturing jobs, and none of them have been union members. They've worked at hotels and in stores. One niece went to community college in a certified nursing assistant program and got a job at a unionized hospital—but it was a temporary contract job for six months, not a permanent union job. Now she works in a nursing home.

Many younger members of my family have moved south again because that's where the jobs are. But companies have a "let me hold my nose, I think I smell a union" attitude. Some of these young people have gone to college and found better-paying jobs—but not everyone can go to college, and the jobs for those without college now have no benefits and no union. Unlike their parents, they can't have a car or purchase a home. No matter what they do, a stable life seems to always be just beyond.

Today as I watch young people of color enter the workforce, it's almost as if we've come full circle, back to that same place my mother started out. She left a state with no opportunity for her and moved to a state with abundant good jobs. The young Black adults coming up today all live in states with a shrinking base of options for those without college educations—but there is now nowhere to move to find abundant good jobs. Where's their boost up the ladder?

Some of the largest layoffs have occurred in areas with large African American populations—in April 2004, for example, 1,000 jobs were cut at a Ford plant in St. Louis and 300 at a Boeing plant in San Antonio. Textile plants with mostly black employees have closed in Roanoke Rapids, N.C., Columbus, Ga., and Martinsville, Va. The states with the greatest number of layoffs of 50 workers or more are black strongholds New York and Georgia.

When Autoliv closed its seat belt plant in Indianapolis in 2003, more than 75% of the laid-off workers were African Americans. Many of these workers are young adults who got their jobs during the labor shortage of the late 1990s even without a high school diploma; now they have few options. "They were taken from the street into decent-paying jobs; they were making $12 to $13 an hour. These young men started families, dug in, took apartments, purchased vehicles. It was an up-from-the-street experience for them, and now they are being returned to their old environment," Michael Barnes, director of an Indiana AFL-CIO training program for laid-off workers, told the *New York Times.*

The Autoliv workers and the many other laid-off black workers are facing an immediate drop in income. Just as important, their lower income weakens their long-term prospects for accumulating assets. This may seem obvious: lower income, lower wealth. But confronted with the fact of the racial wealth gap, many analysts jump to other explanations: African Americans don't save what they do earn; African Americans have dysfunctional family structures. In fact, income *is* the most significant predictor of wealth and of the wealth gap, according to a careful analysis by sociologist Thomas Shapiro. So layoffs represent a double whammy: an immediate loss of income *and* a long-run loss of wealth.

U.S. Chamber of Commerce executive vice president Bruce Josten isn't too worried about layoffs. "We're talking about transformational evolution—successful companies remaking their own operations so they're able to better focus on what their core mission is. It's not a deal where everyone gains instantly. At a micro level, there's always going to be a community that's hurt," Josten told Knight Ridder. The communities that are hurt come in all colors, but several factors make the micro level pain more severe in communities of color.

HARD TIMES HIT BLACKS HARDER

Prolonged unemployment is scary for most families, but it puts the typical African-American family in deeper peril, and faster. The median white family has more than $106,000 in net worth (assets minus debts; the figures exclude vehicles). The median black family has less than $11,000, a far smaller cushion in tough times.

Laid-off workers often turn to family members for help, but with almost a quarter of black families under the poverty line, and one in nine black workers unemployed, it's less likely that unemployed African Americans have family members with anything to spare. Black per capita income was only 57 cents for every white dollar in 2001.

Thanks to continuing segregation and discrimination in housing, it's more difficult for black families to relocate to find work. New jobs are concentrated in mostly white suburbs with little public transportation.

When homeowners face prolonged unemployment, they can take out a home equity loan or second mortgage to tide them over. But while three-quarters of white families are homeowners, less than half of black families own their own homes. And even those black families who do own a home have, on average, less equity to borrow against. In 2001, black homeowners' median home equity was just $29,100, compared to $75,000 for white homeowners, according to an analysis of data from the Panel Study of Income Dynamics by Elena Gouskova and Frank Stafford.

When African Americans *have* been able to build savings, they have made a strong commitment to homeownership. In 2001, according to the Federal Reserve, 43% of the value of black-owned assets were in primary residences. Another 9% were in vehicles. Only 32% were in financial assets such as savings accounts, stocks, and retirement funds. In a term coined by economist Michael Stone, black homeowners are disproportionately "shelter poor"— they have insufficient money left after paying housing costs to afford other necessities. Thus one of the main risks of black job loss is foreclosure and the loss of hard-won wealth in home equity.

HISTORY REPEATS ITSELF

The term "deindustrialization" came into everyday use in the 1970s, when a wave of plant closings changed the employment landscape. From 1966 to 1973, corporations moved over a million American jobs to other countries. Even more jobs moved from the Northeast and Midwest to the South, where unions were scarce and wages lower. New York City alone lost 600,000 manufacturing jobs in the 1960s.

As today, the workers laid off in the 1960s and 1970s were disproportionately African-American. The U.S. Commission on Civil Rights found that during the recession of 1973 to 1974, 60% to 70% of laid-off workers were African-American in areas where they were only 10% to 12% of the workforce. In five cities in the Great Lakes region, the majority of black men employed in manufacturing lost their jobs between 1979 and 1984. A major reason was seniority: white workers had been in their jobs longer, and so were more likely to keep them during cutbacks.

Another reason was geography. The northern cities that lost the most jobs were some of those with the largest populations of people of color,

THE RACIAL WEALTH GAP *HURTS*
BY AMY GLUCKMAN AND ADRIA SCHARF

African-American families own just 15 cents for every dollar of wealth held by white families. The lack of family assets, along with racial discrimination, has a dramatic impact on the education and health outcomes of black Americans. People with assets are able to buy their way into neighborhoods with good schools, and they are able to pay for preventive and emergency health care. While the causal relationships between wealth and life outcomes in areas such as education and health are complex and intertwined with other factors, there's no doubt that the racial wealth gap has fundamental life consequences for black families.

When depressing statistics about black-white gaps—in school achievement, for example—are reported, commentators are quick to attribute them to cultural factors: the higher prevalence of female-headed families in the African-American community, or an "oppositional culture" among African-American teens that equates academic success with selling out. There is no question that African Americans lag behind whites in most measures of educational attainment and academic achievement. Even when family income is accounted for, African-American students demonstrate lower levels of achievement, as measured by standardized tests.

But what about when family wealth is factored in? The ostensibly race-based differences largely vanish, according to sociologist Dalton Conley. Conley analyzed data on high-school and college graduation rates as well as on retention (getting held back a grade), suspension, and expulsion of school-age children. He found that differences in family net worth are a significant explanatory variable for each of these—so much so, for example, that African Americans actually have a higher high-school graduation rate than whites at the same level of family wealth.

"Two families with the same household income [but differing levels of net worth] might have vastly different resources at their disposal to provide advantages to their children. These advantages can be as tangible as extracurricular and private education, financial support during college, or in-kind aid such as supplying educational materials," Conley explains. He also points to research showing that parents' financial contribution to their children's education expenses—whether a computer or a college fund—not only contributes directly to children's academic achievement, it also affects children's educational expectations and, in turn, their own motivation to learn.

The Racial Wealth Divide, Education, and Health

Indicator	Year	White	Black	Black as a % of White
Median Household Net Worth	2001	$121,000	$19,000	15.7%
High School Dropout Rate	2001	4.6%	5.7%	123.9%
Completed High School	2002	88.7%	79.2%	89.3%
Completed Four or More Years of College	2002	29.4%	17.2%	58.5%
Infant Mortality Rate (per 1,000)	2001	5.7	14.0	245.6%
Life Expectancy at Birth	2000	77.4	71.7	92.6%

Sources: Arthur B. Kennickell, "A Rolling Tide: Changes in the Distribution of Wealth in the U.S., 1989–2001," Levy Economics Institute, Nov. 2003; National Center for Health Statistics, National Vital Statistics Reports, Dec. 19, 2002, Table 11; National Vital Statistics Reports, Sept. 18, 2003, Table 31; U.S. Census Bureau, Current Population Survey, Educational Attainment Historical Tables, Table A-2; Educational Attainment Historical Tables, Table A-5; U.S. Census Bureau, Current Population Survey, School Enrollment Historical Tables, Table A-4.

Table excerpted from "The State of the Dream 2004: Enduring Disparities in Black and White," United for a Fair Economy, January 2004.

and those inner-city areas sank deep into poverty and chronically high un-employment as few heavily white areas did.

The race and class politics of deindustrialization are also part of the sto-ry. The pro-business loyalties of the federal government dictated policies that encouraged plant closings and did very little to mitigate their effects. Tax credits for foreign investment and for foreign tax payments encouraged companies to move plants overseas. While Northern cities were suffering from deindustrialization, the federal government spent more in the Southern states than in the affected areas: Northeast and Midwest states averaged 81 cents in federal spending for each tax dollar they sent to Washington in the 1970s, while southern states averaged $1.25. Laid-off black factory workers had no clout, so politicians faced little pressure to address their needs.

As dramatic as the movement of jobs from the North to the South and overseas was the shift from city to suburb. The majority of new manufac-turing jobs in the 1970s were located in suburban areas, while manufactur-ing employment fell almost 10% in center cities. In the Los Angeles area, for example, older plants were closing in the city while new ones opened in the San Fernando Valley and Orange County.

The new suburban jobs were usually inaccessible for African Americans and other people of color because of housing costs, job and housing dis-crimination, lack of public transportation, and lack of informal social net-works with suburban employers. In a study of Illinois firms that moved to the suburbs from the central cities between 1975 and 1978, black employment in the affected areas fell 24%, while white employment fell less than 10%. In another study, some employers admitted to locating facilities in part so as to avoid black workers. One study of the causes of black unemployment in 45 urban areas found that 25% to 50% resulted from jobs shifting to the suburbs. Even the federal government shifted jobs to the suburbs: although the number of federal civilian jobs grew by 26,558 from 1966 to 1973, fed-eral jobs in central cities fell by 41,419. Over time, suburban white people gained a greater and greater geographic edge in job hunting.

LOOKING FORWARD

Mary Clark has been looking for work for nine months now without suc-cess. Stores get applications from hundreds of other laid-off workers; there aren't enough jobs for even a fraction of the unemployed. "It used to be that if one plant shut down, there'd be another one hiring. Now they're all laying off or closing," she says.

For years Clark had helped her grown daughter support her two small children. "Now the roles are reversed, and they help me." She has turned to charities to make ends meet, but some only give aid once a year, and others won't help a single woman without children at home. "It breaks your self-esteem to have to ask for help," Clark says.

Some of her former coworkers are in more desperate straits than she is. Some have lost their homes or gone into bankruptcy. Some people have found jobs far from home and commute for hours a day. Clark sees crime, divorce, and family violence all rising in the area.

What job growth there's been has been concentrated in the low-wage service sector, which pays less than the shrinking manufacturing sector. There's no law of nature that says service jobs are inevitably low paid and without benefits. Or that manufacturing can't revive in the United States. The recent wave of union organizing victories in heavily black industries such as health care represent one source of hope for creating more decent jobs for African Americans.

Dr. Martin Luther King, Jr. said in 1968, "When there is massive unemployment in the black community, it is called a social problem. But when there is massive unemployment in the white community, it is called a depression." The New Deal response to the Great Depression included public works jobs and a strengthened safety net, most of which excluded people of color. Mary Clark clearly recognizes what happens when there is no New Deal for unemployed African Americans: "North Carolina has people who want to work, but we don't have anyone pushing work our way. We need the mills back. We're people used to working, and when you take the work away, what do you have left?"

Why should middle-class people care about wealth inequality? Sam Pizzigati argues that wealth inequality hurts everyone. The concentration of wealth in the United States has promoted excessive consumption among the very rich, raising consumption standards throughout the society. As Pizzigati explains, these rising standards take a financial and psychological toll on middle-class households which must choose between "keeping up with the Joneses" and losing social status.

The Hazards of Life On— and Off—the Luxury Lane

BY SAM PIZZIGATI

How wealthy have the wealthiest Americans become?

This wealthy: A half-century ago, our nation's most affluent loved to fly off to Florida for the winter. Today's wealthy don't just fly their families south. They fly their trees. One deep-pocketed Long Island couple, the *New York Times* reported in 2000, simply could not bear the thought of everyday life without palms eternally swaying. The couple had palm trees installed on its Hamptons estate, then flown, every winter, to Florida.

How wealthy are the wealthy today? This wealthy: A half-century ago, America's wealthiest spent fortunes on country club memberships. Today's fortunate start country clubs just for themselves. Billionaire H. Wayne Huizenga, the *Wall Street Journal* informed us in 1999, founded a private club with only himself and his wife as members. The club features a golf course and 68 boat slips for invited dignitaries.

Wildly excessive consumption, some analysts believe, ought to be a source of entertainment for America's non-rich majority—and nothing more. Rich people, economist Michael Weinstein has quipped, are "fun to watch, fun to ridicule, perhaps even fun to envy." But they aren't, continues Weinstein, "much to worry about."

In fact, rich people—and their consumption patterns—are worth worrying about. What Cornell economist Robert Frank calls "luxury fever" has raised the price of the good life for everyone. In the 1980s and 1990s, as wealth became increasingly concentrated in the United States, luxuries, not basic comforts, came to define the good life. Fancy watches. Expensive cars. Vacation homes. The inevitable result: a general ratcheting up of the sense of what it takes to live a decent life—and more pressure on average Americans. More pressure on middle-income Americans to work the extra hours to make the extra income that affording a decent life demands. More pressure on low-income Americans, already straining just to put food on the table.

Apologists for America's unequal status quo have no sympathy for these pressures. "It's not the high cost of living that gets us, it's the cost of living high," argues W. Michael Cox, chief economist of the Federal Reserve Bank of Dallas. Want a less stressed existence? Just do it. The choice, conservatives assert, is up to every individual.

Some people, to be sure, have been able to jump off the treadmill that has so many Americans getting nowhere fast. But their example has touched off no mass exodus. How could it? Few low-income people can afford to work any fewer hours than they do, not when the cost of renting a decent apartment, in most parts of the United States, now demands a job that pays

JIM WEST

A worker at the North American International Auto Show in Detroit examines one of the luxury automobiles on display.

three times the minimum wage. And all working families, low- and mid-dle-income alike, wherever they live, are still reminded daily, by the media, about the acquisitions that define the life that any self-respecting American ought to desire. Average households may be free, in theory, to ignore these luxury-driven consumption standards, but, in real life, they ignore these standards at their peril.

Take a trivial example. Studies have demonstrated that motorists who delay at a green light "are less likely to be honked" from behind if they're driving a luxury automobile, notes Boston College sociologist Juliet Schor. Most people can tolerate intemperate honking. But few can tolerate the full psychological cost of jumping off the treadmill. Once off the treadmill, people risk losing something important, their status in the groups that matter most to them. And our most valued group identity, in any society split into economic classes, usually involves where we stand, or seek to stand, in the class structure. Consumption is an important marker of that standing.

In a relatively equal nation, a society where minor differences in income and wealth separate the classes, people will be less likely to obsess over meeting consumption standards. If nearly everyone can afford much the same things, things overall tend to lose their significance. People are more likely to judge others by who they are, not what they own, in a society where incomes and wealth are distributed fairly equally.

In an unequal society, people can, of course, decline to play by the consumption rules. But most don't. After all, what right do parents have to expose their children to the "loser" label? What right do people have to force their friends to choose between them and the stigma of hanging out with a failure? So most people keep treading. And this treading will never stop—not as long as wealth remains so concentrated.

SECTION IV
Strategies for Change

According to right-wing pundits, taxing wealth is so crazy an idea that no respectable economist could support it. But economist John Miller shows that some of the most influential political economists of the 19th and 20th centuries did just that. So, too, did Andrew Carnegie, the 19th-century robber baron. Today's supporters of the estate tax and other forms of wealth taxation have plenty of intellectual and historical backing.

Tax Wealth

Great Political Economists
and Andrew Carnegie Agree

BY JOHN MILLER

ART BY NICK THORKELSON

A few years ago, I appeared regularly on talk radio as part of a campaign to block the repeal of the estate tax. As an economist, my job was to correct the distortions and outright hucksterism that the Heritage Foundation and other right-wing think tanks used to demonize the estate tax. In their hands, this modest tax on the inheritance of the richest 2% of U.S. taxpayers became a "death tax" that double-taxed assets in family estates, destroyed family farms and small businesses, and put a brake on economic growth.

Once that was done, assuming anyone was still listening, I was supposed to make the affirmative case for taxing wealth. But before I got very far, whichever conservative expert I was debating would inevitably interrupt and ask, "Isn't what you advocate straight out of Marx's *Communist Manifesto*?" After my first stammering reply, I got pretty good at saying, "Perhaps, but calls for taxing wealth are also straight out of *The Gospel of Wealth* by Andrew Carnegie. Do you think he was anti-capitalist?" Then it was the conservative's turn to stammer.

In fact, Marx, the philosopher of socialism, and Carnegie, the predatory capitalist turned philanthropist, weren't the only ones to call for heavy taxation of estates. Over the 19th and 20th centuries, they were joined by great political economists who, unlike Marx, were more concerned with saving capitalism from its excesses than replacing it. Let's take a look at what all these writers had to say.

KARL MARX

Sure enough, the manifesto of the Communist League, penned by Karl Marx and Fredrick Engels in 1848, called for the heavy taxation and even confiscation of inherited wealth. In the *Communist Manifesto*, Marx and Engels developed a transitional program intended to lead Europe away from the horrors of industrial capitalism—a system guided by "naked self interest"—and toward a socialist society. The ten-step program that Marx and Engels laid out for the most advanced countries began with these demands:

1. Abolition of property in land and application of all rents of land to public purposes.
2. A heavy or progressive graduated income tax.
3. Abolition of all rights of inheritance.

These clauses need to be understood in context of the socialist debate of the day and Marx's other writings. The first clause did not target the capitalist who directed production on the farm or in the mine, but the landowner or rentier who collected a return merely by owning the land or mine. It was their rents, not the capitalist's profits, that Marx and Engels argued should go to the state to be used for public purposes.

A heavy or progressive graduated income tax, the second clause, hardly seems radical. The U.S. federal income tax had a top tax bracket of 90% in the early post-World War II period (prior to 1962), although effective income tax rates were far lower than that.

Abolishing rights of inheritance, on the other hand, would be a radical change. The third clause targeted large estates; despite its wording, it was not intended to apply to small holders of property. "The distinguishing feature of Communism," as Marx and Engels made clear, "is not the abolition of property generally, but the abolition of bourgeois property." Marx and Engels were concerned with the social relation of capital based on the private ownership of the means of production. They saw this as the root of capitalist class power and the basis of class antagonisms that involved "the exploitation of the many by the few." The abolition of capitalist private property was surely the backbone of the *Communist Manifesto*, the most influential economic pamphlet ever written.

JOHN STUART MILL

Writing in the middle of the 19th century as well, the far more respectable John Stuart Mill also called for limitations on inheritance. Mill was a radical, but also a member of the English parliament and the author of the *Principles of Political Economy*, the undisputed bible of economists of his day. Mill regarded the laws of distribution of capitalism (who got paid what) to be a matter of social custom and quite malleable, unlike the inalterable market laws that governed production (how commodities were made). Indeed, he devoted long sections of the later editions of *Principles* to then-novel experiments with workers' cooperatives and utopian communities which he thought could distribute resources more equitably.

Mill openly attacked the institution of inheritance and entered a plea for progressive death duties. Observing the gaping inequalities that the industrial system had produced in England, he wrote that there existed "an immense majority" who were condemned from their birth to a life of "never-ending toil" eking out a "precarious subsistence." At the same time, "a small minority" were born with "all the external advantages of life without earning them by any merit or acquiring them by an any exertion of their own."

To curtail this "unearned advantage," Mill called for the "limitation of the sum which any one person may acquire by gift or inheritance to the amount sufficient to constitute a moderate independence."

He argued for a "system of legislation that favors equality of fortunes" to allow individuals to realize "the just claim of the individual to the fruits, whether great or small, of his or her own industry." Otherwise, as he famously observed, all the mechanical inventions of the industrial revolution would only enable "a greater population to live the same life of drudgery and imprisonment and an increased number of manufacturers and others to make fortunes."

HENRY GEORGE

Henry George, a journalist who taught himself economics, burst onto the American scene in 1879 with the publication of *Progress and Poverty*. This instant bestseller launched a crusade for a "single tax" on land that would put an end to the speculation that George saw as the root cause of the country's unjust distribution of wealth. Although rejected by the economics profession, *Progress and Poverty* sold more copies than all the economic texts previously published in the United States. It is easy to see why. In epic prose, George laid out the problem plaguing U.S. society at the close of the 19th century:

"The association of poverty with progress is the greatest enigma of our times. It is the central fact from which spring industrial, social, and political difficulties that perplex the world… It is the riddle which the Sphinx of Fate puts to our civilization and which not to answer is to be destroyed. So long as all the increased wealth which modern progress brings goes but to build up great fortunes, to increase luxury, and make sharper the contrast between the House of Have and the House of Want, progress is not real and cannot be permanent."

George traced the maldistribution of wealth to the institution of private property in land. To end the association of poverty with progress, he argued that "we must make land common property." But, he argued, "it is not necessary to confiscate land; it is only necessary to confiscate rent." Taxation was his means for appropriating rent, and George proposed "to abolish all taxation save that upon land values."

Henry George's single tax on land (excluding improvements) was meant to lift the burden of taxation from labor and all productive effort and place it on the rising of value of land. That rising value, he wrote, was the product of social advancement, and should be socialized. It was unjust for such gains to remain in the hands of an individual land owner—"someone whose grandfather owned a pasture on which two generations later, society saw fit to erect a skyscraper," as Robert Heilbroner, the historian of economic ideas, put it.

Progress and Poverty spawned an impressive grassroots movement dedicated to undoing the wealth gap. Georgist Land and Labor clubs sprang up across the nation, and despite a concerted counter-attack by the economics profession, Georgists exerted considerable influence on U.S. tax policy. Most recently, Alaska adopted a George-like proposition. The state created the Alaska Permanent Fund and in its constitution vested the ownership of the state's oil and natural resources in the people as a whole. The Permanent Fund distributes substantial oil revenues as citizen dividends to state residents.

JOHN MAYNARD KEYNES

During the Great Depression of the 1930s, John Maynard Keynes, the preeminent economist of the 20th century, warned that a worsening maldistribution of wealth threatened to bring capitalism to its knees. Keynes was no radical. Instead, he was concerned with rescuing capitalism from its

own excesses. Keynes's analysis of the instabilities of capitalist economies, and his prescriptions for taming them, guided U.S. economic policy from the 1940s through the 1970s and are still tremendously influential today.

"The outstanding faults of the economic society in which we live," he wrote in *The General Theory of Employment, Interest, and Money* in 1936, "are its failure to provide for full employment and its arbitrary and inequitable distribution of wealth and incomes."

Keynes argued that income inequality and financial instability made for unstable demand among consumers. Without stable demand for goods and services, corporations invested less and cut jobs. Indeed, during the worst years of the Great Depression, this chain of economic events cost more than one-quarter of U.S. workers their jobs.

By 1936, Keynes wrote, British death duties, along with other forms of direct taxation, had made "significant progress toward the removal of very great disparities of wealth and income" of the 19th century. Still, he thought that much more was needed. In the last chapter of the *General Theory*, Keynes went so far as to propose what he called the "euthanasia of the rentier." By this he meant the gradual elimination of "the functionless investor," who made money not by working but by investing accumulated wealth. Keynes imagined a capitalist economy in which public policy kept interest rates so low that they eroded the income of the functionless investor and at the same time lowered the cost of capital (or borrowing funds) so that it was abundant enough to provide jobs for everyone. This was Keynes's plan to support continuous full employment.

Neither the United States nor Britain ever instituted such a policy, but Keynes provided the theoretical bulwark for the "mixed economy" in which public and private investment complemented one another. He showed how government spending could compensate for the instability of private investment, with government investment rising when private investment fell. The mixed economy, which moderated capitalist instability during the post-war period, remains, in the words of economist Dani Rodrik, "the most valuable heritage the 20th century bequeaths to the 21st century in the realm of economic policy."

Today, just a few years into the 21st century, a conservative movement is trying to rob us of that bequest. The repeal of the estate tax, all but accomplished in 2001, is the sharp end of the axe its adherents are using to cut government down to size. That move is sure to fuel the very excesses that Keynes worried were likely to undo capitalism during the 1930s. It will starve the public sector of revenue, compromising its ability to stabilize the private economy. By showering tax cuts on the richest of our society, it will also exacerbate inequality at a time when the richest 1% already receive their largest share of the nation's income (before taxes) since 1936, the very year that Keynes published the *General Theory*. Finally, repealing the estate tax is unlikely to improve the management of our economic affairs: as Keynes caustically wrote, "the hereditary principle in the transmission of wealth and the control of business is the reason why the leadership of the capitalist cause is weak and stupid."

ANDREW CARNEGIE

It is not easy for me to invoke Andrew Carnegie's defense of the estate tax. For over a decade, I lived in Pittsburgh, where Andrew Carnegie is remembered as the ruthless capitalist who built his public libraries up and down the Monongahela River valley with the money he sweated out of his immigrant workforce, and only after he had busted the union in the local steel mill. Carnegie actually applauded the maldistribution of wealth that Marx, Mill, George, and even Keynes railed against. As he argued, concentrated wealth "is not to be deplored, but welcomed as highly beneficial. Much better this great irregularity than universal squalor."

But despite these apologetics, Carnegie was deeply troubled by large inheritances. "Why should men leave great fortunes to their children?" he asked in his 1889 book, *The Gospel of Wealth*. "If this is done from affection, is it not misguided affection? Observation teaches that, generally speaking, it is not well for the children that they should be so burdened."

Carnegie was also an unabashed supporter of the estate tax. "The growing disposition to tax more and more heavily large estates left at death," Carnegie declared, "is a cheering indication of the growth of a salutary change in public opinion." He added that "of all forms of taxation, this seems the wisest. … By taxing estates heavily at death, the state marks its condemnation of the selfish millionaire's unworthy life." Finally, Carnegie warned that "the more society is organized around the preservation of wealth for those who already have it, rather than building new wealth, the more impoverished we will all be."

FROM HERE TO THERE

Today, whether one is out to save capitalism from its excesses or to bring capitalist exploitation to a halt, taxing accumulated wealth and especially large estates is essential. On that point, Marx, Mill, George, Keynes, and even Carnegie all agreed. But to subject wealth to fair taxation, we will need to do more than resurrect the ideas of these thinkers. We will need a spate of grassroots organizing—from workers' organizations to organizations of the socially-conscious well-to-do—dedicated to the demand that those who have benefited most from our collective efforts give back the most.

This can be done. A hundred years ago, populists concerned about the concentration of wealth forced Congress to enact the original estate tax. They also pushed through a constitutional amendment allowing a progressive income tax that raised revenue for public services. These kinds of advances can happen again.

It will be no easy task. Politics at the beginning of the 21st century are far less progressive than they were at the beginning of the 20th century. But with the greatest of political economists and even a predatory capitalist on our side, perhaps we have a chance.

Chuck Collins and Dedrick Muhammad propose tying the estate tax to a bold set of asset-building initiatives in order to mobilize support for wealth taxation.

Tax Wealth to Broaden Wealth

BY CHUCK COLLINS AND DEDRICK MUHAMMAD

For the past decade, a coalition of business lobbyists and wealthy families has waged a crusade to abolish the nation's only tax on inherited wealth. They've misled the public into believing that the estate tax falls on everyone (when it applies to fewer than the wealthiest 1.5%) and that it destroys small businesses and family farms (it doesn't). In 2001, their multimillion-dollar lobbying effort paid off. Congress voted to phase out the estate tax by gradually raising the exemption level from $1 million in 2002 to $3.5 million in 2009. The tax will disappear in 2010—millionaires and billionaires who die that year will pass on their fortunes tax-free. Its fate after 2010 has yet to be determined. The tax will return to its 2002 levels in 2011 unless Congress revisits the issue.

In a time of state budget crises, a skyrocketing national deficit, and continued cuts to the social safety net, this gift to the richest 1.5% comes at too high a price. Last year, the estate tax added $28 billion to the U.S. Treasury and stimulated an estimated $10 billion in charitable giving. Its abolition is expected to cost the nation $1 trillion over 20 years, and will only deepen the growing wealth divide.

Progressives need to respond to this polarizing economic agenda with a bold economic agenda of their own. One proposal that has real potential to galvanize public support for preserving the tax is a plan to link it to wealth-broadening policies that would directly augment people's personal and household assets. If estate tax revenues were dedicated to a "wealth opportunity fund"—a public trust fund—and used to underwrite wealth-ex-

117

panding programs, the benefits of taxing inherited fortunes would be made clear: the wealth tax would directly reduce asset disparities, including long-standing racial inequities. In the process, the proposal would reassert a positive role for redistributive government spending.

DIVERGING FORTUNES

The concentration and polarization of wealth have reached levels that would have been unfathomable just 30 years ago. Between 1971 and 1998, the share of wealth held by the richest 1% of households grew from 19.9% to 38.1%. Within this top 1%, the largest wealth gains accrued to people with household net worth over $50 million. As New York University economist Edward N. Wolff has observed: "The 1990s also saw an explosion in the number of millionaires and multimillionaires. The number of households worth $1,000,000 or more grew by almost 60%; the number worth $10,000,000 or more almost quadrupled."

Meanwhile, almost one in five households reported zero or negative net worth (excluding the value of their automobiles) throughout the 1990s "boom" years—and racial wealth disparities continued to widen. According to the most recent Survey of Consumer Finances, median net worth for whites rose 16.9% to $120,900 between 1998 and 2001. But median non-white and Hispanic household net worth actually fell 4.5%, to $17,100, during the same period.

British commentator Will Hutton observes that "U.S. society is polarizing and its social arteries hardening. The sumptuousness and bleakness of the respective lifestyles of rich and poor represent a scale of difference in opportunity and wealth that is almost medieval."

SHRINK, SHIFT, AND SHAFT

The drive to abolish the estate tax is just one part of a much broader attack on the progressive tax system. Neo-conservatives are pushing their "shrink, shift, and shaft" fiscal agenda: Shrink the regulatory and welfare states (while enlarging the "warfare" and the "watchtower" states); shift the tax burden from progressive taxes (like the estate tax) to regressive payroll and sales taxes; and shaft the overwhelming majority of the population that depends on government programs and services like public schools, libraries, and roads.

In contrast to the period after World War II, when the federal government carried out massive public investment in wealth-broadening initiatives like the GI Bill, the last three years have seen the Bush administration and Congress institute historic federal tax cuts that disproportionately benefit the very wealthy. In five decades, we've gone from a system of progressive taxation that funded America's biggest middle-class expansion to an increasingly regressive tax system inadequate to fund the most basic of social services.

Democrats have been loath to support anything that looks like a tax hike. Many actually voted for the estate tax phase-out. But taxing wealth is good policy, and in the context of a major wealth-building program, it would make good politics.

Consider how such a program would work: By simply freezing the estate tax at its 2009 level (taxing inherited fortunes in excess of $3.5 million at a rate of 45%), the tax could initially generate $20 to $25 billion a year for a wealth opportunity fund. But in the coming decades, an enormous intergenerational transfer of wealth will occur and estate tax revenue will grow to between $157 billion and $750 billion a year, depending on which estimated annual growth rate one uses. (The lower projection assumes 2% real growth in wealth. The higher figure assumes a 4% growth rate. See <www.bc.edu/research/swri> for more information about these assumptions.) If the estate tax were made more progressive, with a top rate returning to 70% on fortunes over $100 million, it would generate enough revenue for a wealth-broadening program of GI Bill-scale.

ASSET BUILDING SOLUTIONS

How should these revenues be spent? Good proposals and pilot projects already exist to broaden assets and reduce wealth disparities. Taken together, these ideas form the modest beginning of a policy agenda for greater wealth equality.

One example is a new wealth-broadening initiative in England, sponsored by Tony Blair's Labor Party. In 2003, the British Parliament established what have become known as "baby bonds"—small government-financed trust funds for each newborn in the country. Small sums will be deposited and invested for each newborn infant, and available for withdrawal at age 18.

In 1998, then-U.S. Senator Robert Kerrey introduced similar legislation to create what he called "KidSave" accounts. The KidSave initiative would guarantee every child $1,000 at birth, plus $500 a year for children ages one to five, to be invested until retirement. Through compound returns over time, the accounts would grow substantially, provide a significant supplement to Social Security and other retirement funds, and enable many more Americans to leave inheritances to their children.

Another important program is the national Individual Development Account (IDA) demonstration project. This project gives low-income people matching funds for their savings. While the number of households that benefit from IDAs has been small to date, and the amounts that low-income people have managed to save have been modest, the idea is to ramp up this concept, through expanded public funding, to assist many more households.

Nationwide, many community-based organizations are working to expand homeownership opportunities using a patchwork of development subsidies, low-interest mortgages, and down-payment assistant programs.

A challenge for all of these wealth-broadening programs, including the British baby bonds, is that they don't have an adequate or dedicated source of revenue to bring the efforts to a meaningful scale. Here is where some interesting theoretical proposals are emerging as to how to pay for asset programs.

Yale professors Bruce Ackerman and Anne Alstott put forward an "equality of opportunity" proposal in their 2001 book, *The Stakeholder Society.* They advocate imposing an annual 2% tax on wealth, to be paid by the wealthiest

LAST CENTURY'S
WEALTH BROADENING PROGRAM

In the two decades after World War II, federal education and housing programs moved millions of families onto the multigenerational wealth-building train. Between 1945 and 1968, the percentage of American families living in owner-occupied dwellings rose from 44% to 63%, thanks in large part to a massive public commitment to subsidized and insured mortgages from the Federal Housing Authority (FHA), the Veteran's Administration (VA), and the Farmers Home Administration (FmHA).

Prior to the 1940s, mortgages averaged only 58% of property value, excluding all but those with substantial savings from owning homes. FHA and other mortgage subsidies enabled lenders to lengthen the terms of mortgages and dramatically lower down payments to less than 10%. Government guarantees alone enabled interest rates to fall two or three points.

Between World War II and 1972, 11 million families bought homes and another 22 million improved their properties, according to Kenneth T. Jackson's history of the FHA, *Crabgrass Frontier.* The FHA also insured 1.8 million dwellings in multifamily projects. The biggest beneficiary was white suburbia, where half of all housing could claim FHA or VA financing in the 1950s and 1960s. All these housing-subsidy programs

41% of the country. The wealth tax would fund an $80,000 "stake" given to every American at age 21, conditioned on graduating from high school. This notion of "stakeholding," or providing people a piece of the nation's wealth as they come of age, has a long history. In 1797, Tom Paine argued that all new democratic republics, including France and the United States, should guarantee every 21-year old citizen a wealth stake. And in the United States, land grants and subsidized housing loans have been among the ways that the government has helped individuals build personal property.

Sources other than a wealth tax could provide an additional stream of revenue for wealth building—one interesting example is a proposed "sky trust," which addresses both the need for asset building and the problem of environmental degradation. Recognizing that the environmental "commons" is being destroyed, Peter Barnes, in *Who Owns the Sky*, proposes a trust capitalized by pollution credits. Polluting companies would purchase carbon and sulfur permits and the permit revenue would be paid into the

helped finance private wealth in the form of homeownership for 35 million families between 1933 and 1978. The home mortgage interest deduction also benefited suburban homeowners, and interstate highway construction served as an indirect subsidy, as it opened up inexpensive land for suburban commuters.

Unfortunately, for a host of reasons—including racial discrimination in mortgage lending practices, housing settlement patterns, income inequality, and unequal educational opportunities—many nonwhite and Latino families were left standing at the wealth-building train station.

Today, racial wealth disparities persist, and are far more extreme even than disparities in income. Homeownership rates for blacks and Latinos are currently stalled at the level where whites were at the end of World War II. And while over 70% of non-Latino whites own their own homes today, homeownership rates for blacks and Latinos combined average just 48%.

The post-World War II investment in middle-class wealth expansion was paid for by a system of progressive taxation. The top income-tax rate coming out of the war was 91% (it's 38.6% today)—and the estate tax included a provision that taxed fortunes over $50 million at a 70% rate. In turn, many of the widely shared benefits of post-war spending meant that the progressivity of the tax system enjoyed widespread political support.

trust. Barnes compares the idea to the Alaska Permanent Fund, which pays annual dividends to Alaska residents from the state's oil wealth.

By directly contradicting the thrust of the Bush fiscal agenda, which aims to reduce taxation on the wealthiest and dismantle the ladder of economic opportunity for the rest, a wealth-broadening initiative could move progressive constituencies and candidates off of the defense ("We want just half of Bush's tax cut") and behind a positive agenda.

Such an initiative would recapture the possibility of affirmative, activist government, reconnecting the people with the potential for positive government spending—as the GI Bill and homeownership expansion programs did for the post-war generation—and dramatize the limitations of Bush's "want another tax cut?" social policy.

At the same time, this emerging movement must defend existing safety nets and investments in opportunity as a foundation for moving forward. Broadening individual wealth alone has its limitations and is not a substitute for a robust social safety net and adequately funded Social Security program.

THE WEALTH-BROADENING MOVEMENT

From a constituency mobilization perspective, the proposal solves a problem: From the outset, there has been a fundamental imbalance in the estate tax debate. The wealthy individuals and business interests that pay the tax are highly motivated to abolish it. On the other side, the constituencies that would benefit from retaining it are immobilized.

Eliminating the estate tax will lead to budget cuts and a shifting of the tax burden onto those less able to pay—but this has been hard for the public to see. Because the revenues go into the general treasury, its benefits appear remote.

Linking estate tax revenue to a public "trust fund" would help secure support from the vast majority of Americans who are on the wrong side of today's wealth divide by addressing fundamental aspirations of the middle class and the poor alike: the desire for a degree of economic security, a foothold of opportunity, and the means to pass along assets to the next generation.

On the ground, a nascent "wealth broadening movement" already exists, made up of community-development corporations and agencies that promote affordable housing and homeownership, credit unions, and IDAs, as well as savings and investment clubs within religious congregations. These groups aspire to broaden their programs through state and federal legislation, but are hampered by the absence of sizable funding streams. They could provide organizational infrastructure and resources for the effort.

The cumulative impact of a program to broaden wealth by taxing wealth would be to dramatically reduce, over a generation, the disparities of wealth in the United States. This agenda is particularly important for people of color who were themselves excluded, or whose parents or ancestors were excluded, from previous government-led wealth- building opportunities. (See "Last Century's Wealth Broadening Program.")

Wealth is a great equalizing force. Cutting across racial lines, families with equal wealth have similar educational results, economic practices, and health conditions. Asset assistance will be all the more meaningful to those who possess few or no assets, who are disproportionately people of color. Over 11% of African Americans have no assets, compared to 5.6% of white non-Latino households.

In a sense, this agenda would fulfill the next phase of the American civil rights movement. The movement was able to push through legislation that outlawed gross white supremacist practices, but the reforms never adequately addressed the economic dimension of white supremacy. Efforts such as Dr. Martin Luther King's Poor People's Campaign and the War on Poverty were never fully institutionalized. The implementation of asset-building policies that are racially and ethnically inclusive will strengthen the social fabric for future generations.

Obviously, questions about how to design a program to tax wealth in order to broaden wealth remain. Should wealth-broadening go beyond these notions of individual wealth ownership to include community wealth? For instance, public or community-owned housing units with low monthly fees may not represent private wealth for an individual, but are a tremendous source of economic stability and security. Should the wealth-creation vehicles have strings attached, with funds restricted to education, homeownership, and retirement? How should we recognize, in some financial way, the legacy of racial discrimination in wealth-building? How do we protect the ideas from being co-opted by neo-conservatives and avoid risking greater erosion of the welfare state? And what are the politically winnable forms of wealth taxation?

Wealth-building efforts need a revenue stream in order to have a real impact. Organizations working at the state and national levels to defend the estate tax, and progressive taxes more generally, need a positive, galvanizing policy agenda. In sum, wealth taxation and asset development need one another. Taxing concentrated wealth and linking the revenues to programs that will spread wealth in the next generation is the political heart of a winning strategy to expand wealth ownership and build a more equitable society.

Closing the racial wealth divide will require that we not only take strong measures to spread wealth to the poor and middle class regardless of race, but that we also target and address the particular needs of historically disadvantaged groups. Only large-scale redistributive reforms can reduce persistent racial wealth disparities.

Closing the Racial Wealth Gap for the Next Generation

BY MEIZHU LUI

It was only after the civil rights movement opened up new opportunities for people of color that Judith Roderick, an African-American woman, landed a union job in the defense industry in Boston. She worked hard, and, for many years, earned high wages and enjoyed health and retirement benefits.

She saved her money and bought a home in a predominantly black neighborhood. When the local bank denied her a conventional loan to rehab the house, Judith resorted to taking a high-interest loan. She set to work on the home repairs and began making loan payments.

All of that changed in the early 1990s, when company managers, seeking to cut labor costs, laid her off.

As Judith struggled to find a job with a similar wage, the loan caused her to spiral into deeper debt. A few years later, the bank took her house.

As Judith's fortunes declined, the fortunes of many other Boston-area residents—people with advanced degrees, professional jobs, and stock investments—soared. For them, the 1990s economy was booming.

White professionals poured into her neighborhood (which, thanks to her own efforts and those of other local activists, had been fixed up and rid of crime)—sending her rent soaring to $2,000 a month. The bank sold her old house for more than four times what she had originally paid for it.

Judith, who had taken over the care of her grandson, received temporary transitional assistance from the state and managed to get medical benefits for the child. She also qualified for Section 8, a federal rental subsidy. Today, she struggles to pay her bills and keep a roof over her own and her grandson's head.

Unfortunately, Judith's story is not an unusual one among people of color. Better economic times bring small gains, thanks to immense organizing efforts and personal sacrifice. But when there's an economic downturn, racial and ethnic minorities are the first to be, well, turned down.

Whites and people of color move along different economic tracks. Because of past and present discrimination, people of color begin several paces behind the starting line and face more hurdles along the course.

Activists, scholars, and policymakers must bear this in mind as they work to address the national problem of wealth inequality. Policy strategies, whether universal (applying equally to all regardless of race or ethnicity), or targeted to disadvantaged groups, should be examined for their intended and unintended consequences for people of color.

Too often, nonwhites have been excluded from supposedly universal programs. For example, the federal government backed $120 billion in home loans through the Federal Housing Administration between 1934 and 1962, enabling millions of families to attain homeownership. But because of rules that tied mortgage eligibility to race, the vast majority of FHA-backed loans went to whites.

Strategies to close the wealth gap should ensure that minorities have equal access to program benefits, and that programs target not just the overall wealth gap, but the racial wealth gap specifically. Attaining parity will require some catch up.

What follows is a partial list of policies that, if implemented, would go a long way toward putting people of all ethnic and racial backgrounds on the same economic track.

1. HOMEOWNERSHIP

It is said that it is better to have loved and lost than to never have loved at all. The same doesn't hold for homeownership. It's worse to save and purchase a home, only to lose it.

Did Judith really have to lose her home? This question is legitimate given that the federal government props up and protects the nation's two largest mortgage lenders, the Federal National Mortgage Corporation and the Federal Home Loan Mortgage Corporation (better known as Fannie Mae and Freddie Mac). These for-profit corporations were chartered by the government specifically to provide affordable housing for low- and moderate-income people.

These corporations don't make loans directly to individuals; rather, they buy small and medium-sized mortgages from banks, package them together into tradeable securities, and sell these mortgage packages to pension funds and other investors. This arrangement encourages local banks to issue home mortgage loans in low-income communities (because they know they'll be able to resell the loan to these corporations). Fannie Mae and Freddie Mac also work with community organizations to provide credit counseling and other information services in low-income neighborhoods.

The federal government heavily supports Fannie Mae and Freddie Mac with billion-dollar low-interest lines of credit from the Treasury, tax exemptions, and federal insurance, and the federal government could certainly require more of them.

To ensure that Fannie Mae and Freddie Mac reach their mandated quotas of services to low-income people, stronger enforcement mechanisms are needed. In addition, explicit quotas for assistance to people of color and immigrants should be introduced.

Too many immigrants still lack access to information about available housing programs. Many are unfamiliar with the process of purchasing a home, or for that matter, starting a business. This could be reversed if Fannie Mae and Freddie Mac worked with banks to target underserved immigrant communities with multilingual, culturally competent outreach programs. If financial institutions knew they would face repercussions for underserving non-English speaking households, they would design services to better meet their needs.

The 1977 Community Reinvestment Act (CRA) was a major victory for community members mobilized to combat discrimination in home financing. The law requires banks to offer low- and moderate-income people equal access to loans. However, almost 30 years after passage of the CRA, people of color remain less likely than comparable whites to be approved for home mortgages.

Because they buy so many mortgage loans, Fannie Mae and Freddie Mac wield great influence over home-lending practices nationwide. They could impose stricter anti-discrimination requirements on lenders and permit consumers who lack credit histories to submit alternative evidence of their capacity to save and pay bills on time.

Just as important, all regulated lenders should be required to take measures to protect low- and moderate-income borrowers from foreclosure through loan forgiveness programs, payment reductions, and payment waivers. For Judith, the foreclosure took away the asset she had saved to build and literally pushed her from the middle class back into poverty. Rather than profit from layoffs and other economic misfortunes that fall disproportionately on people of color, banks ought to make it their mission to build wealth in households of color and disadvantaged communities.

If Judith could have held on to her home for a few more years, she would have been able to sell the house herself when the market turned, regain her initial investment, and save enough to begin rebuilding her assets.

2. HIGHER EDUCATION

Today, higher education is more important than ever. The wage gap between those with a high school diploma and those with a college degree has continued to widen. Yet the cost of tuition at public and private universities alike has skyrocketed over the last few decades, making college less affordable for those who most need the leg up it provides. At the same time, the mix of federally funded scholarships and loans has shifted: today, 77% of student aid is in loans, so that even those low- and moderate- income students who manage to complete college will start their work lives with tens of thousands of dollars of debt. What's more, aid has become less needs-based and more merit-based, disproportionately benefiting white and wealthier students.

In contrast to today's students, who are left to bear the cost of college largely on their own or with loans, a whole generation of white men in the post-World War II generation got help from the federal government. The 1944 GI Bill subsidized college education for white war veterans, enabling large numbers to move into professional jobs. While African-American and Latino veterans also had formal rights to GI Bill aid, discrimination by universities blocked many from actually using those benefits.

In the 1960s and 1970s, civil rights legislation and affirmative action finally opened college doors for nonwhites—but the rising cost of college, and court challenges to affirmative action, are putting those advances at risk.

We need a new education initiative on the scale of the GI Bill—a massive effort to make higher education affordable to all college-ready students. Short of that, more investment in publicly funded higher education, increased funding for Pell grants and need-based scholarships, and strengthened affirmative action programs would be a good start. Without this sort of educational assistance, Judith's grandson will be unable to pay for college and will likely find himself struggling to get by in a low-wage job.

3. NATIONAL HEALTH CARE

Almost half of all personal bankruptcy filings are due to a lack of adequate health insurance or other health-related expenses. People of color, who make up a third of the nonelderly population, comprise over half of the uninsured, according to the Kaiser Family Foundation. It's no wonder that one of the top policy priorities of the Black Congressional Caucus in 2004 is the provision of health insurance for all.

There is nothing magic about insurance—insurance is basically a system for sharing the risk of unexpected losses. It's an idea that grew from longstanding community practice. Before companies like Blue Cross were formed, extended families would pitch in when any family member had doctors' bills he couldn't pay. In other words, families shared each individual family member's risk of ill health. Today, we're going backwards—each individual is supposed to take care of his or her own costs. When one premature baby can require a half-million dollars of care, this makes no sense. A universal health program would create a huge risk pool comprised of everyone in the country. The more people who share the risk, the more efficient the program, and the more affordable the cost of care.

4. UNIONIZATION AND FAIR TRADE

Union members have higher wages and better benefits than nonunion workers. This is not because union members have better skills, but because they exert collective pressure on employers and thereby gain a greater share of the wealth created by their labor.

Heavy unionization in manufacturing industries like steel and autos gave some African-American workers a foothold of economic security in the middle of the last century, enabling them to earn decent wages, with benefits and pensions, and to begin to realize the American dream.

The decline of U.S. manufacturing began in the 1970s and is accelerating today as global free-trade agreements give corporations the "freedom" to search the world for those most desperate for work at any wage.

During the same period, employers have used increasingly militant tactics to crush the labor movement, with the help of a multibillion dollar industry of anti-union consulting firms. Today, just 13% of the workforce belongs to unions, down from a peak of 35% in the 1950s.

Strengthening workers' right to organize unions would help restart the stalled process of building an African-American middle class—and also benefit immigrant workers. Fair trade agreements guaranteeing worker rights worldwide would, over the long run, also protect workers' job security at home.

5. ASSET DEVELOPMENT POLICIES

Various proposals for asset "starter kits" have been floated in the United States and elsewhere. Independent Development Accounts (IDAs) were launched by a 1998 federal pilot program. Children's Savings Accounts (CSAs) have been established in the United Kingdom, but remain at the proposal stage in the United States.

IDAs are a form of matched savings account in which savings may be withdrawn only for asset-building investments (for example, to buy a home, start a business, or go to school). The matching funds come from the government or a nonprofit organization. IDAs are administered by community-based organizations in partnership with financial institutions that hold deposits. There are now over 500 IDA initiatives across the country, according to the Center for Social Development.

CSAs ensure that every child starts life with a trust fund. At a child's birth, an account is established for her with perhaps $500 to $1,000 of public funds. Parents are encouraged to add roughly that amount to the fund every year, matched by more public and private funds, for up to five years. When the child reaches 18, she would have around $40,000 to use for education, to start a business, or as a down payment on a home.

IDAs should be expanded and funded more heavily and CSAs made available. Both programs should have a progressive matching system to provide larger matching funds to lower-income people. This would enable someone like Judith, who has worked hard all her life but has no cushion of savings, to pass along a financial nest egg to her grandchild. (You never know—he could be an African-American Bill Gates!) Asset starter kits ensure all children, including poor children, have opportunities to develop their talents.

Asset-building programs like these must be designed with and for communities of color and immigrant communities. Many groups already form informal rotating savings and credit associations: individuals put in a certain amount of money every month, and then, in rotation, each has a turn at using all the money in the pot. These accounts have helped to start and expand many businesses, for example, in Korean communities. But "ROSCAs" face certain barriers. Most significantly, banks treat personal deposits as belonging to an individual or household, reporting any deposit of more than $10,000 to the Internal Revenue Service. Reforms should at minimum create a tax exemption for these collective savings pools, and, better still, bolster them with matching funds.

When Martin Luther King traveled to Washington, D.C., in 1963, he didn't go to tell people about a dream. He went to "cash a promissory note"—the Constitution's promise of life, liberty, and the pursuit of happiness for all. This promise cannot be kept without a government commitment to provide some measure of financial opportunity and security for all of us. For centuries, vast private wealth was created from a human rights disaster: the

African slave trade. While this is an uncomfortable topic that most white Americans would just as well put under "file closed," slavery left a legacy that is still very much with us today. African Americans like Judith, whether descended from slaves or not, still suffer from the accumulated effects of the historical social and economic exclusion of their people, and the barriers to wealth creation that persist. If, as a society, we truly believe in equal opportunity for all, then we cannot claim there is a fair race being run when some people have not even approached the starting line. Call it reparations, or restitution, or a chance to catch up—or simply call it justice.

If, by the time Judith Roderick's grandchild is grown, he has access to a good education, health insurance, a financial nest egg, encouragement from an entire society cheering his success, and a guarantee that the color of his skin will not have any bearing on his future, then this nation will at last be on the road to closing the racial wealth gap.

The distribution of wealth in the United States is not likely to change dramatically unless the institutional framework for creating and distributing it is altered. A wide range of community economic development institutions, created by visionary activists and government officials across the country, is beginning to point the way.

Community Economic Development

An Alternative Vision for Creating and Distributing Wealth

BY THAD WILLIAMSON

Inequalities of wealth in the United States result from an economic system that encourages individuals and corporations to accumulate private wealth for private ends. Corporations may rule the world today, but even within modern capitalist economies, there are counter-examples of public, quasi-public, and community-based institutions generating shared, common wealth and using it for shared, common ends. Although these institutions are minute relative to those of the mainstream economy, taken together they are beginning to achieve sufficient size and maturity so as to be able to suggest the outlines of an entirely different economic system.

The most obvious—and perhaps still the most important—example of publicly held wealth is the federal government itself, which owns over 3 billion square feet of building space and millions of acres of undeveloped land. Total federal assets, including land, buildings, infrastructure, and equipment, are estimated to exceed $1.4 trillion. The public also owns the airwaves, a priceless commodity. (Radio and TV networks are tenants of the airwaves, not owners.)

Recognizing just how much federally controlled wealth remains in the United States even today is important—not least because some conservatives and libertarians would like to see the government sell off (or give away) its vast assets. But these assets are of little or no direct value to the people on the wrong side of the wealth gap. The fact that the government owns vast tracts in Wyoming means little in low-income communities around the country where savings and steady work are scarce.

That's where local-scale, community-based economic institutions come in. Under the radar of mainstream media attention, an impressive array of alternative wealth-holding and job-creating institutions has evolved and matured in the past 30 years. While the mechanics of these institutions vary widely, all are built on the principle that profits accumulated through economic activity should be invested in the community or otherwise used to benefit all its members.

Perhaps the best known of these institutional innovations is the **community development corporation** (CDC). CDCs are nonprofit organizations governed by representatives from particular communities (neighborhoods, or entire cities or counties), charged with trying to stimulate economic development in depressed areas. Many CDCs focus on housing development; for example, they may buy abandoned or dilapidated properties, renovate them, then sell them to moderate-income families under special equity rules designed to keep the housing permanently affordable.

Other CDCs have branched out and established their own businesses. CDC-owned businesses both provide jobs to local residents and create a revenue stream that can be used to finance other activities (for example, anti-drug education, child care, or job training) that enhance the local quality of life.

Two CDCs that have been particularly successful in developing a portfolio of community-controlled businesses are the New Community Corporation in Newark, N.J., which employs 2,300 people and generates over $200 million a year in economic activity, and The East Los Angeles Community Union (TELACU), with assets of over $300 million. TELACU employs more than 700 people in businesses such as construction management, telecommunications, and roofing supply.

Closely related to the growth of CDCs are a range of **community development financial institutions** (CDFIs)—banks, credit unions, and microlenders that focus explicitly on assisting community development in depressed areas. Two of the best known examples are Shorebank, a network of financial institutions that invests over $150 million a year in low-income neighborhoods in Chicago, Cleveland, Michigan, and the Pacific Northwest; and Self-Help in Durham, N.C., which has provided over $3.5 billion in assistance to poor people since 1980 in the form of personal loans, business loans, and mortgages. Self-Help also played a critical role in helping pass landmark anti-predatory lending legislation in North Carolina in 1999.

In the 1990s, the federal government established the Community Development Financial Institutions Fund to provide badly needed capital support and technical assistance to fledgling CDFIs. The Bush administration has cut funding for the CDFI Fund; restoring and indeed dramatically expanding support for the fund should be a major policy priority.

Nonprofit-owned businesses are another promising model for broadening wealth. In the last decade, more and more nonprofits have sought to become financially independent by launching business activities. One is Pioneer Human Services in Seattle, a $55 million organization that employs over 1,000 people—most of whom are disadvantaged—in eight businesses, including a precision light-metal fabricator. Pioneer uses revenues from its enterprises to fund a wide range of social services for homeless people and addicts. Another example is Rubicon Programs in Richmond, Calif., which uses revenues from a bakery, a landscaping service, and a home care agency to fund about half of its $14 million budget. The funds are used to provide job training and other assistance to poor people.

Employee ownership is another powerful vehicle for broadening wealth. Over 11,000 firms in the United States are now at least partially employee-owned, and majority employee-owned firms have been successful in a range of sectors, from steel to supermarkets. Research conducted by Peter Kardas, Adria Scharf, and Jim Keogh shows that workers in majority employee-owned firms are better paid than workers in comparable traditional firms, and that these employees get nearly $20,000 more in pension benefits on average than their counterparts in conventional firms. Majority employee-owned firms where workers have full voting rights are unlikely to abandon local communities in search of a higher profit elsewhere; evidence suggests that employee-owned firms are also less likely to declare bankruptcy.

Local public enterprise is surprisingly widespread in the United States, and offers yet another way communities can create jobs and public wealth at the same time. The United States has a long tradition of publicly held electric utilities, which consistently offer lower rates and are generally credited with much more responsible and proactive environmental policies than private, for-profit utilities. The Sacramento Municipal Utility District, which employs more than 2,000 people, spends over $25 million a year on energy efficiency initiatives, discounts to low-income users, and other public programs.

The public utility approach now extends far beyond electricity. Glasgow, Ky., a small rural community, pioneered the concept of a publicly owned and operated telecommunications system. In 1988, the town's electric utility began constructing a citywide communications network to provide cable television, computer networking, and eventually high-speed Internet access. The town's citizens and businesses now enjoy high-speed Internet access and cable television service at a fraction of the rate charged by private providers: residents have saved an estimated $14 million in cable bills alone since 1989. Glasgow's investment in information-technology infrastructure has also attracted many new employers to the city.

By the year 2000, over 250 municipalities had plans in place to own and operate telecommunications systems. One of the largest is in Tacoma, Wash., which in the late 1990s created the Click! Network, part of the public utility Tacoma Power, to compete against AT&T Broadband and other private cable and high-speed Internet providers. By 2001, Click! began turning a profit and now helps bolster Tacoma Power's overall financial position. As in Glasgow, in addition to saving Tacoma residents money, the Click! network has benefited local businesses and helped bolster local economic development. Utility officials also plan to use detailed information transmitted by the network to improve energy management and encourage energy conservation by residents.

Telecommunications is not the only game in town for cities and states wishing to boost revenues and hold down tax rates by establishing public enterprises. Other cities, including Hartford, Seattle, and Oakland, run real estate businesses, using city-owned land to leverage other forms of local economic development. San Diego generates some $43 million a year in revenues from the over 400 properties it leases. Municipalities are also generating revenue through composting systems, methane recovery operations, and retail activities. In addition to the jobs for local residents and other social benefits of many of these ventures, the additional revenue they generate helps pay for vital city services.

Perhaps the most dramatic example of how a public entity can reshape the accumulation and distribution of wealth is the Alaska Permanent Fund. Revenues from oil extraction not only pay for almost the entire Alaska state government, they also fund an annual "dividend" payout to each Alaskan of roughly $1,000 to $2,000. The dividend checks are a major boost to working-class and lower-income Alaskans and are one of the largest sources of income in the state economy as a whole.

Alaska's situation is unique, but its experience points to broader possibilities for asserting public control over natural resources and other public goods in order to provide everyone a steady stream of income and—at least slightly—to level the wealth distribution. It is easy to imagine entrepreneurial cities establishing public control over downtown land and then using revenues from leasing the land to fund dividends for city residents and other public purposes. Or the federal government devoting fees from broadcasters' use of the public airwaves to particular public goods. (Reading programs funded by revenue from TV networks might be appropriate!)

Advocates for a more egalitarian society in which wealth is less concentrated have to do more than critique today's disturbing trends. They must consider alternative mechanisms for producing and distributing wealth that really do lift all boats. Community-based economic institutions have an important role to play: they provide tangible benefits to people right now, they offer models that can be replicated and expanded, and, more broadly, they highlight a new understanding of wealth as a public, shared good that can and should be used for public, shared purposes.

Predatory lenders who charge usurious rates, write loans full of pitfalls in fine print, and push homeowners into foreclosure are literally stripping the wealth out of poor communities and communities of color. Activist David Swanson shows how a grassroots campaign forced the nation's largest predatory lender to pay back the people it swindled and adopt permanent reforms.

Flame-Broiled Shark

How Predatory Lending Victims Fought Back and Won

BY DAVID SWANSON

I f someone told you that a number of low-income people, most of them African-American or Latino, most of them women, most of them elderly, had been robbed of much of their equity or of their entire homes by a predatory mortgage lender, you might not be surprised. But if you heard that these women and men had brought the nation's largest high-cost lender to its knees, forced it to sell out to a foreign company, and won back a half a billion dollars that had been taken from them, you'd probably ask what country this had happened in. Surely it couldn't have been in the United States, land of unbridled corporate power.

And yet it was. In 2001, these families, all members of the Association of Community Organizations for Reform Now (ACORN), launched a campaign against the nation's largest and most notorious predatory lender, House-hold International (also known as Household Finance or Beneficial). The 2003 settlement included a ban on talking about the damage Household had inflicted on borrowers and neighborhoods. That's one reason many people haven't heard this story—the families who defeated Household are in effect barred from publicly criticizing the corporation and teaching others the lessons they learned. (I was ACORN's communications coordinator during much of the Household campaign but left before it ended. No one asked *me* not to tell this story.)

Home Equity as a Percent of Net Worth, by Income Quintile, 2000

	Lowest	Next– Lowest	Middle	Next-to– Highest	Highest
Non-Hispanic Whites	85.6	77.7	70.8	62.9	44.4
Hispanics	90.0	73.5	76.3	70.9	64.9
African Americans	NA	78.7	70.9	73.5	67.8

Source: U.S. Census Bureau, May 2003.

In low-income minority neighborhoods in the United States, the little wealth that exists lies in home equity (see "Home Equity as a Percent of Net Worth"). People of color have made gains in home ownership during the past few decades, thanks in part to efforts by community groups like ACORN and National People's Action to force banks to make loans in communities of color (see "Minority Homeownership Is Growing"). Overall, these gains have been good for the new homeowners and good for their neighborhoods.

But low-income home ownership is fragile. Half of all extremely low-income homeowners pay more than half of their income for housing, according to the National Low Income Housing Coalition. Because low-income homeownership is not protected by additional savings, a temporary loss of income or a sudden large expense, such as a medical bill, can mean the loss of the home.

High-cost lenders—including large national operations like Household, Wells Fargo, and Citigroup, as well as small-time local sharks—strip away, rather than build up, equity in poor neighborhoods. Predatory high-cost lenders turn the usual logic of lending upside down. They make their money by intentionally issuing loans that borrowers will be unable to repay. Their loans invariably leave borrowers worse off, not better off.

Most high-cost (also called "subprime") loans are home-mortgage refinance loans. They carry excessive, and sometimes variable, interest rates and exorbitant fees. The more abusive lenders bundle bogus products like credit insurance into their loans, which accrue more interest and fees. Some lenders quietly omit taxes and insurance costs from monthly mortgage statements, causing crises when the yearly tax and insurance bills arrive. Others encourage borrowers to consolidate credit card and other debt within the mortgage, which further decreases home equity and places the home at greater risk. Loans may even exceed the value of the home, trapping people in debt they cannot refinance with a responsible lender. Hidden balloon payments force repeated refinancing (with fees each time). When borrowers find themselves unable to meet payments, the predatory lender refinances them repeatedly and ultimately seizes the house. Borrowers often have little recourse, as mandatory arbitration clauses written into their loan contracts prevent them from taking lenders to court.

High-cost loans are not made only to people with poor credit. Fannie Mae estimates that as many as half of all subprime borrowers could have qualified for a lower-cost mortgage. After British financial corporation HSBC bought Household International in March 2003, it announced that 46% of Household's real estate-backed loans had been made to borrowers with 'A' credit. But Household had made no 'A' (standard low-cost) loans. In fact, Household was a leading cause of the rows of vacant houses appearing in ACORN neighborhoods in the 1990s.

FIGHTING BACK

ACORN members didn't take this abuse lying down. Their grassroots effort against Household relied on numerous strategies, including shareholder activism, political advocacy, and the old stand-by of direct action. It offers a model for low-income communities seeking to challenge exploitative corporations.

In 2001, ACORN members launched the campaign with simultaneous protests inside Household offices in cities around the country, and then began work to pass anti-predatory lending legislation at local, state, and federal levels.

MINORITY HOMEOWNERSHIP IS GROWING

Over the past decade, homeownership rates among minority households have risen more quickly than among other groups. In 1993, 42.6% of African-American and 40.0% of Latino households owned homes. In 2002, 48.9% and 47.4% of those groups owned homes, respectively. This reflects a more rapid rate of increase than for whites, whose home-ownership grew from an already high 70.4% to 74.7%. Minorities, as a share of all first-time homebuyers, rose from 19.1% in 1993 to 30% in 1999. Indeed, minorities accounted for 41% of net growth in ho-meowners during that same period, according to Harvard University's Joint Center for Housing Studies.

Later that year, ACORN, together with the advocacy group Coalition for Responsible Wealth, introduced a shareholder resolution that proposed to tie Household executives' compensation to the termination of the company's predatory lending practices. When Household held its annual meeting in a suburb of Tampa, Fla., a crowd of ACORN members arrived at the event wearing shark suits and holding shark balloons. The resolution won 5% of the shareholders' vote. In 2002, Household held its meeting an hour and a half from the nearest airport in rural Kentucky. ACORN members weren't deterred by the remote location—they came from all over the country by car. The protest may have been the biggest thing the town of London, Ky., had ever seen. This time, 30% of the shareholders supported the resolution.

ACORN also helped borrowers file a number of class-action suits against Household for practices that were clearly illegal under existing law, and it let Wall Street analysts know what Household stood to lose from these lawsuits. ACORN urged state attorneys general and federal regulators to investigate the firm, and simultaneously put pressure on stores, including Best Buy, that issued Household credit cards. As a result of ACORN agitation, various local and state governments passed resolutions urging their pension funds to divest from the firm.

In the summer of 2002, ACORN members did something that really got the attention of Household executives and board members. On a beautiful day, thousands of Household borrowers poured out of buses onto the lawns of the company CEO and board members in the wealthy suburbs north of Chicago. They knocked on the officials' doors, speaking directly to the people whose policies had hurt them from a distance. When forced to leave, ACORN members plastered "Wanted" posters all over the neighborhood.

Through all of this, ACORN worked the media. It kept a database of borrowers' stories, and put reporters in touch with them, generating several hundred national print articles and television and radio spots. It also maintained an enormous website about Household (which has since been removed as part of the gag-order agreement).

Meanwhile, ACORN Housing Corporation, a nonprofit loan-counseling agency created by ACORN, helped many borrowers cancel rip-off services, such as credit insurance, that were built into their loans, and, when possible, refinance out of their Household loans altogether.

HOUSEHOLD'S CONCESSIONS

For more than two years, a small handful of ACORN staff organized thousands of members in an unrelenting effort, until Household International could no longer sustain the negative attention, shareholder discontent, and

ACORN members from 27 states protest Wells Fargo's predatory lending practices as part of the ACORN national convention in Los Angeles, 2004.

legal and regulatory pressures. In early 2003, the lender agreed to pay $489 million in restitution to borrowers through the 50 state attorneys general. The company later agreed to pay millions more to ACORN to fund new financial literacy programs. This was one of the largest consumer settlements in history, but it amounted to only a fraction of what Household had taken from people, and it could not undo all the damage done to families who had lost their homes. In addition to the payments, the company will:

- Ensure that new loans actually provide a benefit to consumers prior to issuing the loans.
- Reform and improve disclosures to consumers.
- Reimburse states to cover the costs of the investigations into Household's practices.
- Limit prepayment penalties to the first two years of a loan.
- Limit points and origination fees, upfront charges built into the loan, to 5%. (A "point" is one percentage point of the loan amount.)
- Eliminate "piggyback" second mortgages. (When Household issued home loans, it would simultaneously issue a second, smaller, loan at an even higher rate. It often labeled these second loans "lines of credit" in order to avoid federal regulations that limit the rate that can be charged.)
- Implement a "Foreclosure Avoidance Program" to provide relief to borrowers who are at risk of losing their homes due to delinquent payments (for example, reducing interest rates, waiving unpaid late charges, deferring interest, and reducing the principal).

ACORN-led efforts won legislative and corporate reforms as well. Several cities and states (including Arkansas, California, New Mexico, New Jersey, and New York) have banned abusive practices that were once routine. One practice ACORN targeted aggressively was "single-premium credit insurance," a nearly useless and overpriced insurance policy that predatory lenders added to many loans (often falsely describing it as a requirement or failing to tell borrowers it had been included). In 2002, Household and other major lenders announced they would drop the product. This was one of several corporate reforms ACORN won during the course of the campaign.

This campaign demonstrates that a well-organized grassroots effort can combat corporate exploitation and extract significant concessions. By pursuing different strategies at once, ACORN repeatedly hit Household with the unexpected, and put it on the defensive. The outcome is good news for low-income neighborhoods, and bad news for Wells Fargo, the predatory lender who is next on ACORN's list.

The views expressed are the author's alone.

Bill Fletcher, president of TransAfrica Forum and former director of education for SEIU and then the AFL-CIO, talked to Meizhu Lui, executive
director of United for a Fair Economy and former president of AFSCME
Local 1489, about the role unions have played in changing the distribution
of wealth in the United States.

Unions and the Wealth Divide

An Interview with Bill Fletcher

MEIZHU LUI

ML: When we think of unions, we think about their role in increasing wages.
Have they also played a role in increasing the wealth of union members?

BF: If it were up to employers, they would pay subsistence wages, only
enough to keep workers alive and able to reproduce the workforce. Unions
for the most part succeeded in winning wages above the subsistence level,
so that workers could save money, buy homes, and achieve "middle-class"
lifestyles. Unfortunately, many unions explicitly excluded people of color
in their constitutions—some up until the 1950s—and this exclusion contributed to the racial economic and wealth gap. Later, as people of color
not only were allowed to join unions but infused new energy into the labor
movement—African Americans joining public sector unions in the 1960s
and '70s as part of the civil rights movement, and new immigrants today—
they also were able to begin to build up some savings. Union women as a
group have also benefited.

ML: Are there other more explicit wealth-creation activities that unions engaged in? For example, when did they start thinking about the need for pensions—assets for retirement?

BF: The pension idea dates all the way back to Samuel Gompers, who was
the first president of the American Federation of Labor (from 1886 to 1924).

In the 1800s, early unions and guilds provided burial funds for their members, since burial required more savings than some workers could probably muster. In the early 20th century, this old practice went in two new directions. One led toward health insurance, the other toward pensions. Instead of just negotiating wages for actual work hours, labor leaders began to ask employers to create pension funds so that wages would continue into retirement. This kind of asset is important, so that retired workers don't have to spend down their savings, but can still count on income, and can pass along their savings to their children. Pensions allow for the accumulation of family assets over generations.

ML: Originally, unions negotiated "defined benefit" pension plans, where employers committed to pay workers a certain percentage of their income in retirement for the rest of their lives, regardless of the number of years they might live. Workers could calculate their yearly retirement incomes. More recently, the majority of employer pension plans are 401(k)s, or "defined contribution" plans, where employers contribute a certain percent of their workers' wages into investment plans. Workers are at the mercy of the stock market; if stocks go down, their retirement incomes go down as well. What has the unions' role been in this change?

BF: This change began to occur in the 1980s, when Reagan launched an all-out attack on organized labor. Labor did fight back, but lost this battle. It is important to note that nonunion workers were the real losers as unions' power weakened. Today, guaranteed benefit plans are rare; and defined contribution plans compromise economic security for older people. This lesson came home during the Enron scandal.

ML: You mention health insurance as the other "line" coming out of the old burial fund idea. Health insurance paid for by employers was important for workers' economic security; as we know today, most people who lose all their assets do so because they are uninsured and a health crisis occurs in their family.

BF: Yes. For many, this is the most important benefit in their union contracts, especially as health costs rise. Going back to the early labor movement, Gompers felt that every economic benefit should come through the union. Other unions, particularly those in the CIO (Congress of Industrial Organizations), which organized not by craft but by entire workplaces and industries, took up the fight for employers to pay for health insurance. The Gompers notion can work when there are multiple employers and union density is high. But it misses the point that it is a legitimate role of government to provide health care security for its people—that is, national health insurance. Gompers would have been well liked by some of our anti-government, free-market apologists today!

ML: Interesting image—Grover Norquist and Sam Gompers, hand in hand!

BF: If labor had used its clout to bring about a national health plan as happened in a number of European countries, and the uninsured didn't have to spend all their assets for inevitable health crises, then workers as a whole would hold more wealth.

ML: There was an interesting example in Boston where the Hotel Employees and Restaurant Employees union (HERE) won a housing benefit for its workers. How did that happen?

BF: Local 26 in Boston had to change the National Labor Relations Act in order to have the right to bargain around creating an employer-union housing benefit plan. In 1988, they negotiated the first collectively bargained housing trust fund with Boston hotel owners. They then proceeded to take on the federal government, and won the right to bargain such an agreement in 1990—the cart pushing the horse! With union membership as an organizing base and with the support of other community activists, they were able to kick Fleet Bank's butt around its predatory lending practices through research reports and court suits, and by embarrassing the CEO wherever he went. Predatory lending involves charging exorbitant interest rates with the intention of stealing the homes of long-term lower-income homeowners who are property-rich but cash-poor. The settlement of the case against Fleet not only brought a huge amount of money into their loan fund, but set up the Neighborhood Assistance Corporation of America (NACA) to administer the funds. Today, NACA has over $10 billion and provides mortgages with no down payment, no closing costs, no fees, and a below-market interest rate.

Working-class people far beyond Boston are benefiting from the efforts of one union's feisty and far-sighted membership. Since Local 26 has a membership of many people of color and immigrants, they also confronted racial wealth inequality. First, they stopped many discriminatory lending practices which had targeted people of color, for example, by charging them disproportionate interest rates for bank mortgages. Second, they were successful in building wealth for their members, even those who were at the lowest ends of the income and asset scales, who do not have parents who can "gift" them the down payment money. Owning a home became a real possibility for many who would not have been able to do so without this union benefit.

ML: Given the significance of this win, are other unions also using the NLRA to bargain for housing benefits?

BF: Strangely enough, I have not heard of this model spreading to other places. But it is there for unions to take advantage of; the groundwork has been done.

ML: As pension funds have grown into huge pools of dollars, some unions have been using those funds to increase assets for community people. I believe that a construction trade union used pension funds to build affordable housing.

BF: Yes. The Bricklayers Union was one that did build a number of units of housing in Boston. This was great—a way to bridge community and union—but it was on a small scale. A question for labor might be how to bring this kind of project to scale.

An interesting initiative begun a few years ago is the "labor/community strategic partnerships" initiative of the AFL-CIO. The program is called HIT, the Housing Investment Trust, and it uses the clout of union pension fund dollars to be a catalyst for building affordable housing. By bringing investment dollars to the table, and getting matches from local governments and businesses, they have built over 60,000 units of new affordable housing. The projects also have provided 50,000 jobs in the construction industry, and of course, the workers have to be union! But in any case, the AFL-CIO is definitely getting beyond the Gompers model, and thinking about how to provide benefits for more working people than just their own members.

ML: Those pension funds are a potential source of a lot of power!

BF: Yes. Unions have in the last 20 years or so started to develop strategies that use their massive pension funds for investments that can affect corporate behavior and for social change. One of the main architects of this is Randy Barber from the Center for Economic Organizing in Washington, D.C.; he's a real visionary. Pension funds represent the collective wealth of many workers. If used creatively, there is great potential for unions to use this wealth—just as the rich use their dollars—to gain power. Hopefully, unions can use their own wealth to influence the redistribution of wealth in this country, including to close the racial wealth divide. That's a stretch today but hey, keep hope alive!

Pension wealth is one of the most powerful and underused weapons of working people. Most pension wealth is invested by the financial industry with no concern for the impact on working people or their communities. But among union and public-employee pension trustees, there's a growing movement to direct a portion of workers' pension wealth toward worker-friendly investments that bolster the labor movement, save jobs, and build affordable housing.

Labor's Capital

Putting Pension Wealth to Work for Workers

BY ADRIA SCHARF

Pension fund assets are the largest single source of investment capital in the country. Of the roughly $17 trillion in private equity in the U.S. economy, $6 to 7 trillion is held in employee pensions. About $1.3 trillion is in union pension plans (jointly trusteed labor-management plans or collectively bargained company-sponsored plans) and $2.1 trillion is in public employee pension plans. Several trillion more are in defined contribution plans and company-sponsored defined benefit plans with no union representation. (See "Pension Funds and Labor's Voice.") These vast sums were generated by—and belong to—workers; they're really workers' deferred wages.

Workers' retirement dollars course through Wall Street, but most of the capital owned *by* working people is invested with no regard *for* working people or their communities. Pension dollars finance sweatshops overseas, hold shares of public companies that conduct mass layoffs, and underwrite myriad anti-union low-road corporate practices. In one emblematic example, the Florida public pension system bought out the Edison Corporation, the for-profit school operator, in November 2003, with the deferred wages of Florida government employees—including public school teachers. (With just three appointed trustees, one of whom is Governor Jeb Bush, Florida is one of the few states with no worker representation on the board of its state-employee retirement fund.)

The custodians of workers' pensions—plan trustees and investment managers—argue that they are bound by their "fiduciary responsibility" to consider only narrow financial factors when making investment decisions. They maintain they have a singular obligation to maximize financial returns and minimize financial risk for beneficiaries—with no regard for broader concerns. But from the perspective of the teachers whose dollars funded an enterprise that aims to privatize their jobs, investing in Edison, however promising the expected return (and given Edison's track record, it wasn't very promising!), makes no sense.

A legal concept enshrined in the 1974 Employee Retirement Income Security Act (ERISA) and other statutes, "fiduciary responsibility" does constrain the decision-making of those charged with taking care of other people's money. It obligates fiduciaries (e.g., trustees and fund managers) to invest retirement assets for the exclusive benefit of the pension beneficiaries. According to ERISA, fiduciaries must act with the care, skill, prudence, and diligence that a "prudent man" would use. Exactly what that means, though, is contested.

The law does *not* say that plan trustees must maximize short-term return. It does, in fact, give fiduciaries some leeway to direct pension assets to worker- and community-friendly projects. In 1994, the U.S. Department of Labor issued rule clarifications that expressly permit fiduciaries to make "economically targeted investments" (ETIs), or investments that take into account collateral benefits like good jobs, housing, improved social service facilities, alternative energy, strengthened infrastructure, and economic development. Trustees and fund managers are free to consider a double bottom line, prioritizing investments that have a social pay-off so long as their expected risk-adjusted financial returns are equal to other, similar, investments. Despite a backlash against ETIs from Newt Gingrich conservatives in the 1990s, Clinton's Labor Department rules still hold.

Nevertheless, the dominant mentality among the asset management professionals who make a living off what United Steelworkers president Leo Gerard calls "the deferred-wage food table" staunchly resists considering any factors apart from financial risk and return.

This is beginning to change in some corners of the pension fund world, principally (no surprise) where workers and beneficiaries have some control over their pension capital. In jointly managed union defined-benefit (known as "Taft-Hartley") plans and public-employee pension plans, the

ETI movement is gaining ground. "Taft-Hartley pension trustees have grown more comfortable with economically targeted investments as a result of a variety of influences, one being the Labor Department itself," says Robert Pleasure of the Center for Working Capital, an independent capital steward-ship-educational institute started by the AFL-CIO. Concurrently, more public pension fund trustees have begun adopting ETIs that promote housing and economic development within state borders. Most union and public pension trustees now understand that, as long as they follow a careful process and protect returns, ETIs do not breach their fiduciary duty, and may in certain cases actually be sounder investments than over-inflated Wall Street stocks.

SAVING JOBS: HEARTLAND LABOR CAPITAL NETWORK

"It's simple. Workers' assets should be invested in enterprises and construc-tion projects that will help to build their cities, rebuild their schools, and

PENSION FUNDS AND LABOR'S VOICE

The vast majority of defined-benefit pension plans in private industry have no worker representation on their boards of trustees. Only for the 8% of plans that fall under the Taft-Hartley law is worker representa-tion required. Defined benefit plans sponsored by individual employ-ers, which, according to economist Teresa Ghilarducci, represent more than 92% ($1.8 trillion) of private defined benefit plans, have no em-ployee representation. In defined contribution plans like 401(k)s, the structure of the plan is typically set up by the company with little or no worker input, and workers are limited to a predetermined menu of investment choices.

While most of the ETI "action" has been in jointly managed defined benefit and public pensions, the labor movement has extended the fight for increased control over pension assets to rules that affect defined contribution investments as well. Most significantly, the AFL-CIO's Of-fice of Investment led the recent battle for increased public oversight over the mutual fund industry, which ended in victory in early 2003 when the Securities and Exchange Commission (SEC) ruled that the mu-tual fund industry must disclose proxy votes. This is a win for employees with defined contribution plans, as mutual funds cast their proxy votes in line with the desires of corporate managers in order to secure their rebuild America's infrastructure," says Tom Croft of the Heartland Labor Capital Network. The Heartland Network is at the center of a movement to direct labor pension fund dollars into what Croft calls the "heartland" economy.

During the run-up of Wall Street share prices in the 1990s, investment funds virtually redlined basic industries, preferring to direct dollars into hot public technology stocks and emerging foreign markets, which despite the rhetoric of fiduciary responsibility were often speculative, unsound, investments. Even most collectively bargained funds put their assets exclusively in Wall Street stocks, in part because some pension trustees feared that if they didn't, they could be held liable. (During an earlier period, the Labor Department aggressively pursued union pension trustees for breaches of fiduciary duty. In rare cases where trustees were found liable, their personal finances and possessions were at risk.) But in the past five years, more union pension funds and labor-friendly fund managers have begun directing as-

business. Yet, many mutual funds had refused to disclose those votes to the public, including the employees whose dollars they invest.

Estimated Distribution of Capital (late 1990s)

Pension Funds Under Direct or Indirect Influence of Employees (billions of dollars)

	Type of Employee Representation		
Type of Plan	Direct	Indirect	None
Taft-Hartley	est. $247		
Collectively bargained corporate		est. $1,047	
Corporate without a union			est. $1,089
Public sector		$2,094	
Defined contribution			$1,792
Share:	4%	50%	46%
Total: $6,269			

Teresa Ghilarducci, "Small Benefits, Big Pension Funds, and How Governance Reforms Can Close the Gap." *Working Capital: The Power of Labor's Pensions*, Archon Fung, Tessa Hebb, and Joel Rogers, eds. ILR Press, 2001.

sets into investments that bolster the "heartland" economy: worker-friendly private equity, and, wherever possible, unionized industries and companies that offer "card-check" and "neutrality." ("Card-check" requires automatic union recognition if a majority of employees present signed authorization cards; "neutrality" means employers agree to remain neutral during organizing campaigns.) Croft says he and his allies want to "make sure there's an economy still around in the future to which working people will be able to contribute."

Croft estimates that about $3 to $4 billion in new dollars have been directed to worker-friendly private equity since 1999—including venture capital, buyout funds, and "special situations" funds that invest in financially distressed companies, saving jobs and preventing closures. Several work closely with unions to direct capital into labor-friendly investments.

One such fund, New York-based KPS Special Situations, has saved over 10,000 unionized manufacturing jobs through its two funds, KPS Special Situations I and II, according to a company representative. In 2003, St. Louis-based Wire Rope Corporation, the nation's leading producer of high carbon wire and wire rope products, was in bankruptcy with nearly 1,000 unionized steelworker jobs in jeopardy. KPS bought the company and restructured it in collaboration with the United Steelworkers International. Approximately 20% of KPS's committed capital is from Taft-Hartley pension dollars; as a result, the Wire Rope transaction included some union pension assets.

The Heartland Labor Capital Network and its union partners want to expand this sort of strategic deployment of capital by building a national capital pool of "Heartland Funds" financed by union pension assets and other sources. The funds have already begun to make direct investments in smaller worker-friendly manufacturing and related enterprises; labor representatives participate alongside investment experts on advisory boards to many of the funds.

"CAPITAL STEWARDSHIP": THE AFL-CIO

For the AFL-CIO, ETIs are nothing new. Its Housing Investment Trust (HIT), formed in 1964, is the largest labor-sponsored investment vehicle in the country that produces collateral benefits for workers and their neighborhoods. Hundreds of union pension funds invest in the $2 billion trust, which leverages public financing to build housing, including low-income and affordable units, using union labor. HIT, together with its sister fund the Building Investment Trust (BIT), recently announced a new investment program that is expected to generate up to $1 billion in investment in apartment development and rehabilitation by 2005 in targeted cities including

New York, Chicago, and Philadelphia. The initiative will finance thousands of units of housing and millions of hours of union construction work. HIT and BIT require owners of many of the projects they help finance to agree to card-check recognition and neutrality for their employees.

HIT and BIT are two examples of union-owned investment vehicles. There are many others—including the LongView ULTRA Construction Loan Fund, which finances projects that use 100% union labor; the Boilermakers' Co-Generation and Infrastructure Fund; and the United Food and Commercial Workers' Shopping Center Mortgage Loan Program—and their ranks are growing.

Since 1997, the AFL-CIO and its member unions have redoubled their efforts to increase labor's control over its capital through a variety of means. The AFL-CIO's Capital Stewardship Program promotes corporate governance reform, investment manager accountability, pro-worker investment strategies, international pension fund cooperation, and trustee education. (For more details, see "The Wall Street Strategy.") It also evaluates worker-friendly pension funds on how well they actually advance workers' rights, among other criteria. The Center for Working Capital, started by the AFL-CIO in 1997, provides education and training to hundreds of union and public pension fund trustees each year, organizes conferences, and sponsors research on capital stewardship issues including ETIs.

PUBLIC PENSION PLANS JOIN IN

At least 29 states have ETI policies directing a portion of their funds, usually less than 5%, to economic development within state borders. The combined public pension assets in ETI programs amount to about $55 billion, according to a recent report commissioned by the Vermont state treasurer. The vast majority of these ETIs are in residential housing and other real estate.

The California Public Employees' Retirement System (CalPERS) is the single largest pension fund in the country; with $153.8 billion in assets, it provides retirement benefits to over 1.4 million members. CalPERS is an ETI pioneer among state pension funds. In the mid-1990s, when financing for housing construction dried up in California, CalPERS invested hundreds of millions of dollars to finance about 4% of the state's single-family housing market. Its ETI policy is expansive. While it requires economically targeted investments earn maximum returns for their level of risk and fall within geographic and asset-diversification guidelines, CalPERS also considers the investments' benefits to its members and to state residents, their job creation potential, and the economic and social needs of different groups in the state's population. CalPERS directs about 2% of its assets—about $20

THE WALL STREET STRATEGY

Another way labor is deploying its pension capital strategically is through corporate shareholder initiatives. These campaigns target public corporations for proxy battles over executive compensation, board independence, and other corporate governance issues. Whereas ETIs are directed primarily at starting or saving privately held companies, or into construction or real estate projects, shareholder campaigns challenge the large public corporations that workers' pension funds partly own. The AFL-CIO conducts an annual "Key Votes Survey" to track how the investment managers of pension fund assets vote plan proxies on key shareholder proposals. (This helps union trustees, who are elected or appointed to administer pension assets, to monitor the investment managers that actually invest the bulk of union pension dollars.) The AFL-CIO is now pushing the SEC to consider giving long-term shareholders, including pension fund investors, the right to include their own nominees to corporate boards of directors in the proxy materials mailed by corporations to shareholders. If the SEC rules in favor, this would be another useful tool in labor's pension arsenal.

billion as of May 2001—to investments that provide collateral social benefits. It also requires construction and maintenance contractors to provide decent wages and benefits.

Other state pension funds have followed CalPERs' lead. In 2003, the Massachusetts treasury expanded its ETI program, which is funded by the state's $32 billion pension. Treasurer Timothy Cahill expects to do "two dozen or more" ETI investments in 2004, up from the single investment made in 2003, according to the *Boston Business Journal*. "It doesn't hurt our bottom line, and it helps locally," Cahill explained. The immediate priority will be job creation. Washington, Wisconsin, and New York also have strong ETI programs.

In their current form and at their current scale, economically targeted investments in the United States are not a panacea. Pension law does impose constraints. Many consultants and lawyers admonish trustees to limit ETIs to a small portion of an overall pension investment portfolio. And union trustees must pursue ETIs carefully, following a checklist of "prudence" procedures, to protect themselves from liability. The most significant constraint is simply that these investments must generate risk-adjusted returns equal to alternative investments—this means that many deserving not-for-profit efforts and experiments in economic democracy are automatically ruled out. Still, there's more wiggle room in the law than has been broadly recognized. And when deployed strategically to bolster the labor movement, support employee buyouts, generate good jobs, or build affordable housing, economically targeted investments are a form of worker direction over capital whose potential has only begun to be realized. And (until the day that capital is abolished altogether) that represents an important foothold.

As early as the mid-1970s, business expert Peter Drucker warned in *Unseen Revolution* of a coming era of "pension-fund socialism" in which the ownership of massive amounts of capital by pension funds would bring about profound changes to the social and economic power structure. Today, workers' pensions prop up the U.S. economy. They're a point of leverage like no other. Union and public pension funds are the most promising means for working people to shape the deployment of capital on a large scale, while directing assets to investments with collateral benefits. If workers and the trustees of their pension wealth recognize the power they hold, they could alter the contours of capitalism.

SECTION V
Looking Forward

The roots of wealth inequality lie in economic institutions: the corporation and the financial system. Reform movements are already underway in both venues, and, according to William Greider, the transformation of capitalist institutions is not only possible but likely.

Transforming the Engines of Inequality

BY WILLIAM GREIDER

A merican politics has always involved a struggle between "organized money" and "organized people." It's a neglected truth that has resurfaced with ironic vengeance in our own time—ironic because the 20th century produced so much progress toward political equality among citizens, and because the emergence of a prosperous and well-educated middle class was expected to neutralize the overbearing political power of concentrated wealth. Instead, Americans are reminded, almost any time they read a newspaper, that the rich do indeed get richer and that our political system is, as Greg Palast put it, "the best democracy money can buy."

What should we make of this retrogressive turn—a nation of considerable abundance still ruled by gilded-age privilege? A cynic would say it was ever thus, end of story. Political commentators argue it's a sign of the country's maturation that its citizens now accept what they once resisted—gross and growing inequalities of wealth. And many economists simply avert their gaze from the troubling consequences of maldistribution for economic progress and the well-being of society.

I stake out a contrary claim: The United States remains an unfinished nation—stunted in its proclaimed values—so long as it fails to confront the enduring contradictions between wealth and democracy. That is not a utopian lament for radical change, but simply an observation of what our own era has taught us.

Inequality retains its crippling force over society and politics and the lives of citizens, despite the broader distribution of material comforts. We are not the nation of 80 or 100 years ago, when most Americans struggled in very modest circumstances, often severe deprivation. Yet, despite the nation's wealth (perhaps also because of it), the influence of concentrated economic power has grown stronger and more intimate in our lives. Today the social contract is determined more by the needs and demands of corporations and finance than by government or the consensual will of the people.

The federal government and several generations of liberal and labor reformers did achieve great, life-improving gains during the last century. But those reforms and redistributive programs did not succeed in altering the root sources of economic inequality, much less taming them. On the contrary, the U.S. economic system recreates and even expands the maldistribution of incomes and wealth in each new generation.

The root sources of inequality are located within the institutions of advanced capitalism—in the corporation and financial system—with their narrow operating values and the peculiar arrangements that consign enormous decision-making power to a remarkably small number of people. The problem of inequality is essentially a problem of malformed power relationships: Advanced capitalism deprives most people of voice and influence, while it concentrates top-down authority among the insiders of finance and business. Ameliorative interventions by government (for example, through regulation, taxation, and reform) have never succeeded in overcoming the tendency within capitalism toward increased concentrations of economic power.

The drive for greater equality must involve governmental actions, of course, but it cannot succeed unless it also confronts the engines of inequality within the private realm and forces deep changes in how American capitalism functions. The challenge is nothing less than to rearrange power relationships within the corporation and finance capital.

Who has the power to restructure capitalist institutions? In my view, ordinary people do—at least potentially—acting collectively as workers, investors, consumers, managers or owners and, above all, as citizens, to force change. Many are, in small and different ways, already at work on the task of reinventing capitalism.

TRANSFORMING THE WORKPLACE

The workplace is perhaps the most effective engine of inequality, since it teaches citizens resignation and subservience, while it also maldistributes the returns of enterprise. For most Americans, the employment system functions on the archaic terms of the master-servant relationship inherited from feudalism. The feudal lord commanded the lives and livelihoods of serfs on his land and expelled those who disobeyed. The corporate employer has remarkably similar powers, restrained only by the limited prohibitions in law or perhaps by the terms of a union contract. Elaine Bernard, director of Harvard's trade union studies program, described the blunt reality:

> As power is presently distributed, workplaces are factories of authoritarianism polluting our democracy. Citizens cannot spend eight hours a day obeying orders and being shut out of important decisions affecting them, and then be expected to engage in a robust, critical dialogue about the structure of our society.

Where did people learn to accept their powerlessness? They learned it at work. Nor is this stunted condition confined to assembly lines and working-class occupations. The degradation of work now extends very far up the job ladder, including even well-educated professionals whose expert judgments have been usurped by distant management systems.

In most firms, only the insiders at the top of a very steep command-and-control pyramid will determine how the economic returns are distributed among the participants. Not surprisingly, the executives value their own work quite generously while regarding most of the employees below as mere commodities or easily interchangeable parts. More importantly, these insiders will harvest the new wealth generated by an enterprise, while most workers will not. In the long run, this arrangement of power guarantees the permanence of wealth inequalities.

Joseph Cabral, CEO of Chatsworth Products Inc., a successful employee-owned computer systems manufacturer in California, is an accountant, not a political philosopher, but he understands the wealth effects of closely held control in private businesses. "The wealth that's created ends up in too few hands," he said. "The entrepreneur who's fortunate enough to be there at the start ends up really receiving a disproportionate amount of wealth. And the working folks who enabled that success to take place share in little of that wealth. At some point, capitalism is going to burst because we haven't done right for the folks who have actually created that wealth."

But there are other, more democratic, ways to structure the work environment. At Chatsworth, where the workers collectively purchased the enterprise, "Everyone is sharing in the wealth they're creating. … We're not just doing this for some outside shareholder. We're doing it because we are the shareholders."

Employee ownership, worker-management, and other systems of worker self-organization provide a plausible route toward reforming workplace power relations and spreading financial wealth among the many instead of the few.

TRANSFORMING FINANCE CAPITAL

The top-down structure of how Wall Street manages "other people's money" ensures the maldistribution of financial returns. As wealthy people know, those who bring major money to the table are given direct influence over their investments and a greater return on their risk-taking. The rank-and-file investors—because their savings are modest and they lack trustworthy intermediaries to speak for them—are regarded as passive and uninformed, treated more or less like "widows and orphans," and blocked from exerting any influence over how their wealth is invested. To put the point more crudely, the stock market is a casino, and the herd of hapless investors is always the "mark."

Nevertheless, finance capital is, I predict, the realm of capitalism most vulnerable to reform pressures. That's mainly because it operates with other people's money, and most of that money belongs not to the wealthiest families but to the broad ranks of ordinary working people. A historic shift in the center of gravity has occurred in U.S. finance over the past decade: Fiduciary institutions like pension funds and mutual funds have eclipsed individual wealth as the largest owner of financial assets. Their collectivized assets now include 60% of the largest 1,000 corporations. Because these funds invest across the broad stock market, they literally own the economy.

Public pension funds, union-managed pension funds, and shareholder activists are already working to forge an engaged voice for the individuals whose wealth is in play, and to force the fiduciary institutions to take responsibility for the social and environmental effects of how these trillions in savings are invested. The collapse of the stock-market bubble and subsequent corporate scandals have accelerated these reform efforts.

Some of the largest public-employee pension funds including the California Public Employees' Retirement System and the New York State public employees fund, joined by state officials who sit on supervisory boards, are aggressively leading the fight for corporate-governance reform and for stricter social accountability on urgent matters like workers' rights and global warming. The labor movement is organizing proxy battles to press for corporate reforms at individual companies including the Disney Corporation and Royal Dutch Shell, while the AFL's Office of Investment won a victory for mutual-fund investors in early 2003 when it persuaded the Securities and Exchange Commission to require mutual funds to disclose their proxy votes in corporate-governance shareholder fights. (The mutual fund industry is working to resist the measure, and for good reason. Investment firms regularly vote against the interests of their own rank-and-file investors in order to curry favor with the corporations that hire them to manage corporate-run pension funds and 401(k) plans.)

The major banks and brokerages cannot brush aside these new critics as easily as corporate directors often do. Wall Street will respond to fiduciary concerns because it must. It needs the rank-and-file's capital to operate. When six or seven major funds, collectively holding nearly $1 trillion, speak to Wall Street, things do change. Their unspoken threat to scorn companies or financial firms that ignore larger social obligations and shift their money elsewhere sends broad shockwaves across both financial markets and corporate boardrooms.

The more profound tasks are to challenge fraudulent economic valuations (think Enron) and to account for (and internalize) the true costs of products and production processes. Both steps would refocus capital investing toward creating real, long-term value and away from the transient thrill of quarterly returns. The fiduciary funds have the potential power to enforce this new economic perspective, though it is not yet widely understood or accepted by them. As universal owners of the economy, their own portfolios are the losers when individual corporations throw off externalities in order to boost their bottom lines. The costs will be borne by every other firm, by the economy as a whole, or by taxpayers who have to clean up the mess. The compelling logic of this new economic argument is this: what is bad for society cannot be good for future retirees or for their communities and their families.

Citizens, in other words, have more power than they imagine. If they assert influence over these intermediaries, they have the power to punish rogue corporations for anti-social behavior and block the low-road practices that have become so popular in business circles. In coalition with organized labor, environmentalists, and other engaged citizens, they have the capacity to design—and enforce—a new social contract that encourages, among other things, participatory management systems and worker ownership, loyalty to community, and respect for our deeper social values.

While none of this promises a utopian outcome of perfect equality, the redistribution of power within capitalism is certainly a predicate for the creation of a more equitable society.

My conviction is that we are on the brink of a broad new reform era, in which reorganizing capitalism becomes the principal objective. What

I foresee is a long, steady mobilization of people attempting to do things differently, often in small and local settings, trying out new arrangements, sometimes failing, then trying again. As these inventive departures succeed, others will emulate them. In time, an alternative social reality will emerge with different values, alongside the archaic and destructive system that now exists. When that begins to happen and gains sufficient visibility, the politics is sure to follow. If all this sounds too remote to the present facts, too patient for our frenetic age, remember that this is how deep change has always occurred across American history.

This article is adapted from The Soul of Capitalism *(Simon & Schuster, 2003).*

Taxing wealth is a sure way to address the growing wealth gap: it can provide revenue to meet pressing social needs and at the same time slow or reverse the trend toward wealth concentration. But conventional political wisdom says significant wealth taxes simply won't fly in American politics. Political economist Gar Alperovitz takes on the conventional wisdom and explains why he is optimistic about the prospects for a new program of taxing large concentrations of wealth.

The Coming Era of Wealth Taxation

BY GAR ALPEROVITZ

Americans concerned with inequality commonly point to huge disparities in the distribution of income, but the ownership of wealth is far, far more concentrated. This fact is certain to bring the question of wealth taxation to the top of the nation's political agenda as the country's fiscal crisis deepens and, with it, the deterioration of public institutions and the pain of all those who rely on them.

Broadly, in any one year the top 20% garners for itself roughly 50% of all income, while the bottom 80% must make due with the rest. The top 1% regularly takes home more income than the bottom 100 million Americans combined.

When it comes to wealth, these numbers appear almost egalitarian. The richest 1% of households owns half of all outstanding stock, financial securities, trust equity, and business equity! A mere 5% at the very top owns more than two-thirds of the wealth in America's gigantic corporate economy, known as financial wealth—mainly stocks and bonds.

This is a medieval concentration of economic power. The only real question is when its scale and implications will surface as a powerful political issue. A wealth tax is "by definition, the most progressive way to raise revenue, since it hits only the very pinnacle of the income distribution," notes economist Robert Kuttner. But conventional wisdom says that it is impossible to deal with wealth head-on. The battle over repeal of the estate tax, in this view, demonstrated that even the most traditional of "wealth taxes" are no longer politically feasible.

Perhaps. However, a longer perspective reminds us that times can change—as, indeed, they often have when economic circumstances demanded it.

EMERGING SIGNS OF CHANGE

Indeed, times are already beginning to change. One sign: Although many Democrats were nervous about challenging George W. Bush in the first year after he took office, by early 2004 all the Democrats running for president had come to demand a repeal in some form of his tax giveaways to the elite.

It is instructive to trace the process of change. At the outset, only a few liberals challenged the president. The late Paul Wellstone, for instance, proposed freezing future income tax reductions for the top 1% and retaining the corporate Alternative Minimum Tax (AMT), for an estimated $134 billion in additional revenue over 10 years. Ted Kennedy proposed delaying tax cuts for families with incomes over $130,000 and keeping the estate tax (while gradually raising the value of exempted estates from a then-current $1 million to $4 million by 2010). Kennedy estimated this would generate $350 billion over 10 years.

By May 2002, even centrist Democrat Joseph Lieberman urged postponing both the full repeal of the estate tax and reductions in the top income-tax rates. Lieberman estimated his plan would save a trillion dollars over 20 years. The Bush tax cuts were simply unfair, he said, "giving the biggest benefit to those who needed it the least."

The Democrats failed to stop Bush's 2001 and 2003 rounds of tax cuts. But there are reasons to believe that politicians will ultimately come to accept the validity of maintaining and raising taxes on the wealthiest Americans. Just as many Democrats changed their stand on the Bush tax cuts, a similar progression is likely with regard to wealth taxation more generally over the next few years—and for two very good reasons. First, there is an extraordinary fiscal crisis brewing; and second, wealth taxes—like taxes on very high-income recipients—put 95% to 98% of the people on one side of the line and only 2% to 5% or so on the other.

GO WHERE THE MONEY IS

The hard truth is that it is now all but impossible to significantly raise taxes on the middle class. This reality flows in part from the ongoing decline of organized labor's political power, and in part from the Republicans' take-over of the South—another long and unpleasant political story. At any rate, it means that the only place to look for significant resources is where the remaining real money is—in the holdings of corporations and the elites who overwhelmingly own them. Put another way: Raising taxes first on the income and ultimately on the wealth of the very top groups is likely to become all but inevitable as, over time, it becomes clear that there is no way to get much more in taxes from the middle-class suburbs.

Moreover, as Democratic politicians have come increasingly to realize, the "logic of small versus large numbers" could potentially neutralize a good part of the suburbs politically, painting conservatives into a corner where they're forced to defend the very unreasonable privileges of the very rich.

The knee-jerk reaction that taxing wealth is impossible is based upon the kind of thinking about politics that "remembers the future"—in other words, thinking that assumes the future is likely to be just like the past, whether accurately remembered or not. Since wealth has not been taxed, it cannot be taxed now, goes the argument (or rather, assumption).

Of course, taxation of wealth has long been central to the American tax system for the kind of wealth most Americans own—their homes. Real estate taxes, moreover, are based on the market value of the home—not the value of a homeowner's equity: An owner of a $200,000 home will be taxed on the full value of the asset, even if her actual ownership position, with a mortgage debt of, say, $190,000, is only a small fraction of this amount. A new, more equitable form of wealth taxation would simply extend this very well established tradition and—at long last!—bring the elites who own most of the nation's financial wealth into the picture.

Many Americans once thought it impossible to tax even income—until the 1913 passage, after long debate and political agitation, of the 16th Amendment to the U.S. Constitution. Note, however, that for many years, the amendment in practice meant targeting elites: Significant income taxation was largely restricted to roughly the top 2% to 4% until World War II.

Even more important is a rarely discussed truth at the heart of the modern history of taxation. For a very long time now the federal income tax has, in fact, targeted elites—even in the Bush era, and even in a society preoccupied with terrorism and war. In 2000, the top 1% of households paid 36.5% of federal income taxes. The top 5% paid 56.2%. Although detailed calculations are not yet available, the massive Bush tax cuts are not expected to alter the order of magnitude of these figures. Estimates suggest that, ultimately, the tax reductions may modify the figures by no more than two or perhaps three percentage points.

In significant part this results from the rapidly growing incomes of the wealthiest: even at lower rates, they'll still be paying nearly the same share of total income tax. The simple fact is, however, that the record demonstrates it is not impossible to target elites. We need to take this political point seriously and act on it aggressively in the coming period.

FISCAL CRUNCH AHEAD

What makes wealth taxes even more likely in the coming period is the extraordinary dimension of the fiscal crisis, which will force government at all levels to adopt new strategies for producing additional resources. Projections for the coming decade alone suggest a combined federal fiscal deficit of more than $5 trillion—$7.5 trillion if Social Security Trust Fund reserves are left aside.

A worsening fiscal squeeze is coming—and it is not likely to be reversed any time soon. Critically, spending on Social Security benefits and Medicare will continue to rise as the baby-boom generation retires. So will spending on Medicaid. Recent studies project that by 2080 these three programs alone will consume a larger share of GDP than all of the money the federal government collects in taxes. And, of course, the ongoing occupation of Iraq will continue to demand large-scale financial support.

Nor are the trends likely to be altered without dramatic change: The truth is that the Bush tax and spending strategies, though particularly egregious, are by no means unique. Long before the Bush-era reductions, domestic discretionary spending by the federal government was trending down—from 4.7% of GDP a quarter century ago to 3.5% now, a drop during this period alone of roughly 25%.

A radically new context is thus taking shape which will force very difficult choices. Either there will be no solution to many of the nation's problems, or politicians and the public will have to try something new. Suburban middle-class voters, who rely on good schools, affordable health care, assistance for elderly parents, and public infrastructure of all kinds, will begin to feel the effects if the "beast" of government is truly starved. This pain is likely to redirect their politics back toward support for a strong public sector—one which is underwritten by taxes on the wealthiest. Quite simply, it is the only place to go.

TIME TO TAX WEALTH

Ideological conservatives like to argue that all Americans want to get rich and so oppose higher taxes on the upper-income groups they hope to join. In his recent history of taxation, *New York Times* reporter Steven Weisman has shown that this may or may not be so in normal times, but that when social and economic pain increase, politicians and the public have repeatedly moved to tax those who can afford it most. Bill Clinton, for one, raised rates on the top groups when necessity dictated. So did the current president's father! Now, several states—including even conservative Virginia—have seen pragmatic Republicans take the lead in proposing new elite taxation as the local fiscal crisis has deepened.

The likelihood of a political shift on this issue is also suggested by the growing number of people who have proposed direct wealth taxation. A large group of multimillionaires has launched a campaign opposing elimination of taxes on inherited wealth—paid only by the top 2%—as "bad for our democracy, our economy, and our society." Yale law professors Bruce Ackerman and Anne Alstott in their book *The Stakeholder Society* have proposed an annual 2% wealth tax (after exempting the first $80,000). Colgate economist Thomas Michl has urged a net-worth tax, and Hofstra law professor Leon Friedman has proposed a 1% tax on wealth owned by the top 1%. Even Donald Trump has proposed a one time 14.25% net-worth tax on Americans with more than $10 million in assets.

Wealth taxation is common in Europe. Most European wealth taxes have an exemption for low and moderate levels of wealth (especially the value of pensions and annuities). Economist Edward Wolff, who has studied these precedents carefully, suggests that America might begin with a wealth tax based on the very modest Swiss effort, with marginal rates between 0.05% and 0.3% after exempting roughly the first $100,000 of assets for married couples. He estimates that if this were done, only millionaires would pay an additional 1% or more of their income in taxes.

Europe also offers examples of much more aggressive approaches. Wealth taxation rates in 10 other European countries are much higher than Switzerland's—between 1% and 3%—and would yield considerable revenues if applied here. Wolff calculated that a 3% Swedish-style wealth tax in the United States would have produced $545 billion in revenue in 1998. Although an updated estimate is not available, nominal GDP increased about 19% between 1998 and 2002, and wealth taxes would likely produce revenues that roughly tracked that increase.

Some writers have held that wealth taxes are prohibited by the U.S. Constitution. There appear to be two answers to this. The first is legal: Ackerman, a noted constitutional expert, has argued at length in the Columbia Law Review that wealth taxes are not only constitutional, but represent the heart of both original and contemporary legal doctrine on taxation.

The second answer is political. We know that courts have a way of bending to the winds of political-economic reality over time. As the pain deepens, the courts are likely one day to recognize the validity of the legal arguments in favor of wealth taxation. Alternatively, political pressure may ultimately mandate further constitutional change, just as it did in 1913 with regard to income taxation.

There is no way of knowing for sure. But as with all important political change, the real answer will be found only if and when pressure builds up both intellectually and politically for a new course of action. The challenge, as always, is not simply to propose, but to act.

Americans are constantly exhorted to save—but also to spend! Social Security alone is not enough to fund even a modestly comfortable retirement—but many families cannot save enough to fill the gap or meet a financial setback. How should the nation understand and address these dilemmas? Here, economist Ellen Frank looks at how we can both meet individuals' need for economic security and maintain the stability of a modern market economy. Her answer: forget about legislating ever more vehicles for tax-advantaged individual savings, and instead expand the institutions of social wealth.

No More Savings!

The Case for Social Wealth

BY ELLEN FRANK

Pundits from the political left and right don't agree about war in Iraq, gay marriage, national energy policy, tax breaks, free trade, or much else. But they do agree on one thing: Americans don't save enough. The reasons are hotly disputed. Right-wingers contend that the tax code rewards spenders and punishes savers. Liberals argue that working families earn too little to save. Environmentalists complain of a work-spend rat race fueled by relentless advertising. But the bottom line seems beyond dispute.

Data on wealth-holding reveal that few Americans possess adequate wealth to finance a comfortable retirement. Virtually none have cash sufficient to survive an extended bout of unemployment. Only a handful of very affluent households could pay for health care if their insurance lapsed, cover nursing costs if they became disabled, or see their children through college without piling up student loans. Wealth is so heavily concentrated at the very top of the income distribution that even upper-middle class households are dangerously exposed to the vagaries of life and the economy.

With low savings and inadequate personal wealth identified as the problem, the solutions seem so clear as to rally wide bipartisan support: Provide tax credits for savings. Encourage employers to establish workplace savings plans. Educate people about family budgeting and financial investing. Promote home ownership so people can build home equity. Develop tax-favored plans to pay for college, retirement, and medical needs. More leftish proposals urge the government to redistribute wealth through federally sponsored "children's development accounts" or "American stakeholder accounts," so that Americans at all income levels can, as the Demos-USA website puts it, "enjoy the security and benefits that come with owning assets."

But such policies fail to address the paradoxical role savings play in market economies. Furthermore, looking at economic security solely through the lens of personal finance deflects focus away from a better, more direct, and far more reliable way to ensure Americans' well-being: promoting social wealth.

THE PARADOX OF THRIFT

Savings is most usefully envisaged as a physical concept. Each year, businesses turn out automobiles, computers, lumber, and steel. Households (or consumers) buy much, but not all, of this output. The goods and services they leave behind represent the economy's savings.

Economics students are encouraged to visualize the economy as a metaphorical plumbing system through which goods and money flow. Firms produce goods, which flow through the marketplace and are sold for money. The money flows into peoples' pockets as income, which flows back into the marketplace as demand for goods. Savings represent a leak in the economic plumbing. If other purchasers don't step up and buy the output that thrifty consumers shun, firms lay off workers and curb production, for there is no profit in making goods that people don't want to buy.

On the other hand, whatever consumers don't buy is available for businesses to purchase in order to expand their capacity. When banks buy computers or developers buy lumber and steel, then the excess goods find a market and production continues apace. Economists refer to business purchases of new plant and equipment as "investment." In the plumbing metaphor, investment is an injection—an additional flow of spending into the economy to offset the leaks caused by household saving.

During the industrial revolution, intense competition meant that whatever goods households did not buy or could not afford would be snatched up by emerging businesses, at least much of the time. By the turn of the 20th century, however, low-paid consumers had become a drag on economic growth. Small entrepreneurial businesses gave way to immense monopolistic firms like U.S. Steel and Standard Oil whose profits vastly exceeded what they could spend on expansion. Indeed expansion often looked pointless since, given the low level of household spending, the only buyers for their output were other businesses, who themselves faced the same dilemma.

As market economies matured, savings became a source of economic stagnation. Even the conspicuous consumption of Gilded Age business owners couldn't provide enough demand for the goods churned out of large industrial factories. Henry Ford was the first American corporate leader to deliberately pay his workers above-market wages, reasoning correctly that a better-paid work force would provide the only reliable market for his automobiles.

Today, thanks to democratic suffrage, labor unions, social welfare programs, and a generally more egalitarian culture, wages are far higher in industrialized economies than they were a century ago; wage and salary earners now secure nearly four-fifths of national income. And thrift seems a quaint virtue of our benighted grandparents. In the United States, the personal savings rate—the percentage of income flowing to households that they did not spend—fell to 1% in the late 1990s. Today, with a stagnant economy making consumers more cautious, the personal savings rate has risen—but only to around 4%.

Because working households consume virtually every penny they earn, goods and services produced are very likely to find buyers and continue to be produced. This is an important reason why the United States and Europe no longer experience the devastating depressions that beset industrialized countries prior to World War II.

Yet there is a surprisingly broad consensus that these low savings are a bad thing. Americans are often chastised for their lack of thrift, their failure to provide for themselves financially, their rash and excessive borrowing. Politicians and economists constantly exhort Americans to save more and devise endless schemes to induce them to do so.

At the same time, Americans also face relentless pressure to spend. After September 11, President Bush told the public they could best serve their country by continuing to shop. In the media, economic experts bemoan declines in "consumer confidence" and applaud reports of buoyant retail or auto sales. The U.S. economy, we are told, is a consumer economy—our spendthrift ways and shop-til-you-drop culture the motor that propels it. Free-spending consumers armed with multiple credit cards keep the stores hopping, the restaurants full, and the factories humming.

Our schizophrenic outlook on saving and spending has two roots. First, the idea of saving meshes seamlessly with a conservative ideological outlook. In what author George Lakoff calls the "strict-father morality" that informs conservative Republican politics, abstinence, thrift, self-reliance, and competitive individualism are moral virtues. Institutions that discourage saving—like Social Security, unemployment insurance, government health programs, state-funded student aid—are by definition socialistic and result in an immoral reliance on others. Former Treasury Secretary Paul O'Neill bluntly expressed this idea to a reporter for the *Financial Times* in 2001. "Able-bodied adults," O'Neill opined, "should save enough on a regular basis so that they can provide for their own retirement and for that matter for their health and medical needs." Otherwise, he continued, elderly people are just "dumping their problems on the broader society."

This ideological position, which is widely but not deeply shared among U.S. voters, receives financial and political support from the finance industry. Financial firms have funded most of the research, lobbying, and public relations for the campaign to "privatize" Social Security, replacing the current system of guaranteed, publicly-funded pensions with individual investment accounts. The finance industry and its wealthy clients also advocate "consumption taxes"—levying taxes on income spent, but not on income saved—so as to "encourage saving" and "reward thrift." Not coincidentally, the finance industry specializes in committing accumulated pools of money to the purchase of stocks, bonds and other paper assets, for which it receives generous fees and commissions.

Our entire economic system requires that people spend freely. Yet political rhetoric combined with pressure from the financial services industry urges individuals to save, or at least to try to save. This rhetoric finds a receptive audience in ordinary households anxious over their own finances and among many progressive public-interest groups alarmed by the threadbare balance sheets of so many American households.

So here is the paradox. People need protection against adversity, and an ample savings account provides such protection. But if ordinary households try to save and protect themselves against hard times, the unused factories, barren malls, and empty restaurants would bring those hard times upon them.

SOCIAL WEALTH

The only way to address the paradox is to reconcile individuals' need for economic security with the public need for a stable economy. The solution therefore lies not in personal thrift or individual wealth, but in social insurance and public wealth.

When a country promotes economic security with dependable public investments and insurance programs, individuals have less need to amass private savings. Social Security, for example, provides the elderly with a direct claim on the nation's economic output after they retire. This guarantees that retirees keep spending and reduces the incentive for working adults to save. By restraining personal savings, Social Security improves the chances that income earned will translate into income spent, making the overall economy more stable.

Of course, Americans still need to save up for old age; Social Security benefits replace, on average, only one-third of prior earnings. This argues not for more saving, however, but for more generous Social Security benefits. In Europe, public pensions replace from 50% to 70% of prior earnings.

Programs like Social Security and unemployment insurance align private motivation with the public interest in a high level of economic activity. Moreover, social insurance programs reduce people's exposure to volatile financial markets. Proponents of private asset-building seem to overlook the lesson of the late 1990s stock market boom: that the personal wealth of small-scale savers is perilously vulnerable to stock market downswings, price manipulation, and fraud by corporate insiders.

It is commonplace to disparage social insurance programs as "big government" intrusions that burden the public with onerous taxes. But the case for a robust public sector is at least as much an economic as a moral one. Ordinary individuals and households fare better when they are assured some secure political claim on the economy's output, not only because of the payouts they receive as individuals, but because social claims on the economy render the economy itself more stable.

Well-funded public programs, for one thing, create reliable income streams and employment. Universal public schooling, for example, means that a sizable portion of our nation's income is devoted to building, equipping, staffing, and maintaining schools. This spending is less susceptible than private-sector spending to business cycles, price fluctuations, and job losses.

Programs that build social wealth also substantially ameliorate the sting of joblessness and minimize the broader economic fallout of unemployment when downturns do occur. Public schools, colleges, parks, libraries, hospitals, and transportation systems, as well as social insurance programs like unemployment compensation and disability coverage, all ensure that the unemployed continue to consume at least a minimal level of goods and services. Their children can still attend school and visit the playground. If there were no social supports, the unemployed would be forced to withdraw altogether from the economy, dragging wages down and setting off destabilizing depressions.

In a series of articles on the first Bush tax cut in 2001, the *New York Times* profiled Dr. Robert Cline, an Austin, Texas, surgeon whose $300,000 annual income still left him worried about financing college educations for his six children. Dr. Cline himself attended the University of Texas, at a cost of $250 per semester ($650 for medical school), but figured that "his own children's education will likely cost tens of thousands of dollars each." Dr. Cline supported the 2001 tax cut, the *Times* reported. Ironically, though, that cut contributed to an environment in which institutions like the University of Texas raise tuitions, restrict enrollments, and drive Dr. Cline and others to attempt to amass enough personal wealth to pay for their children's education.

Unlike Dr. Cline, most people will never accumulate sufficient hoards of wealth to afford expensive high-quality services like education or to indemnify themselves against the myriad risks of old age, poor health, and unemployment. Even when middle-income households do manage to stockpile savings, they have little control over the rate at which their assets can be converted to cash.

Virtually all people—certainly the 93% of U.S. households earning less than $150,000—would fare better collectively than they could individually. Programs that provide direct access to important goods and services—publicly financed education, recreation, health care, and pensions—reduce the inequities that follow inevitably from an entirely individualized economy. The vast majority of people are better off with the high probability of a secure income and guaranteed access to key services such as health care than with the low-probability prospect of becoming rich.

The next time a political candidate recommends some tax-exempt individual asset building scheme, progressively minded people should ask her these questions. If consumers indeed save more and the government thus collects less tax revenue, who will buy the goods these thrifty consumers now forgo? Who will employ the workers who used to manufacture those goods? Who will build the public assets that lower tax revenues render unaffordable? And how exactly does creating millions of little pots of gold substitute for a collective commitment to social welfare?

Most proposals to address today's yawning wealth gap aim to rechannel more of the world's privately held wealth into the hands of people who now have little or none of it. That is necessary. But in this visionary article, Working Assets founder Peter Barnes reminds us that there is another, vast source of wealth that people are barely aware of and that institutions neglect and abuse: the commons. And in it, he sees the potential to restore a modicum of both equity and ecological sanity to modern capitalist economies.

Sharing the Wealth of the Commons

BY PETER BARNES

We're all familiar with private wealth, even if we don't have much. Economists and the media celebrate it every day. But there's another trove of wealth we barely notice: our common wealth.

Each of us is the beneficiary of a vast inheritance. This common wealth includes our air and water, habitats and ecosystems, languages and cultures, science and technologies, political and monetary systems, and quite a bit more. To say we share this inheritance doesn't mean we can call a broker and sell our shares tomorrow. It *does* mean we're responsible for the commons and entitled to any income it generates. Both the responsibility and the entitlement are ours by birth. They're part of the obligation each generation owes to the next, and each living human owes to other beings.

At present, however, our economic system scarcely recognizes the commons. This omission causes two major tragedies: ceaseless destruction of nature and widening inequality among humans. Nature gets destroyed because no one's unequivocally responsible for protecting it. Inequality widens because private wealth concentrates while common wealth shrinks.

The great challenges for the 21st century are, first of all, to make the commons visible; second, to give it proper reverence; and third, to translate that reverence into property rights and legal institutions that are on a par with

those supporting private property. If we do this, we can avert the twin tragedies currently built into our market-driven system.

DEFINING THE COMMONS

What exactly is the commons? Here is a workable definition: *The commons
includes all the assets we inherit together and are morally obligated to pass on,
undiminished, to future generations.*

This definition is a practical one. It designates a set of assets that have
three specific characteristics: they're (1) inherited, (2) shared, and (3) worthy of long-term preservation. Usually it's obvious whether an asset has
these characteristics or not.

At the same time, the definition is broad. It encompasses assets that are
natural as well as social, intangible as well as tangible, small as well as large.
It also introduces a moral factor that is absent from other economic definitions: it requires us to consider whether an asset is worthy of long-term
preservation. At present, capitalism has no interest in this question. If an
asset is likely to yield a competitive return to capital, it's kept alive; if not,
it's destroyed or allowed to run down. Assets in the commons, by contrast,
are meant to be preserved regardless of their return.

This definition sorts all economic assets into two baskets, the market and
the commons. In the market basket are those assets we want to own privately and manage for profit. In the commons basket are the assets we want
to hold in common and manage for long-term preservation. These baskets
then are, or ought to be, the yin and yang of economic activity; each should
enhance and contain the other. The role of the state should be to maintain
a healthy balance between them.

THE VALUE OF THE COMMONS

For most of human existence, the commons supplied everyone's food, water, fuel, and medicines. People hunted, fished, gathered fruits and herbs,
collected firewood and building materials, and grazed their animals in common lands and waters. In other words, the commons was the source of basic
sustenance. This is still true today in many parts of the world, and even in
San Francisco, where I live, cash-poor people fish in the bay not for sport,
but for food.

Though sustenance in the industrialized world now flows mostly through
markets, the commons remains hugely valuable. It's the source of all natural
resources and nature's many replenishing services. Water, air, DNA, seeds,
topsoil, minerals, the protective ozone layer, the atmosphere's climate regulation, and much more, are gifts of nature to us all.

Just as crucially, the commons is our ultimate waste sink. It recycles water, oxygen, carbon, and everything else we excrete, exhale, or throw away. It's the place we store, or try to store, the residues of our industrial system.

The commons also holds humanity's vast accumulation of knowledge, art, and thought. As Isaac Newton said, "If I have seen further it is by standing on the shoulders of giants." So, too, the legal, political, and economic institutions we inherit—even the market itself—were built by the efforts of millions. Without these gifts we'd be hugely poorer than we are today.

To be sure, thinking of these natural and social inheritances primarily as economic assets is a limited way of viewing them. I deeply believe they are much more than that. But if treating portions of the commons as economic assets can help us conserve them, it's surely worth doing so.

How much might the commons be worth in monetary terms? It's relatively easy to put a dollar value on private assets. Accountants and appraisers do it every day, aided by the fact that private assets are regularly traded for money.

This isn't the case with most shared assets. How much is clean air, an intact wetlands, or Darwin's theory of evolution worth in dollar terms? Clearly, many shared inheritances are simply priceless. Others are potentially quantifiable, but there's no current market for them. Fortunately, economists have developed methods to quantify the value of things that aren't traded, so it's possible to estimate the value of the "priceable" part of the commons within an order of magnitude. The surprising conclusion that emerges from numerous studies is that *the wealth we share is worth more than the wealth we own privately.*

This fact bears repeating. Even though much of the commons can't be valued in monetary terms, the parts that *can* be valued are worth more than all private assets combined.

It's worth noting that these estimates understate the gap between common and private assets because a significant portion of the value attributed to private wealth is in fact an appropriation of common wealth. If this mislabeled portion was subtracted from private wealth and added to common wealth, the gap between the two would widen further.

Two examples will make this point clear. Suppose you buy a house for $200,000 and, without improving it, sell it a few years later for $300,000. You pay off the mortgage and walk away with a pile of cash. But what caused the house to rise in value? It wasn't anything you did. Rather, it was the fact that your neighborhood became more popular, likely a result of the efforts of community members, improvements in public services, and similar factors.

Approximate Value of Natural, Private, and State Assets, 2001 (Trillions of U.S. Dollars)

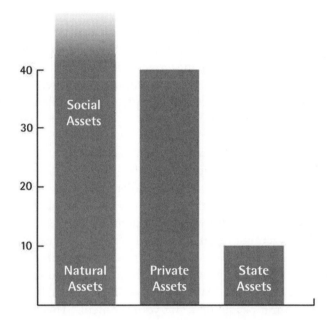

Or consider another fount of private wealth, the social invention and public expansion of the stock market. Suppose you start a business that goes "public" through an offering of stock. Within a few years, you're able to sell your stock for a spectacular capital gain.

Much of this gain is a social creation, the result of centuries of monetary-system evolution, laws and regulations, and whole industries devoted to accounting, sharing information, and trading stocks. What's more, there's a direct correlation between the scale and quality of the stock market as an institution and the size of the private gain. You'll fetch a higher price if you sell into a market of millions than into a market of two. Similarly, you'll gain more if transaction costs are low and trust in public information is high. Thus, stock that's traded on a regulated exchange sells for a higher multiple of earnings than unlisted stock. This socially created premium can account for 30% of the stock's value. If you're the lucky seller, you'll reap that extra cash—in no way thanks to anything you did as an individual.

Real estate gains and the stock market's social premium are just two instances of common assets contributing to private gain. Still, most rich people would like us to think it's their extraordinary talent, hard work, and risk-taking that create their well-deserved wealth. That's like saying a flower's beauty is due solely to its own efforts, owing nothing to nutrients in the soil, energy from the sun, water from the aquifer, or the activity of bees.

THE GREAT COMMONS GIVEAWAY

That we inherit a trove of common wealth is the good news. The bad news, alas, is that our inheritance is being grossly mismanaged. As a recent report by the advocacy group Friends of the Commons concludes, "Maintenance of the commons is terrible, theft is rampant, and rents often aren't collected. To put it bluntly, our common wealth—and our children's—is being squandered. We are all poorer as a result."

Examples of commons mismanagement include the handout of broadcast spectrum to media conglomerates, the giveaway of pollution rights to polluters, the extension of copyrights to entertainment companies, the patenting of seeds and genes, the privatization of water, and the relentless destruction of habitat, wildlife, and ecosystems.

This mismanagement, though currently extreme, is not new. For over 200 years, the market has been devouring the commons in two ways. With one hand, the market takes valuable stuff from the commons and privatizes it. This is called "enclosure." With the other hand, the market dumps bad stuff into the commons and says, "It's your problem." This is called "externalizing." Much that is called economic growth today is actually a form of cannibalization in which the market diminishes the commons that ultimately sustains it.

The Market Assault on the Commons

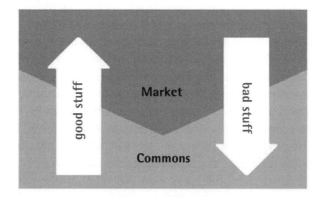

Enclosure—the taking of good stuff from the commons—at first meant privatization of land by the gentry. Today it means privatization of many common assets by corporations. Either way, it means that what once belonged to everyone now belongs to a few.

Enclosure is usually justified in the name of efficiency. And sometimes, though not always, it does result in efficiency gains. But what also results from enclosure is the impoverishment of those who lose access to the commons, and the enrichment of those who take title to it. In other words, enclosure widens the gap between those with income-producing property and those without.

Externalizing—the dumping of bad stuff into the commons—is an automatic behavior pattern of profit-maximizing corporations: if they can avoid any out-of-pocket costs, they will. If workers, taxpayers, anyone downwind, future generations, or nature have to absorb added costs, so be it.

For decades, economists have agreed we'd be better served if businesses "internalized" their externalities—that is, paid in real time the costs they now shift to the commons. The reason this doesn't happen is that there's no one to set prices and collect them. Unlike private wealth, the commons lacks property rights and institutions to represent it in the marketplace.

The seeds of such institutions, however, are starting to emerge. Consider one of the environmental protection tools the U.S. currently uses, pollution trading. So-called cap-and-trade programs put a cap on total pollution, then grant portions of the total, via permits, to each polluting firm. Companies may buy other firms' permits if they want to pollute more than their allotment allows, or sell unused permits if they manage to pollute less. Such programs are generally supported by business because they allow polluters to find the cheapest ways to reduce pollution.

Public discussion of cap-and-trade programs has focused exclusively on their trading features. What's been overlooked is how they give away common wealth to polluters.

To date, all cap-and-trade programs have begun by giving pollution rights to existing polluters for free. This treats polluters as if they own our sky and rivers. It means that future polluters will have to pay old polluters for the scarce—hence valuable—right to dump wastes into nature. Imagine that: because a corporation polluted in the past, it gets free income forever! And, because ultimately we'll all pay for limited pollution via higher prices, this amounts to an enormous transfer of wealth—trillions of dollars—to shareholders of historically polluting corporations.

In theory, though, there is no reason that the initial pollution rights should not reside with the public. Clean air and the atmosphere's capacity to absorb pollutants are "wealth" that belongs to everyone. Hence, when polluters use up these parts of the commons, they should pay the public—not the other way around.

TAKING THE COMMONS BACK

How can we correct the system omission that permits, and indeed promotes, destruction of nature and ever-widening inequality among humans? The answer lies in building a new sector of the economy whose clear legal mission is to preserve shared inheritances for everyone. Just as the market is populated by profit-maximizing corporations, so this new sector would be populated by asset-preserving trusts.

Here a brief description of trusts may be helpful. The trust is a private institution that's even older than the corporation. The essence of a trust is a fiduciary relationship. A trust holds and manages property for another person or for many other people. A simple example is a trust set up by a grandparent to pay for a grandchild's education. Other trusts include pension funds, charitable foundations and university endowments. There are also hundreds of trusts in America, like the Nature Conservancy and the Trust for Public Land, that own land or conservation easements in perpetuity.

If we were to design an institution to protect pieces of the commons, we couldn't do much better than a trust. The goal of commons management, after all, is to preserve assets and deliver benefits to broad classes of beneficiaries. That's what trusts do, and it's not rocket science.

Over centuries, several principles of trust management have evolved. These include:

- Trustees have a fiduciary responsibility to beneficiaries. If a trustee fails in this obligation, he or she can be removed and penalized.
- Trustees must preserve the original asset. It's okay to spend income, but don't invade the principal.
- Trustees must assure transparency. Information about money flows should be readily available to beneficiaries.

Trusts in the new commons sector would be endowed with rights comparable to those of corporations. Their trustees would take binding oaths of office and, like judges, serve long terms. Though protecting common assets would be their primary job, they would also distribute income from those assets to beneficiaries. These beneficiaries would include all citizens within a jurisdiction, large classes of citizens (children, the elderly), and/or agencies serving common purposes such as public transit or ecological restoration. When distributing income to individuals, the allocation formula would be one person, one share. The right to receive commons income would be a nontransferable birthright, not a property right that could be traded.

Fortuitously, a working model of such a trust already exists: the Alaska Permanent Fund. When oil drilling on the North Slope began in the 1970s, Gov. Jay Hammond, a Republican, proposed that 25% of the state's royalties be placed in a mutual fund to be invested on behalf of Alaska's citizens. Voters approved in a referendum. Since then, the Alaska Permanent Fund has grown to over $28 billion, and Alaskans have received roughly $22,000 apiece in dividends. In 2003 the per capita dividend was $1,107; a family of four received $4,428.

What Alaska did with its oil can be replicated for other gifts of nature. For example, we could create a nationwide Sky Trust to stabilize the climate for future generations. The trust would restrict emissions of heat-trapping gases and sell a declining number of emission permits to polluters. The income would be returned to U.S. residents in equal yearly dividends, thus reversing the wealth transfer built into current cap-and-trade programs. Instead of everyone paying historic polluters, polluters would pay all of us.

Just as a Sky Trust could represent our equity in the natural commons, a Public Stock Trust could embody our equity in the social commons. Such a trust would capture some of the socially created stock-market premium that currently flows only to shareholders and their investment bankers. As noted earlier, this premium is sizeable—roughly 30% of the value of publicly traded stock. A simple way to share it would be to create a giant mutual fund—call it the American Permanent Fund—that would hold, say, 10% of the shares of publicly traded companies. This mutual fund, in turn, would be owned by all Americans on a one share per person basis (perhaps linked to their Social Security accounts).

To build up the fund without precipitating a fall in share prices, companies would contribute shares at the rate of, say, 1% per year. The contributions would be the price companies pay for the benefits they derive from a commons asset, the large, trusted market for stock—a small price, indeed, for the hefty benefits. Over time, the mutual fund would assure that when the economy grows, everyone benefits. The top 5% would still own more than the bottom 90%, but at least every American would have *some* property income, and a slightly larger slice of our economic pie.

SHARING THE WEALTH

The perpetuation of inequality is built into the current design of capitalism. Because of the skewed distribution of private wealth, a small self-perpetuating minority receives a disproportionate share of America's non-labor income.

Tom Paine had something to say about this. In his essay "Agrarian Justice," written in 1790, he argued that, because enclosure of the commons had separated so many people from their primary source of sustenance, it was necessary to create a functional equivalent of the commons in the form of a National Fund. Here is how he put it:

> There are two kinds of property. Firstly, natural property, or that which comes to us from the Creator of the universe—such as the earth, air, water. Secondly, artificial or acquired property—the invention of men. In the latter, equality is impossible; for to distribute it equally, it would be necessary that all should have contributed in the same proportion, which can never be the case. ... Equality of natural property is different. Every individual in the world is born with legitimate claims on this property, or its equivalent.

Enclosure of the commons, he went on, was necessary to improve the efficiency of cultivation. But

> The landed monopoly that began with [enclosure] has produced the greatest evil. It has dispossessed more than half the inhabitants of every nation of their natural inheritance, without providing for them, as ought to have been done, an indemnification for that loss, and has thereby created a species of poverty and wretchedness that did not exist before.

The appropriate compensation for loss of the commons, Paine said, was a national fund financed by rents paid by land owners. Out of this fund, every person reaching age 21 would get 15 pounds a year, and every person over 50 would receive an additional 10 pounds. (Think of Social Security, financed by commons rents instead of payroll taxes.)

A PROGRESSIVE OFFENSIVE

Paine's vision, allowing for inflation and new forms of enclosure, could not be more timely today. Surely from our vast common inheritance—not just the land, but the atmosphere, the broadcast spectrum, our mineral resources, our threatened habitats and water supplies—enough rent can be collected to pay every American over age 21 a modest annual dividend, and every person reaching 21 a small start-up inheritance.

Such a proposal may seem utopian. In today's political climate, perhaps it is. But consider this. About 20 years ago, right-wing think tanks laid out a bold agenda. They called for lowering taxes on private wealth, privatizing much of government, and deregulating industry. Amazingly, this radical agenda has largely been achieved.

It's time for progressives to mount an equally bold offensive. The old shibboleths—let's gin up the economy, create jobs, and expand government programs—no longer excite. We need to talk about *fixing* the economy, not just growing it; about *income* for everyone, not just jobs; about nurturing *ecosystems, cultures,* and *communities,* not just our individual selves. More broadly, we need to celebrate the commons as an essential counterpoise to the market.

Unfortunately, many progressives have viewed the state as the only possible counterpoise to the market. The trouble is, the state has been captured by corporations. This capture isn't accidental or temporary; it's structural and long-term.

This doesn't mean progressives can't occasionally recapture the state. We've done so before and will do so again. It does mean that progressive control of the state is the exception, not the norm; in due course, corporate capture will resume. It follows that if we want lasting fixes to capitalism's tragic flaws, we must use our brief moments of political ascendancy to build institutions that endure.

Programs that rely on taxes, appropriations, or regulations are inherently transitory; they get weakened or repealed when political power shifts. By contrast, institutions that are self-perpetuating and have broad constituencies are likely to last. (It also helps if they mail out checks periodically.) This was the genius of Social Security, which has survived—indeed grown—through numerous Republican administrations.

If progressives are smart, we'll use our next New Deal to create common property trusts that include all Americans as beneficiaries. These trusts will then be to the 21st century what social insurance was to the 20th: sturdy pillars of shared responsibility and entitlement. Through them, the commons will be a source of sustenance for all, as it was before enclosure. Lifelong income will be linked to generations-long ecological health. Isn't that a future most Americans would welcome?

APPENDIX

Wealth-Building Strategies

Here is a partial list of promising strategies for asset building—national and local, private and public, large-scale and small.

COMMUNITY DEVELOPMENT FINANCIAL INSTITUTIONS (CDFIs)

CDFIs are nonprofit organizations that provide credit, capital, and financial services to communities neglected by commercial lenders. These "alternative" financial institutions include community development banks, community development loan funds, community development credit unions, micro-credit programs, community development corporations that loan or invest, and community development venture funds. CDFIs have various structures, but all channel resources (from individuals, foundations, religious organizations, unions, and the government) into community-determined development in order to meet the needs of low-income and low-wealth individuals and neighborhoods.

Over 1,000 CDFIs are in operation in the United States, ranging in size from small neighborhood credit unions to institutions with hundreds of millions of dollars in assets. Perhaps the largest CDFI, Self-Help Credit Union, is a national lender that has provided more than $3.5 billion in financing to over 40,000 home buyers, small business people, and nonprofits.

Modern CDFIs grew out of struggles against racial discrimination, gentrification, and community disinvestment in the 1960s and 1970s. Their impact on community development has been enormous, but many communities still lack CDFIs, many community members do not know about their services, and the CDFI sector remains under-capitalized.

For more information:

Coalition of Community Development Financial Institutions	**www.cdfi.org**
Community Development Financial Institutions (CDFI) Fund, U.S. Department of the Treasury	**www.cdfifund.gov**
National Community Capital Association	**www.communitycapital.org**
Nat'l Federation of Community Development Credit Unions	**www.natfed.org**

ROTATING SAVINGS AND CREDIT ASSOCIATIONS (ROSCAs)

Common in immigrant communities, ROSCAs are collective borrowing pools formed among family members or friends. Each person pays in a monthly sum and then has a turn at borrowing the entire pool with no interest. These informal arrangements are adapted from cultural practices indigenous to East Asia, Latin America, the Caribbean, the Near East, and Africa. Though widespread in the United States, they remain below the public radar. Participants are recruited on the basis of trust and are held accountable through community sanctions. In general, the pools of capital are small, although in some cases (for example, in Korean communities) sums large enough to finance small businesses have been collected.

For more information:
Global Development Research Center   **www.gdrc.org**

INDEPENDENT DEVELOPMENT ACCOUNTS (IDAs)

IDAs are matched savings accounts designed to help low-income families accumulate financial assets. An individual participant sets aside savings and receives matching dollars if and only if he or she uses the account for specific wealth-building purposes, for example, to buy a home, pay for college tuition, or start a small business. The match (typically two or three times the amount saved by the individual) comes from public sources or foundations and is capped in order to control program costs. A 1998 federal pilot program launched the first large-scale IDA demonstration projects. Today, about 250 neighborhoods have IDA programs.

So far, the results have been modest. A recent study found that participants saved an average of just $19 a month, producing total assets of about $700 per year, including the match. Many cash-strapped participants have been unable to save at all, or have had to withdraw their savings for nondesignated purposes (with no match).

Nevertheless, if brought to scale and fully funded as a federal program, IDAs would be a useful tool to help low-income families build assets. Washington University's Michael Sherradan and others argue that the existing model should be greatly expanded, making matched savings accounts available to all.

For more information:
Center for Social Development   **www.gwbweb.wustl.edu/csd**
Corporation for Enterprise Development   **www.cfed.org**
Welfare Information Network   **www.financeprojectinfo.org/win/individu.asp**

CHILDREN'S SAVINGS ACCOUNTS

In 2003, the United Kingdom established the Child Trust Fund in order to encourage saving and asset ownership. Each child receives a modest deposit of government funds (known as "baby bonds") at birth and at his or her seventh birthday, with children from lower-income households receiving additional government payments. Family and friends may also contribute to the child's account, which is controlled by the parents until the child reaches 18, at which time the funds may be withdrawn for any purpose. "The CTF account will help to strengthen the savings habit of future generations, spread the benefits of asset ownership to all, educate people in the need for savings, and give young people a basic understanding of financial products," according to the government.

U.S. Senator Robert Kerrey proposed a similar program in 1998. Under the "Kid-Save" initiative, children would have received $1,000 at birth, plus $500 a year from ages one to five, to invest. If a child's parents matched the government's $500 yearly contribution, he or she would have $40,000 at age 18. The legislation has languished.

For more information:

The Aspen Institute Initiative on Financial Security   **www.aspeninstitute.org**
Child Trust Fund of Inland Revenue   **www.inlandrevenue.gov.uk/ctf**
United Kingdom Parliament   **www.parliament.the-stationery-office.co.uk**

HOMEOWNERSHIP

In 1944, the nation made a massive commitment to expand homeownership. The Serviceman's Readjustment Act, better known as the GI Bill, provided veterans easy access to low-interest, long-term mortgage loans that were insured by the Federal Housing Authority and the Veterans Administration. The program was instrumental in building the white middle class in the years after World War II.

Today, the federal government supports homeownership primarily through the tax structure, not direct spending or loan guarantees. The tax deduction for mortgage interest is by far the largest single housing subsidy in the country, and tax advantages for homeownership total $110.5 billion, exceeding direct outlays for housing programs by 236 to 1, according to the Corporation for Enterprise Development report "Hidden in Plain Sight: A Look at the $335 Billion Federal Asset-Building Budget." The problem is, these subsidies don't reach those (mostly lower-income) taxpayers who do not itemize deductions on their tax returns.

Federal homeownership programs include the Department of Housing and Urban Development's HOME program (a federal block grant to state and local governments designed to create affordable housing for low-income households), the Federal Home Loan Bank Affordable Housing Program (which subsidizes long-term financing for very low-, low-, and moderate-income families), certain Community Development Block Grants, and the U.S. Department of Agriculture's rural homebuyers' program. In addition to these programs, government-sponsored mortgage buyers such as Fannie Mae and Freddie Mac provide a secondary market for home mortgage loans by purchasing mortgages from financial institutions.

Major home buying initiatives subsidized by federal dollars, comparable in scale to the GI Bill, are needed to dramatically expand homeownership opportunities. In addition, the Community Reinvestment Act of 1977, which mandated lending in minority neighborhoods, needs to be strengthened in order to end continuing racial discrimination in lending and ensure that low-cost home mortgage loans reach low-income communities and households of color.

For more information:

PolicyLink	**www.policylink.org**
U.S. Department of Housing and Urban Development	**www.hud.gov**

PUBLIC TRUSTS WITH RESIDENT DIVIDENDS

The Alaska Permanent Fund (APF) is a $27.6 billion trust fund that pays approximately $1,100 in dividends (2003 dollars) per year to every Alaska resident. The fourth largest cash infusion into the Alaska economy, the dividend payments account for approximately 10% of annual income for rural Alaskans, which in turn fuels economic growth in the state. The Alaska fund is the largest single example of a type of collective wealth-building strategy in which a public trust generates dividend payments for residents. Under this sort of trust arrangement, profits from the sale or use of public resources are returned to residents though dividend payments (often drawn from the interest on large capital funds created with those profits). Individuals have a right to a stream of income by virtue of membership in the group. In the case of the Alaska Permanent Fund, all Alaska residents receive equal dividends from oil revenues—providing a greater boon to lower-income community members.

Although similar arrangements could theoretically be set up within any group that owns or generates a lucrative resource, only a few dividend-paying public trusts actually exist in the United States: the Alaska Permanent Fund (which began operations in 1976) and some Indian casinos (in which individual tribes distribute dividends to help guarantee equitable division of their casino wealth).

Author Peter Barnes has proposed setting up a national "Sky Trust," which would collect permit fees from carbon-spewing companies. A percentage of the permit revenue would go to Congress and the states, and the remainder would be distributed annually to all U.S. citizens on a one-person, one-share basis. In 2003, Senators Joseph Lieberman (D-Conn.) and John McCain (R-Ariz.) introduced legislation that included elements of the Sky Trust idea. If passed into law, the Sky Trust would be the largest dividend-yielding public trust yet.

For more information:

Alaska Permanent Fund Corporation	**www.apfc.org**
National Indian Gaming Association	**www.indiangaming.org/library/index**
U.S. Sky Trust	**www.usskytrust.org**

PENSIONS AND INDIVIDUAL RETIREMENT PLANS

The federal government gives tax advantages to two general types of retirement policies: employer-sponsored retirement plans and individual savings accounts. Employer-sponsored plans include "defined benefit" pensions, which guarantee retirees a predictable level of income for the rest of their lives, and "defined contribution" plans, favored by most businesses, in which employees or employers contribute a defined amount to the retirement account, then invest the account assets, subjecting future retirement income to market risk. Examples of defined contribution plans are 401(k)s, savings and thrift plans, and employee stock ownership plans.

Fewer than half of all workers are covered by an employer-sponsored pension or retirement plan of either kind at any given time, and fewer than one in five has a defined benefit pension. Coverage rates are even lower among employees of small businesses and lower-wage workers, and because many retirement plans require a waiting period, employees who move between jobs by choice or necessity are not well served by the current pension system.

Individual retirement plans, including Individual Retirement Accounts and Keogh plans (which are specifically for the self-employed), are initiated and controlled by an individual. Pensions and tax-preferred saving plans together provide one-fifth of the income of the elderly, with the bulk of that money going to higher-income people.

For more information:

Employee Benefit Research Institute   **www.ebri.org**
AFL-CIO   **www.aflcio.org**
Employee Benefits Security Administration   **www.dol.gov/ebsa**
Pension Rights Center   **www.pensionrights.org**

SOCIAL SECURITY

Social Security is viewed by most as a source of retirement income, not a form of wealth. But Social Security is very much a form of social, or socialized, wealth—it's the largest component of the nation's social safety net, and it operates much like a national pension and insurance plan. No other government program has had more impact on the lives of the elderly and the disabled.

All workers who pay Social Security taxes for at least 40 quarter-years are eligible for Social Security retirement income. A lesser earning spouse gets 50% of the higher earning spouse or her own benefit, whichever is higher. Money is collected from the paychecks of working people to pay current retirees, with each generation paying for the retirement of the older generation. Forty percent of the elderly rely on Social Security for 90% or more of their income.

In addition to retirement income, Social Security provides survivors' and disability benefits. Of the 44 million people receiving Social Security benefits, 30 million are retirees and their dependents. The rest are disabled workers and their dependents and survivors of deceased workers.

For more information:

AARP   **www.aarp.org/socialsecurity**
Social Security Administration   **www.ssa.gov**
Social Security Network   **www.socsec.org**

WORKER OWNERSHIP

A worker cooperative is a self-managed business in which workers share the fruits of their own labor and have democratic control over the enterprise. Members finance the firm and collectively hold the net worth of the business. They have equal voting rights (on a one-member, one-vote basis), much like citizens in a democratic community. In cooperatives, authority resides in the collectivity as a whole. This is in contrast to the "rule by the few" approach common in other forms of business (e.g., proprietorships, partnerships, and corporations). The number of cooperatives in the United States is estimated to be between 1,000 and 5,000.

Employee stock ownership is a more common form of employee ownership. Less an experiment in economic democracy than the worker cooperative, employee stock ownership nevertheless can be an effective way to spread corporate wealth to working people. By far the most common form of employee stock ownership is the employee stock ownership plan or ESOP, an indirect form of employee ownership in which the company sets up a trust that holds stock on behalf of employees. Trustees, rather than workers themselves, have voting rights over the shares. Studies of ESOP firms in Massachusetts and Washington state found that ESOPs provide employees a significant pool of wealth. The Washington state study found that the average Washington ESOP participant's account was worth $24,260 in 1995. The Massachusetts study found that the per participant wealth held for employees in Massachusetts ESOPs was $39,895 in 2000. The studies suggest that most companies provide ESOPs as a supplement to, rather than a replacement for, wages and other benefits. The average value of total retirement plan assets (for example, 401(k) plus ESOP assets) in ESOP companies is far higher than the average value in comparable non-ESOP companies.

For more information:

Grassroots Economic Organizing (GEO) Newsletter **www.geonewsletter.org**
The ICA Group **www.ica-group.org**
National Center for Employee Ownership **www.nceo.org**
Ownership Associates **www.ownershipassociates.com**

LAND TRUSTS

A community land trust is a nonprofit organization that acquires and holds land for the benefit of the community. These trusts usually provide affordable housing for residents who have been priced out of commercial housing markets. Because the land is held by the trust, not the individual, and is democratically controlled, land trusts enable communities to maintain control over economic development and keep property values affordable for future generations.

Another common type of land trust, sometimes called a conservation land trust, protects open or green spaces from development. Three of the largest urban conservation land trusts in the country were formed in New York in 2004. The Bronx Land Trust, the Brooklyn/Queens Land Trust, and the Manhattan Land Trust will preserve

62 community gardens that the city had planned to destroy. The racially, culturally, and economically diverse trust members will ensure the gardens remain protected neighborhood resources for public use, according to the Trust for Public Land.

For more information:
Institute for Community Economics   **www.iceclt.org**
Trust for Public Land   **www.tpl.org**

THE TAX STRUCTURE

Over the past 20 years, the American tax system has shifted the burden of taxation off the rich and off corporations, and onto everyone else. According to David Cay Johnston, author of *Perfectly Legal: The Covert Campaign to Rig Our Tax System to Benefit the Super Rich—and Cheat Everybody Else,* between 1992 and 2000, when the federal income tax burden on most Americans *rose* by 18%, it *fell* for the top 400 taxpayers, whose incomes had skyrocketed, thanks to tax breaks for the rich passed in 1997. Additional tax cuts for the very rich were passed in 2001 and 2003, subsidized by taxes on the poor and the middle class. Under the current system, most concentrated financial wealth goes untaxed. A major overhaul of the current system of taxation is essential to reducing growing extremes of income and wealth inequality.

For more information:
Citizens for Tax Justice   **www.ctj.org**
Tax Policy Center   **www.taxpolicycenter.org**

References

Ackerman, Bruce and Anne Alstott. *The Stakeholder Society.* New Haven: Yale University Press, 1999.

Ackerman, Bruce. "Taxation and the Constitution." *Columbia Law Review* 99(1):1–58 (January 1999).

Agarwal, Bina and Pradeep Panda. "Spousal Violence in India: Does Women's Property Status Make a Difference?" Paper presented at the Annual Conference of the International Association for Feminist Economics, June 2003.

Agarwal, Bina and Pradeep Panda. "Home and the world: Revisiting violence." *Indian Express,* August 7, 2003.

Aizcorbe, Ana M., Arthur B. Kennickell, and Kevin B. Moore, "Recent Changes in U.S. Family Finances: Evidence from the 1998 and 2001 Survey of Consumer Finances," *Federal Reserve Bulletin* 89 (January 2003).

Amott, Teresa L. and Julie Matthaei. *Race, Gender, and Work: A Multicultural Economic History of Women in the United States.* Boston: South End Press, 1996.

Auerbach, Alan J., William G. Gale, and Peter R. Orszag. "Reassessing the Fiscal Gap." *Tax Notes* (July 28, 2003).

Barnes, Peter. *Who Owns the Sky? Our Common Assets and the Future of Capitalism.* Washington, D.C.: Island Press, 2001.

Blaug, Mark. *Economic Theory in Retrospect.* New York: Richard D. Irwin, 1968.

Boldrin, Michele and David K. Levine. "Perfectly Competitive Innovation." CEPR Discussion Paper No. 3274, 2002. <http://ssrn.com/abstrct=308040>

Bollier, David. *Silent Theft: The Private Plunder of Our Common Wealth.* New York: Routledge, 2003.

Carnegie, Andrew. *The Gospel of Wealth.* 1889. <www.fordham.edu/halsall/mod/1889carnegie.html>

Carnoy, Martin. *Faded Dreams: The Politics and Economics of Race in America.* New York: Cambridge University Press, 1994.

Citizens for Tax Justice. "The Bush Tax Cuts: The Most Recent CTJ Data." December 17, 2003.

Citizens for Tax Justice. "White House Reveals Nation's Biggest Problems: The Very Rich Citizens Don't Have Enough Money & Workers Don't Pay Enough in Taxes." December 2002.

Claessens, Stijn, Simeon Djankov, and Larry H. P. Lang. "Who Controls East Asian Corporations—and the Implications for Legal Reform." Washington, D.C.: World Bank, September 1999.

Collins, Chuck, Mike Lapham, and Scott Klinger. "I Didn't Do It Alone: Society's Contribution to Individual Wealth and Success." Boston: Responsible Wealth, a project of United for a Fair Economy, June 2004.

Collins, Chuck and Dedrick Muhammad. "Tax Wealth to Broaden Wealth." *Dollars & Sense* 251: 22–25 (January/February 2004).

Collins, Chuck and Felice Yeskel with United for a Fair Economy. *Economic Apartheid in America: A Primer on Economic Inequality and Insecurity.* New York: The New Press, 2000.

Conley, Dalton. *Being Black, Living in the Red: Race, Wealth, and Social Policy in America.* Berkeley and Los Angeles, Calif.: University of California Press, 1999.

Congressional Budget Office. "Effective Federal Tax Rates, 1997 to 2001," Table B1-B, April 2004. <www.cbo.gov/ftpdoc.cfm?index=4514&type=1>

Congressional Budget Office. "CBO's Current Budget Projection." March 2004. <www.cbo.gov/showdoc.cfm?index=1944&sequence=0#table5>

Costanza, Robert et al. "The value of the world's ecosystem services and natural capital." *Nature* 387: 253–260 (1997).

Cummings, Sarah et al. *Gender Perspectives on Property and Inheritance: A Global Source Book.* Oxford, U.K.: Oxfam, 2001.

Dixon, John A. and Kirk Hamilton. "Expanding the Measure of Wealth." Washington, D.C.: World Bank, 1996.

Dutta Das, Manju. "Improving the Relevance and Effectiveness of Agricultural Extension Activities for Women Farmers." Rome: U.N. Food and Agriculture Organization, 1995.

Economic Policy Institute. *Snapshot,* February 11, 2004.

Feagin, Joe R. *Racist America: Roots, Current Realities, and Future Reparations.* New York: Routledge, 2001.

Frank, Ellen. "No More Savings!" *Dollars & Sense* 253: 18–20 (May/Jun 2004).

Frank, Robert H. *Luxury Fever.* Princeton: Princeton University Press, 2000.

Freyfogle, Eric. *The Land We Share: Private Property and the Common Good.* Washington, D.C.: Shearwater Books, 2003.

Friedman, Leon. "A Better Kind of Wealth Tax." *The American Prospect* 11(23) (November 6, 2000).

Friedman, Leon. "Trump's Wealth Tax." *The Nation* 269(19): 4–5 (December 6, 1999).

Friends of the Commons. *The State of the Commons 2003/04.*

Fuchs, Lawrence H. *The American Kaleidoscope: Race, Ethnicity, and the Civic Culture.* Middletown, Conn.: Wesleyan University Press, 1990.

Fung, Archon, Tessa Hebb, and Joel Rogers, eds. *Working Capital: The Power of Labor's Pensions*. Ithaca, N.Y.: ILR Press, 2001.

Gale, William G., Peter R. Orszag, and Isaac Shapiro. "The Ultimate Burden Of The Tax Cuts." Washington, D.C.: Center on Budget and Policy Priorities & Tax Policy Center, June 2, 2004.

Gates, Jeff. *The Ownership Solution*. Reading, Mass.: Addison-Wesley, 1998.

Gates, William H., Sr., and Chuck Collins. *Wealth and Our Commonwealth: Why America Should Tax Accumulated Fortunes*. Boston: Beacon Press, 2002.

George, Henry. *Progress and Poverty*. New York: Robert Schalkenbach Foundation, 1948.

Ghilarducci, Teresa. "Small Benefits, Big Pension Funds, and How Governance Reforms Can Close the Gap." In *Working Capital: The Power of Labor's Pensions*, Fung, Hebb, and Rogers, eds. Ithaca: ILR Press, 2001.

Glenn, Evelyn N. *Unequal Freedom: How Race and Gender Shaped American Citizenship and Labor*. Cambridge, Mass.: Harvard University Press, 2004.

Gonzalez, Juan. *Harvest of Empire: A History of Latinos in America*. New York: Penguin Books, 2001.

Gouskova, Elena and Frank Stafford. "Trends in household wealth dynamics, 1999–2001." Ann Arbor: Institute for Social Research, Univ. of Michigan, September 2002.

Greider, William. *The Soul of Capitalism: Opening Paths to a Moral Economy*. New York: Simon & Schuster, 2003.

Hartzok, Alanna. "Henry George's 'Single Tax'." *Econ-atrocity Bulletin*, Center for Popular Economics, April 2004. <www.fguide.org/Bulletin/SingleTax.htm>

Heilbroner, Robert L. *The Worldly Philosophers*. New York: Simon & Schuster, 1999.

Hertz, Thomas. "Rags, Riches and Race: The Intergenerational Economic Mobility of Black and White Families in the United States." In *Unequal Chances: Family Background and Economic Success*, Bowles, Gintis, and Osborne, eds. Princeton University Press and Russell Sage, forthcoming 2005.

Hogarth, Jeanne M. and Chris E. Anguelov. "Descriptive Statistics on Levels of Net Worth, Financial Assets, and Other Selected Characteristics." Paper prepared for the Women & Assets Summit, March-April 2003. <www.heller.brandeis.edu/womenandassets>

Horwitz, Morton. *The Transformation of American Law, 1870–1960: The Crisis of Legal Orthodoxy*. New York: Oxford University Press, 1992.

Internal Revenue Service. "Personal Exemptions and Individual Income Tax Rates, 1913–2002." SOI Bulletin, Data Release, December 10, 2003. <www.irs.gov/taxstats/article/0,,id=96679,00.htm>

"Investment Product Review: Private Capital 2002." Report of the Investment Product Review Working Group, AFL-CIO, November 2002.

Jackson, Kenneth T. *Crabgrass Frontier: The Suburbanization of the United States*. New York: Oxford University Press, 1985.

Johnson, James H., Jr., and Melvin L. Oliver. "Economic Restructuring and Black Male Joblessness in U.S. Metropolitan Areas." *Urban Geography* 12 (1991).

Johnson, Richard W. "The Gender Gap in Pension Wealth: Is Women's Progress in the Labor Market Equalizing Retirement Benefits?" Washington, D.C.: Urban Institute, March 1999.

Johnson, Richard W., Usha Sambamoorthi, and Stephen Crystal. "Gender Differences in Pension Wealth." Unpublished manuscript, quoted in Johnson, "The Gender Gap in Pension Wealth."

Johnston, David Cay. "Dozens of Rich Americans Join in Fight to Retain the Estate Tax." *The New York Times,* February 14, 2001.

Johnston, David Cay. *Perfectly Legal: The Secret Campaign to Rig Our Tax System to Benefit the Super Rich—And Cheat Everybody Else.* New York: Portfolio, 2003.

Keister, Lisa A. *Wealth in America: Trends in Wealth Inequality.* New York: Cambridge University Press, 2000.

Keister, Lisa A. and Alexis Yamokoski. "Single Females & Wealth: The Assets of Young Baby Boomers." Unpublished paper, April 2004.

Kennickell, Arthur B. "A Rolling Tide: Changes in the Distribution of Wealth in the U.S., 1989–2001." Jerome Levy Economics Institute, November 2003.

Keynes, John Maynard. *The General Theory of Employment, Interest, and Money.* New York: Harcourt Brace, 1964.

Kogan, Richard. "Deficit Picture Even Grimmer Than New CBO Projections Suggest." Washington, D.C.: Center on Budget and Policy Priorities, August 2003. <www.cbpp.org/8-26-03bud.htm>

Krehely, Jeff, Meaghan House, and Emily Kernan. "Axis of Ideology: Conservative Foundations and Public Policy." Washington, D.C.: National Committee for Responsive Philanthropy, 2004.

Kuttner, Robert. "Bully For Trump." *The Boston Globe,* November 14, 1999.

Landes, David. *The Wealth and Poverty of Nations.* New York: W.W. Norton, 1999.

Leondar-Wright, Betsy. "Black Job Loss Déjà Vu." *Dollars & Sense* 253: 17 (May/June 2004).

Lipsitz, George. *The Possessive Investment in Whiteness: How White People Profit from Identity Politics.* Philadelphia: Temple University Press, 1998.

Marx, Karl. *The Communist Manifesto.* New York: W. W. Norton, 1988.

Mason, Edward. "Cahill to Boost Pension Fund Investments." *Boston Business Journal,* May 3, 2004.

Massey, Douglas S., and Nancy A. Denton. *American Apartheid: Segregation and the Making of the Underclass.* Cambridge, Mass.: Harvard University Press, 1993.

McCulloch, Heather with Lisa Robinson. "Sharing the Wealth: Resident Ownership Mechanisms: A PolicyLink Report," Oakland, Calif.: PolicyLink, 2001.

Menchaca, Martha. *Recovering History, Constructing Race: The Indian, Black, and White Roots of Mexican Americans.* Austin, Texas: University of Texas Press, 2001.

Michl, Thomas. "Prefunding is Still the Answer," *Challenge* 45(3): 112–116 (May-June 2002).

Mill, John Stuart. *Principles of Political Economy.* London: Longmans Green, 1909.

Mishel, Lawrence, Jared Bernstein, and Heather Boushey. *State of Working America: 2002–03.* Ithaca, N.Y.: ILR Press, 2003.

Muhammad, Dedrick, Attieno Davis, Meizhu Lui, and Betsy Leondar-Wright. "The State of the Dream 2004: Enduring Disparities in Black and White." Boston: United for a Fair Economy, January 2004.

National Urban League, *The National Urban League's Jobs Report*, January 2004.

Office of Management and Budget. *Budget of the United States 2004: Historical Tables.* August 2003. <http://w3.access.gpo.gov/usbudget/fy2004/pdf/hist.pdf>

Oliver, Melvin L. and Tom Shapiro. *Black Wealth/White Wealth: New Perspectives on Racial Inequality.* New York: Routledge, 1995.

Orzechowski, Shawna and Peter Sepielli. "Net Worth and Asset Ownership of Households: 1998 and 2000." *Current Population Reports*, U.S. Census Bureau, May 2003.

Phillips, Kevin. *Wealth and Democracy.* New York: Broadway Books, 2002.

Piketty, Thomas and Emmanuel Saez. "Income Inequality in the United States, 1918–1998." NBER Working Paper #8467, September 2001.

Pizzigati, Sam. *Greed and Good: Understanding and Overcoming the Inequality That Limits Our Lives.* New York: Apex Press, 2004.

Robinson, Randall. *The Debt: What America Owes to Blacks.* New York: Plume Books, 2001.

Rodrik, Dani. "Development Strategies for the Next Century." Paper prepared for the Institute for Developing Economies, Japan External Trade Organization Conference, February 2002.

Roediger, David R. *The Wages of Whiteness: Race and the Making of the American Working Class.* London: Verso, 1999.

Scott, Janny. "Nearly Half of Black Men Found Jobless." *The New York Times*, February 28, 2004.

Seager, Joni. *The Penguin Atlas of Women in the World.* New York: Penguin, 2003.

Shapiro, Thomas M. *The Hidden Cost of Being African American: How Wealth Perpetuates Inequality.* New York: Oxford University Press, 2003.

Sklar, Holly, Laryssa Mykyta, and Susan Wefald. *Raise the Floor: Wages and Policies that Work for All of Us.* Boston: South End Press, 2002.

Squires, Gregory D. "Runaway Plants, Capital Mobility, and Black Economic Rights." In *Community and Capital in Conflict: Plant Closings and Job Loss*, John C. Raines et al., eds. Philadelphia: Temple Univ. Press, 1982.

Thorndike, Joseph J., and Dennis J. Ventry, Jr., eds. *Tax Justice: The Ongoing Debate.* Washington, D.C.: Urban Institute Press, 2002.

Ratner, Sidney. *American Taxation.* New York: W.W. Norton, 1942.

Uchitelle, Louis. "Blacks Lose Better Jobs Faster As Middle-Class Work Drops." *The New York Times*, July 12, 2003.

United Nations Development Programme. *Human Development Report 1995 – Gender and Human Development.*

United Nations Development Programme. *Human Development Report 2003 – Millennium Development Goals.*

United Nations Division for the Advancement of Women. "Women and the Economy." Fact Sheet based on "Review and Appraisal of the Implementation of the Beijing Platform for Action: Report of the Secretary-General," May 2000.

United Nations Food and Agriculture Organization. "FAO Focus: Women and Food Security," no date.

U.S. House Committee on Ways and Means. Tax Revision Compendium, *The Place of the Personal Exemptions in the Present-Day Income Tax,* report prepared by Lawrence Seltzer, 1st Volume, 1959, pp. 493–514.

U.S. Social Security Administration. "The 2004 OASDI [Social Security] Trustees Report," March 23, 2004.

Wagner, Y. and M. Strauss. "The Theoretical Foundations of the Communist Manifesto's Economic Program." In *The Communist Manifesto,* New York: W. W. Norton, 1988.

Williamson, Thad, David Imbroscio, and Gar Alperovitz. *Making a Place for Community.* New York: Routledge, 2002.

Wolff, Edward N. "Changes in Household Wealth in the 1980s and 1990s in the U.S." In *International Perspectives on Household Wealth.* Northampton, Mass.: Edward Elgar, forthcoming.

Wolff, Edward N. "Recent Trends in Wealth Ownership, 1983–1998." Jerome Levy Economics Institute, April 2000.

Wolff, Edward N. *Top Heavy: The Increasing Inequality of Wealth in America and What Can Be Done About It.* New York: The New Press, 2002.

"Women's Property and Inheritance Rights: Improving Lives in Changing Times." Washington, D.C.: Women in Development/WID, March 2003.

Woo, Lillian G., F. William Schweke, and David E. Buchholz. "Hidden in Plain Sight: A Look at the $335 Billion Federal Asset-Building Budget." Washington, D.C.: The Corporation for Enterprise Development, 2004.

Zanglein, Jayne Elizabeth. "Overcoming Institutional Barriers on the Economically Targeted Investment Superhighway." In *Working Capital: The Power of Labor's Pensions,* Fung, Hebb, and Rogers, eds. Ithaca: ILR Press, 2001.

Contributors

Gar Alperovitz is professor of political economy at the University of Maryland and president of the National Center for Economic and Security Alternatives. He is the author most recently of *America Beyond Capitalism: Reclaiming Our Wealth, Our Liberty, and Our Democracy* (John Wiley & Sons, 2004).

Peter Barnes is a successful entrepreneur who co-founded Working Assets and has served on several business boards. He is now a Fellow at the Tomales Bay Institute and author of *Who Owns The Sky?* (Island Press, 2001).

Chuck Collins is co-founder and program director of United for a Fair Economy. His most recent book, co-authored with William H. Gates Sr., is *Wealth and Our Commonwealth: Why America Should Tax Accumulated Fortunes* (Beacon Press, 2003).

Attieno Davis is the Racial Wealth Divide education coordinator at United for a Fair Economy and co-author of UFE's 2004 report *The State of the Dream: Enduring Disparities in Black and White*.

Bill Fletcher is president of TransAfrica Forum and former education director of the AFL-CIO.

Ellen Frank is senior economist at the Institute of Poverty at Rhode Island College. She writes and speaks widely on international economics and on U.S. economic policy.

Amy Gluckman is co-editor of *Dollars & Sense*. She and former *D&S* editor Betsy Reed edited the volume *Homo Economics: Capitalism, Community, and Lesbian and Gay Life* (Routledge, 1997).

William Greider, National Affairs Correspondent for the *Nation*, has been a political journalist for more than 35 years. A former *Rolling Stone* and *Washington Post* editor, he is the author of several books including *The Soul of Capitalism* (Simon & Schuster, 2003), *One World, Ready or Not* (Simon & Schuster, 1997), *Who Will Tell The People* (Simon & Schuster, 1992), and *Secrets of the Temple* (Simon & Schuster, 1987).

Marjorie Kelly is editor and publisher of *Business Ethics: Corporate Social Responsibility Report*, a 17-year-old publication based in Minneapolis. She is also the author of *The Divine Right of Capital: Dethroning the Corporate Aristocracy* (Berrett-Koehler, 2003).

Paul Krugman is an economist at Princeton University and a columnist for the *New York Times*.

Betsy Leondar-Wright is the communications director at United for a Fair Economy and co-author of UFE's 2004 report *The State of the Dream: Enduring Disparities in Black and White*.

Arthur MacEwan teaches economics at the University of Massachusetts–Boston. His most recent book is *Neo-Liberalism or Democracy? Economic Strategy, Markets and Alternatives for the 21st Century* (Zed Books, 1999).

Meizhu Lui is the executive director of United for a Fair Economy. Before joining UFE, she worked for 20 years as a Boston City Hospital kitchen worker, rising through the rank-and-file to become the elected president of her militant AFSCME local. She also organized in communities of color for Health Care for All.

John Miller is an economist teaching at Wheaton College and a member of the *Dollars & Sense* collective.

Dedrick Muhammad coordinates the Racial Wealth Gap program at United for a Fair Economy.

Kevin Phillips is the author, most recently, of the books *Wealth and Democracy: A Political History of the American Rich* (Broadway Books, 2002) and *American Dynasty: Aristocracy, Fortune, and the Politics of Deceit in the House of Bush* (Viking Books, 2004).

Sam Pizzigati is the author of *Greed and Good: Understanding and Overcoming the Inequality That Limits Our Lives* (Apex Press, 2004) and the editor of *Too Much*, a newsletter dedicated to capping excessive income and wealth.

Adria Scharf is co-editor of *Dollars & Sense*. She is pursuing a doctorate in organizational sociology and does research on pensions, worker ownership, and wealth.

Michelle Sheehan is a member of the *Dollars & Sense* collective.

David Swanson is media coordinator at the International Labor Communications Association and formerly communications coordinator at ACORN.

Chris Tilly, an economist teaching at the University of Massachusetts–Lowell, is a member of the *Dollars & Sense* collective.

Thad Williamson is a lecturer in Social Studies at Harvard University and a member of the *Dollars & Sense* collective. He is the author of three books, including most recently (with David Imbroscio and Gar Alperovitz) *Making a Place for Community: Local Democracy in a Global Era* (Routledge, 2002).

THE NEW GLUCOSE REVOLUTION

Low GI Eating
Made Easy

Other **NEW GLUCOSE REVOLUTION** Titles

The New Glucose Revolution:
The Authoritative Guide to the Glycemic Index—
the Dietary Solution for Lifelong Health

The Low GI Diet Revolution

The Low GI Diet Cookbook

The New Glucose Revolution Life Plan

What Makes My Blood Glucose Go Up . . . and Down? And 101
Other Frequently Asked Questions about Your Blood Glucose Levels

The New Glucose Revolution Guide to Living Well with PCOS

■

The New Glucose Revolution Pocket Guide
to the Top 100 Low GI Foods

The New Glucose Revolution Pocket Guide to Peak Performance

The New Glucose Revolution Pocket Guide to Sugar and Energy

The New Glucose Revolution Pocket Guide to
the Metabolic Syndrome and Your Hear

The New Glucose Revolution Pocket Guide to Healthy Kids

The New Glucose Revolution Pocket Guide to Childhood Diabetes

Forthcoming

The New Glucose Revolution Low GI Guide to Diabetes

The New Glucose Revolution Low GI Guide to Losing Weight

The New Glucose Revolution Low GI Guide to Sugar and Energy

The New Glucose Revolution Shopper's Guide to GI Values 2006

THE NEW GLUCOSE REVOLUTION

Low GI Eating Made Easy

The Beginner's Guide to Eating with the Glycemic Index— Featuring the Top 100 Low GI Foods

DR. JENNIE BRAND-MILLER
and KAYE FOSTER-POWELL
with PHILIPPA SANDALL

MARLOWE & COMPANY
NEW YORK

THE NEW GLUCOSE REVOLUTION LOW GI EATING MADE EASY:
The Beginner's Guide to Eating with the Glycemic Index—
Featuring the Top 100 Low GI Foods
Copyright © 2005 by Jennie Brand-Miller, Kaye Foster-Powell, and Philippa Sandall

Published by
Marlowe & Company
An Imprint of Avalon Publishing Group Incorporated
245 West 17th Street • 11th Floor
New York, NY 10011-5300

AVALON
publishing group incorporated

This edition was published in somewhat different form in Australia in 2005
by Hodder Australia, an imprint of Hachette Livre Australia Pty Ltd. This
edition is published by arrangement with Hachette Livre Australia Pty Ltd.

The GI logo Ⓖ is a trademark of the University of Sydney in Australia
and other countries. A food product carrying this logo is nutritious
and has been tested for its GI by an accredited laboratory.

Library of Congress Cataloging-in-Publication Data is available.

ISBN: 1-56924-385-9
ISBN-13: 978-1-56924-385-5
9 8 7 6 5 4 3 2

Designed by Pauline Neuwirth and India Amos, Neuwirth & Associates, Inc.
Printed in the United States of America

Contents

PART ONE

Understanding Low GI Eating

Understanding the GI
helps you choose both the right amount of
carbohydrate and the right type of carbohydrate
for your long-term health and well-being.

"JUST TELL ME WHAT TO EAT!"

These days, figuring out exactly what you should be eating can be confusing. There are so many people and organizations—particularly the media—with an opinion on the best diet, whether it be low-carb, low-fat, high-protein, or any number of fad ideas, that wading through it all seems like mission impossible.

Once upon a time it seemed simple—you just cut down on bread and potatoes if you wanted to lose weight. Then they said fat was the problem and you should eat more "complex" carbs. Now there

> You can read this book from beginning to end if you want to, or just flip through and pick out any tips or ideas that you find interesting.

Feed your well-being

What we eat has a powerful impact on the way our body functions. It affects everything from our heart and bone health to our skin, hair and even our mood. Low-GI foods can:

▶ improve blood glucose control
▶ keep you feeling fuller for longer
▶ help you lose weight
▶ reduce the risk of developing diabetes, heart disease, and certain types of cancer

are the best-sellers telling you to banish carbs altogether—not just refined sugar, but starch too. And we won't even get into grapefruit diets or soup diets . . . So, who is right? What should you eat?

First of all, we human beings are individuals. Being fussy about food doesn't stop with childhood. When it comes to meal times each one of us has likes and dislikes. We are influenced by the traditional foods, recipes, and dietary customs of our family background, and, in addition, some of us have special health requirements that govern what we should or shouldn't eat. That's why one diet or set of food rules can't possibly apply to everybody. When you pause to think about it, the one-diet-fits-all notion doesn't make any sense at all.

There are, however, certain important characteristics of the foods we eat that make some better for us than others. The GI, or glycemic index, is one of those characteristics—one for which we are still learning the relevance to our health. What we do know is that many of the world's traditional staple foods are low GI, which means that they form the basis of a healthy, flexible, diet, whoever you are and wherever you live. A low-GI diet is a way of eating long term that suits everybody, every day, every meal.

The fuels we need for good all-round nutrition

Our bodies run on fuel, just like a car runs on gasoline. In fact, our bodies burn a special mix of fuels that come from the protein, fat, and carbohydrate in the food we eat for breakfast, lunch, and dinner and the snacks we enjoy in between.

Every day (several times a day) we need to fill up our "tank" with the right balance of these fuels.

So, the first step in answering the question "But what should I eat?" is to take a closer look at these fuels—where we find them and what they do.

PROTEIN—KEEP IT LEAN

We need protein to build and maintain our body tissues. Foods rich in protein include:

- lean meat (beef, pork, lamb)
- skinless poultry
- fish and seafood
- eggs
- low-fat dairy foods such as cottage cheese, skim milk, and low-fat yogurt
- legumes including beans, chickpeas, and lentils, and soy products such as tofu and calcium-enriched soy beverages
- nuts

Protein is also a satiating nutrient. Compared with fat and carbohydrate, eating protein will make you feel more satisfied and keep those hunger pangs at bay between meals.

Meat, fish, seafood, and poultry are the richest sources of protein. As long you trim the visible fat and avoid high-fat creamy sauces, batter, and pastry or crumb coatings you can basically eat lean protein as much as you like—but you will probably find there are natural limits on how much of these foods you want to eat.

Because your body can't stockpile extra protein from one day to use up the next, you need to eat it every day. By including a protein-rich food with every meal, you can also help satisfy your hunger between meals.

Protein and GI

With the exception of legumes, milk, and yogurt, protein foods such as meat, chicken, fish, and eggs don't contain carbohydrate, so they do not have GI values.

Protein plus micronutrients

Protein foods are excellent sources of micronutrients such as iron, calcium, zinc, vitamin B_{12} and omega-3 fats.

- Lean red meat is the best source of iron you can get.
- Fish and seafood are important sources of omega-3 fats.
- Dairy foods supply the highest amounts of calcium.
- Eggs are great sources of several essential vitamins and minerals including vitamins A, D, and E and the B vitamins, in addition to iron, phosphorus, and zinc.
- Legumes are nutritional powerpacks—high in fiber, a valuable source of carbs, B vitamins and minerals, and potent phyto-chemicals.
- Nuts are one of the richest sources of "good fats" and the anti-oxidants vitamin E and selenium.

☛ Protein: the bottom line

Keep your protein lean and eat according to your appetite.

**Watch the fat when cooking.
Opt for:**

▶ grilling

▶ barbecuing

▶ pan-frying

▶ stir-frying

▶ baking or roasting

Be wary of coatings such as breadcrumbs, batter, or pastry. You'll end up with something that could have a high GI and is most likely high in fat too.

**When choosing from menus,
hold back on:**

▶ breaded meats or rissoles

▶ breaded or battered fish and seafood

▶ meat and chicken pies

▶ tempura

FOCUS ON THE GOOD FATS

We now know that a low-fat diet is not necessarily the only way to eat for weight loss or overall health. Our bodies need a certain amount of good or unsaturated fat (think nuts, seeds, olive oil, and avocados) to function properly and thrive. Good fats:

▶ provide us with essential fatty acids that form our cell membranes

▶ help us absorb the fat-soluble vitamins A, D, E, and K

▶ form part of our body's hormones

▶ provide insulation
▶ help us absorb some antioxidants from fruits and vegetables
▶ help to make food taste better

The problem with fat is the amount we eat, sometimes without realizing it. Fat provides lots of calories—more than any other nutrient per gram. This may be great for someone who's starving, but it's a real disadvantage to those of us who already eat too much. The main form in which our bodies store those extra calories is, you guessed it, fat.

The most concentrated sources of fat in our diets are butter, margarines, and oils. While it's easy to reduce your fat intake when you can see it, it's difficult with the concealed fats in foods such as cakes, cookies, potato chips, and muffins, regular pop corn or a package of instant noodles. That's why it's important to read the labels on food packaging.

It's not just the quantity of fat in your diet you have to think about—the type of fat can make a big difference to your health and your waistline. Focus on including the good fats in your diet and minimizing foods that are high in saturated fat and trans fatty acids.

Essential fatty acids

Your body actually requires some types of fats—called essential fatty acids—which can't be manufactured by your body and must be obtained through your diet. The best sources are:

▶ seafoods
▶ polyunsaturated oils
▶ flaxseeds
▶ mustard seed oil
▶ canola oil

☞ Health tip:

When shopping, look for products low in saturated fat, rather than just low-fat products. The saturated fat content should be *less than 20 percent of the total fat.*

While a low-fat diet is recommended for weight loss, this doesn't mean a no-fat diet. Studies show that some fats, particularly those found in fish, nuts, and olive oil, are beneficial in reducing abdominal fat when included as part of a weight loss diet.

Choosing the good fats

Emphasize the following mono- and polyunsaturated fats in your diet:

- olive and canola oils
- mustard seed oil
- margarines and spreads made with canola, sunflower, or other seed oils
- avocados
- fish, shellfish, scallops, etc.
- walnuts, almonds, cashews, etc.
- olives
- muesli (not toasted)
- flaxseeds

Giving bad fats the boot

Minimize saturated fats and oils including:

- fatty meats and meat products—e.g. sausages, salami
- full-fat dairy products—milk, cream, cheese, ice cream, yogurt
- coconut and palm oils
- potato chips, packaged snacks
- cakes, cookies, pastries, pies, pizza
- deep-fried foods—fried chicken, french fries, tempura, spring rolls

> ### A word of warning
>
> Some high-fat foods—chocolate, nuts, sausages, pizza, potato chips, and ice cream—have low-GI values. When you are choosing low-GI foods, you're after low-GI carbs, not high-fat foods.

☛ Fat: the bottom line

Focus on monounsaturated and omega-3 fats for long-term health.

CARBOHYDRATE— IT DOESN'T MAKE SENSE TO LEAVE IT OUT!

Carbohydrate is a vital source of energy found in all plants and foods such as fruit, vegetables, cereals and grains. The simplest form of carbohydrate is glucose, which is:

- a universal fuel for our body cells
- the only fuel source for our brain, red blood cells and a growing fetus
- the main source of energy for our muscles during strenuous exercise

So, it *really* doesn't make sense to leave carbs out!

If you were thinking about trying a low-carbohydrate diet, here's just some of what you'll be missing out on:

- vitamin E from whole-grain cereals
- vitamin C from fruits and vegetables

- vitamin B₆ from bananas and whole-grain cereals
- pantothenic acid, zinc and magnesium from whole grains and legumes
- antioxidants and phytochemicals from all plant foods
- and fiber that comes from all the above, and *doesn't come from any animal food*

☞ Health tip

Forget about simple and complex carbohydrates. Think in terms of low GI and high GI.

How your body revs on carbs

When you eat foods such as bread, cereals, and fruit, your body converts them into a sugar called glucose during digestion. It is this glucose that is absorbed from your intestine and becomes the fuel that circulates in your bloodstream. As the level of blood glucose rises after you have eaten a meal, your pancreas gets the message to release a powerful hormone called insulin. Insulin drives glucose out of the blood and into the cells. Once inside, glucose is channelled into various pathways simultaneously—to be used as an immediate source of energy or converted into glycogen (a storage form of glucose) or fat. Insulin also turns off the use of fat

The "carb in"/"carb out" balance

The body attempts to maintain a balance between "carb in" (the carbs you get from food) and "carb out" (the carbs you burn for energy). If you deliberately avoid eating carbohydrates but maintain your normal activity, you are likely to eat more calories than you need as your body drives you to eat more in search of the "carb deficit."

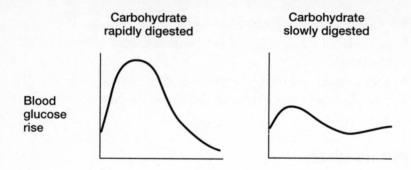

as the cells' energy source. For this reason, lowering insulin levels is one of the secrets to lifelong health. However, cutting carbs is *not the answer.*

What we now know is that not all carbs are created equal. In fact, they can behave quite differently in our bodies. The glycemic index, or GI, is how we describe this difference, ranking carbs (sugars and starches) according to their effect on blood glucose levels. After testing hundreds of foods around the world, scientists have found that foods with a low GI will have less of an effect on blood glucose levels than foods with a high GI. High-GI foods will tend to cause spikes in your glucose levels, whereas low-GI foods tend to cause gentle rises.

- High-GI foods such as white bread, potatoes, jelly beans, and corn flakes are converted to glucose quickly.
- Low-GI foods such as rolled oats, apples, pasta, and yogurt are converted to glucose slowly.

Our diet these days tends to be dominated by high-GI refined and processed carbohydrates—white bread, cookies, light crispy cereals, crackers, potato chips, doughnuts, cakes, and so on. Eating more of these refined carbs means we are eating fewer traditional starchy foods such as truly whole-grain bread (e.g. pumpernickel), fruit, oatmeal, cracked wheat (bulgur and tabbouleh), barley, dried peas, beans, and lentils. These low-GI foods are not only digested more slowly, they are also richer in micronutrients than their high-GI counterparts.

☛ Carbs: the bottom line

Carbohydrate is the most widely consumed substance in the world after water—it's cheap, plentiful, sustainable, and the basis for a healthy diet. Choosing delicious, safe, and satiating low-GI carbs reduces your day-long insulin levels more effectively than any other single dietary change.

Taste test

Try this simple test for yourself. Take a bite of fluffy white bread and keep it in your mouth for two minutes. What's left? Virtually nothing—the enzymes in your mouth have already started breaking down the starch. Now take a cooked (al dente) pasta shell (or other shape) and hold it in your mouth. After two minutes, you'll find you still have a clearly defined piece of pasta left. That's because the carbohydrates in the pasta are resistant to enzyme action. So it is with all the starches in low-GI foods.

SO WHAT DOES GI HAVE TO DO WITH YOU?

Eating a lot of high-GI foods can put pressure on your health because it pushes your body to extremes. This is especially true if you are overweight and sedentary. In the same way that the storm drains of a city are overloaded after a heavy downpour, your body's glucose response mechanisms are stretched after a load of quickly digested carbs.

Switching to eating mainly low-GI carbs that slowly trickle glucose into your bloodstream keeps your energy levels perfectly balanced

Yesterday, today, and tomorrow . . .

About 10,000 years ago, when humans moved from hunting and gathering to farming, our diet was very different from what it is today, and it suited our bodies just fine. We ate a fair amount of meat and seafood, plenty of vegetables and fruits, tree seeds such as nuts and legumes, and coarsely ground cereal grains. We may not have had any labor-saving devices, but preparation was pretty uncomplicated—we ground the grains between stones and cooked food over an open fire. This meant we digested and absorbed food slowly and the blood glucose rise after meals was gradual and prolonged.

That all changed with the 19th-century industrial revolution, which brought prosperity and radical inventions—and a fundamental shift in our diet. We began to eat much more refined carbs and far fewer beans and legumes. And we delved into sponge cakes and fluffy white breads all made with the powdery white flour that the high-speed roller mills were able to produce. We now know that this shift has triggered a string of unintended health effects, many of which are beginning to reach epidemic proportions. This new diet meant the blood glucose rise after a meal was higher and more prolonged, making the pancreas produce more insulin.

Traditional diets all around the world contain slowly digested and absorbed carbohydrate—foods we now know have a low GI. Today we eat more carbohydrate in the form of refined sugars, starches, and cereal products. These high-GI carbs have been shown to spike insulin levels, which can promote hunger and, over the long term, may increase the rates of obesity and other chronic diseases of aging.

and means you will feel fuller for longer between meals. The whole idea is to replace highly refined carbohydrates such as white bread, sugary treats, and crispy, puffed cereals with less-processed carbs such as whole-grain bread, pasta, beans, fruit, and vegetables.

Only foods containing carbohydrates can have their GI measured. And although the GI applies to the carbohydrate, its "value"—high or low—is influenced by how it is packaged in the food, including the presence of protein, fat, and water.

☞ Health tip:

High-GI foods eaten with low-GI foods score somewhere in between, so there's no need to completely avoid eating high-GI foods like baked potatoes. Just include some low-GI foods at the same meal. You can live with a low-GI diet—it's all about moderation.

Not so long ago we believed complex, starchy carbohydrates such as bread and potato were more slowly absorbed than the simple,

GI—whoever thought of that?

It all began with researchers trying to discover the best foods for people with diabetes. The aim was to find out which carbohydrates raised blood glucose the least. Scientists found that when people ate a specified portion of ice cream it raised their blood glucose just as much as the portion of potato did. Up till then everyone with diabetes was being told to avoid all sweets. Everyone just assumed that "simple" sugar would raise their blood glucose more than bread and potatoes. These days we know the GI of hundreds of foods from studies all around the world. In Part 3 (page 101), you can check out the top 100 low-GI foods.

sugary carbohydrate in cakes, cookies, jams, and honey. In learning about the GI of foods we've realized that this isn't true. Foods such as pasta and grain bread are off limits in many low-carb fad diets—but it's precisely these carb foods that fill us up and give us energy. All you have to do is look for the low-GI types.

Did you know?

The foods most strongly associated with high-GI diets are white bread and refined cereals. High intakes of fruits and vegetables are associated with lower-GI diets.

☞ Health tip

When shopping and planning meals, choose smart carbs, the low GI ones that produce only gentle rises in blood glucose and insulin levels because they are slowly digested. Lowering insulin levels is the secret to long-term health.

WHAT ARE THE BENEFITS OF LOW GI EATING?

Low GI eating has science on its side. It's not a diet. There are no strict rules or regimens to follow. It's essentially about making simple adjustments to your usual eating habits—such as swapping one type of bread or breakfast cereal for another. You'll find that you can live with it for life. Low GI eating:

- reduces your insulin levels
- lowers your cholesterol levels
- helps control your appetite
- halves your risk of heart disease and diabetes

Potato chips vs. chocolate bar

Which is better for your blood glucose? Most people with diabetes would see the chocolate bar as taboo, but by measuring the blood glucose rise after different foods scientists have proved this to be unfounded. Potato chips and chocolate have an almost identical effect on blood glucose. Why?

The carbohydrate in chocolate is sucrose, which is 50 percent fructose (which has little effect on blood glucose levels) and 50 percent glucose (high GI), giving it a medium GI overall. In potato chips the carbohydrate is cooked (swollen) starch, which is readily digested to yield 100 percent glucose molecules. Therefore, fully cooked starch has twice the impact on blood glucose levels as the same quantity of sugar.

▶ is suitable for your whole family
▶ means you are eating foods closer to the way nature intended
▶ doesn't defy common sense!

Not only that. You will feel better and have more energy—and you don't have to deprive or discipline yourself. A low-GI diet is easy.

How do you do it?

Low GI eating fits with the first dietary guideline of countries all around the world: "Eat a wide variety of foods." There is a large range of low-GI foods from which to choose. In fact, low-GI foods can be found in four of the five food groups:

▶ whole grains and pasta in the bread and cereal group
▶ milk and yogurt among the dairy foods
▶ legumes of all types in the meat and alternatives group
▶ virtually all fruits and vegetables

This is what makes it so easy to eat the low-GI way every meal, every day.

GETTING STARTED ON LOW GI EATING

To get started, you need to:

▶ *eat* a lot more fruits and vegetables, legumes, and whole-grain products such as barley and traditional oats

▶ *pay attention* to breads and breakfast cereals—these foods contribute most to the glycemic load of a typical American diet

▶ *minimize* refined-flour products and starches such as cakes, crackers, cookies, rolls, and pastries, irrespective of their fat and sugar content

▶ *avoid* high-GI snacks such as pretzels, corn chips, rice cakes, and crackers

In Part 2 (page 35) you'll find step-by-step guidelines for making the switch to everyday low GI eating.

Did you know?

Processing whole grains into flour increases the calorie density by more than 10 percent, reduces the amount of fiber by 80 percent, and reduces the amount of protein by 30 percent. Refining grains leaves a dietary substance that is nearly pure starchy carbohydrate.

Three key habits to ensure a low-GI diet

1. If you eat breakfast cereal, check out the GI of your favorite brand—you might get quite a surprise. Most of the popular big-name cereals have high GI values in the 70s and above.

2. Choose low-GI bread. Try one of the types recommended on page 146 for home use and ask for whole-grain whenever buying sandwiches. Steer clear of cookies, cakes, scones, doughnuts, and bread rolls made of refined flour (except sourdough) as much as you can.

3. Eat fruit for at least one of your daily snacks and have a low-fat milk drink or low-fat yogurt for another.

Getting familiar with the GI of popular carbs

In the table below you will find some common carbohydrate foods, listed according to their GI value. Take a look to see where your favorite carbs fit on the GI scale.

Where does your favorite food fit on the GI scale?

LOW GI <55	MEDIUM GI 56–69	HIGH GI >70
Fruit		
apples	canned apricots	watermelon
oranges	cantaloupe	
pears	mango	
peaches		
banana		
For more low-GI fruits see pages 106–132		
Vegetables		
sweet corn	new potatoes	french fries
sweet potatoes	beets	mashed potatoes
baked beans		baked potatoes
Breads		
whole-grain bread	pita bread	white bread
fruit bread	croissant	whole wheat bread
		doughnuts
Cereals/Grains		
pasta	couscous	jasmine rice
noodles	basmati rice	corn flakes

LOW GI <55	MEDIUM GI 56–69	HIGH GI >70
Cereals/Grains (continued)		
oatmeal		
muesli		
bran cereal		
Sugars		
pure floral honey	sugar	glucose
maple syrup		maltodextrins
Dairy Foods		
ice cream		
yogurt		
custard		
Snacks		
nuts	potato chips	
chocolate		
Beverages		
milk	beer	
juice	cordial	
flavored milk	soft drink	

Note: Some foods such as cheese, eggs, bacon, meat, lettuce, avocado, and fish don't appear on this table—because they don't contain any carbs.

GL (GLYCEMIC LOAD) VS. GI

Your blood glucose rises and falls when you eat a meal containing carbohydrate. How high it rises and how long it remains high is critically important to your health and depends on the *quality* of the carbohydrate (its GI value) as well as the *quantity* of carbohydrate in your meal. Researchers at Harvard University came up with a term that combines these two factors—glycemic load (GL).

GL = GI/100 × carbs per serving

Some people think that GL should be used instead of GI when comparing foods because it reflects the glycemic impact of both the quantity and quality of carbohydrate in a food. But more often than not, it's low GI rather than low GL that best predicts good health outcomes.

So what should you use? Our advice is to stick with the GI in all but a few instances. When you choose low-GI carbs, your diet is invariably healthy with the appropriate quantity and quality of carbohydrate. Following the alternative low-GL path could mean you're eating a decidedly unhealthy diet, low in carbs and full of the wrong sorts of fats and proteins.

You may be wondering what the fuss is all about. Well, some carb-rich foods such as pasta—which have a good satiety factor—have a low GI but *could* have a high GL if the serving size is large. Portion size still counts. And while it's true that a handful of high-GI foods, such as watermelon, have a low GL, we don't want you to restrict *any* fruit or vegetable other than potato.

There's no denying that it is easier to overeat certain foods. This is where low-GI foods are star performers—the versions with the lowest GI values also have the best satiety factor. If you listen to your true appetite, you are far less likely to overeat when you are choosing low-GI foods.

To give you the easy picture of the glycemic impact of foods, we have taken both the GI and the GL into account in our tables (see page 223).

> Don't restrict high-GI fruits and veggies, other than potatoes. Because most are not major sources of carbs, their GI is not that important.

> Don't get carried away with GL: it doesn't distinguish between foods that are **low carb or slow carb.**

EAT LOW-GI CARBS TO LOSE WEIGHT

There is no doubt that reducing portion sizes and eating fewer calories will lead to weight loss. Just *how* you do this is the name of the game. These days, we are eating less fat but getting fatter. Instead of eating fewer calories we are eating more, especially in the form of high-GI refined starches and sugars.

Cutting out all carbs is not the answer (remember the carb deficit problem we mentioned on page 11). The real solution to both weight loss and weight maintenance is to be choosy about the type of carbs you eat. Some good reasons why appear on page 23.

Avoiding the post-lunch dip

Have you ever experienced what nutritionists describe as the "post-lunch dip"? It's that sleepy feeling that hits you, typically mid-afternoon. Your high-carb lunch and the subsequent surge in insulin levels sends your blood glucose plummeting, driving you out to seek a sweet fix and some caffeine. The trick to preventing this dip is lowering the glycemic load of your lunch: eat less carbohydrate, choose lower-GI carbs, and add some protein (such as canned tuna, a couple of eggs, some cottage cheese, or lean meat or chicken). And add as many green, red, and yellow veggies as possible.

How do high-GI carbs make us fat?

▶ Eating high-GI carbs causes a surge of glucose in the blood.

▶ Although the body needs glucose, it doesn't want it all in one hit, so it pumps out insulin to drive the glucose out of the blood and into the tissues.

▶ Insulin switches muscle cells from fat burning to carbohydrate (glucose) burning.

▶ Insulin also directs excess fuels to storage—glucose to glycogen and fats to fat storage.

▶ The action of insulin means blood glucose levels begin to decline rapidly.

▶ The brain detects falling blood glucose and sends out hunger signals.

▶ Low levels of fuel and high levels of insulin then trigger the release of stress hormones such as adrenalin to scour the body for more glucose. This translates to hunger, light-headedness, and feeling shaky. The only way to relieve the state of hunger is with another snack.

How can low-GI carbs help?

If you feel hungry all the time, low-GI foods can help you turn off the switch. Here's how and why . . .

▶ Low-GI foods are rich in carbohydrate—an appetite suppressant far superior to fat.

▶ Many low-GI foods are less processed, which means they require more chewing—helping to signal satiety to your brain.

▶ Low-GI foods often come in the company of fiber so they swell and create a greater feeling of fullness in your stomach.

▶ Low-GI foods are more slowly digested, which means they stay in your intestines longer, keeping you feeling satisfied.

▶ Being slowly digested; low-GI foods trickle glucose into your bloodstream slowly, helping to ward off hunger.

▶ Low-GI foods help overcome the body's natural tendency to slow down fuel usage (your metabolic rate) while dieting.

The satiety factor

Can you imagine feeling satisfied after eating just a fraction of your usual calories? Low-GI foods help make this possible.

In the early days of GI research at the University of Sydney, we discovered a match between the GI of foods and how satisfying they were to eat. Our readers regularly tell us how easy they find low-GI diets because they feel far less hungry. We now know this has a scientific basis—secretion of one of the most powerful satiety hormones (called GLP-1) is higher after consuming the low-GI version of your usual bread, breakfast cereal, or rice.

Test for yourself and feel the difference

You can experience one benefit of low-GI carbs with this simple breakfast challenge. Try out each of the following breakfasts on consecutive mornings, one high-GI and one low-GI, and feel the difference yourself. By mid-morning you'll be thinking better, feeling better, and have more insight into your natural hunger and satiety cues with Breakfast 1.

Breakfast 1—a low-GI option
½ cup natural muesli
with ½ cup low-fat milk
and ½ a banana

Breakfast 2—a high-GI option
1 cup corn flakes
with 1 cup low-fat milk
and a few strawberries

☛ Health tip:

Low-GI foods alleviate hunger, making it easier to eat less. Studies show that, on average, calorie intake is 20 percent greater after consumption of high-GI meals than after low-GI meals.

The weight of the evidence

Studies in adults lasting up to 12 months have consistently shown that people lost more body fat following a diet rich in low-GI carbs compared with conventional diets.

In 2004, a study was published in the prestigious medical journal *The Lancet* confirming that changing *only* the GI of the carbohydrate in a diet (keeping everything else exactly the same), leads to reduced body fat in animals.

☛ The bottom line: 4 keys to long-term weight loss

1. Choose low-GI carbs. Eat regularly and try to include low-GI carbs at every meal. This will stave off hunger and strengthen your resolve against temptation.
2. Reduce your fat intake by cutting out the saturated fat in foods such as chocolate, cookies, and french fries.
3. Snack smarter, snack low GI, and say "no thanks" to high-GI cookies, crackers, candy, and soft drinks.
4. Think *balance and moderation*. Eat a little less. Do a little more.

☛ Health tip:

The evidence from people who have lost weight and maintained it over the long haul is that they:

▸ wanted to change their diet to improve their health
▸ were willing to lose weight slowly
▸ made lasting changes to their diet and activity patterns

LOW-GI CARBS CAN REDUCE
YOUR RISK OF DIABETES

Did you realize that the higher the GI of your diet, the greater your risk of diabetes? Yes, you read it right. An Australian study of 31,000 people over 10 years found that those who had the highest GI diets were more likely to develop diabetes. In fact, they found that eating *white bread* (not sugar!) was the food most strongly related to the development of diabetes.

Foods with a high GI are digested quickly and cause a rapid rise in blood glucose, and an outpouring of insulin (the hormone that removes glucose from the blood and stores it in cells). If you're eating high-GI meals all the time you end up with chronically high insulin levels that could contribute to insulin resistance. This means the cells that normally respond to insulin become insensitive to it, so your body thinks it has to make even more insulin to do the job.

Often, type 2 diabetes is only diagnosed once the pancreas (which produces insulin) is absolutely worn out and cannot maintain sufficient insulin production to normalize blood glucose. Before you get to that point, eating a moderately high-carbohydrate, low-GI diet can actually improve the function of your pancreas, and improved glycemic control can prevent the onset of type 2 diabetes.

In case you still have your doubts . . .

▶ In U.S. studies of thousands of people followed up over eight years, researchers found that those who ate a high-GI diet were almost twice as likely to develop type 2 diabetes. Interestingly, the effect was most pronounced in those with low levels of physical activity, a known way of overcoming insulin resistance.

▶ In the U.S. in the past 100 years, the prevalence of obesity and type 2 diabetes has increased directly in proportion to the consumption of refined carbohydrates.

A meal with a high GI can result in glucose concentrations twice the level compared with the same amount of food with a low GI.

Are you at risk of type 2 diabetes?

More than eighteen million Americans have diabetes or pre-diabetes and are at risk of heart disease and stroke. To find out if you're at risk of type 2 diabetes, answer the following questions.

☐ **1.** Check the box if you have a family history of any of the following:
- diabetes
- heart disease
- high blood pressure
- polycystic ovarian syndrome

☐ **2.** Check the box if you are:
- overweight
- over 40 and of European descent; or over 25 and of Indian, Middle Eastern, African, or Afro-Carribbean heritage
- a woman who has polycystic ovarian syndrome (PCOS)
- a woman who had diabetes in pregnancy

If you have checked either or both boxes above you are at risk of developing type 2 diabetes and should discuss screening tests for this condition with your doctor.

☛ Did you know?

Some diet books demonize sugar and advocate strict avoidance, but a modest serving of 2 teaspoons of sugar actually has a GL of only 7.

What are the key signs and symptoms of diabetes?

▶ increased thirst
▶ going to the toilet all the time—especially at night
▶ extreme tiredness
▶ unexplained weight loss
▶ genital itching or regular episodes of thrush
▶ poor healing of wounds
▶ blurred vision

For more information on diabetes go to www.diabetes.org

Low-GI carbs—giving people with diabetes a new lease on life

When it comes to diabetes, following a low-GI diet can be as effective at lowering your blood glucose as taking diabetic medications. This is not an exaggeration! A scientific analysis of 14 different studies from around the world of people with diabetes showed that low-GI diets improved glycemic control significantly more than high-GI or conventional diets. Improved glycemic control can prevent the onset and progression of diabetes complications.

On a day-to-day basis, low-GI foods can minimize the peaks and valleys in blood glucose that make life so difficult when you have diabetes. Since they are slowly digested and absorbed, low-GI foods reduce insulin demand—lessening the strain on the struggling pancreas of a person with type 2 diabetes and potentially lowering insulin requirements for those with type 1 diabetes. Lower insulin levels have the added benefit of reducing the risk of large blood vessel damage, lessening the likelihood of developing heart disease.

☛ The bottom line: the optimum diet for people with diabetes

There isn't any one optimum diet for all people with diabetes. Whether you eat higher fat, low-fat, high protein, high carb or whatever, certain characteristics are desirable. They are:

▶ Eating regular meals and choosing slowly digested carbs with a low GI.
▶ Including plenty of vegetables and fruits.
▶ Eating only small amounts of saturated fat.
▶ Including a moderate amount of sugar and sugary foods.
▶ Drinking only a moderate quantity of alcohol.
▶ Including a minimum amount of salt and salty foods.

LOW-GI CARBS & A HEALTHY HEART

Eating a high-GI diet isn't only related to diabetes. Heart disease is the single biggest killer of Americans, and having high glucose levels after meals is a predictor of future heart disease. Sound farfetched? Here's how it happens . . .

A high level of glucose in the blood means:

▶ excess glucose moves into cells lining the arteries, causing inflammation, thickening, and stiffening—the making of "hardened arteries"
▶ highly reactive, charged particles called "free radicals" are formed and destroy the machinery inside the cell, eventually causing the cell death
▶ glucose adheres to cholesterol in the blood, which promotes the formation of fatty plaque and prevents the body from breaking down excess cholesterol

▶ higher levels of insulin raises blood pressure and blood fats, while suppressing "good" (HDL) cholesterol levels

Halve your risk of heart attack with a low-GI diet

This might sound like an inflated newspaper headline—it isn't! The results of a Harvard University study of over 100,000 people over 10 years found that those who ate more high-GI foods had nearly twice the risk of heart attack compared with those eating low-GI diets. This was independent of other risk factors such as age, obesity, and smoking, although, surprisingly, in those who were lean, high-GI foods did not pose excess risk.

☛ The bottom line: reduce your risk of heart disease

Along with exercise, a diet rich in slowly digested, low-GI carbs will reduce your risk of heart disease in several ways. By lowering your blood glucose after meals and reducing high insulin levels, you'll have:

▶ healthier blood vessels that are more elastic, dilate more easily, and aid blood flow
▶ improved blood flow and less inflammation
▶ more potential for weight loss and therefore less pressure on the heart
▶ better blood fats—more of the good cholesterol and less of the bad

For more information on heart disease go to www.americanheart.org.

LOW-GI CARBS AND PCOS

Polycystic ovarian syndrome (PCOS) is thought to affect one in four women in developed countries. Characteristics of the syndrome can include irregular periods, infertility, heavy body hair growth, obstinate body fat, diabetes, and cardiovascular disease. In many women it goes undiagnosed because the symptoms may be subtle, such as faint facial hair.

Insulin resistance—where the body resists the normal actions of the hormone insulin—is at the root of PCOS. In an effort to overcome insulin resistance the body secretes more insulin than normal. Among other effects, this leads to growth and multiplication of cells in the ovaries, causing hormonal imbalances.

The problem of insulin resistance

Elevations in blood glucose after eating high-GI foods are followed by elevations in insulin. When insulin levels are chronically raised, the cells that usually respond to insulin become resistant to its signals. The body responds by secreting more insulin, a never-ending vicious cycle that spells trouble on many fronts.

A low-GI diet is invaluable in the management of insulin resistance because it will result in lower blood glucose after meals and thereby *reduce the demand for insulin*, which can help *appetite control* and improve *weight loss*, and normalize fertility hormones.

Managing the symptoms of PCOS

To manage PCOS symptoms effectively you need to take charge of your health by managing your weight (body fat), making the change to low GI eating, and building more activity into your life. The benefits will include:

▶ improving PCOS symptoms
▶ achieving and maintaining healthy weight
▶ controlling blood glucose and insulin levels
▶ boosting fertility
▶ gaining control and quality of life

For more information on PCOS, go to www.pcosupport.org.

☛ The bottom line: Eating well if you have PCOS

If you have PCOS, eating well is not just about managing your weight. It can also improve your overall health and energy levels, and reduce your risk of developing diabetes or heart disease. It's essential to eat in a way that helps to control your insulin levels. This means eating small regular meals and snacks spread throughout the day and choosing low-GI carbs. Your healthy eating plan should include:

- fresh vegetables and salads
- fresh fruit
- whole-grain breads and cereals
- low-fat dairy foods or nondairy alternatives such as soy
- fish, lean meat, skinless chicken, eggs, legumes, and soy products
- small amounts of healthy fats, including nuts, seeds, avocados, olives, olive oil, canola oil, or peanut oil

LOW-GI CARBS & ANTI-AGING

Scientists are beginning to find connections between high blood glucose levels and diseases such as dementia. As we age, abnormal protein deposits form in parts of the brain and eventually interfere with normal mental functioning. High glucose levels accelerate this process. Indeed, the abnormal proteins are called advanced glycosylated endproducts (AGE for short!).

To get a feel for how this happens, think about the browning reactions that occur naturally during cooking—think of toasting, baking, and grilling. When sugar is present, the reactions occur faster, sometimes leading to excess browning, i.e. burning!

The same reactions between sugars and proteins occur very slowly inside the body. Gradually the proteins become burdened by the presence of the freeloading sugar molecules and lose the ability to do their job. When that happens to a long-lived protein like the collagen in skin, the elasticity and natural glow of youthful skin fades. The result: wrinkles. We can't stop it entirely but we can slow it down.

PART TWO

Everyday Low GI Eating: Making the Switch

Don't diet. Focus on eating well and moving more.
Enjoy food and make sure you choose a diet
that will give you energy to burn.
And remember, we all need to be active.
Every day.

LOW GI EATING: FOR EVERYBODY, EVERY DAY, EVERY MEAL

We love hearing our readers' stories of how low GI eating has transformed their lives. Success stories like the woman with gestational diabetes who swapped high-GI for low-GI carbs and found she did not need to take insulin—their stories inspire us all.

These examples and hundreds more have helped us understand what works for people and what doesn't. And that's what this section is about. It covers the sorts of questions our readers and clients actually ask. The answers will show you how easy it is to make simple changes in your food choices that will have a big impact on your overall health—for life.

One of our most frequently received requests is "just tell me what to eat!" So, in this section, we focus on food and give you some simple guidelines about making the switch to everyday low GI eating. You'll find out how to:

> ▶ put together a balanced low-GI meal
> ▶ how to eat low GI when socializing with friends and family and eating out
> ▶ what to buy and how to stock your pantry

Exactly how you incorporate low GI eating into your life is up to you. Some people want to eat low-GI foods all the time, others some of the time. That's OK. There's room for both approaches. And in reality that's how we eat, too.

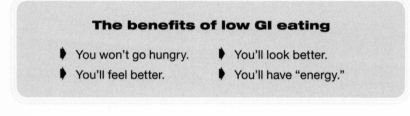

The benefits of low GI eating

▶ You won't go hungry.   ▶ You'll look better.

▶ You'll feel better.   ▶ You'll have "energy."

LOW GI EATING—THE BASICS

First let's show you how easy it is to eat the low-GI way. There's no specific order in which you have to do things, no strict week-by-week list of diet do's and don'ts, no counting, calculating, or measuring. However, there are some basics—daily and weekly eating and activity habits essential to good health. After all, this is not a magic pill. It's an eating plan that will help you nourish your body, feel better, and promote optimum health. So, to help you get started, here are the basics.

Every day you need to:

> ▶ Eat at least three meals—don't skip meals. Eat snacks too if you are hungry.
> ▶ Eat fruit at least twice—fresh, cooked, dried, or juice.
> ▶ Eat vegetables at least twice—cooked, raw, salads, soups, juices, and snacks.

- Eat a cereal at least once—such as bread, breakfast cereal, pasta, noodles, rice, and other grains in a whole-grain or low-GI form.
- Accumulate 60 minutes of physical activity (including incidental activity and planned exercise).

☞ Health tip:

Make healthy eating a habit. Motivation is what gets you started. Habit is what helps to keep you going. Here are some tips.

- Make breakfast a priority.
- If it's healthy keep it handy.
- Don't buy food you want to avoid.
- Make sure temptation is more than an arm's length away—serve meals in the kitchen.
- Focus on the positive—think about what to eat, rather than what not to eat.
- Listen to your appetite—eat when you are hungry and stop when you are full (you don't have to leave a clean plate all the time).

Every week you need to:

- Eat beans, peas, and/or lentils—at least twice. This includes chickpeas, red kidney beans, butter beans, split peas, and foods made from them, such as hummus and dal.
- Eat fish and seafood at least once, preferably twice—fresh, smoked, frozen, or canned.
- Eat nuts regularly—just a tiny handful.

Three tips for making the switch

Here's how you can make it easier to develop and maintain your new low GI eating habits.

Start with something simple

Nothing inspires like success, so attack the easiest changes first, such as eating one piece of fruit every day.

What to choose?

- ❏ Low-GI breads—whole-grain, sourdough and other low-GI breads
- ❏ Low-GI breakfast cereals—muesli, oatmeal, All-Bran, etc.
- ❏ Low-GI cereals—pasta, noodles, basmati or Uncle Ben's converted long-grain rice, whole grains, etc.
- ❏ Lean meat and skinless chicken
- ❏ Low-fat milk, yogurt, or soy-based, calcium-enriched alternatives
- ❏ Omega-3-enriched eggs
- ❏ Olive and canola oils as your main cooking and salad oils

Do it gradually

Choose one aspect of your diet that you want to work on, for example, eating more vegetables, and make that your focus for at least six weeks. It can take at least this long for a new behavior to become habit.

Don't expect 100 percent success

A lapse in your eating habits is not failure. It's a natural part of developing new habits. Falling over is easy, but getting up and keeping going can take real effort. Believe in yourself. You can do it!

How does your daily diet rate?

Try our quick quiz.

1. I mostly eat reduced-fat or low-fat dairy foods.   ☑ YES   ❏ NO
2. I include at least one cup of milk or yogurt or calcium-enriched soy alternative every day.   ☑ YES   ❏ NO

3. When I drink alcohol, I mostly drink no more than two standard drinks per day. (Check YES if you don't drink alcohol.) ☑ YES ☐ NO

4. I generally don't eat take-out/fast food more than once a week. ☑ YES ☐ NO

5. I eat regular meals. ☑ YES ☐ NO

6. I eat skinless chicken. ☑ YES ☐ NO

7. I avoid adding salt to my food. ☑ YES ☐ NO

8. I include fish or some other seafood at least once a week. ☑ YES ☐ NO

9. I rarely eat packaged snacks such as potato chips. ☑ YES ☐ NO

10. I usually eat five or more different vegetables in a day. ☐ YES ☑ NO

11. I use an unsaturated margarine spread rather than butter. (Check YES if you use neither.) ☑ YES ☐ NO

12. I use unsaturated oils such as olive, canola, sunflower, sesame, macadamia, and mustard seed for cooking and food preparation. ☑ YES ☐ NO

13. I eat at least one piece of fruit every day. ☑ YES ☐ NO

14. I limit fatty meats such as sausages, bacon, hot dogs, ground hamburger, and lamb chops or spare ribs to less than once a week. ☑ YES ☐ NO

Score 1 point for each YES.

What Your Score Means:

12–14 Excellent. It looks like you have the balance right and your basic dietary habits are sound. Read on to make sure what you are eating is low GI.

9–11 It sounds like your dietary habits aren't bad but you have work to do in achieving the right balance and lowering the GI of your diet.

Less than 9 Oops! Room for a lot of improvement here—just to boost the basic nutritional quality of your diet. So, back to the basics (page 37) and good luck.

THIS FOR THAT

Simply substituting high-GI foods with low-GI alternatives will give your overall diet a lower GI and deliver the benefits of a low-GI diet. Here's how you can put slow carbs to work in your day by cutting back consumption of high-GI foods and replacing them with alternatives that are just as tasty.

If you are currently eating this (high-GI) food	Choose this (low-GI) alternative instead
Cookies	A slice of whole-grain bread or toast with jam, fruit spread, or Nutella
Breads such as soft white or whole wheat; smooth-textured breads, rolls, or scones	Dense breads with whole grains, whole-grain and stone-ground flour, and sourdough; look for low-GI labeling
Breakfast cereals—most commercial, processed cereals including corn flakes, Rice Crispies, cereal "biscuits" such as shredded wheat	Traditional rolled oats, muesli, and the commercial low-GI brands listed on page 235 look for low-GI labeling
Cakes and pastries	Raisin toast, fruit loaf, and fruit buns are healthier baked options; yogurts and low-fat mousses also make great snacks or desserts
Chips and other packaged snacks such as Twinkies, pretzels, Pop-Tarts	Fresh grapes or cherries, or dried fruit and nuts
Crackers	Crisp vegetable strips such as carrot, pepper, or celery
Doughnuts and croissants	Try a skim milk cappuccino or smoothie instead
French fries	Leave them out! Have salad or extra vegetables instead. Corn on the cob or coleslaw are better fast-food options
Candy	Chocolate is lower GI but high in fat. Healthier options are raisins, dried apricots, and other dried fruits

If you are currently eating this (high-GI) food	Choose this (low-GI) alternative instead
Muesli bars	Try a nut bar or dried fruit and nut mix
Potatoes	Prepare smaller amounts of potato and add some sweet potato or sweet corn. Canned new potatoes are an easy and lower-GI option. You can also try sweet potato, yam, taro, or baby new potatoes—or just replace with other low-GI or no-GI vegetables
Rice, especially large servings of it in dishes such as risotto, rice salads, fried rice	Try basmati or Uncle Ben's converted long-grain rice, Japanese sushi rice with salmon and vinegar, pearl barley, cracked wheat (bulgur), quinoa, pasta, or noodles
Soft drinks and fruit juice drinks	Use a diet variety if you drink these often. Fruit juice has a lower GI (but it is not a lower-calorie option). Water is best
Sugar	Moderate the quantity. Consider pure floral honey (not commercial blends), apple juice, fructose, and grape nectar as alternatives

LOW GI EATING GIVES YOU A HEALTHY BALANCE

Everyday low GI eating is easy. Although the glycemic index itself has a scientific basis, you don't need to crunch numbers or do any sort of mental arithmetic to make sure you are eating a healthy low-GI diet.

By following the low-GI-eating basics we described earlier (page 37) you'll find you are enjoying foods from all the food groups and reaping the benefits of 40-plus nutrients. You'll also be taking in the protective anti-oxidants and phytochemicals your body needs each day for long-term health and well-being.

FAQs about the GI

Are sugary foods all high GI?

No. This is one of the most widely perpetuated myths, even by so-called proponents of the GI—the sweeter it is the more it spikes your blood glucose. Long-held beliefs are hard to shift. In our food finder (page 101) you'll discover many deliciously sweet low-GI foods from ice cream and chocolate milk to honey and fresh fruit.

Should I add up the GI each day?

No. In some of our early books we included sample menus and calculated an estimated GI for the day. As our understanding of the GI grew and we talked to our clients and heard from our readers, we realized how unnecessary and misleading this was. The GI value of a food can be altered by the way it is processed or cooked, so we don't believe it is possible to calculate a precise GI value for recipes or to predict the GI of a menu for the whole day. That's why we now prefer simply to categorize foods as low, medium, or high GI in most circumstances. We have also found that many people who simply substitute low-GI foods for high in their everyday meals and snacks reduce the overall GI of their diet, gain better blood glucose control, and lose weight.

Should I avoid all high-GI foods?

No. There is no need to eat only low-GI foods. While you will benefit from eating low-GI carbs at each meal, this doesn't have to be at the exclusion of all others. High-GI foods such as potatoes and whole wheat bread make a valuable nutritional contribution to our diet, and when eaten with protein foods or low-GI carbs, the overall GI value of the meal will be medium.

What's the GI of meat, chicken, fish, eggs, and cheese?

There is no point wondering about the GI of meat, eggs, fish and cheese—these foods don't have one. The same goes for most of the vegetable kingdom—foods such as broccoli, tomatoes, pumpkin, and parsnips contain so little carbohydrate that their GI is either impossible to measure or irrelevant. But these foods are part of a healthy, balanced diet and we're asked about them all the time, so we have included them in our tables.

Should I be pedantic about GI values?
No. Whether a food's GI is 56 or 64 isn't biologically distinguishable. Normal day-to-day variation in the human body could obscure the difference in these values. Generally, a variation of more than 10 could be considered different.

Does a food's GI value make it good or bad for you?
No. When choosing foods, the glycemic index is not intended to be used on its own. A food's GI value doesn't make it good or bad for you. The nutritional benefits of different foods are many and varied. Meat and fish are protein rich, whole grains are rich in carbs, while fruits and vegetables are rich in vitamins, minerals, and antioxidants. We suggest you base your food choices on the overall nutritional content, along with the amount of saturated fat, salt, fiber, and, of course, the GI value. In the food finder we highlight some of the many important nutritional benefits of the top 100 low-GI foods.

Avoid these common mistakes about food and eating

Giving food a low priority
People who give food a low priority often skip meals, grab food on the run, or become overhungry and then overindulge to compensate. Usually all three and in this order! Some people take better care of their cars than their bodies. Remember, food is our fuel for a healthy life—we need it to live, breathe, and go about our everyday tasks. So schedule choosing, preparing, and eating healthy food into your day.

Not eating enough vegetables

Three vegetables on your dinner plate is not enough. You need to eat a variety of vegetables in different forms at different times of day. When you follow our "1, 2, 3 . . . putting it on the plate" plan (see page 48), you'll find it easy to enjoy fruit or vegetables at every meal.

Comparing your food intake with others

This is a pointless exercise. First, it's almost impossible to get an accurate picture of what other people really eat (they lie). Second, food requirements vary so much between people. Gender, size, activity, and age all come into play, along with a range of individual factors. Some lucky people just need to eat more than others.

Going on a restrictive diet

If you want to lose body fat and keep it off, restrictive dieting isn't the answer. This kind of dieting that has you obsessively counting calories and cutting out whole food groups is almost impossible to stick to in the long term and can set you on the dreaded "yo-yo" dieting cycle. Instead of trying to control every urge to sneak a morsel of chocolate or feeling guilty when you fall off the dieting wagon, give yourself a treat and enjoy a regular splurge. It's a more sensible approach to eating—and living.

The only way to lose weight and body fat permanently is to change your eating habits and include regular physical activity in your day. We know this can mean changing the habits of a lifetime. We know this is hard. That's why we suggest you make gradual changes, one step at a time, that fit in with your way of living and that you can maintain for life.

Filling the shopping cart with "fat-free" foods

Low fat or no fat is a recent trend in food manufacturing. But "99% fat free" doesn't mean calorie free; all too often much of it is high GI and will still cause weight gain if eaten to excess. Here's an example. Take a regular 1¾-ounce scoop of vanilla ice cream:

- regular ice cream (10% fat) = 90 calories (average)
- reduced-fat ice cream (6.5% fat) = 85 calories (average)
- low-fat ice cream (less than 4% fat) = 30 calories (average)

So, enjoy a scoop of low-fat ice cream, but say "no thanks" to seconds.

☛ **Health tip:**

Commit time to exercise. This is just as important as committing to three meals a day, or substituting low GI for high. In our modern lifestyle, exercise seldom just happens. Like anything else that we want to do, we have to plan it and allocate time for it. It's not "optional."

Food minus exercise = fat

SIMPLE STEPS TO DEVELOPING GOOD EATING HABITS

Listen to your appetite

Eat when you are hungry and put your knife and fork down when you are full (not stuffed). If you have a tendency to overeat, serve food in the kitchen and bring it to the table to remove the temptation of helping yourself to seconds and thirds at the table. Also, be aware that we all have "hungry days," so it's normal to eat more on some days and less on others.

Watch for signs of non-hungry eating

It's also normal to reach for food when you are tired, bored, or stressed. We call this "non-hungry eating." It isn't wrong, but it tends to contribute to overeating. If you are aware of it, you can do something about it—such as drink a glass of water or make yourself busy.

Think about what to eat, rather than what not to eat

Be positive. Make planning and preparing meals fun. Our food finder on page 101 is packed with hundreds of delicious foods, meal ideas, and recipes you can enjoy every day.

Eat regularly

Remember the basics: three meals a day is a must. It's probably easier to stick to regular meal and snack times to start with, too. So make meals a time to relax and enjoy food whether you are on your own or with family or friends—you are more likely to feel satisfied if you do.

If it's healthy, keep it handy

Stock your cupboards and fridge with healthy low-GI foods and snacks. Increase your chances of eating them by keeping them handy!

Keep occasional foods out of sight

Make overeating as hard as possible by putting occasional and snack foods well out of sight, preferably out of easy reach.

☞ Health tip:

Low-GI foods can form the basis of a healthy and flexible diet whoever you are and wherever you live.

1, 2, 3 . . . PUTTING IT ON THE PLATE

Main meals for most Americans consist of some sort of meat (or chicken or fish) with vegetables and potato (or rice or pasta). This is a good start, and a little fine-tuning will ensure a healthy, balanced meal. All you need to do is adjust your proportions to match our "plate." Here are the three simple steps to put together a balanced low-GI meal.

1 is for carb

It's an essential, although sometimes forgotten, part of a balanced meal. What do you feel like? A grain like rice, barley, or cracked wheat? Pasta, noodles, or whole wheat spaghetti? Or perhaps a high-carb vegetable like sweet corn, sweet potato, or legumes? Include at least one low-GI carb per meal.

2 is for protein

Include some protein at each meal. It lowers the glycemic load by replacing *some* of the carbohydrate—not all! It also helps satisfy the appetite.

3 is for fruits and vegetables

This is the part we often go without. If anything it should have the highest priority in a meal, but a meal based solely on fruit and low-carb vegetables won't be sustaining for long. A plain salad is a recipe for hunger.

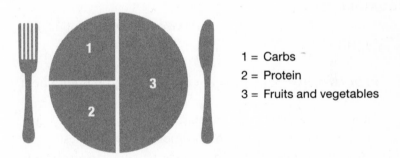

1 = Carbs
2 = Protein
3 = Fruits and vegetables

The plate model is adaptable to any serving sizes.

▶ As long you keep food to the proportions shown here, the meal will be balanced.
▶ As long as the types of food you choose fit within the guidelines for healthy eating, then you should have a healthy diet overall.

☛ **Health tip:**

Choose healthy foods that you like eating—put them together to make balanced, low-GI meals.

BREAKFASTS THAT SUSTAIN YOU THROUGH THE MORNING

No doubt you know it's a good idea to eat breakfast if you want to keep healthy, but did you realize that your food choices may also be a critical factor? Firing up your engine with high-GI crispy flakes or soft, light toast provides a short-lived fuel supply that will send you in search of a snack within a few hours. If you want something to nourish your body and sustain you right through the morning, follow our breakfast basics.

Breakfast basics
Choose foods from each group—carbohydrate, protein, and fruits and vegetables.

1. **Carbohydrate**—breakfast cereal, bread, buckwheat pancakes
2. **Protein**—low-fat milk, calcium-enriched soy milk, low-fat yogurt, eggs, tofu, lean ham or bacon, sardines or a little cheese
3. **Fruits and vegetables**—the choice is yours, fresh, frozen, or canned fruits and vegetables, dried fruit, fruit or vegetable juice

☛ **Health tip:**

A healthy breakfast including whole grains and fruit is a great start in meeting your daily fiber intake.

Eating breakfast can improve:

▶ speed in short-term memory tests

▶ alertness, which may help with memory and learning

▶ mood, calmness, and reduce feelings of stress

Breakfast also helps schoolchildren do better in creativity tests.

Seven everyday low-GI breakfasts

Kaye's Favorite Breakfast

1. **Carbohydrate**: natural muesli
2. **Protein**: skim milk, low-fat plain yogurt
3. **Fruit**: strawberries

Add a little skim milk to a big bowl of natural muesli to moisten, plus a generous dollop of low-fat plain yogurt. Top with a handful of chopped strawberries (or any other fruit).

Creamy Oatmeal

1. **Carbohydrate**: rolled oats
2. **Protein**: skim milk
3. **Fruit**: raisins, honey

Cook traditional rolled oats according to the package instructions in skim milk to make a creamier cereal. Serve topped with a scattering of raisins and a drizzle of honey.

Fruit Toast with Ricotta and Pear

1. **Carbohydrate**: dense fruit and-nut-bread
2. **Protein**: reduced-fat ricotta cheese
3. **Fruit**: pear

Spread thick slices of a dense fruit-and-nut bread with reduced-fat ricotta cheese and top with sliced fresh pear (peeled if you prefer). Sprinkle with cinnamon sugar to serve.

Eggs with Mushrooms and Parsley
1. **Carbohydrate**: soy-and-flaxseed bread
2. **Protein**: eggs
3. **Vegetables**: mushrooms, parsley

Slice a generous handful of mushrooms and cook in a little olive oil. When softened, add some fresh chopped parsley and season with salt and pepper if desired. Serve on toasted soy-and-flaxseed bread with poached or scrambled eggs. A grilled tomato alongside makes this breakfast extra tasty.

Oats with Apple, Raisins, and Almonds
1. **Carbohydrate**: rolled oats
2. **Protein**: skim milk
3. **Fruit and nuts:** apple, raisins, almonds

Soak traditional rolled oats in skim milk in the refrigerator overnight. Next morning add 1 grated Granny Smith apple, a small handful of raisins, and a sprinkle of slivered almonds, stir and serve.

Smoothie On the Go
1. **Carbohydrate**: processed bran cereal
2. **Protein**: low-fat milk, low-fat yogurt
3. **Fruit**: banana, honey

Something to think about . . .

At the same time that obesity in American adults doubled, the proportion of adults skipping breakfast increased twofold.

Combine 1 banana, 1 tablespoon of bran cereal, 1 cup of low-fat milk, 2 teaspoons of honey, and 3½ ounces of low-fat yogurt in a blender. Blend until smooth and thick.

Lazy Weekend French Toast
1. **Carbohydrate**: sourdough bread
2. **Protein**: eggs, skim milk
3. **Fruit**: pear or apple

Beat together 2 eggs, ¼ cup of skim milk, and 1 teaspoon of pure vanilla extract. Dip 4 thick slices of sourdough bread in the egg mixture, then cook over medium heat in a lightly greased nonstick fryingpan for 2–3 minutes on each side until golden. Serve topped with pan-fried pear or apple slices and a sprinkling of cinnamon.

Did you know?

Highly processed breakfast cereals are some of the highest-GI foods and cost a lot more than traditional cereal grains such as oatmeal.

LIGHT & LOW, THE SMART CARB LUNCH

It is important to take a break and refuel properly at lunchtime. A healthy low-GI lunch will help maintain energy levels and concentration throughout the afternoon and reduce the temptation to snack on something indulgent later in the day. It does not need to be a big meal. In fact, if you find yourself feeling sleepy in the afternoon, cut back on the carbs and boost the protein and light vegetables at lunchtime. (Of course a cup of coffee may help too!). Try these light meal suggestions for lunch—or for dinner if you prefer to eat your main meal at lunchtime.

Lunch and light meal basics

Choose a food or foods from each group—carbs, protein, and fruits and vegetables.

1. **Start** with a low-GI carb such as whole-grain or sourdough bread, pasta, noodles, sweet corn, or canned mixed beans.
2. **Add** some protein, such as fresh or canned salmon or tuna, lean meat, sliced chicken, reduced-fat cheese, or egg.
3. **Plus** vegetables or salad to help fill you up. A large salad made with a variety of vegetables would be ideal. Round off the meal with fruit.

Seven everyday low GI lunches and light meals

Minestrone and Toast
1. **Carbohydrate**: beans, pasta, sweet potato, barley, rice, low-GI bread
2. **Protein**: Parmesan, beans
3. **Vegetables**: tomato, carrots, onion, celery, and other soup vegetables

When making minestrone yourself or buying it ready-made, choose a filling combination that includes legumes and plenty of chopped vegetables. Serve topped with some freshly shaved Parmesan and enjoy with low-GI toast or a crusty grainy roll.

☛ Health tip:

Of all foods eaten by populations around the world, legumes are associated with the longest lifespan. Aim to include them at least twice a week.

Snack Bar Sandwich
1. **Carbohydrate**: mixed-grain, soy and flaxseed, or seeded bread, such as rye bread
2. **Protein**: canned salmon, tuna, or hardboiled egg
3. **Vegetables**: tomato, sprouts, grated carrot, finely sliced onion rings, mixed salad greens

Try a smear of mayonnaise on the bread instead of margarine.

Vegetarian Roll-ups
1. **Carbohydrate**: whole-grain flatbread, hummus
2. **Protein**: reduced-fat cheese, hummus
3. **Vegetables**: tabbouleh, shredded lettuce

Spread flatbread with hummus, roll up around a filling of tabbouleh and shredded lettuce sprinkled with grated cheese, and warm through in a toaster oven.

Mexican Bean Tortilla
1. **Carbohydrate**: Mexican beans (red kidney beans in a tomato and mild chili sauce), corn tortilla
2. **Protein**: reduced-fat cheese, red kidney beans
3. **Vegetables**: avocado, shredded lettuce, sliced tomato

Warm ½ cup of beans and serve in a corn tortilla with 2–3 avocado slices, lots of shredded lettuce, tomato slices, and grated reduced-fat cheese.

Egg-Drop Soup
1. **Carbohydrate**: vermicelli noodles, creamed sweet corn
2. **Protein**: chicken stock, chicken, egg
3. **Vegetables**: carrot, shallots

Bring 2 cups of chicken stock to a boil, add a handful of dry vermicelli noodles, and 1 finely diced carrot. Cook the noodles and carrot for 3–4 minutes, then stir in ½ cup of creamed corn, strips of cooked chicken (a great way to use leftovers), and chopped shallots. Heat through. Beat 1 egg and slowly pour it into the boiling soup in a thin stream, stirring quickly.

Tasty soups for light meals and lunches

▶ lentil and spinach soup

▶ split pea and ham soup

▶ chicken and sweet corn soup

▶ miso broth with noodles and tofu

▶ bean soup

▶ barley soup

▶ pumpkin soup

▶ mushroom soup

Frittata

1. **Carbohydrate**: sweet potato, sweet corn kernels
2. **Protein**: egg, skim milk, lean ham, reduced-fat cheese
3. **Vegetables**: zucchini, red and green pepper, tomato, onion, mushroom, shallots, and parsley

Stir-fry about 1 cup of chopped vegetables with 2 slices of chopped ham in a little oil until soft. Beat 2 eggs with ½ cup of skim milk and season with freshly ground black pepper and 1 tablespoon of chopped parsley. Pour the egg mixture over the vegetables and cook over a low heat (preferably covered) until set. Sprinkle a little grated cheese over the top and brown under a broiler.

Legumes

Versatile, filling, nutritious legumes are low in calories and provide a valuable source of protein and carbs, which is why we include them as both a carb and protein food in our ingredient list.

Salmon Salad with Chili Dressing

1. **Carbohydrate**: sourdough or whole-grain bread
2. **Protein**: salmon
3. **Vegetables**: cherry tomatoes, red onion, red and yellow pepper, mixed salad, and baby spinach leaves

Combine 1 small can of red salmon (drained and flaked) with ½ pint of cherry tomatoes, slices of red onion, red and yellow pepper strips, and mixed salad and baby spinach leaves. Toss in a chili dressing made from olive oil, lemon juice, and minced chili pepper and serve with bread or a crusty roll.

TAKE TIME OVER ONE MAIN MEAL EVERY DAY

What to make for dinner is the perennial question. Most people know that eating well is important, but it can be hard to get motivated to cook at the end of a long day. You don't have to spend hours preparing. If your cupboards and refrigerator are stocked with the right foods, you should be able to put a meal together in under 30 minutes.

Involve everybody at mealtimes

When you can, involve everybody in the household in choosing and preparing meals. Even if you love cooking, it's fun having a helper—someone to spin the lettuce, turn the meat, set the table, or simply talk to while you chop or stir, etc. It's also a great opportunity to find out about what's happening in other family members' lives! Lots of our readers say they hate cooking, but preparing and cooking meals is an integral part of healthy eating. Easy meals for family and friends can revolve around platters of foods on the table from which everyone can serve themselves. This avoids any complaints about being served foods they don't like.

If you live alone . . .

If you live alone, why not prepare food for two and put a meal away for another night? To avoid overeating on the night you cook, divide up all the food before you sit down to eat. Make use of partially prepared convenience foods such as chopped salads, filled pastas, and frozen mixed vegetables to make meal preparation a little easier.

If you like using frozen meals, choose a low-fat type and add your own cooked vegetables to fill in the gaps. Make a point of taking time over your meal and enjoy what you're eating. Don't gulp it down without thinking in front of the television—you can end up eating more than you should. The experts have even given this habit a name: "mindless eating."

Eating together as a family not only improves relationships but eating habits, too. In a recent study, researchers found that children who regularly ate dinner at home had:

▶ higher intakes of fruits and vegetables
▶ higher nutrient intakes
▶ lower intakes of soft drinks and fried food
▶ lower saturated fat intakes as a proportion of their total energy intake

Main meal basics

Choose a food or foods from each group—carbs, protein, and fruits and vegetables.

1. **Start** with a low-GI carb such as sweet potato, pasta, noodles, sweet corn, legumes.
2. **Add** some protein such as lean meat or chicken, fish, or seafood, eggs and legumes.
3. **Plus** plenty of vegetables and salad to help fill you up—remember our plate model (page 49). A large salad made with a variety of vegetables would be ideal. Round out the meal with fruit.

Seven everyday low-GI main meals

Peppered Steak with Sweet Potato Mash
1. **Carbohydrate**: sweet potato (allow 4 ounces per person)
2. **Protein**: fillet, rump, or top round steak (allow 5 ounces per person)
3. **Vegetables**: mushrooms, green beans, salad vegetables, including tomato

Sprinkle steak with pepper seasoning and grill or pan-fry. Serve with steamed sweet potato mashed with low-fat milk, sliced mushrooms

Alcohol

If you like to have a drink, that's OK—there might even be some health benefits. Both red and white wines contain powerful antioxidants, which may work to reduce heart disease risk. But go easy. While studies show some health benefits in those who drink one to two standard drinks a day, compared to none at all, there is a very steep increase in health risk from increased consumption. 3½ ounces (for women) to 7 ounces (for men) of wine per day is the maximum recommended by health authorities. Keep in mind that alcohol:

▶ is addictive
▶ can be fattening
▶ contributes to dehydration

cooked in a little olive oil, steamed green beans, and a crisp salad tossed in a vinaigrette dressing.

Lamb and Veggies

1. **Carbohydrate**: canned or baby new potatoes (allow 2–3 per person), sweet corn on the cob (allow 1 small cob per person)
2. **Protein**: trimmed lamb loin chops or cutlets (allow 7 ounces per person) or lean lamb fillet (allow 5 ounces per person)
3. **Vegetables**: carrots, broccoli (allow ½ cup per person)

For extra flavor, coat the meat with a spice blend such as chermoula (a Moroccan marinade) or garlic and rosemary and allow to "dry marinate" for about 20 minutes. Barbecue or grill lamb (trim off the fat if you are cooking chops). Serve with steamed vegetables—baby new potatoes, corn on the cob, sliced carrots, and broccoli florets—and your favorite condiments.

Thai-style Kebabs

1. **Carbohydrate**: basmati rice
2. **Protein**: chicken, beef, firm white-fleshed fish, or tofu (allow 1 pound for 4 kebabs)
3. **Vegetables**: zucchini, onion, mushrooms (add extra vegetables such as red pepper if you like)

Prepare a marinade using the following ingredients: juice and grated rind of 2 limes, 1 teaspoon of crushed garlic, 1 tablespoon of grated ginger, 2 teaspoons of chopped chili, 1 tablespoon of chopped lemongrass and 1 tablespoon of chopped cilantro.

Marinate 1 pound of diced chicken, beef, firm fish, or tofu, 2 zucchinis sliced into rounds, 1 onion quartered and layers separated, and 8 mushrooms, halved (or quartered if they are large) for at least 20 minutes, longer if you have the time. Thread the different ingredients alternately on skewers, brush with a little oil and barbecue or grill for about 10 minutes, turning regularly and basting with the marinade. Serve with basmati rice and lime wedges.

Honey and Mustard Pork

1. **Carbohydrate**: baby new potatoes (allow 2–3 per person), or sweet potato (allow 4 ounces per person)
2. **Protein**: pork cutlets (allow 7 ounces per person)
3. **Vegetables**: red pepper, broccoli

Prepare a marinade with the following: 1 tablespoon of olive oil, 1 tablespoon of seeded mustard, 2 teaspoons of honey, 2 tablespoons of lemon juice, and freshly ground black pepper. Trim the fat off the pork cutlets, marinate for an hour, then pan-fry for about 5 minutes on each side. Cut the pepper into strips lengthwise and stir-fry in the remaining marinade. Serve with steamed broccoli florets and potato or sweet potato, spooning the juices over the meat. Serve with additional mustard or applesauce.

Spicy Fish with Rice and Vegetables

1. **Carbohydrate**: basmati rice
2. **Protein**: firm white fish fillets (allow 5 ounces per person)
3. **Vegetables**: frozen vegetable combination (peas, carrots, beans, sweet corn, etc.)

Brush firm white fish fillets with your favorite curry paste blended with some lemon juice. Pan-fry and serve with basmati rice and steamed vegetables.

Spaghetti with Tomato Salsa and Feta

1. **Carbohydrate**: spaghetti (or your favorite pasta shapes)
2. **Protein**: feta cheese
3. **Vegetables**: tomato, onion, basil, olives, salad vegetables

To make about 2 cups of salsa (enough for 4 people), chop 4 tomatoes, ½ red onion, a bunch of basil leaves, and 15 ounces of pitted kalamata olives and combine in a bowl. Toss cooked spaghetti in a little olive oil and top with the tomato salsa and 5 ounces of crumbled feta. Serve with a crisp green salad.

Red Lentil and Vegetable Curry

1. **Carbohydrate**: split red lentils, basmati rice
2. **Protein**: lentils, yogurt
3. **Vegetables**: onion, pumpkin, carrots, vegetable stock, spinach, cilantro

Cook 1 finely chopped onion in a little oil in a large frying pan until soft and golden. Add 2 tablespoons of curry paste, 14 ounces of diced pumpkin, 2 diced carrots, and ½ cup of split red lentils. Stir in 2 cups of vegetable stock and simmer, uncovered, until just cooked. Stir in the leaves from a bunch of spinach and simmer gently just until they wilt. Serve over steamed basmati rice with plain yogurt, topped with finely chopped fresh cilantro. Serves 4 people.

DESSERTS FOR
SWEET FINISHES

The idea of dessert puts a smile on everyone's face, but so often we keep sweet treats for special occasions. Well, you don't need to worry with these recipe ideas—they are easy, everyday fare made with just a few ingredients in a matter of minutes. Finishing your meal with something sweet can help signal satiety/satisfaction to the brain's appetite center, and keep you from hunting around the kitchen afterward. They're also a great source of fruit and calcium- and protein-rich dairy foods.

Seven everyday low-GI desserts

Caramelized Apples
Cut 4 apples into quarters, remove the core and seeds, and slice thinly. Cook in 1 tablespoon margarine for 4–5 minutes, or until golden. Reduce the heat and add 2 tablespoons brown sugar, stirring until it dissolves. Increase the heat and add ⅔ cup light evaporated milk and stir to combine and heat through. Serve the apples with the sauce and a dollop of low-fat plain yogurt.

Honey Banana Cups
Slice a large banana and halve 2 fresh passionfruit. Divide an 8-ounce container of low-fat honey-flavored yogurt between 2 small cups or glasses. Top with half the banana and one of the passionfruit. Top with the rest of the yogurt and remaining banana, finishing with the passionfruit. Serve with a coconut macaroon alongside.

☛ **Health tip:**

Low-fat dairy products generally contain more calcium, phosphorus, potassium, and magnesium than their full-fat counterparts. So, do your heart and your health a favor and eat lots of low-fat dairy.

Sugar

Many people pride themselves on not keeping sugar in their pantry, yet they have a bottle of fruit juice in the fridge. Sure, fruit juice does provide vitamin C and other phytonutrients, but it also contains about five teaspoons of sugar per glass, the same as a soft drink.

Sugar can be a concentrated source of calories, with few nutrients, but no moreso than a bottle of oil or alcoholic spirits or a stick of butter. It isn't advisable to consume sugar to excess, but you can use it in moderation without adversely affecting your health.

Strawberries with Honey Yogurt

Toss 2 pints of washed, hulled strawberries with 2 tablespoons of sugar in a frying pan for 5 minutes. Serve with low-fat plain yogurt combined with 1–2 tablespoons of honey, to taste.

Peaches with Cinnamon Ricotta

Beat 10½ ounces of low-fat ricotta cheese with 2 tablespoons of powdered sugar, ½ teaspoon of cinnamon, and ½ teaspoon of vanilla extract. Divide dollops of the mixture between 4 side plates and add a halved fresh peach (or any other fruit) and 2 almond biscotti.

Banana Split

Cut 4 bananas in half lengthwise and place in dessert bowls. Add 2 scoops of low-fat ice cream and top with the pulp of ½ passionfruit.

Summer Fruit Salsa

Dice a large mango, a handful of strawberries, and a peeled orange into ½ inch pieces. Mix with fresh passionfruit pulp and serve with low-fat ice cream or frozen yogurt.

Fruit Toast

Toast thick slices of raisin bread and spread with light cream cheese or ricotta sweetened with a teaspoonful of sugar and a few drops of vanilla extract. Top with fresh fruit: sliced banana, peach, or strawberries, or whole fresh blueberries or raspberries. Sprinkle with powdered sugar to serve.

TIME FOR A SNACK

Most people feel like eating every three to four hours. Eating frequently can help you avoid becoming too hungry and lessen the chance of overeating when meal times come around. Depending on what you choose, snacks can also make a valuable contribution to your vitamin and mineral intake.

How to make pita chips

Open out pita bread, spread lightly with bottled sweet chili sauce and grill until just crisp.

Quick snacks you can make anytime

- fresh fruit salad
- ice cubes made with fruit juice
- a handful of fresh or frozen grapes
- vegetable sticks with hummus or yogurt-based dip: cut fresh celery, cucumber, carrots, red pepper, and zucchini
- low-fat plain yogurt with fresh fruit
- a smoothie made with fruit and low-fat milk and yogurt
- a scoop (just one!) of low-fat ice cream
- hummus with pita bread
- a bowl of cereal with low-fat milk (Note: eating sweetened cereals dry is hazardous for teeth—always add milk.)

- a slice of fruit or raisin toast
- an apple muffin
- 2 oatmeal cookies with a slice of cheese and an apple
- whole-grain breakfast bars with milk

Bag lunch snacks

- a juicy orange
- a small banana
- a large peach or pear
- single-serving applesauce
- a handful of dried fruit and nut mix
- a handful of dried apricots, apple rings, or raisins
- a container of low-fat yogurt or a dairy dessert
- a nutrigrain bar
- low-fat cheese or cheese sticks
- popcorn
- 4 squares (1 ounce) of chocolate (very occasionally for a treat)

Hot snacks for cold days

- a small baked potato with reduced-fat sour cream
- a cup of vegetable soup with toast or crackers
- toasted sandwich on low-GI bread
- a small bowl of bean soup
- small serving of instant noodles with vegetables
- toasted fruit loaf or raisin bran lightly spread with margarine or low-fat ricotta
- low-GI toast lightly spread with Nutella, peanut butter, honey, or fruit spread

Nibbles

- a small handful of unsalted, roasted nuts
- a small handful of dried fruit and nut mix
- carrot, celery, and other vegetable sticks
- fruit platter—berries, orange segments, dried fruit, nuts, etc.
- marinated vegetable platter (use paper towel to soak up some of the oil before arranging the platter) with pita bread

Drinks

▶ a small glass of fruit juice (¾ cup)
▶ low-fat milk or calcium-enriched soy milk
▶ low-fat flavored milk
▶ warm flavored milk drink (Nestlé's Quik, etc.)
▶ a low-fat smoothie
▶ café latte or cappuccino with low-fat milk

☛ Health tip:

Make a delicious low-fat milkshake by combining a cup of low-fat milk with a tablespoon of skim milk powder, 2 tablespoons of low-fat vanilla yogurt, and a tablespoon of ice cream topping. Blend until frothy.

WHAT TO DRINK?

Water

It's calorie-free and cheap—surely two good reasons for drinking water. However, it isn't necessary to drink eight glasses a day. Food contributes at least one-third of our daily fluid requirement, so we need five to seven cups of fluid to make up the remainder. Aim to make at least two or three of these water.

Fruit juice

It's widely considered a healthy drink, but if your diet includes fruits and vegetables, fruit juice really isn't necessary. If you like to include it, one glass a day is enough, and think of it as a (low-fiber) serving of fruit.

Tea

Drinking a cup of tea often provides the opportunity to take time out and relax—there is a benefit in this. Tea has also been recognized recently as a valuable source of antioxidants that may protect against several forms of cancer, cardiovascular disease, kidney stones, bacterial infection, and dental cavities. A maximum of three cups of tea a day is recommended.

Coffee
Did you know that 80 percent of the world's population consumes caffeine daily? For most people two cups of coffee a day is recommended, but if you are pregnant, caffeine sensitive, or have high blood pressure it is probably best to cut down to one cup per day. Both tea and coffee are a major source of antioxidants in the diet, simply because they are so widely and frequently consumed.

Milk
Milk is a valuable source of nutrients for adults and children, but, being a liquid, it is easily overconsumed. Think of it as food in liquid form. Recommended intakes vary for different ages, but for normal, healthy, nonpregnant adults, around 1¼–2 cups (or 10–15 fluid ounces) of low-fat milk a day is suitable.

> Some sports drinks, such as Gatorade, have a high GI. To "beat the heat" with a low-GI drink, opt for low-carb sports drinks or mineral water with freshly squeezed fruit juice to hydrate and to sustain energy without excess calories.

LIVING EVERYDAY LOW GI EATING

Five typical menus
Wondering if you can really make this low-GI diet work for you? Here's how some of our readers have changed to everyday low GI eating.

Three tips for making the switch

1. Start with something easy.
2. Do it gradually.
3. Don't expect 100 percent.

Barbara, 65, small eater

"When I gave up work to become a full-time homemaker I found I piled on the weight—and I wasn't happy about that at all! I keep myself busy looking after the house, my husband, and my three young grandchildren several times a week. To get myself back into shape, I go for a brisk walk for at least 20 minutes, sometimes 40 minutes, in the morning, as often as I can. I've been eating low-GI food for a year now and I'm used to it. That's just the way I (and my husband) eat now. I've lost 22 pounds so far—down to 180 pounds, but I'd like to lose a lot more!"

Breakfast
▶ small cranberry juice
▶ ⅔ cup Grapenuts with ½ cup low-fat milk
▶ green tea with 1 sugar

Mid-morning
▶ low-fat yogurt
▶ 1 fresh apricot

Lunch
▶ cheese and tomato sandwich on multigrain bread (with light margarine)
▶ white or green tea

Mid-afternoon
▶ peach

Dinner
- grilled trout fillet
- 2 small baked potatoes
- mixed salad
- low-fat ice cream in cone

After-dinner snack
- small bunch of grapes
- 6 almonds

Harry, 55, medium eater

"I am on the road as a sales rep. I'd like to lose weight to look better—I actually need to lose about 45 pounds. Because my job is quite sedentary—I spend so much time sitting at a desk or behind the wheel of a car—I make the effort to walk for half an hour most weekday mornings. On the weekend I'll do a longer walk for an hour or so. So far I have lost 18 pounds. I'm now a three-meals-a-day person and I'll eat in between if I get hungry. It was a big change for me to start eating breakfast."

Breakfast
- 2 slices of multigrain toast spread with light margarine plus 2 slices of low-fat processed cheese and half a tomato
- 1 banana

Mid-morning
- small cappuccino

Lunch
- 1 bowl miso soup
- grilled chicken without the skin
- salad
- 1 cup boiled long-grain rice

Dinner
- 1 cup spaghetti
- 1 cup meat and tomato sauce
- 1 cup green salad
- 1 banana
- 1 peach
- 3½ ounces fat-free yogurt
- glass of chardonnay

Fiona, 38, medium eater
"I have a more-than-full-time, stressful job and work long hours. I have little time for planned exercise, so rely on 'incidental exercise' around the office or shopping, etc. I am not trying to lose weight—but I don't want to gain any! So I am careful with my diet and fussy about the food I eat. I take my lunch to work—it saves time and I know I am eating healthily!"

Breakfast
- small freshly squeezed orange juice
- ½ cup muesli with plain yogurt
- a nectarine
- tea with low-fat milk

Mid-morning
- nut bar
- tea with low-fat milk

Lunch
- 2–3 slices multigrain bread, no butter
- mixed salad
- 3½-ounce can tuna or salmon
- salad dressing
- grapes

Mid-afternoon
- coffee with low-fat milk, no sugar
- low-fat fruit yogurt
- an apple

Dinner
- 5 ounces chicken strips
- 1 cup stir-fried noodles
- 2 cups stir-fried vegetables

After-dinner snack
- 2 scoops of low-fat ice cream or a chocolate chip cookie

Did you know?

Eating just half a cup of broccoli each week is enough to boost your health. Imagine what more could do!

David, 50, bigger eater

"I work full time as a warehouse manager, which I guess could be classified as 'light activity'—my job certainly gives me a good level of incidental activity. I socialize a fair bit and go square dancing twice a week. I have lost 22 pounds and am now maintaining stable weight. I wouldn't really say I'm on a diet. We just eat well, we made a few changes to our bread, and I eat more fruit than I used to."

Breakfast
- ¾ cup Special K with ¼ cup All-Bran with ¾ cup low-fat milk
- ½ sliced banana

Mid-morning
- an apple and a banana

Lunch
- 4 slices 9-grain bread
- low-fat cheese and ham
- pickles, tomato, lettuce
- diet drink

Mid-afternoon
- 3–4 oatmeal cookies or homemade muesli
- coffee with low-fat milk, no sugar

Dinner
- lean steak
- 2 new potatoes, plus a chunk of sweet potato
- mini corn on the cob
- broccoli, carrots, pumpkin, beans

Dessert
- canned fruit and ½ cup low-fat custard

Vicki, 29, medium eater
"I am a vegetarian but I do eat dairy foods. I work full time in an office. I catch a train to work so I accumulate about 30 minutes of walking each day. On the weekends I do lots of outdoors things—go to the beach, swim, walks. Although I don't need to watch my weight, I am aware that I need to get plenty of iron from my diet. Eating low-GI foods, I just feel better and have more energy to do things. It's the ideal way of eating to me!"

Breakfast
- 1 cup All-Bran cereal with 1 teaspoon flaxseeds, 2 tablespoons low-fat plain yogurt, skim milk, and a small handful of raisins
- skim latte (decaf!)

Mid-morning
- nectarine
- herbal tea

Lunch
▸ Avocado sushi roll, tofu sushi roll

Mid-afternoon
▸ a peach and a small handful of cashews
▸ tea with milk

Dinner
▸ 2 tortillas with red kidney bean and lentil chili sauce with light sour cream, grated cheese, and lettuce
▸ Green side salad with vinaigrette

Did you know?

A 3-ounce package of instant noodles supplies as many calories as five slices of bread. Low-GI they may be, but low-calorie they definitely are not.

CLUED IN ON EATING OUT?

Often it's the high-calorie foods you unknowingly choose from the menu that tip your healthy eating plans out of balance. If you eat out more than once a week, it's worth thinking about what you're actually eating. Check out your knowledge with this quick quiz.

Which of these has the lowest fat content?
a) combination Chinese meal with fried rice/lemon chicken/sweet and sour pork
b) lasagna with meat
c) Japanese bento box including beef with rice, sushi, and salad
d) fish and chips, including battered fish

Which is the lowest-calorie option for a coffee break?
a) skim-milk hot chocolate
b) cappuccino
c) skim-milk latte

Which drink is less fattening?
a) vodka and orange juice
b) Corona beer
c) glass of wine

Which is the healthiest fast-food snack?
a) 2 slices of super-supreme pizza
b) roast chicken Subway sub with cheese
c) chicken burger

Which light meal is a low-GI choice?
a) grilled chicken, avocado, pepper and cheese toasted Italian bread sandwich
b) potato wedges with sour cream and sweet chili
c) fettuccine Napolitana

Which makes the healthiest café snack?
a) chunky raisin toast and butter
b) skim-milk banana smoothie
c) carrot cake

The secrets revealed

Which of these has the lowest fat content?
The meat lasagna is the lowest fat option here, with an average serving containing only 16 grams of fat. Next is the Japanese bento box at 33 grams; fish and chips at 35; and a massive 40 grams in the Chinese meal.

Which is the lowest-calorie option for a coffee break?

The skim latte is the winner here in terms of calories (80 calories, 0.5 grams fat) and has the added bonus of extra calcium. Although the hot chocolate is made with skim milk it has twice the calories (160 calories) and eight times the fat. The cappuccino is in between at 90 calories and 5 grams of fat.

Which drink is less fattening?

Depending on your knowledge of alcoholic beverages, you might have guessed that the glass of wine is least fattening, containing the lowest number of calories. It's closely followed by the beer at 130 calories, and the Screwdriver (vodka and orange juice) tops the list at 210 calories per serving. That's as much as three slices of bread!

Which is the healthiest fast-food snack?

Subway fast food can be a lower-calorie snack, depending on your toppings, but it whacks a pretty high glycemic load on your plate with even the standard sub containing 44 grams of carbohydrate, and bread that is probably high GI (it hasn't been tested). None of the other options here are any better in the GI stakes and are all higher in calories.

Which light meal is a low-GI choice?

Pasta has a low GI, so the fettuccine is the best option. Potato and refined flour in the other choices make them high GI. All of these options will have a high GL because of their large carbohydrate content, so team the pasta with salad and pass on the garlic bread!

Which makes the healthiest café snack?

Sustaining, nutritious, and delicious—how can you beat a banana smoothie for a premium low-GI snack? The raisin toast also has a low GI, but is best with the butter served separately so you control the amount.

MAKING THE RIGHT CHOICES WHEN EATING OUT

Fast-food restaurants

Burgers and french fries are a bad idea—quickly eaten, high in saturated fat, and rapidly absorbed high-GI carbs that fill you with calories that don't last long. Some fast-food chains are introducing healthier choices but read the fine print. Look out for lean protein, low-GI carbs, good fats, and lots of vegetables.

You can choose:

▶ marinated and barbecued chicken, rather than fried
▶ **salads** such as coleslaw or garden salad; eat the salad first
▶ **corn on the cob** as a healthy side order
▶ **individual menu items** rather than buffets, and never super-size

Lunch bars

Steer clear of places displaying lots of deep-fried fare and head toward fresh-food bars offering fruits and vegetables. Containers of garden or Greek salad topped with fruit and yogurt make a healthy, low-GI choice.

With sandwiches and melts, choose the fillings carefully. Including cheese can make the fat exceed 20 grams per sandwich (that's as much as chips!).

Make sure you include some vegetables or salad in or alongside the sandwich.

You can choose:

▶ **mixed-grain** bread rather than white
▶ **salad** fillings for sandwiches or as a side order instead of fries
▶ **pasta** dishes with both vegetables and meat
▶ **kebabs** with tabbouleh and hummus

- **grilled fish** rather than fried
- **vegetarian pizza**
- **gourmet wraps**

In cafés

Whether it's a quick snack or a main meal, catching up with a friend for coffee doesn't have to tip your diet off balance. Pass on breads, but if you really must, something like a dense Italian bread is better than a garlic or herb bread.

Whatever you order, specify: "no french fries—extra salad instead" so temptation does not confront you. If you want something sweet try a skim iced chocolate or a single little biscotti.

You can choose:

- skim milk for your coffee rather than whole milk
- **sourdough or whole-grain bread** instead of white or whole wheat
- **bruschetta** with tomatoes, onions, olive oil, and basil on a dense Italian bread rather than buttery herb or garlic bread
- **salad** as a main course or side order, with the dressing served separately so you control the amount
- **grilled steak or chicken breast** rather than fried or breaded
- **vegetable-topped pizza**—such as pepper, onion, mushroom, artichoke, eggplant
- **lean-meat pizza**—such as ham, fresh seafood, or sliced chicken breast
- **pasta** with sauces such as marinara, bolognese; napolitana, arrabiata (tomato with olives, roasted pepper, and chili), and piccolo (eggplant, roasted pepper, and artichoke)
- **seafood** such as marinated calamari, grilled with chili, and lemon, or steamed mussels with a tomato sauce
- **water, mineral water, or freshly squeezed fruit and vegetable** juices rather than soft drinks

Asian meals

Asian meals, including Chinese, Thai, Indian, and Japanese, offer a great variety of foods, making it possible to select a healthy meal with some careful choices.

Keeping in line with the 1, 2, 3 steps to a balanced meal, seek out a low-GI carb such as basmati rice, dal, sushi, or noodles. Chinese and Thai rice will traditionally be jasmine, and although high GI, a small serving of steamed rice is better for you than fried rice or noodles.

Next, add some protein—marinated tofu, stir-fried seafood, tandoori chicken, fish tikka, or a braised dish with vegetables. Be cautious with pork and duck, for which fattier cuts are often used; and avoid Thai curries and dishes made with coconut milk because it's high in saturated fat.

And don't forget, the third dish to order is stir-fried vegetables!

You can choose:

▶ **steamed dumplings, dim sums, or fresh spring rolls** rather than fried entrées
▶ **clear soups** to fill you up, rather than high-fat laksa (a curry-based noodle dish)
▶ **noodles** in soups rather than fried in dishes such as pad Thai
▶ **noodle and vegetable stir-fries**—if you ask for extra vegetables you may find that one order feeds two
▶ **seafood** braised in a sauce with vegetables
▶ **tofu (bean curd), chicken, beef, lamb, or pork fillet** braised with nuts, vegetables, black bean, or other sauces
▶ **salads** such as Thai salads
▶ **smaller servings of rice**
▶ **vegetable dishes** such as stir-fried vegetables, vegetable curry, dal, channa (a delicious chickpea curry), and side orders such as pickles, cucumber, and yogurt, tomato, and onion
▶ **Japanese dishes** such as sushi, teriyaki, sashimi, salmon steak, or tuna, teppanyaki (which is grilled) in contrast to tempura, which is deep-fried

Did you know?

In supermarkets, more expensive items tend to be placed in the line of sight of consumers. So look up and down.

Airlines and airports

Airports are notoriously bad places to eat. Fast-food chains, a limited range, premade sandwiches, sad-looking cakes, a lack of fresh fruits and vegetables, and expensive!

In airline lounges you will do better, although, again, the range is limited. Fresh fruit is always on offer and usually some sort of vegetables either as salad or soup. The bread is usually the super-high-GI white French type and with crackers as the only other option, you would do better to rely on fruit, fruit juices, yogurt, or coffee with skim milk for your carbs.

In-flight, unless you have the privilege of a sky chef, meals are fairly standard fare, including a salad and fruit if you're lucky. Many airlines offer special diets with advance bookings, and although there's no guarantee it meets your nutritional criteria, it may give you healthier choices compared to what everyone else is having.

Traveling coach these days, it's probably best to eat before you leave, take your own snacks with you, and decline the in-flight snack (you really will be better off without that mini chocolate bar, cookie, cake, or muffin, and on some airlines you have to pay for it).

You can choose to eat:

- **fresh fruit, soup, and salad items** in airline lounges rather than white bread, cheese, cakes, and salami
- **small meals** in-flight, rather than eating everything put in front of you
- **water** to drink, wherever you are
- **dried fruit, nut bars, bananas, or apples** that you have taken along yourself

WHAT TO PUT IN THE SHOPPING CART

The perfect place to get started on healthy low GI eating is the supermarket, whether you are pushing a cart up and down the aisles, or shopping online. This is where we make those hurried or impulsive decisions that have a big impact. Cadbury's milk chocolate is on sale, do you stock up or keep walking? One little decision—what a big impact.

Make a list

Spend a little time each day, or weekly if it suits, planning what to eat when. It makes life simpler. Meal planning is just writing down what you intend to eat for the main meals of the week, then checking your fridge and pantry for ingredients available and noting what you need to purchase. We've included more ideas on meal planning in the menu section on pages 50–67. So study the GI tables, look at the meal ideas in this book, and browse through some recipes with a notepad handy.

The list on pages 87–91 is just to get you started. Bear in mind that it doesn't contain all low-GI foods, and individual choices will be dictated by your tastes and budget. Make a photocopy and take it with you to the store if you like, or just use it for ideas. For more tips on what to pop in the cart and stock in your pantry, check out Part 3: Top 100 Low GI Food Finder.

WHY IT'S IMPORTANT
TO READ THE LABEL

Often we're asked questions like: "What should I look for on the label?" and "Can I believe what it says?"

Reading the fine print

Remember, the GI alone doesn't identify a healthy food. If you like to keep some numbers in your head when you're shopping, then the following details are for you. Keep in mind that they are a general guide and shouldn't be used definitively to exclude or include foods in your diet.

☞ Health tip:

Remember, if you don't buy it, you can't eat it.

Nutritional Information

Servings per package: 3
Serving size: 5.29 ounces (150 grams)

	Quantity per serving	Quantity per 100 g
Energy	145 cal	96 cal
Protein	4.2 g	2.8 g
Fat, total	7.4 g	4.9 g
—saturated	4.5 g	3.0 g
Carbohydrate, total	18.6 g	12.4 g
—sugars	18.6 g	12.4 g
Sodium	90 mg	60 mg
Calcium	300 mg (30%)*	200 mg

*Percentage of recommended dietary intake

Ingredients: Whole milk, concentrated skim milk sugar, strawberries (9%), gelatine, culture, thickener (1442).

Energy—This is a measure of how many calories we get from a food. For a healthy diet we need to eat more foods with a low energy density and combine them with smaller amounts of higher-energy foods. To assess the energy density of a packaged food, look at the kcals per 100 grams. A low energy density is less than 120 kcals per 100 grams.

Fat—Seek low saturated fat content, ideally less than 20 percent of the total fat. For example, if the total fat content is 10 grams, you want saturated fat less to be than 2 grams. A food can be labeled as being low in saturated fat only if it contains less than 1 gram of saturated fat per 100 grams and the saturated fat provides less than 10 percent of the total energy of the product.

Total carbohydrate—This is the starch plus any naturally occurring and added sugars in the food. There's no need to look at the sugar figure separately, since it's the total carbohydrate that affects your blood glucose level. You could use the total carbohydrate figure if you were monitoring your carbohydrate intake and to calculate the GL of the serving. The GL = grams of total carbohydrate × GI/100.

Can I believe what it says?

Consumers are increasingly interested in what is in the food they eat. That's where the FDA's Office of Nutritional Products, Labeling, and Dietary Supplements (ONPLDS) comes in. As part of the Center for Food Safety and Applied Nutrition they are responsible for developing standards for food labeling to help us make informed choices about the food we buy and eat. Their principal role is to protect the health and safety of people in the United States through the maintenance of a safe food supply. For more information visit www.cfsan.fda.gov.

Fiber—Most of us don't eat enough fiber in our diet, so seek out foods that are high in fiber. A high-fiber food contains more than 3 grams of fiber per serving.

Sodium—This is a measure of the nasty part of salt, in our food. Our bodies need some salt, but most people consume far more than the 6 grams a day they need. Canned foods in particular tend to be high in sodium. Check the sodium content per 100 grams next time you buy—a low-sodium food contains less than 140 milligrams of sodium per 100 grams. Many packaged foods and convenience meals are well above this. Aim for less than 300 milligrams per 100 grams with convenience and ready-to-eat foods.

☞ Health tip:

Seventy-five percent of most people's salt intake comes from the supermarket (in processed foods and ready-to-eat meals) and from take-out. What can you do to cut down?

▶ check the labels for sodium content.

▶ never add salt to your food.

▶ minimize the frequency with which you eat salty foods.

How do you know if it's low, medium, or high GI?

When you're scanning the supermarket shelves, there's an easy way to identify nutritious foods that have been GI tested. This certification mark on a food label means that the food has been properly tested (according to the standardized method) and you can trust the GI value that's posted near the nutrition information panel. Unfortunately, some manufacturers make unverified and even false low GI claims.

Importantly, foods that carry the GI certification mark have been scientifically tested not just for their GI, but against a range of strict nutrient criteria. So you can be sure that the food is a healthier choice within its food group, no matter what the GI.

Things you should know about the GI symbol

▶ Foods that carry the certification mark are healthy in many respects. To be eligible, foods must meet other strict nutrient criteria relating to carbohydrate, total fat, salt, calories, and be a good source of fiber.

▶ Manufacturers pay a license fee to use the certification mark on their products. The fee is paid to GI Limited, a non-profit partnership between the University of Sydney, Diabetes Australia, and the Juvenile Diabetes Research Foundation. The fee helps to fund sensible, balanced communication about the GI, healthy eating, and research.

▶ High-GI foods can carry the symbol. Remember, you don't need to eat low GI all the time—an informed person can mix and match as he or she sees fit.

▶ If you have type 1 diabetes, you may need to consider the quantity of carbohydrate in each serving of food, in addition to the GI. Calculating the GL (grams of carbohydrate × GI/100) is one way of estimating the total glycemic effect.

▶ Beware of "low glycemic" claims. "Low glycemic" is a fuzzy term that can mean "low carb," not "slow carb." Only slow carbs deliver the "feel full" feeling and a host of other health benefits.

▶ A food may be reliably tested and not carry the certification mark. It's the manufacturer's choice, but as a consumer you may find it hard to distinguish between reliable and unreliable claims. Look for the GI symbol as your trusted signpost to healthier food choices.

▶ A comprehensive listing of the GI values of foods can be found in *The New Glucose Revolution Shopper's Guide to GI Values 2006*. The *Shopper's Guide* is updated every year. The 2006 edition will be available in November 2005.

▶ For more information about the certification mark, go to www.gisymbol.com.au

▶ To search a reliable GI database, go to www.glycemicindex.com

EVERYDAY LOW-GI SHOPPING

Having the staples on hand

Our shopping list will help you stock the pantry and fridge with the staples you require to turn out a meal in minutes. It includes everything you'll need for the low-GI meal ideas in the food finder.

To make your own shopping list, use the same headings. They will take you to the appropriate aisles of the supermarket or to the shops you usually favor.

We've included convenience foods such as canned beans, bagged salads, bottled sauces and pastes, canned fruits, and chopped vegetables (fresh and frozen) in the list. There's no need to feel guilty about using these items. Remember, this book is about making eating a healthy, low-GI diet as easy as possible and although some convenience items such as frozen vegetables or canned beans may be a little more expensive, the time savings and health benefits can outweigh the costs.

If you want to know more about some of the foods on the shopping list, check the food finder in Part 3. We have included lots of meal ideas and even some recipes in this section.

☞ Health tip:

We need to eat foods with fiber for bowel health and to keep regular. In fact, we need about 18 grams of fiber a day (most of us fall short of that—about 6 grams short). It's deliciously easy to increase your intake. Just make sure your shopping list includes high fiber breakfast cereals and oatmeal, whole-grain or granary breads, fresh fruits and vegetables, and canned (or dried) beans, peas, and lentils. You'll find plenty of ideas for using these low-GI high-fiber foods in our Top 100 Food Finder.

Your checkout choice

The GI Symbol program helps consumers make healthier food choices. Foods with the symbol are healthy nutritional choices for their food group have been through rigorous testing procedures.

The bakery

Fruit loaf
Low-GI bread
  Whole-grain

Sourdough
English muffins
Pita bread

The refrigerator section

Milk
  Low-fat
  Skim
  Low-fat flavored
Margarine, canola
Cheese
  Reduced-fat grated cheese
  Parmesan cheese
  Reduced-fat ricotta or cottage
    cheese
  Reduced-fat cheese slices
Yogurt
  Low-fat plain
  Low-fat fruit or vanilla
    flavored
  Low-fat drinking yogurt or
    kefir

Soy alternatives
  Low-fat calcium-enriched soy
    milk
  Soy yogurt
Dairy desserts
  Custard
Fruit juice
  Apple juice
  Orange juice
  Grapefruit juice
  Cranberry juice
Fresh noodles
Fresh pasta
  Ravioli
  Tortellini
Tofu
Sushi
Dips such as hummus

☛ Health tip:

Seventy-five percent of most people's salt intake comes from the supermarket (in processed foods) and from take-out meals. Check the labels for sodium content (see page 82), never add salt to your food, and minimize the frequency with which you eat salty foods.

☞ Health tip:

If they have been stored and cooked carefully, frozen vegetables can provide similar levels of nutrients to those of fresh vegetables, sometimes even more.

The freezer

Ice cream
  Reduced or low-fat vanilla or
    flavored
Frozen yogurt
Frozen fruit desserts or gelato
Frozen vegetables
  Peas
Beans
Corn
Spinach
Mixed vegetables
Stir-fry mix
Broccoli
Cauliflower

Fresh fruits and vegetables

Basics
  Sweet potato
  Taro
  Yam
  Sweet corn
  Lemons or limes
  Onions
  Carrots
  Garlic
  Ginger
  Chilis
Leafy green and other seasonal
  vegetables
  Spinach
  Cabbage
  Broccoli
  Cauliflower
  Asparagus
Asian greens such as
    bok choy
Leeks
Fennel
Snowpeas
Beans
Zucchini or squash
Brussels sprouts
Eggplant
Mushrooms
Salad vegetables, depending on
  season
  Lettuce (choose a variety)
  Arugula
  Tomato
  Cucumber
  Pepper
  Spring onions

Celery
Bagged mixed salad greens
Sprouts—mung bean,
   snowpea, alfalfa, etc.
Avocado
Fresh herbs, depending on
season
   Parsley
   Basil
   Mint
   Chives
   Coriander, cilantro

Fresh fruit, depending on
season
   Apples
   Oranges
   Pears
   Grapes
   Grapefruit
   Peaches
   Apricots
   Strawberries
   Mango

General groceries

Eggs
Beverages
   Tea
   Coffee
   Flavored milk powders such
      as Nestlé's Quik
Herbs, spices, condiments and
sauces
   Jar of minced ginger, garlic,
      chili
   Mustard
   Horseradish
   Tomato sauce

Asian sauces
   Soy sauce
   Bottled pasta sauce
   Jar of curry paste
Deli items or pre-packed jars
   Sundried tomatoes
   Olives
Spreads
   Pure honey
   Apricot jam
   Nutella
   Peanut butter

Did you know?

Highly processed breakfast cereals have high GI values,
not because they're high in sugar but because they're
high in refined starch.

Oils and vinegars
  Canola or olive oil cooking
    spray
  Olive oil
  Canola or vegetable oil
  Balsamic vinegar
  White wine vinegar
Breakfast cereals
  Traditional rolled oats
  Natural muesli
  Low-GI breakfast cereals
Cereals and whole grains
  Pasta
  Noodles, rice, buckwheat
  Rice—basmati or Uncle
    Ben's long-grain con-
    verted rice
  Couscous
  Bulgur/cracked wheat
  Pearl barley
  Oatmeal cookies
Dried legumes
  Beans—keep a variety in
    the cupboard including
    cannellini, navy, lima,
    kidney, soy, pinto, etc.
  Chickpeas
  Lentils
  Split peas

Canned foods
  Mexi-beans
  Chickpeas
  Lentils
  Beans—keep a variety in the
    cupboard including can-
    nellini, butter, navy, lima,
    kidney, soy, pinto, etc.
  Four-bean mix
  Corn kernels
  Tomatoes, whole, crushed,
    and tomato paste
  Tomato soup
  Tuna packed in spring water
    or oil
  Salmon packed in water
  Sardines
Canned fruit and single serv-
  ing containers
  Pears
  Peaches
  Mixed fruit salad
Dried fruit and nuts
  Apricots
  Raisins
  Prunes
  Apple rings
  Unsalted natural almonds,
    walnuts, cashews, etc.

Your everyday checkout choice

To increase iron intake choose lean red meat.

Butcher/meat department

Lean ham

Lean beef for grills, barbecues, and casseroles

Lean lamb fillets

Lean pork fillets

Lean ground beef

Chicken

Skinless chicken breast or drumsticks

Fish

Any type of fresh fish

Your everyday checkout choice

To cut back the fat, choose:

▶ lean cuts of meat and skinless chicken

▶ low-fat dairy and soy milk products

▶ vegetable oils and cooking sprays

▶ "lite" spreads and dressings

▶ tomato and pepper sauces and salsas to serve with pasta

☛ Health tip

Low iron levels can cause tiredness, physical weakness, and increased sensitivity to cold. Lean red meat is a rich and highly bio-available source of iron, so aim to include it in your diet at least three times a week.

READY . . . SET . . . GO— MOVE IT & LOSE IT!

When we explained the basics of everyday low GI eating at the beginning of this section, we mentioned that one of the golden rules is to accumulate 60 minutes of physical activity every day, including incidental activity and planned exercise. This will help you control your weight for a whole host of reasons. To make a real difference to your health and energy levels, exercise has to be regular and some of it needs to be aerobic. But every little bit counts—and, best of all, any extra exercise you do is a step in the right direction.

> Remember, all you have to do is accumulate 60 minutes of physical activity every day.

Though some people can make a serious commitment to 30-plus minutes of planned exercise three or four times a week, most of us have a long list of excuses. We're too busy, too tired, too rushed, too stressed, too hot, too cold to go to the gym or take a walk or do a regular exercise routine. But there's good news. Research tells us that the calories we burn in our everyday activities are important too, and that any amount of movement is better than none at all.

Changing the habits of a lifetime isn't easy. We know how hard it can be to find time to fit everything into a day, especially if you are working and have a family. That's why we suggest you move it *and* lose it with our "1, 2, 3 one step at a time, in your own time" approach.

1. **Start** with extra incidental activity.
2. **Add** time to move more.
3. **Plus** planned exercise—it's worth it.

> Think of extra incidental activity as an opportunity, not an inconvenience.

1. Start with extra incidental activity

Incidental activity is the exercise we accumulate each day as part of our normal routines—putting out the garbage, making the bed, doing chores, walking to the bus stop, going out for a coffee, and walking up a flight of stairs. If you make a conscious effort to increase the amount of this kind of activity in your day, it will eventually become second nature.

With just a little extra effort, here's how you can build more incidental physical activity into your life. You've probably heard these ideas before, so read this list as a timely reminder. It would be great if you could use just one of these ideas regularly.

▶ Use the stairs instead of taking the elevator. Walk up them as quickly as you can. Try taking them two at a time—to strengthen your legs.

▶ Don't stand still on the escalator—walk up and down.

▶ Take the long way around whenever you can—popping down to the corner store, getting a drink from the office water cooler, going to the bathroom.

▶ Make the time to walk your children to or from school.

▶ Catch up with a friend by meeting for a walk, rather than talking on the phone or over coffee.

▶ Get off your chair and talk to your colleagues rather than sending endless emails.

▶ Walk the dog instead of hitting tennis balls for him or her to chase and retrieve.

▶ Get rid of the leaf blower and rake the leaves or sweep the steps the old-fashioned way.

▶ Park the car at the opposite end of the parking lot and walk to the ATM, post office, or dry cleaners.

▶ Walk to a restaurant (or park a good distance from it) to force yourself to take a walk after dinner.

Think of extra incidental activity as an opportunity, not an inconvenience. The following table shows how "spending" five minutes here and there every day can add up to potential fat "savings" in the long term.

Take 5 minutes every day to:	Potential savings in grams of fat*	
	in 1 year	in 5 years
Take the stairs instead of the elevator	3,700	18,500
Vacuum the living room	700	3,500
Walk 1/10 of a mile from the car to the office	700	3,500
Carry the groceries 500 feet to the car	900	4,500

* Figures based on a 154-pound person

2. Add time to move more

Exercise is more likely to be achieved when scheduled into your day, just like any other appointment. So think about your day, make a note in your planner, and prioritize exercise. To reap the benefits, exercise doesn't have to be intense: exercise of moderate duration and intensity—including walking—is associated with reduced risk of disease. While brisk walking is best, even slow walkers benefit!

For most of us, walking fits the bill perfectly. It keeps us fit, it's cheap and convenient, it gets us out and about, and it becomes even more important as we grow older. You can walk alone, or with friends. In fact, talking while you walk can have important emotional benefits: Not only do our bodies produce calming hormones while we walk, but the talk itself can be great therapy—and good for relationships in general. But don't hesitate to walk alone if you prefer, or with your dog—your pet will love you all the more for it. And you'll be able to take some time to think and relax.

How often? Try to walk every day. Ideally you should accumulate 30 minutes or more on most days of the week. The good news is, you can do it in two 15-minute sessions or six 5-minute sessions. It doesn't matter.

How hard? You should be able to talk comfortably while you walk. Find a level that suits you. If you feel sore at first, don't worry; your body will adapt and the soreness will decrease. Stretching for 2 minutes before and after your walk will help minimize aches and pains.

Getting started Before beginning a walking (or any exercise) program, see your doctor if you have:

‣ been inactive for some time
‣ a history of heart disease or chest pains
‣ diabetes
‣ high blood pressure

Or if you:

‣ smoke
‣ weigh more than you should

☛ Health tip

For more information, step out and check out these walking programs:

www.thewalkingsite.com
www.walk.diabetes.org
www.pbs.org/americaswalking/

3. Plus planned exercise—it's worth it

Exercise and activity speed up your metabolic rate (increasing the amount of energy you use) which helps you to balance your food intake and control your weight. Exercise, and activity also make your muscles more sensitive to insulin and increase the amount of fat you burn.

A healthy low-GI diet has the same effect. Low-GI foods reduce

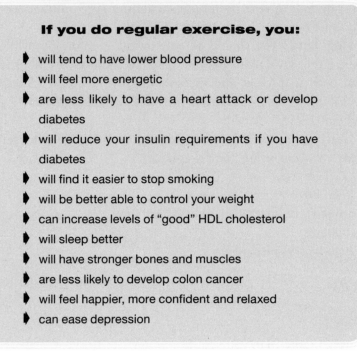

If you do regular exercise, you:

- will tend to have lower blood pressure
- will feel more energetic
- are less likely to have a heart attack or develop diabetes
- will reduce your insulin requirements if you have diabetes
- will find it easier to stop smoking
- will be better able to control your weight
- can increase levels of "good" HDL cholesterol
- will sleep better
- will have stronger bones and muscles
- are less likely to develop colon cancer
- will feel happier, more confident and relaxed
- can ease depression

the amount of insulin you need, which makes fat easier to burn and harder to store. Since body fat is what you want to get rid of when you lose weight, exercise or activity in combination with a low-GI diet makes a lot of sense.

Best of all, the effect of exercise doesn't end when you stop moving. People who exercise have higher metabolic rates and their bodies burn more calories per minute even when they are asleep!

If you are ready to improve your fitness, making a commitment to a planned exercise program, including aerobic, resistance, and flexibility/stretching exercises will give you the best results. Variety is also important.

Planned exercise doesn't mean having to sweat it out in a gym. The key is to find some activities you enjoy—and do them regularly. Just 30 minutes of moderate exercise each day can improve your health, reducing your risk of heart disease and type 2 diabetes. If

To achieve:

▶ 4,000 steps you need about 30 minutes of moderately paced walking

▶ 7,500 steps you need about 45 minutes of moderately paced walking

▶ 10,000 steps you need about 60 minutes of briskly paced walking

you prefer you can break this into two 15-minute sessions or three 10-minutes sessions. You'll still see the benefits. Remember, every little bit counts.

What about personal trainers?

Working with a personal trainer can be a great way to improve your health and fitness and work toward your goals. A good trainer will design an exercise program tailored to your needs and fitness level as well as providing motivation and support. Many personal trainers now provide services at a reasonable rate and you can choose to use a health club or train at home or outdoors. If cost is an issue, you could train with a small group of three or four others with similar fitness levels, or you could just have a few sessions initially. If you can, try to budget for at least 10 sessions. This will help you achieve your goals and increase your confidence with the new exercises.

To help you achieve your walking goal, clip a pedometer to your waistband or belt in the morning and start counting. Of course, the pedometer only counts steps and not any other activities.

How many steps will make a difference?

Go out and buy a cheap pedometer (step counter). Research has shown that every day we need to take about:

- ❑ 7,500 steps to maintain weight
- ❑ 10,000 steps to lose weight
- ❑ 12,500 steps to prevent weight regain

For most of us this means taking a walk on top of our incidental activity. In the normal course of a day—just living and working—it is virtually impossible (unless you deliver the mail or walk other people's dogs for a living!) to achieve that 10,000 steps a day.

The following table gives you an idea of how many steps are equivalent to 15 minutes of certain activities.

15 minutes of activity	Equivalent number of steps
Moderate sexual activity	500
Watering the garden	600
Vigorous sexual activity	750
Clearing and washing the dishes	900
Standing cooking at the grill	950
Standing while playing with kids	1100
Carpentry—general workshop	1200
Playing golf at the driving range	1200
Food shopping with a cart	1400
General house cleaning	1400
Sweeping and raking	1600
Digging the garden	2000
Mowing the lawn with a hand mower	2350
Moving furniture	2350
Carrying bricks or using heavy tools	3150

How to find a good personal trainer

Many trainers are attached to health clubs, but if you don't belong to one or you would prefer to train at home or outdoors, look in your local newspaper or search online for someone in your area. Ask to see their qualifications—they should have a certificate in personal training. A good trainer should offer you at least one complimentary session to "try before you buy."

Before starting . . .

If you have any concerns about your health, or any illnesses such as diabetes or heart problems or an injury, discuss your activity plan with your doctor first.

What to expect when you see a personal trainer

In your first session, a good personal trainer will ask you about your current lifestyle, your goals and expectations, and any health or medical problems. He or she will then work out a program to help you reach your goals and work closely with you to implement the plan, supervising each of your exercise sessions to make sure you are performing the exercises correctly and pushing you to next the level. He or she will also help to motivate you when you the going gets tough.

☛ Health Tip

Did you know that the benefits of exercise don't stop when you stop? People who exercise have higher metabolic rates and their bodies burn more calories per minute—even when they are sound asleep!

Here are some ideas to get you started

- aerobics
- aqua-aerobics
- cycling
- dancing
- exercise balls
- exercise bikes
- exercise classes
- exercise DVDs and videos
- golf
- health clubs and gyms
- paddling, rowing, and kayaking
- Pilates
- spinning classes
- surfing and bodysurfing
- swimming
- Ping-Pong
- tai chi
- team sports
- tennis, squash, and other racket sports
- treadmills
- weight training
- yoga

PART THREE

The Top 100: Low GI Food Finder

Everyone can benefit from the low-GI approach to eating.
It is the way nature intended us to eat—
slow-burning, nutritious foods that satisfy our hunger.

$\mathcal{J}$o pick the top 100 low-GI foods for healthy eating and to give you plenty of choice, we pushed our shopping cart up and down the supermarket aisles. We have listed the foods in this section from A to Z within the appropriate food group to make meal planning and shopping easier.

We are often asked about foods such as lean red meat, chicken, eggs, fish, and seafood—foods that don't have a GI because they don't contain carbs. As a result we have also included brief sections on these protein-rich foods because they are an important part of a healthy diet.

The food groups

When planning meals, choose foods from all the groups to make sure you gain the benefits of the 40+ essential nutrients along with

> ▶ Fruits and vegetables (page 106)
> ▶ Breads and cereals (page 146)
> ▶ Legumes including soybeans, chickpeas and lentils (page 185)
> ▶ Nuts and seeds (page 200)
> ▶ Fish and seafood (page 204)
> ▶ Lean red meat, poultry, eggs and tofu (page 206)
> ▶ Low-fat dairy products and dairy alternatives (page 208)

the protective antioxidants and phytochemicals your body needs each day for long-term health and well-being.

We have also included a few "borderline" low- to medium-GI foods as they are great additions to your diet.

Which brand?

Low GI eating often means making a move back to staple foods—legumes, whole-grain cereals, vegetables, and fruit—which naturally have a low GI, so it doesn't matter what brand you buy.

Knowing which brand to buy is important, however, when it comes to choosing carb-rich processed foods such as breads and breakfast cereals, whose GI values can range from low to high.

To find the GI of your favorite brands you can:

▶ Look for the certified GI symbol on foods. Ⓖ
▶ Check the nutritional label—some manufacturers include the GI.
▶ Visit **www.glycemicindex.com** to search a reliable database of GI values.
▶ Check the GI tables on page 223.

If you can't find the GI of your favorite breakfast cereal or bread, contact the manufacturer and suggest they have the food tested by an accredited laboratory.

GI values

A low GI value is 55 or less
A medium value is 56–69
A high GI value is 70 or more

Are you eating enough fiber?

Many low-GI foods are good sources of dietary fiber, which is a terrific bonus, since we need about 30 grams of fiber a day for bowel health and to keep regular. Filling, high-fiber foods can also help you maintain a healthy weight by reducing hunger pangs.

Dietary fiber comes from plant foods—it is found in the outer bran layers of grains (corn, oats, wheat and rice and in foods containing these grains), fruits and vegetables and nuts and legumes (dried beans, peas, and lentils). There are two types—soluble and insoluble—and there is a difference.

- *Soluble fibers* are the gel, gum, and often jelly-like components of apples, oats, and legumes. By slowing down the time it takes for food to pass through the stomach and small intestine, soluble fiber can lower the glycemic response to food.
- *Insoluble fibers* are dry and bran-like and commonly thought of as roughage. All cereal grains and products made from them that retain the outer layer of the grain are sources of insoluble fiber, e.g., whole-grain bread and All-Bran, but not all foods containing insoluble fiber are low GI. Insoluble fibers will only lower the GI of a food when they exist in their original, intact form, for example in whole-grains of wheat. Here they act as a

physical barrier, delaying access of digestive enzymes and water to the starch within the cereal grain.

A word on processed food

Try to avoid highly processed foods as much as possible. Think of it this way: you should do the processing, not the food company!

FRUITS & VEGETABLES

Fruits and vegetables play a central role in a low-GI diet. While we all remember being told to eat our greens, we now know that it's important to eat seven or more servings of fruits and vegetables every day for long-term health and well-being. The greater the variety, the better.

When it comes to fruits and vegetables think color, think variety, think protective antioxidants, and give these foods a starring role in your meals and snacks.

Green

▸ artichokes, arugula, Asian greens, asparagus, avocados, green beans, bok choy, broccoli, broccolini, Brussels sprouts, cabbage and Chinese cabbage, green pepper, celery, chard, chicory, cucumber, endive, green onions, leafy greens, leeks, lettuce, mesclun, okra, peas (including snowpeas and sugar snap peas), spinach, spring onions, sprouts, squash, watercress, zucchini
▸ green apples, figs, green grapes, honeydew melons, kiwi fruit, limes, green pears

Red/pink

▶ red pepper, radishes, red onions, tomatoes, yams
▶ red apples, blood oranges, cherries, cranberries, red grapes, pink/red grapefruit, guavas, plums, pomegranates, raspberries, rhubarb, strawberries, tamarillo, watermelon

White/cream

▶ bamboo shoots, cauliflower, celeriac, daikon, fennel, garlic, Jerusalem artichoke, kohlrabi, mushrooms, onions, parsnips, potatoes (white-fleshed), shallots, taro, turnips, white corn
▶ bananas, lychees, nectarines, white peaches, brown pears

Orange/yellow

▶ butternut squash, cantaloupe, carrots, yellow/orange pepper, pumpkin, squash, sweet corn, sweet potato, winter squash, yellow beets, yellow tomatoes
▶ yellow apples, apricots, cherimoya, gooseberries, grapefruit, lemons, mandarins, mangoes, nectarines, oranges, papaya, peaches, persimmons, pineapple, tangerines

Blue/purple

▶ beets, eggplant, purple asparagus, radicchio, red cabbage
▶ blackberries, blackcurrants, blueberries, boysenberries, purple figs, purple grapes, plums, raisins

Wash first

Wash all fruits and vegetables before you eat or cook them. If you are going to eat the skins, use a scrubbing brush on vegetables such as potatoes and carrots. For leafy vegetables such as cabbages and lettuce, remove the outer leaves first, then wash leaves individually and dry in a salad spinner.

Why are fruits and vegetables so important?

A high fruit and vegetable intake has been consistently linked to better health. It could be because they are packed with antioxidants—nature's personal bodyguards—which protect body cells from damage caused by pollutants and the natural aging process.

Here's how you can eat seven or more servings of fruits and vegetables a day.

☐ Top muesli or *breakfast* cereal with sliced fruit.

☐ Sip a small juice for a *morning snack*.

☐ Enjoy a vegetable soup or salad for *lunch*.

☐ Boost your brainpower *mid-afternoon* with a snack such as a handful of grapes, or crispbread topped with ricotta and tomato slices.

☐ Brighten your *dinner* plate with a variety of vegetables such as sweet potato, green beans, and red and yellow pepper plus a big salad.

☐ Finish your meal with a fruity *dessert* or a fruit platter.

Some key antioxidants

Beta-carotene—the plant form of vitamin A, used to maintain healthy skin and eyes. A diet rich in beta-carotene may even reduce damage caused by UV rays. Apricots, peaches, mangoes, carrots, broccoli, and sweet potato are particularly rich in beta-carotene.

Vitamin C—nature's water-soluble antioxidant found in virtually all fruits and vegetables. Some of the richest sources are guavas, pepper, oranges, kiwi fruit, and cantaloupe. Vitamin C is used to make collagen, the protein that gives our skin strength and elasticity.

Anthocyanins—the purple and red pigments in blackberries, blueberries, pepper, and eggplant also function as antioxidants, minimizing the damage to cell membranes that occurs with aging.

Fruits

Naturally sweet and filling, fruit is widely available, inexpensive, portable, and easy to eat—just like other snack foods, but without the added fat and sugar. So, buy the best you can and enjoy a lifetime of benefits.

The sugars in fruits and berries have provided energy in the human diet for millions of years. It shouldn't come as too much of a surprise, therefore, to learn that these sugars have low GI values. Fructose, in particular—a sugar that occurs naturally in all fruits and in pure honey—has the lowest GI of all. Fruit is also a good source of soluble and insoluble fibers, which can slow digestion and provide a low GI. And as a general rule, the more acidic a fruit is, the lower its GI value.

Temperate climate fruits—apples, pears, citrus (oranges, grapefruit), and stone fruits (peaches, plums, apricots)—all have low GI values.

Tropical fruits—pineapple, papaya, banana, canteloupe, and watermelon tend to have higher GI values, but their glycemic load (GL) is low because they are low in carbohydrate. So keep them in the fruit bowl and enjoy them every day if you wish, as they are excellent sources of antioxidants.

How much?
One serving is equivalent to:
- 1 medium piece of fresh fruit such as an apple, banana, mango, orange, peach or pear (about 4 ounces)
- 2 small pieces of fresh fruit such as apricots, kiwi fruit, or plums (about 2 ounces each)
- 1 cup of fresh diced or canned fruit pieces, including grapes and chopped berries and strawberries

▶ 4–5 dried apricot halves, apple rings, figs or prunes (about 1 ounce)
▶ 1½ tablespoons raisins (about 1 ounce)
▶ ¾ cup fruit juice, homemade or unsweetened, 100 percent juice

> People who eat three of four servings of fruit a day, particularly apples and oranges, have the lowest overall GI and the best blood glucose control.

How much a day?
▶ Smaller eaters: 2 servings
▶ Medium eaters: 3 servings
▶ Bigger eaters: 4 servings

Serving suggestions
1. Fruit is nature's take-out food. Carry fresh fruit or a small container of fruit pieces or dried fruit to snack on.
2. Top your breakfast cereal with fresh fruit such as berries and sliced bananas or add diced fruit to low-fat yogurt snacks.
3. Whip up smoothies or frappés with fresh fruit, juice, and low-fat yogurt or make fresh fruit ice cubes with juice or simply freeze some fruit!
4. Toss fresh fruit slices (apples, citrus segments, strawberries, pears) or whole grapes into crisp green salads. Add a few nuts and serve with a light oil and vinegar or citrus dressing.
5. Prepare a fruit platter (including grapes, strawberries, slices of melon, apple or pear, orange segments, etc.) for dessert or to nibble on while watching television; or keep a bowl of your favorite fruit within reach.
6. It's more likely to tempt you if it's right in front of you, so store fruit or vegetable pieces (such as diced melon or carrot sticks) in a clear container in the refrigerator.

7. Sliced pear, apple, banana, or pineapple make great toasted sandwich fillings.
8. Serve fresh fruit salsa with meat, chicken, or fish, or use as a salad dressing or dip.
9. Make fruit compotes for desserts or toppings for low-fat ice cream, pancakes, and waffles.
10. Try apple or pear slices with some cheese and whole-grain crackers or top grainy toast with thinly sliced peaches, strawberries, apples, or pears and a dollop of ricotta or cottage cheese.

Thirst-quencher

Eating fruit regularly is a great way to keep hydrated: some fruits such as watermelon contain up to 90 percent water. If you're not well hydrated, all your body functions, from joint lubrication and muscle contraction through to digestion and mental performance can be compromised.

Apples
GI 38

Apples are the ultimate portable snack. It's said that the Roman legions munched them as they marched and the *Mayflower* Pilgrims packed them when they set sail for America. Just one fresh apple will give you about one-third of your vitamin C needs for the day and by stimulating saliva it can also help prevent dental decay. Apples are a good source of dietary fiber, particularly pectin, which promotes a healthy balance of bacteria in the intestine. On top of this, apples, particularly the skins, are packed with antioxidants.

Simply wash, dry, and enjoy as a snack, skin and all (some people even eat the core), or eat one for a sweet finish to meals. Cooking apples is likely to raise the GI *slightly*.

Serving suggestions

▶ Add coarsely grated apple to your muesli or favorite low-GI breakfast cereal, or to muffin mixes when baking.

▶ Bake or microwave whole apples for a warm and filling dessert, or core and stuff with dried fruit, a little honey, and a sprinkle of cinnamon, then bake.

▶ Add apple slices to sandwiches and salads or serve apple slices with fruit and cheese platters.

▶ Slice into segments and use to make stewed apple with cloves, open apple tarts or apple crumbles with a crunchy toasted muesli topping.

Apple Rings, Dried
GI 29

A rich source of fiber, dried apple rings are great for lunch boxes, and a tasty ingredient to chop and add to muesli and other breakfast cereals, fruit and nut mixes, health bars and fruit slices, and desserts. Drying concentrates the calories, so count about 10 rings as a serving.

Serving suggestions

▶ Make a compote by microwaving or simmering dried apple with other fruits and a cinnamon stick in just enough water to cover.

▶ Soak dried apple in boiling water for about 30 minutes and use in desserts or baking or to make an applesauce for serving with meat.

Apple Juice
GI 40 (unsweetened)

Apple juice is a good source of vitamin C and potassium. The fiber, however, is lost during processing, along with many of the other nutrients in apple skin. When buying juice, look for unsweetened, 100 percent juice. To make your own, quarter and core two apples and cut into pieces that will fit into the food tube of your juicer, process, and enjoy a small glass of juice (¾ cup) as a snack or to finish a meal. Add sticks of celery, carrot, or a little fresh ginger for variety.

> For maximum health benefits, be choosy about the apple juice you buy. Look for brands with no added sugar and that are pressed whole including the skins, pips, and cores.

Serving suggestions

▶ Sip on a long apple spritzer made with ½ cup of juice plus plenty of crushed ice, seltzer, and fresh mint leaves.

▶ Make apple juice ice cubes to cool down on hot days.

▶ Start the day with muesli moistened with apple juice rather than low-fat milk.

▶ Use apple juice to sweeten breakfast cereal and other foods.

> Using the whole apple for juicing (except the stem and the core) retains more of the naturally occurring phytonutrients found in the fruit.

Apricots
GI 57

For fragrance and flavor, fresh apricots are almost irresistible. This sweet "borderline" low–medium GI fruit is delicious as a snack or to finish a meal. Like all orange–yellow fruits and vegetables, they are rich in beta-carotene and a good source of vitamin C, fiber, and potassium.

Cooking apricots draws out their flavor, so they are delicious stewed. If they are not quite ready for eating when you buy them, they should ripen in a day or two at room temperature in your fruit bowl (or in a paper bag away from heat and light). To eat your fill of apricots year round, choose canned or dried apricots. Canned apricots have a medium GI (64). Or, for a delicious topping on grainy toast, use apricot fruit spread (GI 56) in moderation.

Serving suggestions

▶ Grill apricot halves (stones removed) and serve with custard, ice cream, or yogurt.

▶ Halve fresh apricots, remove the stones, stuff with a teaspoon of ricotta, and top with chopped nuts.

▶ Gently poach whole or halved apricots in fruit juice with cloves or a cinnamon stick.

Apricots, Dried
GI 30

Dried apricots can be so addictive it's often hard to stick to just a handful—five or six halves is the equivalent of a serving. However, if you do overindulge, remind yourself of their health benefits: they are high in fiber, a rich source of beta-carotene, and provide reasonable amounts of calcium, iron, and potassium.

Dried apricots are a delicious snack food whether you are on the run or desk bound. They also bring a natural sweetness to many recipes: soaked and pureed for desserts, added whole to casseroles, or chopped and mixed with couscous or rice as a main meal accompaniment.

Serving suggestions

▶ Simmer dried apricots in a little water, white wine, or fruit juice to soften and plump up and serve on their own or with a dollop of low-fat yogurt or ice cream.

▶ Add chopped apricots and other dried fruits to homemade muesli.

▶ Dice and add dried apricots to the mix when baking fruit slices and cookies.

▶ Make a Moroccan-flavored casserole with diced lamb or chicken, onions, dried apricots, and spices such as paprika and cumin.

Bananas
GI 52

Bananas are one the world's most popular fruits. Eat this versatile fruit raw or cooked; whole, sliced, or mashed; or as a snack or part of a dessert, fruit salad, or meal. They are also a nutritional gold mine: high in fiber, folate, and vitamin C and rich in potassium, which is why sportspeople consume them in great numbers after intense exercise to replace nutrients and help maintain peak performance.

Unlike most other fruit, bananas contain both sugars and starch. The less ripe the banana, the lower its GI—ripening causes the starch to turn to sugars and the GI increases. The starch in raw bananas is resistant to digestion and reaches the large intestine intact, where it is fermented by the resident microflora. The products of fermentation are believed to be important for large intestine health and may reduce the risk of bowel cancer. Cooking bananas increases the GI because it gelatinizes the starch so that it becomes easily digested.

> Did you know that if you place bananas in a mixed fruit bowl they'll help other fruit ripen?
> To prevent a peeled banana from going brown, brush it with a little lemon juice.

Serving suggestions

▶ If the bananas in your fruit bowl are looking overripe, freeze them in their skins, then peel and add to the blender. They make the most delicious ice cream alternative for creamy shakes and smoothies.

▶ Enjoy banana custard or ice cream made with low-fat milk or soy drink.

▶ Add mashed banana to the mixing bowl for muffins and fruit breads.

Berries—enjoy them by the bowlful

Apart from strawberries (GI 40), most berries have so little carbohydrate it's difficult to test their GI. Their low carbohydrate content means their glycemic load (GL) will be low, so enjoy them by the bowlful. They are a good source of vitamin C and fiber, and some berries also supply small amounts of folate and essential minerals such as potassium, iron, calcium, magnesium, and phosphorus.

Berries are best eaten as soon as possible after purchase. If you need to keep them for a day or two, here's how to minimize mold. Take them out of the container and store in the refrigerator on a couple of layers of paper towel and cover loosely with plastic wrap.

Serving suggestions

❑ Combine your favorite berries with a little sugar and a tablespoon or two of balsamic vinegar or a little white wine or orange juice. Let the flavors develop for 30 minutes or so at room temperature, then serve.

❑ Top gelato, low-fat ice cream, or yogurt, with a spoonful or two of berries for a snack or dessert.

❑ Make berry smoothies with low-fat milk, soy milk, or yogurt for breakfast or a meal in a glass when you are on the run.

❑ Puree berries for coulis, salsas, sauces, sorbets, and ice creams.

❑ Serve berries for breakfast with muesli or your favorite low-GI cereal and a dollop of low-fat vanilla or honey yogurt.

See also Strawberries (page 132).

◗ Gently fry banana slices in a little margarine and brown sugar and serve with pancakes or a dollop of low-fat yogurt—or both.

◗ Bake or steam green bananas (about 30 minutes) and serve as a vegetable accompaniment with barbecued meats.

Cherimoya
GI 54

Juicy cherimoyas taste like a tropical fruit salad and are virtually a complete low-GI food source on their own. They also provide some protein, carbohydrate, and fiber along with many essential vitamins and minerals, including vitamin C, potassium, and magnesium.

If you haven't tried a cherimoya before, choose one that's just soft to touch (like an avocado) without splits or bruises. To open one, place your thumbs in the indentation where the stem joins the fruit, and then you can separate the segments. Discard the black seeds, remove the fibrous center if it is still hard, and eat fresh or add to salads. Because cherimoya flesh discolors fast, brush with a little lemon juice if you aren't using the segments immediately. You can also freeze the peeled segments.

Add fresh cherimoya segments or puree to desserts such as cheese cake, sorbets, parfait, and ice cream. Cooking alters the flavor, so stir segments into savory dishes or curries just before serving to heat through.

Serving suggestions

◗ Power your day with an energy breakfast of muesli moistened with fresh orange juice and topped with cherimoya segments.

◗ For a meal on the run, sip a cherimoya smoothie made with low-fat yogurt and milk and honey to sweeten.

◗ Fold cherimoya puree into low-fat yogurt for a quick and creamy dessert.

◗ Serve segments of cherimoya with fruit and cheese platters— remembering to lightly brush them with a little lemon juice first to prevent discoloring.

‣ Sleep soundly after a cherimoya eggnog made with low-fat milk and honey to taste.

Citrus fruit— nutritional powerpacks

Citrus fruit—oranges, mandarins, lemons, grapefruit, and limes—have among the highest levels of antioxidants of all fruit. They are also rich in folate, fiber, vitamin C, and vitamin A. We know that oranges and grapefruit have a low GI, while the juice of lemons and limes provides acidity that slows gastric emptying and lowers the overall GI of a meal. Try a fresh squeeze of lemon or lime on vegetables with a twist of black pepper just before serving, or toss salad in a dressing made with oil, lemon juice, and salt and pepper to taste.

See Grapefruit (page 119); Oranges (page 126).

Cranberry Juice
GI 52 (unsweetened)

Cranberries have earned a reputation for promoting urinary tract health, and research is now confirming this. Whole cranberries are an excellent source of iron, vitamin C, and fiber and are packed with antioxidant power. Cranberry juice is a healthy option, but, like all juices, drink it in moderation. Remember, drinking a large glass can mean you are taking on board more energy (calories) than you intended—or need. As an alternative, try a cranberry spritzer with ice and seltzer.

Serving suggestions

‣ Blend a tangy cranberry cooler by combining 1 cup of cranberry juice with ½ banana, a container of low-fat yogurt, ½ cup fresh or frozen raspberries, and 1 cup of crushed ice

‣ Whip up a creamy cranberry-banana smoothie for two. Blend 1 small banana with ½ container vanilla low-fat yogurt, 1 cup of cranberry juice, and ½ cup skim milk. Add more yogurt if you like it when the straws stands up straight!

Dried dates update

Dates are one of the oldest cultivated fruits and a staple food throughout the Middle East. Rich in carbohydrate, dried dates are a good source of fiber, minerals such as iron, potassium. and magnesium, and vitamins B_6, niacin, and folate. Unlike most fruits they contain almost no vitamin C. It would appear that the GI value of dried dates could vary significantly depending on the variety (and there are approximately 600 varieties).

When dried dates were first tested their GI value was 103. This high value was puzzling and was rechecked a number of times. It may be that the amount of carbohydrate per serving on the packaging label was incorrect. A team in the Faculty of Medicine and Health Sciences at the United Arab Emirates University tested the khalas variety of dates in 2004 and found that the average GI value was 39.

Dried dates are a delicious snack or addition to stuffings, pilafs, muffins, and desserts. Like all dried fruits, a little goes a long way.

Grapefruit
GI 25

Just half a grapefruit contains about 35 mg of vitamin C, which is almost 60 percent of your recommended daily intake. This is one of the lowest-GI fruits and provides some fiber too. Choose fruit that feels "heavy" for its size—this tends to indicate a thinner skin and plenty of juice. Store in your fruit bowl, as they are juicier eaten at room temperature.

Serving suggestions

▶ Start your day with zest with juicy grapefruit's refreshing tang. Halve a grapefruit, loosen the segments, and eat as is, or sweeten with a little sugar or a drizzle of honey.

▶ Toss segments in salads with smoked salmon and avocado; shrimp and avocado; radicchio, beets, and avocado; or simply add to Asian greens and a citrus dressing.

▶ Combine with chopped pepper, finely chopped onion, and a little chili for a tangy salsa to accompany grilled or barbecued meats.

▶ Enjoy as part of a winter fruit salad with sweeter ingredients such as oranges and raisins and a drizzle of honey.

Dried fruit—concentrated flavor

Drying is the oldest known method of preserving fruit. It often happens naturally on the tree or vine and animals love the results too. It intensifies the flavor and sweetness and at the same time effectively concentrates the nutrients and retains the fiber. If you are watching your weight, keep in mind that the calorie content of dried fruit is higher than for fresh fruit.

Make a fruit compote with 2 cups of your favorite dried fruits, 1–2 cups of fresh orange juice (to cover), a cinnamon stick, and a little sugar or honey to taste. Simmer gently for about 10 minutes or until the fruit has plumped up. Cover and set aside to cool. Serve with breakfast cereal or as a dessert for a sweet finish.

For snacks and school lunch boxes, try 100 percent dried fruit bars.

See also Apple Rings (page 112); Apricots, Dried (page 114); Prunes (page 130); Raisins (page 131).

Grapefruit Juice
GI 48 (commercial)
Cool and refreshing as a snack or after a workout, one small glass of grapefruit juice is rich in vitamin C. The grapefruit juice you buy in the supermarket has a much higher GI than the whole fruit, possibly because manufacturers reduce its acidity to produce a juice with wide consumer appeal. If you squeeze your own grapefruit for juice, however, the GI will be similar to that of whole fruit.

Serving suggestions
▶ Combine with seltzer or mineral water for a cool, tangy spritzer.
▶ Add juice to desserts such as sorbets and mousses.

Grapes
GI 46 (green)
Grapes are a perfect low-GI finger food fruit—grab a small bunch and enjoy as a no-mess, no-fuss snack or with a fruit or cheese platter to finish a meal. They are a good source of vitamin C, provide some fiber, and red-skinned grapes contain protective antioxidants called anthocyanins. They have one of the highest sugar contents of all temperate fruits, which is one reason why they make such a good starter for alcoholic drinks—more sugar means more alcohol. The first wine (recorded in Mesopotamia and Egypt around 3000 B.C.E.) was probably made by accident by allowing a container of grapes to ferment naturally.

Choose bunches with plump, undamaged fruit (avoid split, sticky, or withered grapes) and don't be shy about asking if you can taste-test for flavor.

Serving suggestions
▶ Top cereal with low-fat vanilla yogurt and a handful of fresh grapes to start the day.
▶ Put a bowl of grapes on the table after dinner.
▶ Add red and green grapes to fruit salads and side salads.
▶ Cool off with frozen fruit skewers—grapes, strawberries,

Fruit juice—watch how much you drink

It's all too easy to overdo the calories when drinking juice. For example, if you buy a "large" orange juice in a café or fast-food chain that offers value-saving portions, you may find you are consuming the equivalent of ten oranges (720 cals)! Remember, one serving is ¾ cup.

Freshly squeezed juice can be an effective way to boost your fruit intake, and apart from fiber, retains many of the nutrients you'll find in its whole counterpart. Manufacturers add vitamin C to fruit juice so that their product has the equivalent vitamin C of fresh juice. However, you do miss out on one of the big benefits of whole fruit—the skin (or the fibrous material next to it) which is normally discarded during processing. This contains much of the fiber and trace minerals along with some of the protective anti-oxidants. Some manufacturers throw nothing away.

It's wise to be a little wary when buying juice as there are many products on the market, some of which don't contain much fruit at all. Look for labels that say:

❑ "100 percent pure fruit juice"
❑ "unsweetened"

And of course check the sell-by date.

If you have a juice extractor and make your own, you know exactly how much fruit you have used, you can throw in some pulp for fiber, and you can conjure up fruit and vegetable concoctions with herbs or spices for extra zing.

See also Apple Juice (page 112), Cranberry Juice (page 126), Grapefruit Juice (page 121); Orange Juice (page 126).

banana slices, and melon or pineapple chunks make a colorful combination.

Honey, Pure Floral
GI 55 (average)

It could be said that we are all born with "a sweet tooth." We don't know why, but it may have something to do with the brain's dependence on glucose as its sole source of fuel. Our hunter-gatherer ancestors relished honey and all sorts of other sources of concentrated sugars such as maple syrup, dried fruits, and honey ants and went to great trouble to obtain them. So, if you like to sweeten your food with honey or use it as a spread, you are following a long tradition!

Honey

The color and flavor of honey differs depending on the nectar source (the flowers) visited by the honey bees. We now know from our testing in Australia that the GI of honey can vary too, depending on where the bees have been buzzing. We found that in Australia the lower GI honeys are what are called pure floral honeys (average GI 55) from the blossoms of particular eucalyptus nectar sources rather than the mass market blended honeys from a variety of nectar sources (GI more than 70).

Did you know, however, that honey comes in both high and low GI forms? Most commercially available honey is blended for a mass appeal and often has a high GI (more than 70). If you're after guaranteed low GI ones, then seek out "pure floral" or "monofloral" honeys. Bioactive components of these honeys appear to reduce their GI naturally.

Jam
GI 55 (average)

A dollop (1–2 teaspoons) of jam or fruit spread on grainy bread or toast contains fewer calories than lightly spreading it with butter or margarine. So enjoy a little jam on your bread or toast and give fat the boot.

▶ Strawberry jam GI 51
▶ Apricot fruit spread GI 56

Kiwi Fruit
GI 53

The furry kiwi fruit provides plenty of vitamin C—just one will meet your daily requirements. They are also rich in fiber, a good source of both vitamin E and potassium, and a moderate source of iron. They are renowned as a meat tenderizer thanks to the enzyme actinidin—simply rub cut or mashed fruit over the meat and leave for about 30–40 minutes before barbecuing or grilling.

Shop for kiwis with care. Choose plump, firm fruit with just a little give—if it feels soft to the touch the flesh will be mushy. The best way to eat them is simply to cut them in half and scoop out the flesh. Alternatively, peel and slice or dice and add to fruit and green salads, and fruit and cheese platters, or puree and serve with low-fat yogurt, ice cream, gelato, and sorbets.

Serving suggestions

▶ Toss kiwi fruit slices with watercress and avocado chunks in a light citrus dressing.
▶ Add slices of kiwi fruit to chunks of pineapple, papaya and mango, strawberry halves, passionfruit, and a dash of lime juice to make a colorful tropical fruit salad.
▶ Bring color and variety to a cheese platter with slices of kiwi

fruit, small bunches of purple-red grapes, dried apricot halves, and walnuts.

Mangoes
GI 51

Mangoes are one of the few tropical fruits that squeeze into the low-GI range. They are also a rich source of vitamin C (one provides your recommended daily intake) and beta-carotene, and a useful source of fiber and potassium.

This versatile fruit is delicious fresh, sliced and pureed in desserts, or combined with fish, meat, or poultry along with flavors such as lime juice, chili, and cilantro for main meals. You can even eat them green in Asian-style salads and pickles, although you need to choose the right variety of mango. Ask your grocer to recommend a green eating mango, or visit an Asian produce store.

If you find mangoes messy to eat, try slicing off a "cheek" lengthwise, cutting as close to the stone as you can. Now score the flesh horizontally and then vertically with a sharp knife just to the skin to make 2½ inch squares. Half turn "inside out" so that the mango cubes pop up for easy eating.

Serving suggestions

▶ Stir-fry strips of duck or chicken breast and make a warm salad tossed with golden mango slices, bean sprouts, chopped onion, chili, fresh mint leaves, and a tangy Thai dressing.

▶ Combine diced mango with chopped red onion, tomatoes, red pepper and cilantro and a dash of lime juice to serve as a salsa with seafood.

▶ Try chopped fresh mango with a scoop of low-fat chocolate ice cream and an almond cookie for a delicious and easy dessert.

Oranges
GI 42

One orange is something of a personal protection powerhouse, providing you with your whole day's vitamin C requirement. Oranges are rich in antioxidants and are good sources of folate and potassium. Much of their sugar is sucrose, a "double" sugar made up of glucose and fructose. When digested, only the glucose molecules have an impact on your blood glucose levels. This, plus the high acid content, account for the low GI.

Serving suggestions

▶ Peel and enjoy the juicy segments with breakfast cereal, as a snack, or as an after-dinner palate cleanser.
▶ Chop into fruit salads, toss into salads, add to soups or casseroles or to couscous.
▶ Slice and add to fruit punch.
▶ Carrot and orange make a great couple—enjoy this perfect partnership in soup, salad, or juice.
▶ Oranges make delicious desserts—jellies, sorbets, souffles, crepes, ice cream
▶ Try a citrus salad with orange and grapefruit segments, a can of chickpeas, cherry tomatoes, and peppery arugula tossed in an oil and lemon juice dressing.

Orange Juice
GI 50 (unsweetened)

Freshly squeezed juice has most of the health benefits of a whole orange, but lacks the fiber unless you throw in the pulp. Its GI will be similar to that of whole fruit. If you are buying oranges specifically for juicing, choose ones that are firm and heavy for their size.

The juices you buy from the supermarket tend to have a slightly higher GI than the whole fruit because they contain equal amounts of fructose, glucose and sucrose. During processing, much of the original sucrose is partially split or "hydrolyzed" to glucose and fructose. When shopping look for unsweetened, 100 percent juice.

Use orange juice to moisten breakfast cereal as a change from milk, or add to meat dishes, couscous, or spinach salads to help increase iron absorption. And remember, it's all too easy to overdo your juice intake—a serving is just ¾ cup.

Serving suggestions
▶ Add juice to fruit punches, fruit salad, milk shakes, and eggnog.
▶ Use orange juice's zesty flavor in marinades, sauces, and dressings.
▶ Freeze juice to make summer treats such as ice cubes and ice pops.

Papaya/Pawpaw
GI 56
You can be forgiven for being confused about whether to call this large, oval-shaped tropical fruit papaya or pawpaw, or even whether it's the same fruit as the names are used interchangeably even by the experts. Native to the Americas, the tropical papaya (*Carica papaya*) is a completely different fruit from *Asimina triloba*—the true pawpaw (see sidebar). Papayas range in color from a deep orange to a pale green and in size from looking rather like a small football to an overgrown pear, depending on the variety. Whichever you buy, however, it will be rich in vitamins A and C, a moderate source of fiber and will have a low–medium GI.

Like many tropical fruits, a ripe papaya is best raw. Simply cut it in half lengthwise, scoop out the seeds, peel away the skin, cut the flesh into slices or wedges and enjoy. The green or unripe fruit can be cooked as a vegetable or cut into strips or grated and added to Asian-style salads. The shiny black–gray seeds are usually thrown away, but they are also edible (they have a peppery flavor)—crush them and add to dressings or sprinkle over salads.

Serving suggestions

▶ Serve papaya slices for breakfast sprinkled with lemon or lime juice for a fresh-tasting start to the day, or dice papaya and add to tropical fruit salads with mangoes, kiwi fruit, passionfruit, and berries.

▶ Puree ripe papaya and use as a sauce or topping or to flavor sorbets and ice creams (but not jellies—fresh papaya will not set in gelatine desserts).

▶ Serve seafood or chicken with a coriander and papaya salsa.

▶ Puree ripe papaya and add to marinades (it contains papain, a protein-splitting enzyme that can be used as a meat tenderiser) or just rub a little juice over meat and leave for about 20 minutes before cooking.

> The true pawpaw, or papaw as it is often called, (*Asimina triloba*) is a North American native from the same family as cherimoyas. It has creamy yellow, sweet flesh with a custard-like texture and looks rather like a fat, brown banana.

Peaches
GI 42

It's nice to know that something as juicy and delicious as a ripe, fresh peach is so healthy. Peaches are good sources of vitamin C, potassium, and fiber.

For eating, look for bruise-free peaches with a fragrant aroma that give a little to touch. For cooking, freestone peaches (ask your grocer if unsure) are probably the better choice. The easiest way to peel a peach is to dip it in boiling water, then in cold water. The peel should slide off easily. To prevent discoloration if you are not eating the cut fruit immediately, brush with a little lemon or lime juice.

Canned peaches have many of the nutritional benefits of fresh fruit (with a little less vitamin C) along with a low GI and the convenience of being available year round. Try single-serving cans or containers as a snack.

Serving suggestions
- Top grainy toast with ricotta and thinly sliced fresh peaches for an easy breakfast or a tasty snack.
- Halve, stone, and poach peaches in champagne, white wine, or fruit juice with or without the skin and serve with low-fat yogurt or ice cream.
- Sip on a fruity whip of pureed peaches or nectarines blended with ice and orange juice.
- Sprinkle fresh peach halves with a little cinnamon and lightly grill.

Pears
GI 38

Juicy, sweet pears are one of the world's most loved fruits—they've even been immortalized in poetry, paintings, and a Christmas carol! They are renowned as a nonallergenic food, thus a favorite when introducing babies to solid foods. An excellent source of fiber and rich in vitamin C and potassium, fresh pears have a low GI because most of their sugar is fructose. Canned pears in "natural juice" also have a low GI (44) because the fructose remains in high concentration during processing. Single-serving containers and cans are also available. Again, look for those in natural juice.

Although they are often hard when you buy them, pears will ripen at room temperature in a few days. Pack a pear for lunch or to snack on during the day—there's no need to peel, as the skin is a good source of fiber.

Serving suggestions
- Dip pear slices in lemon juice and serve with cheese and walnuts.
- Toss in salads—try pear, avocado, arugula or radicchio, and walnuts.

- Poach or bake pears in a light citrus syrup or red wine with a touch of cardamom.
- Try topping a bowl of oatmeal with grilled pear slices and a drizzle of honey or some brown sugar.

Plums
GI 39

Plum pudding, plum jam, Chinese plum sauce—this fruit is popular the world over. It's also a good source fiber and provides small quantities of vitamins and minerals. Fresh plums have a low GI and it's likely that canned plums in natural juice will also have a low GI. However they have not been tested yet.

Choose plump, undamaged fruit (no splits, bruises, or signs of decay) with a slight whitish bloom, and enjoy fresh as a snack or to finish a meal.

Serving suggestions

- Halve, remove stone, and add to fruit salads and compotes or serve with cheese or fruit platters.
- Puree for making sauces and delicious sorbets and ice cream.
- Top stewed plums with a sprinkle of toasted muesli and a dollop of yogurt for a breakfast with a difference.
- Poach plums in red or white wine with a stick of cinnamon and serve hot or cold.

Prunes
GI 29

Prunes have a reputation for keeping us regular, but there's more to this tasty dried fruit than that. They are a concentrated source of many nutrients, including beta-carotene, B vitamins, potassium, and phosphorus. Prunes are also a useful source of iron for vegetarians. Their sugar content, naturally occurring acids and fiber make them a great low-GI food for snacks on their own or as part of a fruit and nut mix.

You can buy prunes with stones or pitted—but check for the

occasional stone as the processing is not always perfect. Soften or "plump" by simmering or soaking and enjoy in desserts, or add to lamb, pork, chicken, and game dishes for a Moroccan flavor.

Serving suggestions

▶ Combine prunes with an equal amount of water in a small pan and gently simmer for about 5–10 minutes. Add a slice of lemon or some spices for extra flavor.

▶ To soften in the microwave, pour fruit juice or water over prunes, cover, and cook.

▶ To soften overnight, place prunes in a heat-resistant bowl and just cover with boiling water. When cool, cover and store in the refrigerator.

Raisins
GI 56

For a quick and easy low-GI snack it's hard to beat raisins. The are a good source of fiber and also provide some potassium and vitamin E. They are juicier, softer, and sweeter than their cousins the currant, which may account for their popularity in breakfast cereals, muesli, and mixes with nuts and apricots. They also make a versatile cooking ingredient—add to all sorts of dishes from casseroles and compotes to couscous, cakes, cookies, and granola.

Serving suggestions

▶ A mini-box of raisins is ideal for school lunch boxes.

▶ Spread grainy bread with a little peanut butter and make a salad sandwich with grated carrot, cucumber slices, raisins, and shredded lettuce.

▶ Sweeten breakfast cereal and yogurt with a spoonful of raisins.

▶ Simmer raisins in apple or orange juice with peeled and grated ginger to make a tasty compote for breakfast or dessert.

▶ Add raisins to your favorite bread pudding recipe along with chopped dates.

Strawberries
GI 40

It's no wonder deliciously versatile strawberries are the world's most popular berry fruit. You can eat them fresh, add them to fruit salads and frappés, use them in a delicious dessert, decorate cakes with them, or make them into jams, fruit spreads, and sauces.

Fresh strawberries are rich in vitamin C, potassium, folate, fiber, and protective antioxidants. Because the average serving has very little impact on blood glucose levels, people with diabetes can eat them freely. So reap the health benefits as you enjoy them by the bowlful, but hold the cream! A word of warning: don't eat too many in a single day. They can have diuretic and laxative effects if you overdo it.

If you aren't eating them immediately, spread the berries out in a single layer on paper towel on a plate and lightly cover with plastic wrap. Remove any damaged or moldy ones first.

Serving suggestions

▶ For a perfect parfait, take a tall glass and arrange layers of sliced strawberries, whole blueberries, and dollops of low-fat vanilla yogurt. Mango slices are delicious with this combination, too

▶ Blend strawberries for a bright and refreshing coulis to serve with low-fat ice cream or poached pears. Freeze for fruity ice cubes.

▶ Add strawberries to smoothies and shakes with low-fat yogurt or ice cream.

▶ Serve whole with fruit and cheese platters or dip in chocolate for a sweet treat with coffee at the end of a meal.

▶ Quarter fresh strawberries and soak in balsamic vinegar with a little sugar.

▶ Add to green salads with baby spinach and a light balsamic dressing.

▶ Enjoy a dollop of strawberry jam (GI 51) on grainy fresh bread or toast in moderation.

Vegetables

Think of vegetables as "free" foods—they are full of fiber, essential nutrients, and protective antioxidants that will fill you up without adding extra calories. And most are so low in carbohydrate that they will have no measurable effect on your blood glucose levels.

Leafy green and salad vegetables, for example, have so little carbohydrate that we can't test their GI. Even in generous serving sizes they will have no effect on your blood glucose levels.

Higher-carbohydrate vegetables include sweet corn, potato, sweet potato, taro, and yam, so you need to watch the portion sizes with these. Most varieties of potato tested to date have a high GI, so if you are a big potato eater, try to replace some with low-GI alternatives such as sweet corn, sweet potato, yam, or legumes. Vegetables such as pumpkin, carrots, peas, and beets contain some carbohydrate, but a normal serving size contains so little that it won't raise your blood glucose levels significantly.

> Pile your plate high with leafy green and salad vegetables and eat your way to long-term health and vitality.

How much?
One serve is equivalent to:
- ½ cup cooked vegetables (other than potato, corn, and sweet potato)
- 1 cup raw salad vegetables
- 1 cup vegetable soup (without cream!)
- 1 cup pure vegetable juice

How much a day?
Even the smallest eater should aim to eat five or more servings of vegetables every day, including fresh and frozen vegetables, vegetable juices, and soups. This is a minimum of 2½ cups of cooked vegetables or 4 cups of salad.

Starchy vegetables—how much a day?

Starchy vegetables such as sweet potato, potato, and sweet corn are higher in carbohydrate so their GI and serving size is more relevant. One serving is equivalent to:

▶ 1 medium (4 ounces) potato (a touch smaller than a tennis ball)
▶ ½ cup mashed potato
▶ 4 ounces sweet potato
▶ ½ cup corn kernels
▶ ½ cob sweet corn
▶ 3 ounces taro
▶ 1 large (6 ounces) parsnip

In addition to the five or more servings of other fresh or frozen vegetables:

▶ Smaller eaters: 1 serving
▶ Medium eaters: 3 servings
▶ Bigger eaters: 4 servings

Salad as an appetizer

Enjoy a mixed salad (lettuce, tomato, cucumber, celery, pepper) tossed in an oil and vinegar dressing before moving on to your main course. A recent study reported that eating a salad like this as an appetizer helps to fill you up and you will eat less overall.

Serving suggestions

1. Pile vegetables on your favorite sandwiches. Try sliced pepper, cucumber, onion, tomatoes, broccoli, zucchini, spinach, and mushrooms. Or include salad ingredients or chopped up

leftover vegetables in a pita pocket, sandwich, or tortilla wrap. Top grainy toast with leftover veggies.

2. Add vegetables to stir-fried meat, chicken, prawns, fish, or tofu dishes.

3. Make a meal of stuffed vegetables—pepper, tomato, eggplant, and onion all make great "containers."

4. Use herbs and spices for flavor and serve two or three portions of different vegetables such as broccoli, carrots, and cauliflower or even a ratatouille of mixed vegetables, including tomatoes, pepper, eggplant, and onions.

5. Throw some vegetables on the grill or on the barbecue with meat. Try zucchini, corn, pepper, mushrooms, eggplant, onion, or thick slices of parboiled sweet potato. (Use vegetable oil spray or a little olive oil on a cold grill to prevent sticking.)

6. Make homemade vegetable soups. Try combinations like onion, carrot, celery, and tomato in a chicken or vegetable stock. Puree if you prefer a creamy texture.

7. Try a vegetarian main dish at least once a week, such as creamy vegetarian lasagna with ricotta, onions, mushrooms, tomatoes, lentils, and spinach.

8. Add grated carrot and zucchini to breads and muffins, or grated carrot and onion to rissoles and burgers.

9. For quick munching, keep celery, pepper, baby carrots, cucumbers, broccoli or cauliflower florets, and cherry tomatoes on hand. Dip them in hummus, low-fat eggplant or tuna dip or a homemade tomato salsa.

10. Buy a vegetable cookbook packed with recipes you can't wait to try out, and buy and try vegetables you haven't cooked before.

Storage and cooking tips

Vegetables are best fresh, so shop two or three times a week if you can and use them within two to three days.

Ethylene gas produced by aging fruits and vegetables leads to their deterioration. You can minimize the effect of ethylene by storing vegetables in the fridge in Evert-Fresh reusable produce bags, which are available in the produce section of supermarkets, or you can use special cartridges (available in some supermarkets) designed to absorb ethylene. Fruits give off more ethylene than vegetables, but vegetables are more sensitive to its effects, so if you have two crispers, keep fruit in one and vegetables in the other.

Wash green leafy vegetables well to remove any soil or grit, then rinse before cooking. They are best steamed or cooked with a minimum of water. Tear salad leaves into small pieces and dry them thoroughly before adding to the salad bowl—the water will dilute the dressing. Salad spinners are great for this purpose, or simply use a clean dish towel.

To make sure you gain the benefit of all those essential nutrients when cooking:

- leave the skins on whenever you can, or peel very finely
- avoid soaking vegetables in water
- use a steamer or microwave for best results
- cook vegetables in big chunks rather than coarsely chopped
- reduce the amount of water you use, cover the pan and cook quickly and as close to serving time as possible; *never* add baking soda to the cooking water
- cook vegetables until they're softened but still firm to bite

Take-out tips

When you are ordering take-out food opt for choices that include vegetables, such as:

- regular hamburger with salad
- pizza piled with vegetable toppings—mushrooms, tomatoes, pepper, spinach, artichoke
- salad with sandwiches, wraps, or rolls
- pasta with a tomato-based sauce and plenty of vegetables
- stuffed potato with Mexican-style beans, tomato salsa, and cheese
- sweet corn on the cob

- vegetarian nachos
- salad as a side order or a main course (hold the fries!)
- meat and vegetable fajitas
- corn tortilla with beans and salsa

Salad on the side

A side salad tossed in an oil and vinegar dressing with your meal, especially a high-GI meal, will help to keep blood glucose levels under control.

Carrots
GI 41

"Eating your carrots will help you see in the dark"—sound familiar? Carrots are rich in beta-carotene, a plant form of vitamin A or retinol, which we need to maintain normal vision. A deficiency in vitamin A produces night blindness (an inability to see in dim light). Carrots also provide some vitamin C and fiber, so add them when you're cooking soups, salads, stir-fries, stews, casseroles, and cakes.

Because they make a deliciously crunchy raw snack, it's worthwhile being fussy when shopping, and choose firm, bright orange carrots. Avoid the ones with cracks, soft patches, or discolored skin if you can. Grate and add to salads and sandwiches, cut into sticks for dips or snacks, or boil, steam, or bake (whole or sliced) and serve with main meals.

Serving suggestions

- Enjoy a freshly grated carrot salad with a bunch of chopped chives and a dressing of oil and lemon juice.
- For a Middle Eastern flavor toss cooked carrot slices in a little oil and lemon juice with roasted cumin seeds crushed in a mortar and pestle.

▶ Make a creamy, pureed carrot soup with leeks, a potato, and a good-quality chicken stock served with a dollop of low-fat yogurt.

▶ Peel and juice a couple of carrots or add other vegetables or fruit such as celery, apple and orange to start your day with a healthy glow.

Keep a look out for cassava

Although you may never have seen this starchy tuber in your local supermarket, you may well use one of its best known by-products, tapioca (GI 70), when thickening sauces or making puddings. Cassava (GI 46), also called yuca, manioc, and mandioca, is a high-carbohydrate staple for millions of people around the world. It looks rather like an elongated potato (about 12 inches long) with coarse brown skin and white, fibrous flesh. The roots are usually peeled and boiled, baked, or fried. They are also dried and processed into granules, pastes, flours—and even alcohol. The young leaves can be eaten as a vegetable, while the larger, older leaves are sometimes used for wrapping food before cooking.

Corn
See Sweet corn, page 140.

Peas, Green
GI 48
There's nothing like the aroma of shelling and eating fresh, green peas straight from the pod. Today, most of us buy them in frozen packages—the manufacturer has done the hard work. Green peas are actually a legume, but we have included them here, as most of us think of them as a green vegetable. They are rich in fiber and

vitamin C and higher in protein than most vegetables. Although a good source of thiamin, niacin, phosphorus, and iron when fresh, cooking will reduce the nutrient levels. Frozen peas have about 60 percent more beta-carotene than fresh peas that have been exposed to light during their trip to market.

If you do buy peas in the pod, you'll need about 12 ounces of pods to fill a cup with shelled peas. And tempting as it is to pick up a pack of "freshly" shelled peas from your supermarket, only do so if you know they really have been freshly shelled and you plan to use them immediately.

Boil, steam, or microwave peas for about 4–5 minutes (remember, cooking destroys the nutrients) or add to rice dishes such as risottos, pasta dishes, omelettes, soups and stews (at the last minute), or combine with mashed potato or sweet potato.

Peas with edible pods such as snowpeas and sugar snaps (immature pods) only need the minimum of cooking time, too, and are

Have you heard about nopal?

The fleshy pads or "paddles" (nopales) of the prickly pear cactus (nopal) with the spines removed are a traditional ingredient in Mexican cuisine. They are a good source of calcium and vitamin C and contain beta-carotene and iron. They have a small amount of carbohydrate and an amazingly low GI—7. Sometimes called "edible cactus," nopales are usually sold in Mexico and the U.S. "despined" although you'd probably have to trim the eyes with a vegetable peeler to remove any remaining "prickers." They can be diced for salads; steamed quickly as an accompaniment (the texture should be crunchy); added to soups, salsas, stews, stir-fries, fillings for scrambled eggs or tortillas; or stirred into Mexican-style recipes with chili, tomatoes, and corn.

delicious in stir-fries, or steamed or cooked in the microwave for a side dish.

Serving suggestions

▶ Whip up an omelet with onion, a little ham or lean bacon, and fresh peas.

▶ If you feel like comfort food, puree or mash cooked peas with chicken stock and a little margarine.

▶ Add blanched snowpeas or sugar snaps to salads or serve with vegetable platters and dips.

See also Split Peas (page 197).

Sweet Corn
GI 48 (on the cob)

Sweet corn is actually the seed of a type of grass that grew in the Americas for thousands of years before Christopher Columbus arrived on the scene. It is rich in vitamin C and a good source of fiber, folate, and beta-carotene. It also has higher amounts of protein and vitamin B than most other vegetables because it's actually a cereal grain. Canned and frozen kernels have a similar GI to corn on the cob.

Corn is often used as a base for gluten-free products. However, many products made from corn don't have a low GI at all—cornflakes (GI 77), popcorn (GI 72), cornmeal (GI 68), and corn pasta (GI 87). Corn chips do (GI 42), but they are also very high in salt and fat.

For the sweetest flavor, buy corn on the cob with the fresh green husk intact, because the natural sugar in the kernels starts converting into starch the moment the husk is removed. To avoid disappointment, stay away from cobs with dry yellow husks and small shrinking kernels.

Boil, steam, or microwave briefly, or bake or grill and serve piping hot topped with the merest hint of margarine or butter. Toss whole baby corn into stir-fries or cut kernels off the cob (slicing as close to the cob as possible) and add to soups and stews, fritters and frittata, chowders and crepes, salsa and salads. You can substitute canned kernels in recipes calling for fresh, but remember that the flavor won't be quite as sweet.

Serving suggestions

▶ Spice up barbecued meats with a tangy corn salsa made from diced tomato, pepper, onion, chopped chili (to taste), fresh cilantro, and a lime dressing.

▶ Barbecue cobs by pulling back the husk, removing the silk, and then pulling the husk back over the kernels to cover before cooking. When grilling, the experts recommend plunging the whole cobs into iced water for an hour before cooking to help the corn cook slowly and evenly.

▶ Make a sweet corn frittata with chopped onion, lean bacon, eggs, low-fat milk, and parsley, and top with a sprinkle of reduced-fat tasty cheese.

▶ Add the finishing touch to a warm salad of roast sweet potato, red onion, red pepper, baby eggplant, and baby spinach with small corn cob chunks.

Sweet Potato
GI 44

Sweet potatoes aren't a "potato" at all, they are the roots of a vine from the sprawling morning glory family, and a staple food in many parts of the world. There are several varieties: orange-fleshed with red skin; red-purple-skinned with yellow flesh; and white-skinned with yellow skin and flesh. All are rich in nutrients, including beta-carotene, vitamin C, and fiber plus vitamin E, thiamin, and folate. A versatile vegetable with a low GI, they make a great substitute for potatoes and, like pumpkin, you can use them in sweet dishes, too. A big advantage over potatoes is that the skin does not develop green patches (which makes them inedible) when exposed to light.

They are as easy to prepare and cook as potatoes—peel or simply scrub the skins and steam, boil, bake, or microwave. Try mashing peeled sweet potatoes with a little mustard oil or wrapping small chunks in foil and cooking them on the grill. Sliced or cut into chunks, they make a tasty addition to soups, stews, stir-fries, and salads (roasted first); cooked and pureed you can add them to scone or cake mixes.

Serving suggestions

▶ Tuck into a winter-warming shepherd's pie with a sweet potato mash topping.

▶ Make a spicy stir-fry with onions, ginger, garlic, sweet potato slices, peas, and water chestnuts.

▶ Create casseroles and stews by adding a variety of vegetables including sweet potatoes, tomatoes, onions and carrots to chicken or lean meat.

▶ Make a creamy soup with sweet potatoes and Granny Smith apples flavored with cumin and cinnamon and topped with a dollop of low-fat plain yogurt.

Taro
GI 55

Taro, sometimes called "elephant ear," is an important food throughout the Pacific Islands. It's a good source of vitamin C and fiber and, like other traditional staples such as sweet potato and yam, it is slowly digested, which is probably why it offered protection against diabetes to at-risk populations such as Pacific Islanders, Maoris, and Australian Aborigines. The increased incidence of diabetes in these groups today is linked to increased consumption of modern quickly digested starches.

If you haven't tried taro before, look for firm, hairy tubers with no wrinkling of the skin. Wear rubber gloves when peeling as the juices occasionally cause a skin irritation. Taro flesh is similar to sweet potato in flavor and you can use it the same way—steamed, boiled, or cut into wedges and baked.

What about potatoes?

Boiled, mashed, baked, or fried, everybody loves potatoes. However, we now know that the GI value of potatoes can vary significantly depending on variety and cooking method (GI 56 to 89)—according to University of Toronto researchers reporting in the *Journal of the American Dietetic Association* in 2005. Their study found that precooking and reheating potatoes or consuming cold cooked potatoes (such as potato salad) reduces the glycemic response. The highest GI values were found in potatoes that were freshly cooked and in instant mashed potatoes.

In our testing so far in Australia, the only potatoes to make the moderate GI range are tiny, new canned ones (GI 65). The lower GI of these potatoes may be due to differences in the structure of the starch. As potatoes age, the degree of branching of their amylopectin starch increases significantly, becoming more readily gelatinized and digested, thus producing a higher GI. New potatoes are also smaller and there seems to be a correlation between size and GI—the smaller the potato the lower the GI.

There's no need to say "no" to potatoes altogether just because they may have a high GI. They are fat free (when you don't fry them), nutrient rich and filling. Not every food you eat has to have a low GI. So enjoy them, but in moderation. Try steaming small new potatoes (with their skin for added nutrients), or bake a potato and add a tasty topping based on beans, chickpeas, or corn kernels. Add variety to meals and occasionally replace potatoes with sweet corn, sweet potato, or yams, or serve pasta, noodles, basmati rice, or legumes.

Serving suggestions

Try a taro, chickpea, and sweet potato curry as a side dish (serves 6) or with cooked rice as a main meal (serves 4). Peel and chop 14 ounces each of taro and sweet potato into 1-inch chunks and steam for about 10 minutes until half cooked. Remove from the heat and set aside. Heat 2 tablespoons of olive oil in a large pan and lightly sauté 1 tablespoon of freshly grated ginger and 3 cloves of crushed garlic over a medium heat for 2–3 minutes. Add the taro and sweet potato, 2 cups of cooked chickpeas, 1 tablespoon of curry powder, and 1 red chili (peeled, seeded, and very finely sliced). Stir gently to coat the vegetables and chickpeas in the curry mix, then cover and cook until the vegetables are tender. Serve topped with 2 or 3 tablespoons of freshly chopped cilantro.

Tomatoes

As with most vegetables you can dig into tomatoes without thinking about their GI. They are so low in carbohydrate that they have no measurable effect on your blood glucose levels, but they do provide plenty of fiber, vitamins, minerals, and health-giving lycopene, an anticancer antioxidant.

Products made with tomatoes, such as tomato juice and tomato soup, are more concentrated and can be a useful source of carbohydrate for light meals and snacks.

Canned Tomato Soup GI 38

While canned tomato soup is a quick and easy meal with a slice or two of grainy toast, it is also great for quick casseroles and sauces—try it as a bolognese sauce base. Many brands contain large amounts of sodium, so look for reduced-sodium ones. A serving is 1 cup.

Commercial Tomato Juice GI 38

You can feel good about drinking tomato juice (no sugar and minimal sodium added) on the rocks or straight from the can. A thirst-quenching glass provides vitamins A and C, potassium, and folic acid. A serving is 1 cup.

Serving suggestions

▶ Add beans to your favorite homemade tomato soup recipe and top with finely chopped fresh herbs for a satisfying meal.

▶ Oven-roast tomatoes and serve with pasta shapes or stir a fresh tomato sauce through spaghetti for a meal in minutes.

Vegetable juices

Watch the sodium content in commercial vegetable juices—look for brands with low- or reduced-sodium labels. Or make your own!

Yam
GI 37

Like sweet potato and taro, yams are high in fiber, nutrient dense, and a good source of vitamin C and potassium. They have long been a staple food in Asia, throughout the Pacific Islands, and in New Zealand. In Australia the Aborigines ate many species of yam, and when they led their traditional "bush tucker" lifestyle they were protected from diabetes.

Use yams in your cooking in the same way you would use sweet potatoes, although yams tend to have an "earthier" flavor. Wash and peel before baking, steaming, boiling, or microwaving to serve as an accompaniment or add to salads, soups, and stews.

Serving suggestions

▶ Puree yam cooked with leeks and chicken stock to make a creamy soup and flavor with fresh herbs such as dill or chives.

▶ Toss cooked bite-sized chunks of yam with mesclun, onion slices, pepper, and chives in a light oil and vinegar dressing for a satisfying salad.

▶ Steam and mash yam chunks with skim milk and a teaspoon or two of margarine and season with salt and a few twists of freshly ground black pepper to taste.

▶ Bake au gratin at 350°F with overlapping yam slices moistened with chicken stock, sprinkled with a teaspoon of dried sage topped with grated cheddar cheese and freshly grated nutmeg.

BREADS & CEREALS

Did you know that the type of bread and cereal you eat affects the overall GI of your diet the most? Why? Well, cereal grains such as rice, wheat, oats, barley, and rye and products made from them such as bread, pasta, and breakfast cereals are the most concentrated sources of carbohydrate in our diet.

These days, supermarket shelves are packed with products based on quickly digested, high-GI flours and grains. Breakfast cereals are a good example. Once, a bowl of slowly digested porridge made with traditional rolled oats gave most of us the energy to keep going from breakfast through to lunchtime. Nowadays we are more likely to fill that breakfast bowl with high-GI crunchy flakes that will spike our blood glucose and insulin levels and leave us needing a mid-morning snack to keep going.

A simple swap is all it takes to reduce the GI of your diet. To get started, replace some of those high-GI breads and breakfast cereals with low-GI carbs that will trickle fuel into your engine. Here's how on the opposite page.

How much?
One serving is equivalent to:
▶ 1 slice bread (sandwich thickness) or ½ English muffin
▶ ½ cup (1 ounce) breakfast cereal, rolled oats, or muesli
▶ ½ cup cooked rice or other small grains such as bulgur or couscous; or cooked pasta or noodles

> High in fiber, rich in nutrients, bulky and filling, whole-grain cereal foods serve us well.

How much a day?
▶ Small eaters: 4 servings
▶ Medium eaters: 6 servings
▶ Bigger eaters: 8 servings

Switch from this high-GI food	To this low-GI alternative
Bread—whole wheat or white	Bread and bread rolls containing visible grainy bits, multigrain, 100 percent whole-grain stone-ground, whole wheat, sourdough, sourdough rye, pumpernickel, soy and flaxseed, and fruit breads.
Processed breakfast cereal such as cornflakes and Kellogg's Rice Crispies	Rolled oats (not instant), and oat-based cereal such as muesli, a fiber-based cereal such as All Bran, or the lower-GI processed cereals such as Kellogg's Special K and Frosted Flakes.
Plain cookies and crackers; wafers, rice cakes	Cookies made with dried fruit, whole grains and oats such as old-fashioned oatmeal raisin cookies, or make your own "crisp" breads with baked or toasted thin slices of low-GI breads.
Cakes and muffins, doughnuts and scones	Add fruit, oats, and whole grains to the mix. Look for recipes on whole-grain cereal boxes. Go halves in a slice of fruit and nut cake or fruit and muesli muffin in a café.
Rice	Choose low-GI varieties (basmati, Uncle Ben's converted long-grain rice, or long-grain and wild rice) or try buckwheat noodles or barley instead—you can even make a barley risotto.

Serving suggestions
1. Start the day with oatmeal or muesli, fruit, and a dollop of low-fat yogurt.
2. Top grainy toast with creamed sweet corn or grilled mushrooms for something savory; or ricotta and slices of peaches or apples for a fruity flavor.
3. When buying lunch, choose a whole-grain or low-GI bread or roll for sandwiches.
4. Pack pita pockets with a bean or chickpea salad, tomato and onion slices, and lots of fresh basil or cilantro.

> ## What's a serving?
>
> A serving is not necessarily the portion you put on your plate. It's a standard reference dietitians use to help give you an idea of the total amount of each of the different types of food you should eat each day. The number of servings you need of particular types of food such as cereal or dairy foods depends on your age and how active you are, and whether you are male or female, pregnant, etc.

5. Serve noodles, pasta, low-GI rice, bulgur, or quinoa with main meals instead of potato.
6. Add barley, pasta, or a low-GI rice to soups, stews, and casseroles for a filling one-dish wonder.
7. Add bulgur or oats to homemade burger patties or rissoles and serve with a whole-grain bun.
8. Develop a taste for whole-grain bread (try toasting it to begin with), and commit to eating it as your main bread choice.
9. Develop a repertoire of low-GI snacks—raisin toast or fruit loaf with a dollop of ricotta; pita crisps dunked in hummus or salsa.
10. Get hold of a natural whole foods cookbook, stock your pantry with whole-grain staples, and try a new recipe each week.

What about gluten?

People with celiac disease have a permanent intolerance of gluten, a type of protein in wheat, rye, barley, millet, triticale, and oats. Even eating tiny amounts can cause a problem. There are a number of gluten-free products on the market, but with their refined corn or rice starch content many have intermediate or high GI values. Some have been tested for their GI—but not all. If you are on a gluten-free diet and need to reduce the overall GI of your diet, opt for basmati rice, Uncle Ben's converted long-grain rice, pastas made from soy, noodles made from rice, or mung beans and legumes in any form.

Check the tables (page 246) or go to www.glycemicindex.com to find the latest GI values. Or contact manufacturers for information on the GI of their products.

Bread

Brown or white, whole wheat or multigrain, sourdough or soy and flaxseed, sliced or in loaves or rolls, bread is truly a staple food—it's inexpensive, low in fat and a useful source of protein, carbohydrate, and fiber, along with essential vitamins and minerals. In the United States it represents at least 60 percent of our cereal intake. Most breads sold today have a high GI because they are made from quickly digested refined flours—white or whole wheat. Choose a low-GI bread and you are on your way to reducing the overall GI of your diet. Here's how.

Look for really grainy breads, granary, 100 percent stoneground whole wheat, sourdough, or breads made from chickpea or other legume-based flours such as soy, or with added soybeans. Look for these breads in the bread or bakery section of your supermarket, in specialty bakeries or delis, and in health, natural, and organic food stores. Check out the ingredient list on the package. Good choices

Don't overindulge yourself

Breads, rolls, and pita breads are not fattening in themselves. It's what goes on (or in) them that can pile on the calories. A smear of margarine is all you need—or none at all. For a change, try Nutella, peanut butter, almond or cashew butter, or avocado. Or you can opt for low-fat alternatives like ricotta or cottage cheese or a fresh fruit spread.

will list grains such as barley, rye, triticale, oats, or oat bran and kibbled wheat; or seeds such as sunflower or flaxseed; and legumes such as soybeans. If you want a general rule of thumb: the coarser textured, denser, and less processed a bread is, the lower its GI is likely to be.

Low-GI breads to look for

Manufacturer and Brand	GI
Con Agra, Soy and Linseed, made from mix in bread machine	50
Con Agra, Muesli, made from mix in bread machine	54
Con Agra, Healthy Choice Hearty 7 Grain	55
Con Agra, Healthy Choice, Hearty 100% Whole Grain	62
Natural Ovens, 100% Whole Grain	51
Natural Ovens, Hunger Filler, whole grain	59
Natural Ovens, Nutty Natural, whole grain	59
Natural Ovens, Cinnamon, Raisin, and Pecan	63
Rudolph's Specialty Ltd., Linseed Rye	55

Chapatti
GI 27 (made with besan flour)

Chapatti is an unleavened bread eaten every day by millions of people throughout India and Sri Lanka, and found on the menu in Indian restaurants worldwide. When made with besan flour, chapatti has a low GI. Besan flour is made from ground, dried chickpeas and is also used to make roti and other Indian breads. It's a heavy-textured flour with a distinctive nutty flavor, and you can often find it in health food stores, Asian produce stores, and the Asian foods section of supermarkets. Nutrient rich thanks to its legume origins, besan is an excellent source of protein and the minerals potassium, calcium, and magnesium.

Chapatti is also made from barley flour and from atta, a wheat flour with a higher GI (63) due to the nature of the starch—so if you are ordering chapattis in a restaurant, ask about the ingredients.

If you are making them yourself, use a recipe that specifies besan or gram flour. One chapatti could be equivalent to as much as 3 bread servings, depending on size.

Serving suggestions

▶ Serve a curry with chapattis instead of basmati rice, or to mop up a delicious dal.

▶ Use chapattis to wrap a curry mixture made from lean ground meat browned with your favorite curry paste, a chopped onion, and a can of brown lentils or chickpeas. Heat through and stir in a couple of tablespoons of low-fat plain yogurt and freshly chopped mint. Spoon onto one side of the chapatti, roll up, and serve while still warm.

Fruit Loaf
GI range 44–54

There are several types of fruit loaves or breads that include raisins, dried apricots or apple, figs, and sometimes nuts and seeds. The dried fruit content means they can be a useful source of iron, protein, fiber, thiamin, niacin, riboflavin, and magnesium. Generally, the heavier, dense fruity breads will have a lower GI. Enjoy fresh or toasted for breakfast or as a snack.

Serving suggestions

▶ Snack on toasted fruit loaf with a dollop of ricotta.

▶ Add flavor to a bread pudding by making it with slices of fruit loaf—great comfort food. Spread 8 slices of fruit loaf with a tablespoon of margarine. Cut into triangles and place in layers in a round casserole dish. Whisk 3 eggs with 2 cups of low-fat milk or soy milk and 2 tablespoons of sugar or honey and pour over the bread layers. Stand the casserole dish in a baking pan filled with enough water to come halfway up the sides of the dish. Bake in a moderate oven (350°F) for 40 minutes or until browned on top.

Pita Bread
GI 57

Top it, stuff it, wrap it, cut it into wedges and dip it, or split it open and bake it to make "crisps"—pita is the ultimate meal-in-a-bread to have around for all occasions. With all the health benefits of ordinary bread, this traditional Middle Eastern flat two-layered bread splits open horizontally, making the perfect pocket for your favorite fillings.

Serving suggestions

- Wrap up with hummus, shredded lettuce, falafel, tabbouleh, and a tangy tomato salsa; or avocado, mushrooms, bean salad, shredded lettuce, and pepper strips; or tuna, white beans, onion rings, cucumber, feta, and a drizzle of oil and vinegar.
- Use pita bread as an instant pizza base—top with tomato paste, mushrooms, pepper, finely sliced onion, olives, and a sprinkle of Parmesan cheese.
- For breakfast, toast and top with fresh light ricotta and a dollop of blackberry all-fruit preserves.
- Serve dips such as hummus and baba ghanoush with pita crisps—simply cut the pita bread into triangles, open out the "halves" and spray with a little olive oil, sprinkle over paprika for extra flavor, and bake at 350°F for about 5 minutes, or until crisp.

Pumpernickel
GI 50

This traditional rye bread from Germany can be something of an acquired taste. It's a very good source of fiber and, thanks to its high proportion of whole cereal grains, has a low GI value. Also known as rye kernel bread, pumpernickel contains 80–90 percent whole and cracked rye kernels.

Pumpernickel (no one is quite sure of the origins of the name) has a strong flavor and is dark, dense, and compact—not "airy" like some breads. It is usually sold thinly sliced and vacuum packed for long shelf life. You can crumble it to use in stuffings and for making desserts, but it is most popular as an appetizer.

Serving suggestions

▶ For an appetizer, top pumpernickel with tangy cheese and apple or pear slivers, spicy sausage and salsa, or smoked salmon, horseradish cream, and dill.

▶ For breakfast, toast pumpernickel, spread lightly with margarine, and accompany with a hot chocolate drink made with low-fat milk.

Sourdough
GI 54

Crusty, chewy white sourdough's characteristic flavor comes from the slow fermentation process, which produces a buildup of organic acids. It's about the best low-GI bread substitute for people who absolutely insist they can only eat white bread. Use for sandwiches and toast (with sweet or savory spreads and toppings) or serve with main meals, soups, and salads.

Serving suggestions

Make bruschetta for a quick and easy light meal or snack. Simply brush slices of crusty sourdough with a little olive oil, then lightly grill or bake on both sides and top with:

▶ fresh tomato and basil salsa with a dash of balsamic vinegar
▶ grilled red and yellow pepper with roasted artichoke hearts
▶ grilled eggplant with semidried tomatoes
▶ mushrooms sautéed with garlic, lemon juice, and parsley
▶ tuna, arugula, and capers

Sourdough Rye
GI 54

Sourdough rye is made with rye instead of wheat flour. Slices of chewy, low-GI sourdough rye piled with tasty hot or cold fillings make great sandwiches for workdays, picnics, or travel. This bread's compact structure keeps the sandwich with all its fillings intact, while the slightly sour flavor combines well with a wide range of meat, poultry, fish, and salad fillings.

Keep them cool

If you plan to make sandwiches ahead of time or pack them for your lunch, be sure to include an ice pack. If you're taking your sandwiches on a picnic, park the cooler in the shade. Foods most susceptible to bacteria growth are meats, poultry, eggs, and mayonnaise, so be sure they are not left at room temperature for more than an hour.

Serving suggestions

Try these sandwich fillings:

- salad (the works) with rare roast beef and horseradish, or smoked ham and grainy mustard
- smoked turkey with cranberry, avocado, and sprouts
- egg salad with fresh chopped chives and crisp lettuce
- chicken breast with watercress, apple slices, and walnuts
- tuna melt—flaked tuna, finely sliced onion rings, and a slice of Gruyère cheese
- BLT—lean grilled bacon, lettuce, and tomato slices

Tested low-GI soy and linseed breads with low GI values include (at the time of this writing): Rudolph's Specialty Ltd. linseed rye bread (GI 55) and Con Agra soy and linseed bread made from package mix, in a bread mixer (GI 50).

Soy and Flaxseed Bread
GI range 36–57

These moist breads with good keeping qualities are made by adding kibbled soy beans or soy flour and flaxseeds to bread dough. These phytoestrogen-rich ingredients have been shown to help relieve the symptoms of menopause. They are also rich in omega-3 fatty acids (the good essential oils). Unless you are on a very low-fat diet, don't be deterred from enjoying soy and flaxseed breads as their fat content is unsaturated. They are a good source of fiber. Remember, the grainier the bread, the lower the GI.

Serving suggestions

▶ Club sandwiches, open-faced sandwiches with cold meats and salad, and toasted or grilled sandwiches for light meals and lunches.

▶ For a satisfying salad in a sandwich, take two slices of soy and flaxseed bread with a little avocado and fill with a slice of lean ham, tomato, arugula, grated carrot, grated beets, spring onions, and sprouts.

▶ To make a cheesy melt, spread a slice of soy and flaxseed bread with whole-grain mustard. Add chopped sun-dried tomatoes, grilled eggplant, and a slice of mozzarella cheese. Melt the cheese under the broiler, add salad greens and another slice of soy and flaxseed, slice diagonally, and serve.

Stoneground 100% Whole Wheat Breads
GI 53

"Stoneground 100% whole wheat bread" means that the flour has been milled from the entire wheat berry—the germ, endosperm, and the bran—and the milling process slowly grinds the grain with a burrstone instead of high-speed metal rollers to distribute the germ oil more evenly. As a result, virtually none of the nutrient-rich ingredients are lost in the processing, making this bread a rich source of several B vitamins, iron, zinc, and dietary fiber. If you can't find stoneground breads in the bakery section of your supermarket, try specialist bakeries or health, natural, or organic food stores.

Serving suggestions

▶ Fill toasted sandwiches with tomato and a slice of cheese or banana, light cream cheese, and honey.

▶ Top toast with a slice of lean ham, spinach, a perfectly poached egg, and a drizzle of oil and vinegar.

Tortilla
Corn tortilla GI 52
Wheat tortilla GI 30

Mexicans use them as plates, forks, and spoons. They dip their tortillas into stews and use torn-off pieces to scoop up sauces. Tortillas are a flat (unleavened) bread traditionally made from corn (maize) flour. A staple of Mexican cuisine, they are quite different from the Spanish tortilla, which is a type of omelette. And when made in the traditional Mexican way, whether from corn or wheat flour, they have a low GI.

Almost any kind of food that is not too liquid—beans, corn, or chicken, chili or salsa—can be placed on or wrapped in the versatile tortilla for a complete meal. Make the most of them with your favorite recipes for burritos, enchiladas, fajitas, and quesadillas (but hold the creamy dips) or use as rolls, wraps, or scoops. Corn tortillas are also a good alternative to bread if you are gluten intolerant.

Serving suggestion
▶ To make bean and corn burritos, preheat the oven to 350°F. Combine a 14-ounce can of corn kernels, drained, a 14-ounce can of red kidney beans, rinsed and drained, 2 large ripe tomatoes, chopped, 2 shallots, finely sliced and 2½ ounces prepared taco sauce in a bowl. Wrap four 6-inch white corn tortillas in foil and warm in the oven for 5 minutes. To assemble, spread shredded lettuce over a warmed tortilla, and top with the bean mixture and a little grated reduced fat cheese. Fold the bottom of the tortilla over the filling, and roll up to enclose. Serve immediately. Makes 4.

Whole-Grain Bread
GI range 43–54

Whole-grain breads such as "multigrain" or "granary" breads contain lots of "grainy bits" in the bread (not just on top for decoration). They tend to have a slightly grainy, chewy texture and provide a good source of fiber, vitamins, minerals, and phytoestrogens, although this will depend on the flour mix. These are usually made from whole wheat or white flour (or a combination of the two) with kibbled and whole grains added to the dough.

Choose breads with whole or kibbled grains such as barley, rye, triticale (a wheat and rye hybrid), oats, soy, cracked wheat, and seeds such as sunflower seeds or flaxseeds.

> There are a number of whole-grain breads available, including Natural Ovens Hunger Filler (GI 59), Natural Ovens 100% Whole Grain (GI 51), and Con Agra Healthy Choice Hearty 100% Whole Grain (GI 62).
>
> These are great everyday breads. Keep a loaf in the freezer so you don't run out.

Serving suggestions

▶ Make your own "submarines" with whole-grain rolls or muffins
▶ Top a vegetable gratin with grainy breadcrumbs
▶ Enjoy a beef or chickpea burger on a grainy bun

Breakfast Cereals

Whether you like waking up to a crisp, crunchy cereal, a warming bowl of oatmeal or a chewy, nutty muesli, a good breakfast can set you up for the day. Given the solid evidence that people who eat breakfast are calmer, happier, and more sociable, the number of people skipping breakfast is an alarming trend. Studies regularly show that eating breakfast improves mood, mental alertness, concentration, and memory. Nutritionists also know that having breakfast helps people lose weight, can lower cholesterol levels, and helps stabilize blood glucose levels.

Breakfast cereals and bars to look for

Manufacturer	Brand	GI
Kellogg's	All-Bran	34
	All-Bran Fruit 'n' Oats	39
	Bran Buds with psyllium	47
	Frosted Flakes	55
	Special K	56
	Mini-Wheats Whole Wheat	58
Swiss Alpen	Muesli	55

All-Bran
GI 30

With its malty taste, Kellogg's All-Bran is a good source of B vitamins and an excellent source of insoluble fiber. Made from coarsely milled wheat bran, it's among the most fiber-rich of all breakfast cereals on the market. It is also low in sodium and a good source of potassium.

Serving suggestions

▶ Top a bowl of All-Bran with banana slices or canned pear slices and serve with low-fat milk.

▶ Sprinkle a few tablespoons over low-fat yogurt as a fiber booster.

▶ Blend yourself a honey banana smoothie—a cup of low-fat milk, a small banana, honey to taste, and ¼ cup of All-Bran (or more if you like).

▶ Warm up in winter with a fruity blend of canned plums or apricot halves, low-fat milk, honey to taste, and ¼ cup of All-Bran; microwave for 30 seconds.

▶ Add ½ cup of All-Bran to muffin mixes, banana, and other fruit or vegetable breads, and cookies when baking.

Rise and shine with breakfast

Skipping breakfast is not a good way to cut back your food intake, and it can leave you feeling fatigued, dehydrated, and without energy for the day's decisions. Breakfast-skippers tend to make up for the missed food by eating more snacks during the day, and more food overall.

Bran
GI 19 (extruded rice bran)
GI 55 (unprocessed oat bran, average)

You can buy unprocessed oat bran in the cereal section of supermarkets and in health, natural, and organic food stores. Its carbohydrate content is lower than that of oats, and it is higher in fiber, particularly soluble fiber. Bran is a soft, bland product useful as an addition to breakfast cereals and as a partial substitution for flour in baked goods to help boost fiber and lower the GI. You can also add a tablespoon or two to meatball and burger mixes, use it in making muesli, or add to oatmeal for extra fiber.

Cereals with bran

When shopping in the supermarket, you will find a number of low-GI breakfast cereals that include bran: Kellogg's All-Bran (34) All-Bran Fruit 'n' Oats (39) Bran Buds with psyllium (47)

Serving suggestion

Enjoy one of these low-GI Cherry Oat Crunchies made with fruit, nuts, oats, and bran flakes. Just two delicious cookies will give you 2 grams of fiber.

Preheat the oven to 350°F. Lightly spray two baking trays with olive oil. Put 2 ounces soft brown sugar, 3 ounces pure honey, 4½ ounces reduced fat margarine or butter, 2 eggs, ½ teaspoon of baking soda, and 2 teaspoons of vanilla in a large mixing bowl. Beat using electric beaters on medium speed for 2 minutes. Fold in 5½ ounces wholemeal flour, 7 ounces rolled oats, 3 ounces chopped dried apricots, 2 ounces roughly chopped walnuts, 2¾ ounces bran flakes cereal, crushed. Mix thoroughly. Drop spoonfuls of the mixture onto the prepared baking trays, spacing them about 2 inches apart. Bake for 15 minutes, or until light brown. Leave for 5 minutes before lifting off the tray and placing on a wire rack to cool. Store in an airtight container. Makes around 42.

Muesli
GI 49 (natural muesli made with rolled oats, dried fruit, nuts, and seeds)

Muesli originated as a Swiss health food, developed by Dr. Max Bircher-Brenner, who was a passionate advocate of the benefits of a vegetarian, especially raw, diet. It currently rates as one of the few relatively unprocessed breakfast cereals on the market. A good source of thiamin, riboflavin, and niacin, its low GI value is the result of the slower digestion of raw oats. Oats also contain fiber that increases the viscosity of the contents of the small intestine, thereby slowing down enzyme attack. This same fiber has also been shown to reduce blood cholesterol levels.

There are essentially three basic types of muesli: toasted, natural (untoasted), and moist (Swiss or Bircher) muesli, but the list of possible ingredients is endless and generally includes:

- cereals: rolled oats, flakes of barley or rice, plus a processed bran cereal if you need to boost the fiber
- nuts: chopped almonds, walnuts, macadamias, or hazelnuts
- seeds: sesame seeds, sunflower seeds, flaxseeds, pepitas
- dried fruit: raisins, raisins, chopped dried apricots or figs, pears, bananas, apple rings, cranberries

▶ spices: cinnamon and other spices are sometimes added for extra flavor

Any muesli will fuel your day, but check the nutrition label when buying toasted muesli, as it can contain extra fat and sugar.

Mueslis on the market

There are a number of mueslis available in the supermarket with GI values ranging from 49 to 55. Look for a natural muesli (49), low-fat muesli (54), or Swiss Alpen muesli (55).

For a gluten-free muesli, look for Glutano foods, organic muesli, or Swiss-style muesli.

Serving suggestion

Try our low-GI simple Swiss muesli:

Combine 1 cup of traditional rolled oats, ½ cup of low-fat milk and 2 tablespoons of raisins in a bowl; cover and refrigerate overnight. Next morning add ½ cup of low-fat vanilla yogurt, 2 tablespoons of slivered almonds, and ½ an apple (grated). Mix well, adjusting the flavor with a little lemon juice if you wish. Serve with your favorite berries, such as strawberries or blueberries. Serves 2.

Oatmeal
GI 42 (traditional rolled oats)

The first farmers back in Neolithic times knew that the best way to cook any grain was to make an "oatmeal"—all they had to do was crack the grain, add water, and cook the mixture in a pot on the edge of the fire. The basic recipe hasn't changed much over the years. The classic oatmeal we associate with Scotland was made from stoneground oats simmered in milk or water until cooked, and served with salt or sugar and milk.

For a high-energy breakfast it's hard to beat a hot cereal made with traditional oats—a good source of soluble fiber, B vitamins, vitamin E, iron, and zinc. The GI value for oatmeal has been tested on a number of occasions and the published values range from 42 (for rolled oats made with water) to 82 (for instant oats).

Traditional rolled oats are hulled, steamed, and flattened, which makes them a 100 percent whole-grain cereal. The additional flaking to produce quick cooking or "instant" oats not only speeds up cooking time, it increases the rate of digestion and the GI. This is why traditional rolled oats are preferred over instant in the low-GI diet.

Oatmeal connoisseurs advocate steel-cut oats—the whole grains are simply chopped into chunks. These oats are hard to find but worth the hunt if you like a chewier texture—and it has a GI value of 51.

Follow the instructions on the package (or use your favorite recipe) to make oatmeal. A fairly standard rule is one part rolled oats to four parts water. Cooking oats in milk (preferably low-fat or skim) not only produces a creamy dish but supplies you with calcium and reduces the overall GI.

Serving suggestions

Don't skimp on finishing touches for perfect oatmeal. Choose toppings such as:

▶ fresh fruit slices in season
▶ mixed berries
▶ unsweetened canned plums
▶ a teaspoon or two of maple syrup
▶ a tablespoon or two of dried fruit such as raisins or chopped apricots

Noodles

Noodles have long been a staple food in China, Japan, Korea, and most of Southeast Asia. Today, their meals-in-minutes value has made them popular worldwide—they are a great stand-by for quick meals. They are also a good source of carbohydrate, provide some protein, B vitamins, and minerals, and will help to keep blood glucose levels on an even keel.

Noodles are made from flour, water, and sometimes egg that is mixed into a dough, rolled out to the appropriate thickness, and cut into long ribbons, strips, and strings—long noodles symbolize long life. Their dense texture and shape whether they are made from wheat flour, buckwheat, mung beans, soybeans, rice, or sweet potatoes contribute to their low to intermediate GI values (33 to 62). Choose lower-GI noodles for everyday use.

You can buy noodles fresh, dried, or boiled (wet). Fresh and boiled noodles will be in the produce or refrigerated specialty section in your supermarket or Asian grocery store. Use them as soon as possible after purchase or store in the refrigerator for a day or two.

Dried noodles are handy to have in the pantry for quick and easy meals in minutes. They will keep for several months, provided you haven't opened the package.

Egg noodles are made from wheat flour and eggs. They are readily available dried, and you can find fresh egg noodles in the refrigerated specialty section of the supermarket or Asian grocery store. Hokkien noodles are "wet" egg noodles and will be in the refrigerator section too. Instant noodles are usually precooked and dehydrated egg noodles. Check the label as they are sometimes fried.

Served with fish, chicken, tofu, or lean meat and plenty of vegetables, a soup, salad, or stir-fry based on noodles gives you a healthy balance of carbs, fats, and proteins plus some fiber and essential vitamins and minerals. Enjoy them hot or cold in soups, salads, and stir-fries. If they are served crisp, it means that they have been deep-fried.

To cook, follow the instructions on the package, as times vary depending on types and thickness. Some noodles only need swirling under running warm water to separate, or soaking in hot (but not boiling) water to soften before you serve them or add to stir-fries.

Others need to be boiled. Like pasta, they are usually best just tender, almost al dente, so keep an eye on the clock.

As it's all too easy to slurp, gulp, twirl, and overeat noodles, keep those portion sizes moderate. While they are a low-GI choice themselves, eating a huge amount will have a marked effect on your blood glucose. Instead of piling your plate with noodles, serve plenty of vegetables—a cup of noodles combined with lots of mixed vegetables can turn into three cups of a noodle-based meal and fit into any adult's daily diet.

Remember when planning meals that the sauces you serve with noodles and how you cook them can provide a lot more calories than the noodles themselves.

Buckwheat Noodles
GI 46 (soba noodles)

Japan's soba noodles are like spaghetti in both color and texture. They are usually made from a combination of buckwheat and wheat flour and are a better source of protein and fiber than rice noodles. You can buy them fresh or dried, but fresh is better if available. Serve soba hot or cold. One of the classic soba recipes is zaru soba, in which boiled soba noodles are eaten cold with a soy dipping sauce.

Serving suggestions

▶ For a satisfying pork and noodle soup, season a pork fillet with freshly ground Szechuan pepper, then sear on all sides in a little vegetable oil to get a crust. Cook about 7 ounces of buckwheat noodles following the instructions on the package, then drain and add to 2 cups of simmering chicken stock. Stir in a seeded and sliced dried red chili, ½ cup of thinly sliced shiitake mushrooms, and 2 teaspoons of mushroom soy sauce. Add the thinly sliced pork, ½ a cup of cilantro leaves, heat through, and serve.

▶ Make a buckwheat noodle salad by tossing 2 cups of cooked noodles in a dressing made with about 1 tablespoon of light soy sauce, 2 tablespoons of white wine vinegar, 1 teaspoon of sesame oil, 2 teaspoons of mirin, ½ teaspoon of finely chopped ginger, 1 clove of crushed garlic, and a pinch of chili (or to taste). Top with finely chopped spring onions and serve. If you like, add thinly sliced pieces of tofu, too.

Cellophane Noodles
GI 33

Cellophane noodles, also known as Lungkow bean thread noodles or green bean vermicelli, are fine, translucent threads made from mung bean flour, which is why they have the lowest GI value of noodles tested to date. When soaked they become shiny and slippery and are sometimes called slippery noodles or glass noodles. They are often used in soups, salads, and stir-fries. They can also be deep fried. To soften, simply soak them in hot (not boiling) water for a couple of minutes before adding them to the dish.

Serving suggestions
▶ Make a spiced seafood salad using seafood mix from the fish shop (including calamari, crab meat, and shrimp) with cellophane noodles, chopped Asian greens, snowpeas, and a chili-lime dressing.
▶ Use leftover chicken to whip up a salad with noodles, blanched snowpeas, blanched green beans, arugula, and a light sesame and hoisin dressing.

Instant Noodles
GI 46

Asian-style dried noodles are very popular as a quick meal or snack. They are a high-carbohydrate convenience food but they also contain a substantial amount of fat—over 35 percent of their calories, in fact. The flavor packets supplied tend to be based on salt and flavor enhancers, including monosodium glutamate. Keep them for occasional use and add fresh or frozen chopped vegetables when preparing. These noodles can also be added to soups and stir-fries.

Serving suggestions

▶ For a meal in minutes, make a quick Thai noodle curry. Stir-fry sliced onion, red pepper, baby corn, broccoli florets, and snow-peas in a large pan or wok. Add a tablespoon of Thai red curry paste. Prepare instant Asian noodles according to the instructions on the package. Add to the vegetables with enough stock to make a sauce. Stir in a tablespoon of light coconut milk, heat through, and serve.

▶ Make up a single serving of instant noodles with half the flavor packet. Add a couple of tablespoons each of frozen peas and corn kernels and then microwave to heat through.

Rice Noodles
GI 40 (fresh)

Made from ground or pounded rice flour, rice noodles are available fresh and dried. Run hot water through fresh rice noodles to loosen them, then drain and combine with other ingredients. Dried rice noodles are a little brittle and need to be soaked for 10 to 15 minutes before adding to soups, salads, and stir-fries.

Serving suggestions

▶ Enjoy rice noodles in broth served with a little lean meat, chicken, or tofu, and vegetables, including chopped Asian greens, bean sprouts, mint leaves, and some finely sliced chili.

▶ Make up some fresh rice paper rolls: mix together softened chopped rice vermicelli with grated carrot, fresh bean sprouts, chopped roasted peanuts (unsalted), chopped fresh mint, and cilantro or parsley and a dressing of sesame oil and lime juice with minced garlic, chili and a pinch of sugar. Roll up spoonfuls of the mixture in softened rice paper rounds and serve alongside sweet chili sauce for dipping.

Wheat Flour Noodles
GI 62 (udon noodles)

Japanese udon noodles are white and usually firmer and thicker than soba noodles. They are available dried, ready boiled, and fresh.

Cook them according to the instructions on the package, as times will vary depending on the type. Enjoy them hot in soup or cold with dipping sauces and salads.

Serving suggestions

▶ Combine cooked udon noodles with seared tuna and cucumber slices and toss in a tangy dressing made with soy sauce, lime juice, sesame oil, and a dash of wasabi.

▶ Serve cooked udon noodles cold with a dipping sauce made from soy sauce, mirin, and Japanese dashi soup stock and other accompaniments such as sesame seed, grated fresh ginger, dried seaweed, chopped green onion, and wasabi.

Pasta

It's said that pasta (Italian for "dough") comes in more shapes and sizes than there are days of the year. Whatever the shape, it's perfect for quick meals and scores well nutritionally as a good source of protein, B vitamins, and fiber. Pasta in any shape or form has a relatively low GI (30 to 60)—great news for pasta lovers, but portion size is important. Keep it moderate.

Initially we thought that pasta's low GI was due to its main ingredient, semolina (durum or hard wheat flour). Scientists have now shown, however, that even pasta made with plain wheat flour has a low GI and the reason for the slow digestion is the physical entrapment of ungelatinized starch granules in a spongelike network of protein (gluten) molecules in the pasta dough. Pasta and noodles are unique in this regard. Adding egg to the dough lowers the GI further by increasing the protein content.

As a general rule, commercial dried pasta is made from durum wheat semolina and no eggs; commercial fresh pasta is made with durum wheat semolina and eggs. Homemade pasta tends to be made with plain wheat flour and eggs. There is also some evidence that thicker types of pasta tend to have a lower GI than thinner types, perhaps due to their dense consistency and because they cook more slowly (and are less likely to be overcooked).

A number of pasta shapes and types have been tested. Note

that canned spaghetti in tomato sauce and packaged macaroni and cheese are not low GI—they have medium to high GI values.

Watch that glucose load. While pasta is a low-GI choice, eating too much will have a marked effect on your blood glucose. That's because if you eat too large a portion of even a low-GI food, the glucose load becomes too large. So, instead of piling your plate with pasta, fill it with vegetables—a cup of cooked pasta combined with plenty of mixed vegetables can turn into three cups of a pasta-based meal and fit easily into any adult's daily diet.

A moderate portion of pasta served with vegetables or tomato sauce or accompaniments such as olive oil, fish, and lean meat, plenty of vegetables, and small amounts of cheese provides a healthy balance of carbs, fats, and proteins.

Pasta salads are ideal for people with busy lives. You can make them in minutes, or prepare beforehand and keep in the fridge until serving time.

Gluten free

Gluten-free pastas based on rice and corn (maize) have moderate to high GI values. Serve with plenty of vegetables, a little pasta sauce, and grated Parmesan to help lower the GI.

Al dente

Cooked al dente, pasta does not cause sugar spikes when you eat moderate portions. Al dente ("firm to the bite") is the best way to eat pasta—it's not meant to be soft. It should be slightly firm and offer some resistance when you are chewing it. Its GI is lower, too—overcooking boosts the GI. Although most manufacturers specify a cooking time on the package, don't take their word for it. Start testing about 2–3 minutes before the indicated cooking time is up.

Cappellini
GI 45

This is the thinnest form of pasta (cappellini literally means "fine hairs") and is made from semolina. Angel-hair pasta is similar in shape, but its dough is made with eggs. Because cappellini is so thin, it is all too easy to overcook it. For a perfect al dente product, the optimal cooking time is around 4 minutes. Cappellini comes fresh or dried and is best served with light, smooth, or spicy sauces such as tomato, marinara, or pesto.

Serving suggestion

A basic marinara sauce is essentially tomatoes and garlic to which seafood (most often these days) is added. To make a basic marinara, cook 2 cloves of crushed garlic and a finely sliced onion in a little olive oil until soft and golden. Add chopped fresh herbs such as parsley and basil (about ½ cup), 2 14-ounce cans of Italian tomatoes, a splash of white wine, a pinch of sugar and salt, and freshly ground black pepper to taste. Simmer uncovered until the sauce is thick, rich, and red—about half an hour. Add ½ pound of shrimp (shelled and deveined) toward the end of the cooking time. Cook until the shrimp lose their translucency—just a few minutes depending on the size. Makes about 3 cups of sauce.

Fettuccine
GI 40

This is the familiar flat, long, ribbon-shaped pasta usually about ¼ inch wide. Fettuccine is the term that Romans use for "noodles." It's made from semolina and other ingredients such as spinach, squid ink, tomato paste, and even cocoa. Available fresh and dried, it's best with tomato- or cheese-based sauces.

Serving suggestions

‣ Toss cooked fettuccine in a tablespoon of pesto with diced tomatoes and top with a little grated Parmesan cheese. Try using a sun-dried tomato pesto as an alternative and top with some pitted black olives.

▶ Fettuccine is delicious with seafood. While the pasta is cooking, combine a little finely chopped garlic, chopped red chilies, and flat-leaf parsley in a bowl (adjust the quantity to suit your tastebuds). Pan-fry about four scallops per person in a little olive oil for 2–3 minutes, then add the garlic mixture and heat through. Stir in the drained pasta and serve topped with more freshly chopped parsley.

Linguine
GI 46 (thick)
GI 52 (thin)

With its flat shape, linguine is great with many kinds of pasta sauces—pesto and clam or seafood sauces are ideal. It's available fresh and dried and in a variety of flavors, including spinach and whole wheat.

Serving suggestions

▶ Toss al dente linguine with peppery arugula (stems removed), halved or quartered baby tomatoes, canned tuna, and a little oil and lemon juice. Season with salt and freshly ground black pepper and serve warm topped with a little freshly grated Parmesan.

▶ Red pesto is a piquant coating sauce for all kinds of pasta shapes and ribbons. Combine the following ingredients in a food processor and blend: ½ ounce of drained anchovy fillets, a clove of crushed garlic, a tablespoon of toasted pine nuts, a tablespoon of dried breadcrumbs (from grainy bread), a 6-ounce can of red pimiento (drained) or a small jar of roasted pepper, 1 large peeled and seeded tomato, 2 teaspoons of capers, 1 teaspoon of dried oregano, and 1 tablespoon of chopped fresh parsley. Add 2 tablespoons of red wine and blend. Slowly add about ½ cup of olive oil and blend in bursts until the sauce has the consistency of pesto. Makes about 1 cup.

Macaroni
GI 47

These short, hollow pasta tubes of "macaroni and cheese" fame combine well with tomato- or other vegetable-based sauces. They are often used in baked dishes, soups, and salads.

Serving suggestions

To make macaroni and cheese, preheat the oven to 350°F, then cook 14 ounces of macaroni following the instructions on the package. Combine an 8-ounce container of ricotta with 1¼ cups of low-fat milk, 2 beaten eggs, 2 teaspoons of smooth Dijon mustard, 1 teaspoon of Tabasco sauce (or to taste), and freshly ground black pepper in a food processor and blend. Combine the cooked macaroni with 1 cup of shredded low-fat cheddar cheese and 2 cups of baby spinach leaves in a bowl. Stir in the ricotta mixture, then spoon into a baking dish. Top with grated Parmesan cheese, grainy breadcrumbs, and a little paprika, and bake for 20–25 minutes. Serve with a crisp green salad. Serves 4.

Pastina
GI 38 (star-shaped)

Small pasta or "pastina" comes in many shapes: stars, orzo, acini di pepe, and many more. But just like the larger pasta shapes, pastina is made from durum wheat semolina. It is used in vegetable, chicken, and beef soups to provide some bulk and added calories to the soup. Children particularly love the shapes of these smaller pastas.

Serving suggestion

Cook 3½ ounces of pastina according to the package instructions and drain. Heat 6 cups of chicken stock and add the cooked pasta plus 2 cups of cooked shredded chicken fillet. Season with salt and freshly ground black pepper and serve with a little grated Parmesan cheese and chopped flat-leaf parsley.

Ravioli
GI 39 (meat-filled)
Ravioli are small, square pasta "pillows" with fillings such as meat, cheese and spinach, mushroom, pumpkin, and tofu. Buy them fresh, frozen, or vacuum packed and serve with a sauce that brings out the flavor of the fillings.

Serving suggestions
▶ A homemade tomato and basil sauce with a sprinkling of Parmesan cheese is a classic ravioli dish. What makes it even better is that by adding a large salad and fruit dessert you will have created a low-GI meal in less than 20 minutes!
▶ Top a homemade tomato and basil soup with floating ravioli and grated Parmesan cheese.

Spaghetti
GI 44 (plain)
GI 42 (whole wheat)
Probably the most popular pasta of all, spaghetti's round, long strands are available fresh and dried and in a variety of flavors such as spinach and whole wheat. With its sturdy texture, spaghetti's versatility is endless. It blends beautifully with cooked and raw vegetables; any mixture of herbs and spices; meats, poultry, fish, and shellfish; sauces containing olive oil, margarine, butter, or light cream; and even nuts such as walnuts, pine nuts, and sunflower seeds—all of which fit in a healthy, balanced diet.

All the low-GI virtues of regular spaghetti apply to whole wheat

Pasta makes a quick and easy meal with many prepared pasta sauces on the market (although it's easy to make your own). Stick to tomato-based sauces or toss with vegetables rather than the creamy ones laden with fat. And use a modest sprinkling of cheese on top.

spaghetti and they can be used interchangeably in any recipe with the same sauces and accompaniments. Just keep mind that you'll be taking in more than double the amount of dietary fiber when you opt for whole wheat spaghetti.

Serving suggestions

▶ Serve spaghetti with a low-fat meat sauce made from lean cuts of beef, pork, or veal plus chopped tomatoes, carrots, onions, celery, and fresh herbs.

▶ Toss al dente spaghetti with smoked salmon, capers, and a little olive oil and finish with a few drops of lemon juice.

▶ Make a spaghetti and tomato salad—enjoy as a light meal and use leftovers for lunch the next day. Dice 3 medium tomatoes and combine in a bowl with 1 tablespoon of olive oil, 1 table-spoon of capers, 1 crushed garlic clove, the juice of a lemon, a sprinkle of chili powder (or to taste), a few pitted black olives, freshly ground black pepper to taste, and a handful of torn basil leaves. Combine with a cup of cooked spaghetti and serve cold or warm. Serves 2.

Spirali
GI 43

There are so many dried pasta shapes—from spirals (spirali), shells (conchiglie), bows (farfalle, literally butterflies), pencil-shaped tubes (penne and penne rigate), small wheels (rotelle), twists (gemelli, literally twins) to round tubes such as cannelloni, which are stuffed then baked. Everyone has their favorites. The great news for pasta lovers is that they all have a relatively low GI. Whether you serve them with tomato- or vegetable-based sauces, simply fold in your favorite vegetables or use them in salads, they are ideal for creating healthy, balanced meals in minutes.

Serving suggestions

▶ Serve your favorite shapes with lightly steamed cauliflower or broccoli florets and diced lean crisp bacon (pancetta is even better) cooked with a sliced red chili. Top with chopped parsley and a little grated Parmesan.

▶ Enjoy a quick pasta and red bean salad. Combine 1 cup of cooked pasta shapes with 1 cup of canned red kidney beans (drained), 3 finely chopped spring onions, and a tablespoon of chopped fresh parsley. Toss with an oil and vinegar dressing made from 1 tablespoon of olive oil, 1 tablespoon of white wine vinegar, 1 teaspoon of Dijon mustard, a crushed clove of garlic, and freshly ground black pepper. Serves 4.

Tortellini
GI 50 (cheese)

Tortellini are a small, crescent-shaped, filled pasta available in a range of fillings—including spinach and ricotta, chicken, veal, ham, mushrooms, and cheese in a variety of combinations. The overall nutrient content will vary depending on the fillings. You can usually buy it fresh, frozen, or vacuum packed and all you have to do is cook and serve.

Serving suggestions

▶ Toss cooked tortellini with fresh chopped herbs such as parsley and basil, a minced garlic clove and a little olive oil.
▶ Try this time-saving tortellini meal. Cook spinach and cheese tortellini according to the package instructions until al dente and serve with bought or homemade tomato sauce topped with a little grated Parmesan cheese. Serve with a big garden salad for a complete meal in minutes.

Vermicelli
GI 35

Rather like cappellini, vermicelli is a thin type of spaghetti that's available fresh and dried. Because it is so fine it cooks quickly, so watch the times. Serve with light sauces or add to soups and stir-fries.

Serving suggestions

Toss al dente vermicelli with:

▶ lightly steamed strips of zucchini, finely chopped parsley, a few walnut halves, a twist of black pepper, and a little grated Parmesan cheese

▶ a store-bought or homemade tomato sauce with yellow and red marinated pepper slices, anchovies, flaked canned tuna, olives, capers, and basil

Rice

Carb-rich rice is one of the world's oldest and most cultivated grains—there are some 2,000 varieties worldwide—and the staple food for over half the world's population. A soup, salad, or stir-fry based around rice with a little fish, chicken, tofu, or lean meat and plenty of vegetables will give you a healthy balance of carbs, fat, and protein plus some fiber and essential vitamins and minerals.

Rice can have a very high GI value, or a low one, depending on the variety and its amylose content. Amylose is a kind of starch that

Why "gelatinization" means high GI

The starch in raw carb-rich foods such as rice grains is stored in hard, compact granules that make the food difficult to digest unless you cook it. This is why eating raw potatoes can give you a stomachache. During cooking, water and heat expand starch granules to different degrees; some actually burst and free the molecules. This happens when you make gravy by heating flour and water until the starch granules burst and the gravy thickens. If most of the starch granules have swelled during cooking, we say that the starch is fully gelatinized. It is now also easy to digest, which is why the food will have a high GI.

resists gelatinization. Although rice is a whole-grain food, when you cook it, the millions of microscopic cracks in the grains let water penetrate right to the middle of the grain, allowing the starch granules to swell and become fully "gelatinized," thus very easy to digest.

So, if you are a big rice eater, opt for the low-GI varieties with a higher amylose content such as basmati, or Uncle Ben's converted long-grain rice. These high-amylose rices that stay firm and separate when cooked combine well with Indian, Thai, and Vietnamese cuisines.

Brown rice is an extremely nutritious form of rice and contains several B vitamins, minerals, dietary, fiber, and protein. Chewier than regular white rice, it tends to take about twice as long to cook. The varieties that have been tested to date have a high GI, so enjoy it occasionally, especially combined with low-GI foods. Arborio risotto rice releases its starch during cooking and has a medium GI. Wild rice (GI 57) is not actually rice at all, but a type of grass seed.

As with pasta and noodles, it's all too easy to overeat rice, so keep portions moderate. Even when you choose a low-GI rice, eating too much can have a marked effect on your blood glucose. A cup of cooked rice combined with plenty of mixed vegetables can turn into three cups of a rice-based meal that suits any adult's daily diet.

Uncle Ben's Converted Long Grain Rice GI value: 38

It has a higher than average amylose content. This not only means it has a low GI, but it is easier to cook fluffy, non-sticky rice. You will find it on your supermarket shelf.

Basmati Rice
GI 58

basmati is a long-grain aromatic rice grown in the foothills of the Himalayas and is especially popular in India. When cooked, the grains are dry and fluffy, so they make the perfect bed for curries and sauces. You can buy brown or white basmati rice—brown basmati has more fiber and a stronger flavor, but it takes twice as long to cook. It also has a higher GI.

Serving suggestions

▶ Toss rice in an oil and vinegar dressing with raisins, chopped red and green pepper, corn kernels, and finely sliced red onion and celery to make a simple salad.

▶ Rice on the run is great for lunch the next day, too. Pour a lightly beaten egg into an oiled fryingpan and cook over a medium heat until bubbly. Flip over to cook on the other side, turn onto a cutting board, and chop into slices. Sauté finely diced zucchini and red pepper, a stick of thinly sliced celery, and a grated carrot in a little oil in the pan. Add minced garlic, ginger, and chopped shallots, stir till aromatic, then add a cup of cooked basmati rice and stir until heated through. Sprinkle with soy sauce to serve.

Sushi
GI 48–55

Ideal for snacks and light meals, these bite-sized pieces are usually made with combinations of raw or smoked fish, chicken, tofu, and pickled, raw, and cooked vegetables and wrapped in dried seaweed and rice seasoned with vinegar, salt, and sugar. Even though the rice used to make sushi is short-grain and somewhat sticky, sushi still has a low GI, possibly because of the vinegar (acidity puts the brakes on stomach emptying) and the viscous fiber in the dried seaweed. In addition, sushi made with salmon and tuna boosts your intake of healthy omega-3 fats. Sushi served with miso is a delicious light and low-GI lunch.

> Freshly cooked rice has a higher GI than cold, reheated rice. This is one of the reasons for sushi's low GI.

Serving suggestions

▶ On occasion, try short-grain rice, or rice puddings or creamed rice. Boil ½ cup of rice with 1 cup of water for 5 minutes until the water is absorbed. Add 2 cups of low-fat milk and cook over a low heat for 20–25 minutes until the rice is tender. Stir in sugar, honey, or other sweetener to taste. (Adding the milk will help to lower the GI).

Whole Cereal Grains

Whole-grain simply means grains that are eaten in nature's packaging—or close to it—traditional rolled oats, cracked wheat, and pearl barley, for example. The slow digestion and absorption of these foods will trickle fuel into your engine at a more usable rate and therefore keep you satisfied for longer.

There are countless reasons to include more whole cereal grains in your diet, but it's hard to beat the fact that because you are eating the whole grain, you get all the benefits of its vitamins, minerals, protein, dietary fiber, and protective antioxidants. Studies around the world show that eating plenty of whole-grain cereals reduces the risk of certain types of cancer, heart disease, and type 2 diabetes.

A higher-fiber intake, especially from whole cereal grains, is linked to a lower risk of cancer of the large bowel, breast, stomach, and mouth. Eating these higher-fiber foods can help you lose weight because they fill you up sooner and leave you feeling full for longer. They improve insulin sensitivity, too, and lower insulin levels. When this happens, your body makes more use of fat as a source of fuel—what could be better when you are trying to lose weight?

Barley
GI 25

One of the oldest cultivated cereals, barley is nutritious and high in soluble fiber, which helps to reduce the post-meal rise in blood glucose—it lowers the overall GI of a meal. In fact, barley has one of the lowest GI values of any food. Look for products such as pearl

What's the difference?

❑ Whole-grain foods contain the whole grain—the bran, germ and endosperm. Even when processed, much of the grain is intact—"whole" or "cracked." It's these grainy bits that slow down the rate of digestion. A rule of thumb: if you can't see the grains then it's probably not low GI.

❑ Whole wheat foods contain all the components of the grain, but they have been milled to a finer texture and we digest them faster. Whole wheat foods usually have the same GI as their white counterparts. For example, white bread's GI is 70, whole wheat's is 71. Whole wheat foods are an important source of fiber and nutrients in a balanced diet.

barley to use in place of rice as a side dish, in oatmeal, or to add to soups, stews, and pilafs. You can also use barley as a substitute for rice to make risotto. Barley flakes, or rolled barley, which have a light, nutty flavor, can be cooked as a cereal and used in baked goods and stuffing.

Serving suggestion

To make a zesty and satisfying chunky lentil and barley soup, cook a finely chopped onion gently in a little olive oil for about 10 minutes, or until soft and golden. Add 2 crushed cloves of garlic, ½ teaspoon of turmeric, 2 teaspoons of curry powder, ½ teaspoon of ground cumin, and a teaspoon of minced chili (or to taste), then add 4 cups of chicken stock or water. Stir in ½ cup of pearl barley, ½ cup of red lentils and a 14 ounce can of tomatoes. Bring to a boil, cover, and simmer for about 45 minutes or until the lentils and barley are tender. Season to taste and serve sprinkled with chopped fresh parsley or cilantro. Serves 4

Buckwheat
GI 54

Gluten-free buckwheat is not a type of wheat or a true cereal at all—it's a herbaceous plant that produces triangular seeds. However, because the seeds are used in exactly the same way as cereal grains, that's what people think they are. Buckwheat has a rather nutty flavor and is a good source of protein, B vitamins, magnesium, potassium, and soluble fiber.

It is easy to cook and you can use it in place of rice or other whole-grain cereals such as bulgur, or add it to soups, stews, and casseroles. Buckwheat flour is widely used for making pancakes, muffins, biscuits, and is an indispensable ingredient for Russia's blini and Japan's soba noodles.

Serving suggestion

To make buckwheat and buttermilk pancakes with berries, combine 4½ ounces buckwheat flour, 1¼ ounces whole meal flour, 1½ teaspoons baking powder, and 2 tablespoons of raw sugar in a mixing bowl. Make a well in the center and pour in 2 lightly beaten eggs, 1 cup buttermilk, and 1 teaspoon of vanilla and whisk until smooth. Add a little more milk if the pancake batter is too thick. Heat a frying pan over medium heat and lightly spray with olive oil. Pour just enough batter into the pan to make a 4-inch pancake and cook for 1–2 minutes each side, or until the pancakes are golden and cooked. Repeat with the remaining mixture. Top the pancakes with a spoonful of yogurt and some blueberries. Serves 4—two pancakes per person.

Bulgur
GI 48

Also known as cracked wheat, bulgur is made from whole wheat grains that have been hulled and steamed before grinding to crack the grain. The wheat grain remains virtually intact—it is simply cracked—and the wheat germ and bran are retained, which preserves nutrients and lowers the GI. With its wheaty flavor you can use bulgur instead of rice or other grains in a range of recipes. Use it as a breakfast cereal, in tabbouleh, or add it to pilafs, vegetable burgers, stuffing, stews, salads, and soups.

Serving suggestions

▶ Try this super-nutritious, high-fiber mushroom and bulgur salad. Make a marinade with 3 tablespoons of lemon juice, 3 tablespoons of olive oil, a crushed garlic clove, and a tablespoon each of freshly chopped parsley and mint (or more if you like). Marinate 4½ ounces of sliced mushrooms and 2 chopped spring onions in the mixture for about an hour. Place 1 cup of bulgur in a bowl, cover with hot water, and let it stand for about 20–30 minutes until the water is absorbed and the bulgur softens. Drain well, squeezing out excess water. Toss the bulgur with the marinated mushrooms and spoon into a serving dish. Serves 4.

▶ To make tabbouleh, cover ½ cup of bulgur with hot water and soak for 20–30 minutes to soften. Drain well and squeeze out the excess water. Add a cup of finely chopped flat-leaf parsley, 3 or 4 chopped spring onions, 2 tablespoons of chopped mint, and a chopped tomato. Stir in a dressing made with 2 tablespoons each of lemon juice and olive oil. Tabbouleh is best made ahead of time to let the flavors develop. Serves 4.

▶ Pilaf made with bulgur has a far lower GI than rice pilaf. Serve it with casseroles or as a meal on its own with chopped vegetables. Sauté a thinly sliced brown onion in 1½ tablespoons of olive oil until it is translucent. Add a handful of crushed dry egg noodle vermicelli and stir until it is pale gold in color. Add ½ cup of

Whole grains on the side

Try barley, buckwheat, bulgur, or quinoa as a change from rice—vegetarian or whole food cookbooks will give you some tasty recipes.

bulgur and 1 cup of hot chicken stock. Cover and simmer on low heat for about 7 minutes or until it looks dry. Cover and let stand for 10 minutes before serving. Makes about 2 cups.

Quinoa
GI 51

Quinoa (pronounced keen-wah) is a small, round, quick-cooking grain somewhat similar in color to sesame seeds. It's a nutritional powerpack—an excellent source of low-GI carbs, fiber, and protein, and rich in B vitamins and minerals, including iron, phosphorus, magnesium, and zinc. You can also buy quinoa flakes and quinoa flour, but the GI of these products has not yet been published.

Health and organic food stores and larger supermarkets are the best places to shop for quinoa. You may find it's a little more expensive than other grains. The whole grain cooks in about 10–15 minutes and has a light, chewy texture and slightly nutty flavor and can be used as a substitute for many other grains. It is important to rinse quinoa thoroughly before cooking—the grains have a bitter-tasting coating designed by nature to discourage hungry hordes of birds.

Serving suggestion

▶ Make the most of this supergrain—substitute gluten-free quinoa for rice, couscous, cracked wheat, or barley in soups, stuffed vegetables, salads, stews, and even in "rice" pudding.

▶ To serve as a side dish, thoroughly rinse 1 cup of quinoa (if not prewashed). Drain, place the grains in a medium-sized pot with 2 cups of water, and bring to the boil. Reduce to a simmer, cover, and leave to cook until all the water is absorbed.

▶ If you want a richer flavor, toast quinoa (but don't let it burn) in a dry pan for a few minutes before cooking as above.

▶ Give your day a hearty start with quinoa "oatmeal" by adding about ½ cup of finely sliced apples and a couple of tablespoons of raisins to the pot while the quinoa is simmering. Add ½ teaspoon of cinnamon for extra flavor if you like. Serve with low-fat milk and sweeten with honey or sugar to taste.

Rye
GI 34
Whole-kernel rye is used to make bread, including pumpernickel and some crispbreads. It's an excellent source of fiber and also a good source of vitamins and minerals. It is more usually sold as rye flakes, which are the hulled, steamed, and rolled rye grains. Like rolled oats, you can eat the flakes as an oatmeal or sprinkle them over bread before you bake it.

Serving suggestion
To make spicy stuffed tomatoes, gently cook 1 chopped onion in 1 tablespoon of olive oil for a minute or two. Add 2 crushed cloves of garlic and continue cooking until the onion is soft and golden. Add 1 diced medium-sized eggplant, 1 cup of rye flakes, 2 cups of water, and 1 tablespoon of curry powder (or to taste). Stir, cover, and simmer about 30 minutes or until the eggplant and rye flakes are tender and water is absorbed. Cut the tops off 4 large tomatoes and scoop out the insides; set the "cups" aside. Chop the remaining tomato and add to the curry mixture. Remove the mixture from the heat and stir in ⅔ cup of plain low-fat yogurt and season with salt and freshly ground black pepper to taste. Spoon the curry mixture into the tomato cups and serve.

Semolina
GI 55 (cooked)
Semolina is the coarsely milled inner part of the wheat grain called the endosperm. It is granular in appearance. The large particle size of semolina flour (compared with fine wheat flour) limits the swelling of its starch particles when cooked, which results in slower digestion, slower release of glucose into the bloodstream, and a lower GI.

Couscous

Semolina is also used to make couscous (GI 65), a coarsely ground semolina pasta that's quick and easy to prepare. With a GI in the medium range, we suggest you enjoy this convenient food in moderation. Alternatively, adding low-GI legumes such as chickpeas to couscous recipes is not only delicious, it reduces the overall GI of the dish.

You'll find durum wheat semolina in most supermarkets. You can use it to make homemade pasta or gnocchi or simply cook it and eat it as a hot cereal or make it into a traditional milk pudding. Use semolina to thicken sauces and gravies instead of plain flour.

Serving suggestion

To make semolina oatmeal, mix about 1 tablespoon of semolina with 3 tablespoons of low-fat milk or water into a smooth paste. Slowly stir in ¾ cup of low-fat milk. Cook over a low heat, stirring continually for about 10 minutes to the desired consistency. Sweeten with a little honey or maple syrup, or serve with chopped fresh or canned fruit.

Whole Wheat Kernels
GI 41

As the most important cereal crop in the world, wheat—mainly in the form of bread and noodles—nourishes more people than any other grain. The bulk of the world's wheat is milled into flour—usually white flour. But there are forms of wheat, with their bran and germ intact, that can be eaten as a main or side dish. Whole wheat kernels (also called "groats" or wheat berries) are a highly nutritious food, packed with B vitamins, protein, and minerals, including iron, magnesium, and manganese. Think of them as the wheat version of rice—but allow for much longer cooking times. They have a strong, nutty flavor. Add them to hearty soups and stews, or use them when baking bread.

Serving suggestion

To cook whole-kernel wheat, wash 1 cup of wheat, then soak in 2 cups of water overnight. Place the rehydrated wheat in a pan with a little extra water if necessary and bring to a boil. Turn down the heat and simmer gently for about an hour until soft and the water is mostly absorbed. The cooked wheat will keep in a covered container in the refrigerator for about two weeks. Prepared this way, whole wheat kernels can be used for many dishes such as pilafs, tabbouleh, and side dish substitutes for rice or noodles.

LEGUMES, INCLUDING BEANS, PEAS & LENTILS

Humans have long known about the benefits of eating legumes. Not only do they keep in the cupboard for a year or more, they are an excellent source of protein, easy to prepare, and cost very little. When you cook them, they more than double in weight—1 cup of dry beans makes 2½ cups of cooked beans—and when you eat them, you'll feel satisfied for longer.

So, what are they? Also known as pulses, legumes are the edible dried seeds found inside the mature pods of leguminous plants. Legumes include various types of beans, peas, chickpeas, and lentils. Green peas are legumes, but we most often eat them fresh

> For a low-GI food that's easy on the budget, versatile, filling, low in calories, and nutritious, look no further than legumes—beans, chickpeas, and lentils.

as a green vegetable, so we have included them in the vegetable section. Peanuts are legumes, too, but since they are usually thought of as nuts we have included them in that section.

Whether you buy them dried, or opt for canned convenience, you are choosing one of nature's lowest-GI foods. They are high in fiber and packed with nutrients, providing protein, carbohydrate, B vitamins, folate, and minerals. When you add legumes to meals and snacks, you reduce the overall GI of your diet because your body digests them slowly. This is primarily because their starch breaks down relatively slowly (or incompletely) during cooking and they contain tannins and enzyme inhibitors that also slow digestion.

Although they have an excellent shelf life, old beans take longer to cook than young, which is why it's a good idea to buy them from shops where you know turnover is brisk. Once home, store them in airtight containers in a cool, dry place—they will keep their color better.

Canned bean convenience

Don't feel guilty about using canned beans—the main aim is to enjoy these low-GI superfoods. The only disadvantage of canned beans is that they generally tend to be soft. If you like a firmer texture, especially in salads, you'll probably need to cook your own.

What about gas or flatulence?

Legumes of all sorts, including baked beans, are renowned for producing flatulence (gas) and many jokes. The components responsible are indigestible sugars called raffinose, stachyose, and verbascose that reach the large bowel intact, where they are fermented by resident flora. Believe it or not, this is good for colonic health, increasing the proportion of good bifidobacteria and reducing potential pathogens. However, not all legumes will make you gassy, and not everyone has the problem to the same extent. If you are worried about the social implications, cooking legumes in fresh water (not the water you soaked them in) reduces the problem, as does eating small amounts regularly—your body becomes used to them. Alternatively, to prevent the problem, add a minute amount of powdered asafoetida spice to the pot during cooking—no more than a quarter of a teaspoon per cup of dried beans or lentils. We have also been told that adding a teaspoon of powdered gelatin to the pot during cooking will help—but we haven't tried this one ourselves.

How much?

Legumes are an important part of a low-GI diet, which is why it's a good idea to try to include them in your meals at least twice a week as a starchy vegetable alternative—more often if you are vegetarian. One serving is equivalent to ½ cup of cooked bean lentils, chickpeas, or whole dried or split peas.

Serving suggestions

You can substitute one 14-ounce can of beans for ¾ cup of dried beans.

▶ Drain and rinse canned beans and add them directly to soups, stews, salads, or curries.
▶ Top lettuce with kidney beans or chickpeas marinated in an oil and vinegar dressing.
▶ Add beans or chickpeas to vegetable soups or minestrone.
▶ Make a pureed bean dip and serve with carrot or celery sticks, blanched snowpeas, or cucumber strips.
▶ Create your own bean filling for tacos and burritos by mashing canned chili beans with a fork.
▶ Puree cooked yellow split peas or canned navy beans to use as a base for soups or chowders.

Preparing dried legumes

1. **Wash.** Wash thoroughly in a colander or sieve first, keeping an eye out for any small stones or "foreign" material (especially with lentils).

2. **Soak.** Soaking plumps the beans, makes them softer and tastier, and reduces cooking times a little. Place them in a saucepan, cover with about three times their volume of cold water, and soak overnight or for at least four hours. As a rule of thumb, the larger the seed, the longer the soaking time required. There's no need to soak lentils or split peas.

3. **Cook.** Drain, rinse thoroughly, then add fresh water—two to three times the volume of the legumes. Bring to a boil, then reduce the heat and simmer until tender. Generally, you will need to simmer lentils and peas for 45–60 minutes and beans and chickpeas for 1–2 hours, but check the recipe instructions. A couple of points to keep in mind:

Baked Beans
GI 48 (canned in tomato sauce)

Baked beans are a popular ready-to-eat form of legume, an easy way to introduce children to the world of beans, and available in convenient single-serving cans. Haricot (navy) beans are most commonly used for baked beans. If you make your own baked bean recipe, it will have a lower GI.

Serving suggestions

▶ Top half a baked potato cooked in the microwave with a scoop or two of canned or homemade baked beans sprinkled with a little grated cheese.

❑ Adding salt to the water during cooking will slow down water absorption and the legumes will take longer to cook.

❑ Make sure that legumes are tender before you add acidic flavorings such as lemon juice or tomatoes. Once they are in an acid medium they won't get any softer no matter how long you cook them.

Time-saving tips

❑ If you don't have time to soak legumes overnight, add three times the volume of water to rinsed beans, bring to a boil for a few minutes, then remove from the heat and soak for an hour. Drain, rinse, add fresh water, then cook as usual.

❑ Cooked legumes freeze well. Prepare a large quantity of beans or chickpeas and freeze in meal-sized batches to use as required.

❑ Store soaked or cooked beans in an airtight container in the fridge. They will keep for several days.

▶ A scoop or two of baked beans is a healthy addition to any meal.

Black Beans
GI 30 (home-cooked)

The black bean or black kidney bean is the small, shiny bean with an earthy sweet flavor often used in South and Central American and Caribbean cooking, and Mexican dishes such as refried beans. Add them to chili con carne or to bean soups and salads for extra flavor and texture. In Latin American–style dishes, a spicy bean mix made with black or red kidney beans is often served over rice.

Where to buy beans?

These days supermarkets stock a wide range of dried and canned beans. For the more unusual beans, check out your local health food store or Greek, Turkish, Middle Eastern, South American, or kosher delicatessen or produce market.

Serving suggestion

Use leftover chicken and rice to make these tasty burritos. Preheat the oven to 350°F. Wrap 6 large tortillas in foil and warm in the oven. Cook 1 chopped onion and 1 crushed clove of garlic in a tablespoon of vegetable oil, stirring occasionally until softened. Add 1 cup of chopped cooked chicken, 1 cup of cooked or canned black beans, 1 cup of cooked basmati rice, and 1 can of diced tomatoes. To serve, spoon about ¾ cup of the filling into the center of the warmed tortilla. Sprinkle 1 tablespoon of grated low-fat cheese on top, fold in the ends, then roll the tortilla around the filling. Place in a large shallow baking dish. Sprinkle ½ cup of grated low-fat cheese on top of burritos, then cover with foil and heat in the oven for about 10 minutes, or until the cheese is melted and the filling is hot. Serve topped with chopped cilantro. Makes 6.

Black-Eyed Beans
GI 42

Also known as cowpeas, Southern peas, and black-eyed peas, these beans are medium-sized, kidney-shaped, and cream-colored with a distinctive black "eye" and a subtle flavor. They are a popular "soul food" in the South, where they are traditionally served with pork. Add black-eyed beans to soups and stews or serve as a side dish.

Serving suggestions

▶ Cook chopped leeks, onions, and carrots with crushed garlic in a little olive oil. Add cooked or canned black-eyed, kidney and white beans, canned tomatoes plus fresh thyme and bay leaves, and a chopped red chili to make a Mediterranean-style vegetable casserole.

▶ Soak a cup of black-eyed beans overnight, then simmer in fresh water for about 30 minutes until tender. Drain and cool, then add chopped tomato and celery. Toss with a dressing of 2 tablespoons chopped parsley, 1 tablespoon seeded mustard, 1 crushed clove of garlic, and 3 tablespoons each of olive oil and wine vinegar.

Butter Beans
GI 31 (home cooked)
GI 36 (canned)

Sometimes called large lima beans, butter beans are a flat-shaped white bean with a smooth, creamy, slightly sweet flavor. Add to soups, stews, and salads or simply heat and serve as a side dish topped with finely chopped fresh herbs.

Serving suggestions

▶ Add a cup of cooked butter beans and a crushed clove of garlic to steamed sweet potato (or taro or yam) and mash as usual. Season to taste with a little salt and freshly ground black pepper and add enough water or low-fat milk or soy milk for a creamy consistency.

▶ Dip pita crisps into a butter bean puree. Puree a drained can of butter beans (or any white bean) with a crushed clove of garlic in the food processor slowly, pouring in just enough oil and lemon juice to create the desired consistency.

Cannellini Beans
GI 31 (canned)

Also known as white kidney beans, cannellini beans are large, smooth-textured, mild-flavored, kidney-shaped beans with a creamy white skin. They are used in soups, salads, stews, casseroles, bean pots such as the French cassoulet, and in many Italian dishes.

Serving suggestions

▸ Add cannellini beans to pureed vegetable soups for a creamy texture. Simmer cauliflower florets until tender in chicken stock, then blend with a cup of cooked beans and season to taste with salt and freshly ground black pepper. Top with freshly grated nutmeg and finely chopped parsley and serve.

▸ Make a salad of cannellini beans and finely sliced fennel tossed in a tangy lemon, oil, and vinegar dressing and top with finely chopped flat leaf parsley.

Chickpeas
GI 28 (home cooked)
GI 40 (canned)

Also known as garbanzo beans or ceci, these versatile caramel-colored legumes have a nutty flavor and firm texture. Popular in Middle Eastern, Mediterranean, and Mexican cooking, they are the main ingredient in specialties such as hummus and falafel, and are the basis for many vegetarian dishes. Keep a can in the pantry or cooked chickpeas in the fridge and add them to soups, stews, and salads or to a tomato-based sauce served with couscous or rice. After soaking, whole chickpeas can be roasted with salt and spices to make a crunchy low-GI snack that's every bit as tasty as potato chips!

Serving suggestions

▸ Combine 2 oranges separated into segments, a drained and rinsed 14-ounce can of chickpeas, and a finely sliced fennel bulb (or two if small ones). Toss in a dressing made with olive oil, vinegar, and orange juice for a tangy salad.

▸ To make a spicy pilaf, simmer a finely chopped onion in a little olive oil until soft, then add a cup of chopped button mushrooms and a crushed clove of garlic. Stir in ⅔ cup of basmati rice, a teaspoon of garam masala, and a cup of cooked chickpeas. Pour over 1½ cups of chicken stock, bring to a boil, then reduce the heat to very low, cover, and simmer gently for 10–12 minutes or until the rice is tender and all the liquid is absorbed.

Canned Mixed Beans
GI 37 (canned)

Canned bean mixes that include red kidney beans, chickpeas, and lima and butter beans make it easy to add protein and boost flavor and fiber to meals, including soups and stews. You can also add canned mixed beans to your salad wraps, sandwiches, and rolls for a lunch that lasts.

Serving suggestions

▶ For a meal in minutes, combine drained and rinsed mixed beans with baby spinach leaves, chopped spring onions, cucumber, yellow pepper, sliced radishes, finely sliced celery, and halved or quartered cherry tomatoes and toss in a light lemony oil and vinegar dressing.

▶ Boost the flavor and fiber of a homemade tomato soup by adding a can of drained, rinsed four-bean mix.

Haricot Beans
GI 33 (homecooked)
GI 38 (canned)

These small, white, oval-shaped beans, sometimes called navy beans, are the ones most often used in the manufacture of commercial baked beans. They have a mild flavor and combine well in soups and stews.

Serving suggestion

Make your own baked beans to serve on a special occasion such as a picnic or pot luck. Combine a small chopped onion, 2 small diced peppers (red or green), and 3 cups of cooked or canned haricot beans in a large casserole dish. Add ⅓ cup of pure honey,

2 tablespoons of Dijon mustard, 1 tablespoon of white wine vinegar, ½ cup of tomato sauce, and a few twists of freshly ground black pepper. Mix well, then cover and cook in a preheated oven (350°F) for about 45 minutes to an hour. Serves 6–8 as a side dish.

Hummus
GI 6 (regular)

Hummus—pureed chickpeas, lemon juice, tahini, olive oil, garlic, and sometimes ingredients such as roasted red peppers—is one of the most popular foods to emerge from the Middle East. It can be served as part of a mezze platter or used as a dip with pita bread, or raw or blanched vegetables such as carrot and celery sticks. It's widely available in the refrigerator section of supermarkets and fresh produce stores, in specialty delis, or as a take-out from Middle Eastern restaurants.

Serving suggestions

▶ Use hummus as a spread for sandwiches, as a topping on grilled fish, chicken, with baked potatoes, or in a wrap with kebabs and salad or a falafel roll.

▶ To make your own, combine a 14-ounce can of chickpeas (drained, reserving the liquid), ½ cup of tahini (sesame seed paste), a large clove of garlic, chopped, ⅓ cup of lemon juice, plus a little salt and freshly ground black pepper to taste. Process in a blender or food processor, adding enough of the reserved chickpea liquid to make a smooth consistency.

Lentils
GI 26 (red, homecooked)
GI 30 (green, homecooked)
GI 48 (green, canned)

Lentils are one food that people with diabetes should learn to love—they can eat them until the cows come home. In fact, we have found that no matter how much of them people eat, they have only a small effect on blood glucose levels. They are one of nature's superfoods—rich in protein, fiber, and B vitamins and often used as substitutes for meat in vegetarian recipes.

All colors and types of lentils have a similar low GI value, which is increased slightly if you opt to buy them canned and add them toward the end of cooking time. Lentils have a fairly bland, earthy flavor that combines well with onions, garlic, and spices. They cook quickly to a soft consistency and are used to make Indian dal, a spiced lentil puree. Lentils also thicken any kind of soup or extend meat casseroles.

Serving suggestions

▶ Make a meal of lentil soup and low-GI bread—you will feel completely satisfied. Canned lentil soup (GI 44) is a convenient, quick meal when you don't have time to prepare your own.

▶ To make a vegetarian lentil burger, simmer a chopped onion in olive oil for a few minutes to soften. In a bowl thoroughly combine 2 cups of canned and drained lentils with the onion mix and 2 cups of mashed potato or sweet potato, season to taste with salt and freshly ground black pepper, adding a dash of Tabasco or chili sauce for flavor. Form into patties and cook them on both sides until browned, in the oven, on the barbecue, or in a pan and combine with salad, tomato slices, chutney, and grainy rolls.

▶ For an easy alternative to mashed potato, bring to a boil 1 cup of chicken or vegetable stock, ⅔ cup of split red lentils, and 1 bay leaf, then simmer until the lentils are mushy and thick. Season with salt and freshly ground black pepper. You may also like to add a teaspoon of curry powder for extra flavor.

Lima Beans
GI 32 (baby frozen)

The lima bean, a larger variety of the butter bean, comes from Peru. Baby lima beans, also called sieva beans, cook faster. They are sometimes served as a vegetable side dish. Dried and canned lima beans have a buttery flavor and are used in soups, stews, and salads. If you are cooking your own, bring them to a boil slowly to prevent the skin from slipping off.

Serving suggestions

▶ Toss a cup of cooked beans with ½ cup of sun-dried tomatoes, ¼ cup of raisins, and ¼ cup of chopped pecan nuts in a dressing made with the juice of a lemon and 2 tablespoons of olive oil. Season to taste and serve with finely chopped fresh dill.

▶ Gently warm 1 cup of cooked or canned lima beans in a pan with ¼ cup of freshly squeezed lemon juice, a tablespoon of olive oil, 2 finely chopped cloves of garlic, and 2 teaspoons of fresh thyme (leaves picked) until just heated through. Toss in a salad bowl with 8 cooked baby beets cut into quarters, and a handful each of arugula and baby spinach leaves. Top with crumbled feta and serve.

Marrowfat or "mushy" peas

Marrowfat peas (GI 39) are a completely different variety from the green or garden pea. They are large yellow peas that, like all legumes, are rich in nutrients and have a low GI. The maro pea was introduced to the UK from Japan over 100 years ago because the climate was suitable for pea growing. It then became known as "marrowfat" because of its plump shape. You can buy marrowfat peas dried, in cans, or as canned "mushy peas." They make delicious pea soup.

Mung Beans
GI 39 (homecooked)

Also known as green gram or golden gram, dried mung beans are small, olive green beans that are used in many Asian cuisines for savory dishes such as India's green gram dal or to make a paste for popular sweets. The starch from mung beans is used in making bean thread and cellophane noodles. Like all legumes, they are a good source of fiber, iron, and protein. You can buy sprouted mung beans in cans, or packaged in the produce section—a useful source of vitamin C.

Serving suggestions

▶ Add mung bean sprouts as an extra vegetable to a stir-fry or fried rice at the end of cooking.

▶ Combine 1 cup of mung bean sprouts, 1 cup of baby spinach, 1 cup of arugula, 1 sliced cucumber, 1 pint of baby tomatoes, halved, ½ an avocado, sliced, 1 small finely sliced red onion, and ½ cup of pitted black olives in a large salad bowl with a dressing made from olive oil, balsamic vinegar, and a dash of lemon juice. Serves 4.

Peanuts

See page 203.

Peas

GI 22 (whole dried, homecooked)
GI 32 (yellow or green split peas)

Like other legumes, dried peas are a nutritional storehouse, and because they are slowly digested, a little goes a long way. Whole dried or blue peas are the dried version of garden peas and are traditionally used in English dishes such as "pease pudding" and mushy peas. Soak them before cooking.

Dal

Dal can refer to dried legumes (Bengal gram, split peas, channa, and lentils) as well as the puree that's usually served with Indian meals.

Yellow or green split peas come from a variety of garden pea with the husk removed. They tend to disintegrate and are traditionally used for green split pea and ham soup and yellow split peas for making Indian dal.

Serving suggestions

▶ Your local Indian grocery store will sell prepared dals. Combined with flat bread and basmati rice, dal makes a delicious low-GI light vegetarian meal. To make your own dal, rinse and drain 1 cup of red lentils and place in a saucepan with ½ teaspoon of turmeric and a pinch of chili powder. Add 1½ cups of boiling water and cook for 15 minutes or until the lentils are very soft but still retain their shape. Season to taste with salt. Heat 1 tablespoon of margarine or olive oil in a small frying pan and gently cook a small finely chopped onion until soft and golden—about 10 minutes. Stir 1 teaspoon of garam masala into the onion mixture, stir briskly for 30 seconds, then add 1 teaspoon of coriander and combine with the lentils. Season to taste with salt and freshly ground black pepper. You may also like to add a squeeze of lime.

▶ Make split pea soup with 2 cups of split peas, 2 finely chopped onions, 2 finely chopped carrots, and 2 finely sliced sticks of celery. Add a bay leaf for flavoring, season with freshly ground black pepper and, for extra oomph, add a bacon bone or two while the soup is cooking.

See also Green Peas, page 138.

Pinto Beans
GI 39 (homecooked)
GI 45 (canned)
This medium-sized mottled bean ("pinto" means painted) turns pinkish-brown when cooked. It's a staple in Latin American cooking and used whole or made into refried beans as a filling for burritos or tacos.

Serving suggestion

▶ Make a colorful and crunchy bean mix for tacos. Combine 2 cups of cooked pinto beans with a finely diced green pepper, a cup of juicy red chopped tomatoes, 2 sliced spring onions, 1 cup of sweet corn kernels (straight off the cob is best), ½ teaspoon of ground cumin, and salt and freshly ground black pepper to taste. Serve with tacos and bowls of guacamole, shredded lettuce, and grated low-fat cheese. Serves 4.

▶ To make refried beans, heat a little olive or sesame oil in a frying pan over medium heat. Add 1 finely sliced onion and 2 cloves of crushed garlic and cook very gently until soft and golden (about 10 minutes). Stir in 2 cups of cooked pinto (or black) beans, 2 teaspoons of cumin, and ½ cup of water or vegetable stock. Mash the beans into the liquid, adding more stock if the mixture seems too dry. Season to taste with salt and freshly ground black pepper.

Red Kidney Beans
GI 36 (canned)

These tasty red beans are a popular addition to vegetarian and meat chili dishes and nachos, tacos, and burritos. Not only do red kidney beans play a leading role in Mexican and "Tex-Mex" cuisines, a scoop is a sustaining side dish with main meals and adds substance to soups, stews, and salads.

Serving suggestions

▶ Stir into a homemade or bought tangy tomato salsa to add a Mexican flavor.

▶ Create a colorful bean salad by combining a 14-ounce can of kidney beans (drained) in a serving bowl with 1 cup each of cooked green beans and cooked yellow beans sliced on the diagonal. Finely slice half a red pepper, half a green pepper, and 2 stalks of celery. Toss the beans and vegetables in a light dressing made with balsamic vinegar and olive oil. Coat the salad well—you will need about ½ cup of dressing. Serves 4–6 as a side dish.

Soybeans
GI 14 (canned)
GI 18 (homecooked)

Soybeans and soy products are the nutritional powerhouse of the legume family. They have been a staple part of Asian diets for thousands of years and are an excellent source of protein. They're also rich in fiber, iron, zinc, and vitamin B. They are lower in carbohydrate and higher in fat than other legumes, but the majority of the fat is polyunsaturated. Soybeans are a rich source of phyto-chemicals, especially phytoestrogens, and have been linked with improvements in blood cholesterol levels, relief from menopausal symptoms, and lower rates of cancer in many studies.

Serving suggestions
▶ Use canned soybeans in place of other beans in any recipe.
▶ Make a quick soybean and vegetable curry with chopped onions, garlic, carrots, tomatoes, cauliflower, and broccoli using vegetable stock and your favorite curry paste.

Tofu

Tofu has little or no carbs. It's a cheese-like curd made from soybeans, and although it is not high in fiber, it's a low-cost, high-protein, low-fat bean food that will surprise you with its versatility. By itself, tofu is bland, so marinate it in soy sauce, ginger, chili, and garlic, or try it as part of a well-seasoned dish such as a stir-fry.

NUTS

People who eat nuts once a week are less likely to have heart disease than those who don't eat any nuts. There are probably several reasons. Nuts contain a variety of antioxidants, which keep blood vessels healthy; arginine, an amino acid that helps keep blood flowing smoothly; folate; and fiber, both of which can lower cholesterol levels. Although nuts are high in fat (averaging around 50 percent), it is largely unsaturated, so they make a healthy substitute for foods such as cookies, cakes, pastries, potato chips, and chocolate. They also contain relatively little carbohydrate, so most do not have a GI value.

Nuts are one of the richest sources of vitamin E, with a small handful of mixed nuts providing more than 20 percent of the recommended daily intake. The vitamin E content may explain the findings from a recent study from the Harvard University School of Public Health that found that increased nut consumption, including natural peanut butter, may improve the body's ability to balance glucose and insulin.

> How do you halve your risk of developing heart disease? By eating a small handful of nuts five to seven times a week!

How much?
One serving provides 10 grams of fat and is equivalent to:

▶ ½ ounce (about 10 small or 5 large) nuts or a tablespoon of seeds
▶ 3 teaspoons peanut butter or Nutella

How much a day?
Aim for a small handful (no fingers) of nuts most days.

▶ Smaller eaters: 1 serving most days
▶ Medium eaters: 1 serving a day
▶ Bigger eaters: 1–2 servings most days

Serving suggestions

▶ Use nuts and seeds in food preparation. Try toasted cashews in a chicken stir-fry; sprinkle walnuts over a pear and radicchio salad with a light blue cheese dressing; or top fruit desserts or muesli with natural almonds.

▶ Add toasted pine nuts to your favorite pasta dish.

▶ Sprinkle a mixture of chopped nuts and flaxseeds over cereal or salads, or add to baked goods such as muffins and breads.

Cashews
GI 22

Cashews, like all nuts, are cholesterol free and high in protein. Their carbohydrate content is quite low, which accounts for their low GI value. They do have a high fat content (almost half their total weight) but it is less than any other type of nut and three-quarters of it is heart-healthy polyunsaturated and monounsaturated fat. Cashews are also rich in several B vitamins and the minerals copper, magnesium, and zinc. Because of their high nutrient content and calorie density, you can eat cashews several times a week, but keep the amounts you eat small and look for unsalted varieties.

Serving suggestion

Cashews make a healthy addition to salads, rice dishes, and desserts, and are a popular ingredient in Asian stir-fries.

Nutella
GI 33

Nutella is a sweetened chocolate spread made from hazelnuts, cocoa, skim milk powder, and peanut oil, and is a favorite even with non-chocoholics. About half its sugar content is milk sugar (lactose). Its fat content is high, but the fats are mainly mono- and polyunsaturated (just like peanut butter), so it can be a healthy addition to the balanced diet of any active person.

Serving suggestions

▶ Add to banana smoothies, or stir a little through plain yogurt for a chocolate fix.

▶ Soften a little Nutella in the microwave and serve with a scoop of low-fat ice cream sprinkled with crunchy natural or toasted muesli.

Peanuts
GI 14

A low-carb but high-fat, high-protein food (50 percent fat and 25 percent protein), peanuts grow under the ground—they are also known as groundnuts. Technically a legume, they are an excellent source of vitamins B and E and so low in carbohydrate that their GI doesn't really count—although their fat content does! Because peanuts are such a tasty and convenient finger food they are easily overeaten, so give yourself a specific ration. And stick to it!

All processed peanuts are quality-controlled for the presence of fungus that produces a toxin called aflatoxin, one of the most carcinogenic substances known. Because peanuts in the shell are not screened, throw away any moldy ones. And a word to the wise: choose dry roasted peanuts and avoid salt.

Peanut allergy is an increasingly common food allergy, especially in children. It occurs in approximately 1 in 50 children and 1 in 200 adults and is the allergy most likely to cause anaphylaxis (which involves swelling in the gut, respiratory tract, and/or cardiovascular system) and death. Symptoms of allergy include itching, especially around the mouth, swelling tongue, flushed face, cramping, difficulty breathing, diarrhea, and vomiting. If peanut allergy is suspected, urgent medical attention should be sought. One-third of all peanut-allergic people are also allergic to tree nuts such as brazil nuts, hazelnuts, walnuts, almonds, macadamia nuts, pistachios, pecans, pine nuts, and cashews.

Serving suggestions

▶ Make up trail mixes with peanuts, raisins, dried fruit, and sunflower seeds for a no-fuss snack on the run.
▶ Sprinkle crushed nuts over salads for flavor and crunch or stir crushed nuts and chopped dried fruit through low-fat yogurt.
▶ Add crushed peanuts to the mix when baking cookies.

Peanut Butter
GI 14

This delicious treat is made from groundnuts. The healthiest type of peanut butter has no added salt and is made from fresh, unroasted peanuts. Peanut butter is an excellent source of niacin and a good source of magnesium. The best way to include more peanut butter in your diet is to use it in place of butter or margarine.

Serving suggestions

▶ Top toast with peanut butter and banana or grated apple.
▶ Make a salad sandwich with lettuce, tomato, grated carrot, sprouts, and cucumber, using peanut butter as the spread.
▶ Use peanut butter to make a satay sauce and serve with vegetables and kebabs.

FISH & SEAFOOD

We can't measure a GI for fish because it doesn't contain any carbohydrate. However, it is an important part of a balanced diet

> Increased fish consumption is linked to a reduced risk of coronary heart disease, improvements in mood, lower rates of depression, better blood fat levels, and enhanced immunity.

Mercury in fish

The U.S. Food and Drug Administration (FDA) recommends limiting or avoiding consumption of some types of fish that may contain higher levels of mercury, a toxic heavy metal. Although two to three serves of fish and seafood is recommended per week, pregnant women and women thinking of becoming pregnant should avoid swordfish, shark, King mackerel, and tile fish. The fish can contain potentially risky levels of mercury.

Pregnant women, women of child-bearing years, and children are also advised to limit their intake of albacore (white) tuna to 6 ounces per week. For children, the recommended serve size is 2½ ounces.

and we now know that just one serving of fish or seafood a week may reduce the risk of a fatal heart attack by about 40 percent. The likely protective components of fish are the very long-chain omega-3 fatty acids. Our bodies only make small amounts of these fatty acids, which is why we rely on dietary sources, especially fish and seafood.

How much?
Eat fish, including fresh, frozen, canned, and smoked, one to three times a week as an alternative to a serving of meat, chicken or egg.

One serving is equivalent to:

- 5 ounces raw fish or seafood
- 4 ounces grilled or steamed fish
- 3½ ounces canned fish (drained)

Which fish?

Oily fish, which tend to have darker colored flesh and a stronger fish flavor, are the richest source of omega-3 fats.

▶ Fresh fish with higher levels of omega-3s are: Atlantic salmon, smoked salmon, Atlantic and Pacific mackerel, bluefin tuna, and swordfish. Eastern and Pacific oysters and squid (calamari) are also rich sources.

▶ Canned pink and red salmon (including the bones), sardines, mackerel, and, to a lesser extent, tuna, are all rich sources of omega-3s; look for canned fish packed in water, canola oil, olive oil, tomato sauce, or brine, and drain well.

Fish Sticks
GI 38

Fish sticks have a measurable GI because of their breadcrumb coating. Although low GI, they may be high in saturated fat, depending on the oil used in manufacturing. Check the food label carefully. Oven baking or grilling are the healthiest ways to cook them and, of course, serve them with plenty of vegetables or salad.

LEAN MEAT, CHICKEN, & EGGS

As with fish and seafood, GI is not relevant to protein-rich meat, chicken, and eggs. These foods are valuable inclusions in a healthy diet, however, not only for protein, but also for essential vitamins and minerals. Red meat is the best dietary source of iron, the nutrient used in carrying oxygen in our blood, and the main source

> Lean meat, chicken, and eggs are valuable additions to a healthy diet thanks to their protein, and nutrients such as iron, zinc, vitamin B_{12}, niacin, and other B vitamins.

of zinc, which is a part of over 100 enzymes throughout the body. Good iron and zinc status can improve your energy levels and exercise tolerance. A chronic shortage of iron leads to anemia, with symptoms including pale skin, excessive tiredness, breathlessness, and decreased attention span. Even mild iron deficiency can cause unexplained fatigue.

Although chicken contains about one-third as much iron as meat, it is readily absorbed, as it is from red meat, and provides a versatile, nutrient-rich alternative. Eggs also contain valuable amounts of the nutrients found in meat, although the iron is not as well absorbed. The cholesterol content of eggs is only a concern if you have high cholesterol levels and/or your total diet is high in saturated fat. Omega-3-enriched eggs, meat, and chicken also make a significant contribution to long-chain omega-3 fats, which are so vital in human brain development and function.

How much?

Although nutritious, meat, chicken, and eggs do not have to be a part of everyone's diet. After all, there are countless healthy vegetarians in the world! If you are not vegetarian, we suggest eating lean meat three times a week in addition to eggs or skinless chicken once or twice a week, accompanied by plenty of salad and vegetables. One serving is equivalent to:

- 3½ ounces raw lean meat or chicken
- 2 medium eggs
- 1 small chop
- ½ cup cooked ground lean meat
- ½ skinless chicken breast
- 1 large chicken drumstick

How much a day?

One or two servings a day is appropriate for most people; bigger eaters may want a little more.

▶ Smaller eaters: 1–2 servings a day
▶ Medium eaters: 2–3 servings a day
▶ Bigger eaters: 3 servings a day

Shopping tips

▶ Choose lower-fat meat products such as pastrami, and rolled turkey breast.
▶ Choose lean cuts of meat.
▶ Cut visible fat including skin from meat and poultry and drain away the fat after cooking.

Serving suggestions

▶ Marinate skinless chicken or lean meat to add flavor and moisture before grilling or baking. Try combinations of olive oil, red wine, and garlic or lemon juice, olive oil, fresh herbs, and pepper.
▶ Try cooking fresh fish in the microwave for a quick meal, basted with soy sauce, lemon juice, or yogurt, and seasoned with fresh dill, paprika, or curry spices. One fillet takes 60–90 seconds on a high setting.
▶ Pan-fry or stir-fry strips of lean meat or chicken in a nonstick pan using small amounts of olive or canola oil. Add flavor with ginger, garlic, chili, and lemon zest, adding sauces such as soy, oyster, hoisin, etc., after cooking.
▶ Enjoy poached eggs with grainy bread and baby spinach; scrambled eggs with salmon; or an omelet or frittata with lots of vegetables.

LOW-FAT DAIRY FOODS & CALCIUM-ENRICHED SOY PRODUCTS

Calcium is the most abundant mineral in our bodies. It builds our bones and teeth and is involved in muscle contraction and relaxation, blood clotting, nerve function, and regulation of blood pressure. If we don't get enough calcium in our diet, our bodies

> The key to strong, healthy bones is making sure you have plenty of calcium in your diet. Milk, cheese, yogurt, ice cream, buttermilk, pudding, and custard are among the richest sources and, for most of us, the easiest way to get the calcium we need.

will draw it out of our bones. Over a period of time, this can lead to osteoporosis, loss of height, curvature of the spine, and periodontal disease (disease of the bones supporting our teeth).

Studies are now showing that calcium:

- can help lower high blood pressure
- may protect against cancer, particularly cancer of the bladder, bowel, and colon, and possibly against breast, ovarian, pancreatic, and skin cancers
- can favorably influence blood fat levels and reduce the risk of stroke
- can reduce the risk of kidney stones
- can assist in weight regulation

Dairy Foods

Dairy foods are recommended throughout childhood and beyond. Not only are they an important source of calcium, they also provide energy, protein, carbohydrate, and vitamins A, B, and D. Virtually all dairy foods have low GI values—largely thanks to lactose, the sugar found naturally in milk, which has a low GI of 46.

By choosing low-fat varieties of milk, yogurt, ice cream, pudding, and custard, you will enjoy a food that provides you with sustained energy, boosting your calcium intake but not your saturated fat intake. Although cheese is a good source of calcium, it is not a source of carbohydrate, as its lactose is drawn off in the whey during production. This means that GI is not relevant to cheese.

What about lactose intolerance?

Lactose, the sugar in milk, is a disaccharide ("double sugar") that needs to be digested into its component sugars before our bodies can absorb it. The two sugars (glucose and galactose) compete with each other for absorption. Once absorbed, the galactose is mainly metabolized in the liver and produces very little effect on our blood glucose levels. The remaining sugar, glucose, is present in a small enough amount not to cause a spike in blood glucose.

Some people are lactose intolerant because the enzyme lactase is not active in their small intestine. Children who are lactose intolerant often outgrow this by five years of age. If you are lactose intolerant, you should still be able to enjoy cheese—which is virtually lactose free—and yogurt. The microorganisms in yogurt are active in digesting lactose during passage through the small intestine. Alternatively, try lactose-reduced or lactose-free milk and milk products, or low-GI, low-fat, calcium-enriched nondairy alternatives such as soy milk. Note that rice milk has a high GI value (GI 92).

Boning up

We build our maximum bone strength by the time we reach about 20 years old. From our early 30s, bone calcium starts decreasing, but an adequate calcium intake, among other things, can help stop the decline.

Nondairy calcium sources

If you eat only plant foods or want to avoid dairy products, you may turn to soy beverages, yogurts, and desserts as an alternative. Soy products are not naturally high in calcium so look for calcium-fortified products if you are relying on them as a source of calcium.

Other nondairy options that will boost your calcium intake are foods such as almonds, brazil nuts, sesame seeds, dried figs, dried apricots, soybeans, Asian greens such as bok choy, fish with edible bones such as salmon and sardines, calcium-enriched tofu, and calcium-fortified breakfast cereals.

How much?
One serving is equivalent to:

- 1 cup low-fat milk
- 1 cup calcium-enriched low-fat soy milk
- 6-ounce container low-fat yogurt or calcium-enriched soy yogurt
- 1 ounce reduced-fat hard cheese
- 1 cup low-fat custard or 8 scoops (1⅔ cup) of low-fat ice cream are calcium-equivalent options but are higher in calories, so don't rely on them routinely.

How much a day?
Everyone should aim to eat or drink at least two servings of dairy foods or calcium-enriched soy products per day to meet calcium needs.

- Smaller eaters: 2 servings
- Medium eaters: 2 servings
- Bigger eaters: 3 servings

Weight control

Recent research suggests that people who include more dairy foods in their diet are better able to control their weight. Calcium is required to burn fat but it's also possible that some components of dairy inhibit fat absorption.

Cheese—a great source of calcium

Perfect for sandwich fillings, snacks, and toppings for pasta and with gratin dishes, cheese also contributes a fair number of calories. Most cheese is around 30 percent fat, much of it saturated.

Ricotta and cottage cheese are good low-fat choices—usually less than 7 percent fat. Use them as an alternative to butter or margarine for sandwiches. It's worth trying fresh ricotta from a deli—you may find its soft creamy texture and fresh flavor tastier than prepackaged ricotta. When making lasagna, use creamy ricotta instead of white sauce. Flavored cottage cheese or natural cottage cheese with freshly snipped chives or basil and a twist of black pepper make ideal low-fat toppings for toast and crackers for snacks and light lunches.

Although there are a number of good reduced-fat cheeses available, others can lose out in the flavor just to save a relatively small reduction in fat. If you are a

Serving suggestions

The experts tell us that it only takes 21 days to start building a new health habit. Here are some simple ways to get started and make sure you get at least two servings of dairy foods each day.

- Start your day with a fruit smoothie.
- Top your breakfast cereal with yogurt.
- Relax with a caffè latte mid-morning.
- Add a slice of cheese or a dollop of ricotta to your sandwich.
- Reach for a glass of cool milk for a refreshing snack.
- Follow your main meal with a dairy dessert.
- End the day with warm milk and honey to ensure a good night's sleep.

real cheese lover and having a hard time finding a tasty low-fat one, try these tips for making the most of your higher-fat cheese choices.

❑ Consider eating a little of a strong-flavored cheese rather than a lot of something bland and tasteless.
❑ Shave a few strips of fresh Parmesan over pasta—a vegetable peeler does the job nicely. Grating and shaving helps a little cheese go a long way.
❑ Enjoy full-fat cheeses in small amounts occasionally. This includes regular types of cheddar, blue cheese, Swiss, brie, camembert, Colby, gouda, and havarti.
❑ Try some mozzarella cheese—whole milk or part skim. It may contain less fat than some reduced-fat cheeses. Grate and sprinkle over stuffed veggies such as pepper or eggplant, baked potatoes, and pizzas before cooking.

Chocolate Milk

GI 24 (low-fat, sweetened with NutraSweet or Splenda)
GI 34 (low-fat, sweetened with sugar)

Flavored milks are available in regular or low-fat varieties with relatively modest amounts of added sugar (about 4 percent) compared with soft drinks (11–12 percent). Adding a moderate amount of sugar in the form of chocolate syrup or powder or other flavors does not significantly raise the GI of low-fat milk. For many people, children and adults alike, who don't like the taste of plain milk or prefer something sweeter, this dairy choice can add some extra vitamins and minerals to the day's nutrient intake. However, the choice of a low-fat type is important, as is a smaller, rather than larger, serving size if you're watching your calorie intake.

Boning up

The best way to safeguard your bones is to pack in enough calcium before your mid to late twenties and thereafter eat a well-balanced diet with plenty of weight-bearing activity like walking, running, aerobics, tennis, soccer, and dancing, which will strengthen your bones.

Although some parents might be concerned that flavored milk simply adds extra sugar to their child's diet, it is a far more nutritious drink than a soft drink. A study in Canada has shown that children and teenagers who drink flavored milk consume fewer soft drinks and fewer fruit drinks than those who do not, and have far better calcium intakes. This is significant when you consider that maximum bone strength is built up in our younger years and 82 percent of our children aren't getting the recommended three daily servings of dairy foods they need.

Serving suggestions

◗ Make flavored milk ice cubes for snacks after school or on hot days.
◗ Blend flavored milk with fruit and a dollop of low-fat yogurt for a quick smoothie.

Custard
GI 43 (made with powder)

Custard is a good source of calcium and protein, especially for young children who don't like drinking milk. Packaged custard made with wheat starch is quick and easy to prepare. Make it with low-fat milk or low-fat calcium-enriched soy milk and sprinkle a little freshly grated nutmeg on top for that traditional "baked custard" look. Serve hot or cold with fresh or canned fruit—especially peaches or nectarines—or with a sliced banana stirred in.

Serving suggestions

▶ Refuel with a chilled single-serving container of custard from the dairy section in the supermarket. Look for low-fat varieties.

▶ Top winter warming desserts like apple and rhubarb crumble with a creamy custard sauce or use as a filling for pastries.

▶ For that special occasion, make a "real" custard with milk, vanilla bean, and egg. Bring 2 cups of milk almost to the boil, remove from the heat, add a vanilla pod and set aside for 15 minutes to infuse. Meanwhile, whisk 5 egg yolks and 4 ounces of sugar in a bowl until thick and creamy. Remove the vanilla bean from the milk and pour the milk into the egg mixture, stirring vigorously. Place in a heavy-based saucepan and cook over a medium heat (do not allow to boil), stirring constantly, until the custard thickens. Strain if the custard becomes lumpy.

Dairy Desserts
GI 32–48 (chilled, low-fat)

From parfaits to mousse, rice pudding to tiramisu, today's refrigerated dairy section is filled with tempting, ready-to-eat, light, creamy, even aerated, desserts packaged in single-serving containers, cartons, and pouches. Without the effort needed to whip up a pudding from scratch, they provide a guilt-free after-dinner indulgence or a convenient snack on the run and without adding too many calories. Because they are milk based they can be a useful source of calcium and provide an alternative to yogurt or ice cream when you want something sweet. Choose low-fat, low-GI products and enjoy in moderation.

Serving suggestions

▶ Lightly grill fresh fruits and serve topped with a dollop of a chocolate or vanilla dairy dessert as an alternative to ice cream or yogurt.

▶ Enjoy single-serving dairy desserts as a satisfying snack when you need to refuel on the run or as an alternative to other morning or afternoon snacks.

Flavored Milk Powders
GI 40 (Nestlé's Quik made with reduced-fat milk)

Milk is an important source of calcium throughout life. Adding a moderate amount of refined sugar in the form of NesQuik or other flavored powders or syrups (chocolate, vanilla, strawberry, malt, etc.) does not significantly raise the GI of low-fat or skim milk. As with flavored milks from the chilled dairy section, this is an excellent dairy choice for children and adults that can help add some extra vitamins and minerals to the day's nutrient intake.

Ice Cream
GI 37–49 (low-fat)

Ice cream is not just a treat, it's a useful source of bone-building calcium plus some protein and the other essential vitamins and minerals found in milk. Because it contains added sugar, the GI generally tends to be a little higher than milk and yogurt. See the tables for the low-GI brands. Look for low-fat varieties when you shop—you'll find that some taste as good if not better than their full-fat counterparts. Add a scoop to milkshakes and smoothies and enjoy a small portion as a snack or dessert with fruit.

Serving suggestions

For a satisfying snack or quick breakfast in a glass, whip up a nutritious smoothie. Start with your fruit combination and add about a cup of milk and a scoop of low-fat ice cream or yogurt to make it creamy. Boost the vitamin and fiber content with a little wheat germ or bran. For a thicker texture, blend with frozen fruit. If you don't have time to freeze the fruit, simply blend in some crushed ice until the smoothie is as thick as you like. Here are some combinations to try:

▶ Tangy banana and apple—blend until smooth: 1 frozen banana, ½ cup of orange juice, 1 gala apple, peeled and cut into chunks, ½ cup of milk, and a scoop of low-fat ice cream or yogurt.

▶ Raspberry and peach—blend until smooth: ½ cup of apple juice,

½ cup of low-fat ice cream, 1 peeled, sliced and partially frozen peach, and ½ cup of partially frozen raspberries. Blend in ½ cup of crushed ice and serve.

▸ Creamy banana and strawberry—blend until smooth: 1 banana, ½ cup of sliced strawberries, 1 cup of low-fat milk, and 1 scoop of low-fat ice cream. Blend in ½ cup of crushed ice and serve.

Instant Puddings
GI 40–47

Instant puddings, like custard, are useful in helping children and teenagers (and adults) achieve the three servings of dairy foods a day they need to build strong bones. These dried package mixes come in a range of flavors and are the speediest way to whip up a nutritious, satisfying, and economical dessert, and because they are so easy to make, even young children can help in the kitchen. Choose low-fat milk or low-fat calcium-enriched soy milk for these dairy desserts and serve with fresh or canned fruit.

Serving suggestions

▸ Make instant pudding iced treats for after-school snacks. Combine pudding and milk in a deep bowl and beat with a mixer following the package instructions. Spoon the mixture into individual cupcake pans and leave to set for about a minute. Insert ice cream sticks into the center and freeze.

▸ Whip up banana smoothies with extra flavor by blending a tablespoon of instant pudding mix per cup of milk.

Milk
GI 27–34 (range of skim to whole milks)

Nutritionally, milk packs a punch. It's long been valued for protein, the bone-building minerals calcium and phosphorus, and vitamins such as riboflavin (vitamin B_2). Milk also has a low GI—a combination of the moderate glycemic effect of its sugar (lactose) plus the milk protein, which forms a soft curd in the stomach and slows down the rate of stomach emptying. Regular whole milk is

Fat count

▶ Whole milk contains about 3½ percent milk fat.

▶ Low-fat milk comes in two basic types: 2 percent, meaning 98 percent of the fat has been removed, and 1 percent, which is 99% fat free

▶ Low-fat milk contains less than 1.5 percent fat and boosted calcium content.

▶ Nonfat or skim milk contains less than ½ percent milk fat.

▶ Skim milk contains no more than 0.15 percent fat.

high in saturated fat, but these days there is a wide range of milk to suit everybody's needs, including reduced-fat, low-fat, or skim varieties. So enjoy a glass of milk or a milkshake or smoothie and use milk in your cooking for desserts and sauces, but opt for the reduced-fat, low-fat, and skim types.

We sometimes include buttermilk in our recipes. Despite its name, buttermilk isn't high in fat—it's made from skim milk. Specially chosen bacterial cultures are added in its manufacture to give the traditional texture and slightly sour taste that makes it popular for baking.

Serving suggestions

▶ Hot milk and honey makes a nutritious nightcap. Research shows that people do sleep more soundly after a warm milk drink at night. Warming the milk activates an amino acid called tryptophan, which the body converts to serotonin, the hormone associated with calmness and well-being

▶ When you're out for a coffee choose a skim milk caffè latte or cappuccino and get a calcium boost!

▶ White sauce is used in dishes such as mornay, lasagna, and savory soufflés and is the base for many sauces. To make it, the traditional method is to melt 2 tablespoons of butter or margarine in a small saucepan over a low heat. Blend in 2 tablespoons of plain flour and cook over a low heat for 1–2 minutes, then slowly add 1 cup of milk, stirring constantly until smooth and thickened. Season to taste with salt and freshly ground black pepper, celery salt, nutmeg, or a few tablespoons of chopped chives or parsley. You can make a lower-fat version by heating 1 cup of low-fat milk with 1 whole peeled onion and a bay leaf. When hot, stir in 1 tablespoon of cornstarch blended with a little cold milk and stir over a low heat until thickened. Remove the onion and bay leaf and discard and season as above.

Soy Milk
GI 36–44 (reduced fat, calcium fortified)

Drinking this completely dairy- and lactose-free beverage is an easy way to include soy protein in your diet. Whole soybeans—which are usually neither genetically modified nor genetically engineered (check the label)—are mixed with filtered water and flavorings to produce a milk-like product. Once enjoyed only by vegetarians, soy milk has become increasing popular, possibly because it tastes good and is recognized to be rich in phytoestrogens, nutrients that are known to have health benefits.

Soy milk is available fresh from the dairy section, in aseptic containers and in powdered forms. You can also buy flavored products. To ensure it is a suitable alternative to regular dairy milk, soy milk is often enriched with a range of vitamins and minerals including calcium and riboflavin (vitamin B_{12}). Choose a low-fat calcium-enriched milk and use it exactly as you would regular milk—on your breakfast cereal, with hot or cold drinks, or in your cooking when making desserts and sauces.

Serving suggestions

If you haven't tried calcium-enriched low-fat soy milk before, here are some easy ways to get started.

▶ Mix it in with mashed sweet potato, pumpkin, or potato, or in a combination of all three vegetables.
▶ Try a soy latte or soy banana smoothie or use in other flavored milk drinks.
▶ Use it to make white sauce for lasagna or moussaka.
▶ Make dairy desserts with soy milk.

Soy Yogurt
GI 50 (fruit flavored, sweetened with sugar)

Soy yogurt is usually made from soybeans or soy protein rather than soy milk. Look for calcium-enriched, low-fat varieties and use in exactly the same way as you would dairy yogurts as a snack or dessert, or added to smoothies and shakes. Unflavored soy yogurt can be used in dips, sauces, and spreads.

Look for the symbol Ⓖ

When faced with the bewildering array of yogurts in your supermarket's dairy section, look for this symbol Ⓖ

Yogurt
GI range 14–43
GI 14–21 (low-fat, flavored, no added sugar)
GI 26–43 (low-fat, flavored, sweetened with sugar)

Yogurt is a concentrated milk product rich in calcium, riboflavin, and protein, and all varieties have low GI values, mainly due to the combination of acidity and high protein. Artificially sweetened, flavored yogurts have the lowest GI values and contain fewer calories than the naturally sweetened flavored versions. Drinking yogurts are also available and will have similar GI values. Low-fat yogurt provides the most calcium for the least calories (520 mg calcium in a 6-ounce container).

People who are lactose intolerant can usually safely consume yogurt without experiencing abdominal distress. Special types of bacteria added to some yogurts (e.g., bifidobacteria) may colonize the large intestine and provide health benefits. Research in this area is still controversial.

Eating a 6-ounce container of yogurt is equivalent to drinking 1 cup of milk. As with other dairy products, choose the low-fat varieties and enjoy throughout the day with breakfast cereals or as a snack or dessert.

Serving suggestions

Always keep a container of low-fat plain yogurt in the fridge, trying different brands until you find one you like. It's a great base for dips, salad dressings, and sauces—sweet and savory.

- Serve chicken salad with a yogurt dressing made from a 6-ounce container of low-fat plain yogurt, 2 tablespoons of lemon juice, a couple of teaspoons of a tangy mango chutney, and 2 tablespoons of finely chopped mint.
- Spice plain yogurt with a little ground cumin and cardamom to make a sauce for topping burgers or falafel rolls. Add fresh mint for a finishing touch.
- Make a spicy Indian "lassi" drink by blending 1 cup of low-fat plain yogurt with ½ teaspoon of ground cumin and a pinch of salt to taste. Chill. Just before serving, stir in ¼ teaspoon of finely minced onion and a few strips of finely sliced green chili. Pour into a tall glass over ice cubes and serve—delicious as an appetizer before an Indian meal.
- For a sweeter taste, mango lassis are a meal in a glass or a delicious way to finish a spicy dinner. You can make this lassi in about 5 minutes by combining in a blender 1½ cups of diced mango with ½ cup of freshly squeezed orange juice, ½ cup of ice cubes, 1 tablespoon of honey or a little more to taste, and 1 teaspoon of rosewater if you have it. Process for about 30 seconds until the ingredients are just blended. Add 1½ cups of low-fat plain yogurt and blend for another 30–40 seconds until it's frothy. Makes 4 cups.

PART FOUR

Low GI Made Easy Tables

*H*ere's your easy and reliable reference to the GI of foods. Use these tables to choose the best carbs for your health and to enjoy low-GI foods every meal, every day.

Remember, it is carb quality that counts.

We have categorized the foods A to Z under the following headings:

- Bakery products—including cakes and muffins
- Beans, peas, and lentils—including split peas, chickpeas, and baked beans
- Beverages—including fruit and vegetable juices, soft drinks, flavored milk, and sport drinks
- Cookies—including savory crispbreads and plain crackers

- Bread—including sliced white and whole wheat bread, fruit breads, flat breads
- Breakfast cereals—including processed cereals, muesli, oats, and oatmeal
- Cereal grains—including couscous, bulgur, barley
- Dairy products—including milk, yogurt, ice creams, and dairy desserts and soy products
- Fruits—including fresh, canned, and dried fruit
- Miscellaneous—including various fast foods
- Pasta, noodles, and rice
- Snack foods—including muesli bars, candy, and nuts
- Sweeteners and spreads—including sugars, honey, jam
- Vegetables—including green vegetables, salad vegetables, root vegetables

Foods that meet the strict nutritional criteria of the GI Symbol Program are indicated Ⓖ.

All you need to do for everyday low GI eating is make **MOST** of your carbohydrate choices from the **EVERYDAY** food, taking into account the serving sizes shown. Remember, larger servings will increase the glycemic load of the food and may change its ranking.

Note: We have organized the **EVERYDAY** foods into those you can eat according to your appetite and those where you need to exercise a bit of restraint and some sensible portion caution.

EVERYDAY foods

These "eat according to your appetite" foods have a **low GI** and a **low GL** (depending on how much you put on your plate). They are slowly digested, long-lasting foods, which are the best sources of sustained energy. Their low GI gives them a high satiety factor, which means you can eat them according to appetite. Some of your **EVERYDAY** foods—multigrain bread, fresh fruit, low-fat yogurt, split peas, soy beans, rolled oats, honey, and sourdough bread.

EVERYDAY CAUTION WITH PORTION foods

These foods have a moderate or low GI and a moderate to high GL, again, depending on your serving size. They're great sources of carbohydrate but it's sensible to give some thought to the quantity of these foods, because of their potential to have a high GL if you overload your plate or go back for seconds or thirds. Some of your **EVERYDAY CAUTION WITH PORTION** foods—fruit juices, noodles, pasta, rice, soft drinks, flavored milks, fruit breads, muesli bars, raisins

OCCASIONAL foods

These foods have high GI values but a moderate GL. Their high GI makes them rapidly digested and much less satisfying than the **EVERYDAY** foods so keep them occasional. Some foods that are higher in saturated fat have also been included in this group. Some of your **OCCASIONAL** foods—potatoes, crackers, and processed cereals.

SAVE FOR A TREAT foods

These are high GI and high GL or are high in saturated fat. Many of them are common foods in our American diet but by stimulating blood glucose and insulin spikes they contribute to our risk of obesity, diabetes, and heart disease. Don't be fooled by the low-fat nature of some of them! Some of your **SAVE FOR A TREAT** foods—puffed cereals, white bread, bagels, jelly beans, chocolate.

BAKERY PRODUCTS

Everyday foods	Everyday caution with portion foods	Occasional foods	Save for a treat foods
	Apple muffin, home-made 2 ounces	Angel food cake, plain 1¾ ounces	Banana cake, home-made 2¾ ounces
		Bran muffin, commercially made 4½ ounces	Blueberry muffin, commercially made 4½ ounces
		Carrot cake, commercially made 4½ ounces	Chocolate cake, made from packaged mix with frosting, Betty Crocker 4 ounces
		Crumpet, white 1¾ ounces	
		Scones, plain, made from package mix 1¾ ounces	Croissant, plain 2 ounces
			Cupcake with strawberry icing 1½ ounces
		Sponge cake, plain, unfilled 2¼ ounces	
		Waffles, plain 1¾ ounces	Oatmeal muffin, made from packaged mix, 2 ounces
			Pound cake, plain, Sara Lee 1¾ ounces
			Vanilla cake made from packaged mix with vanilla frosting, Betty Crocker 4 ounces

BEANS, PEAS, AND LENTILS

Everyday foods	Everyday caution with portion foods	Occasional foods	Save for a treat foods
Baked beans, canned in tomato sauce, Heinz ⅔ cup	Black-eyed beans, soaked, boiled ⅔ cup		
Black beans, boiled ⅔ cup	Fava beans ⅓ cup		
White beans, canned, drained ⅓ cup	Haricot beans, cooked, canned ⅔ cup		
Butter beans, canned, drained ⅓ cup	Kidney beans, red, canned, drained ⅔ cup		
Butter beans, dried, boiled ⅔ cup			
Cannellini beans ⅓ cup			
Chickpeas, canned ⅔ cup			
Chickpeas, dried, boiled ⅔ cup			
Dark red kidney beans, canned, drained ⅔ cup			
Four bean mix, canned, drained ⅓ cup			
Green lentils, canned ¼ cup			
Green lentils, dried, boiled ¼ cup			
Haricot beans, dried, boiled ⅔ cup			
Kidney beans, red, dried, boiled ⅔ cup			
Lima beans, baby, frozen, reheated ⅔ cup			
Mung beans ⅔ cup			
Peas, dried, boiled ⅔ cup			

Beans, Peas, and Lentils, *continued*

Everyday foods	Everyday caution with portion foods	Occasional foods	Save for a treat foods
Red lentils, dried, boiled ⅔ cup			
Soy, canned, drained ⅔ cup			
Soybeans, dried, boiled ⅔ cup			
Split peas, yellow, boiled 20 mins ⅔ cup			

BEVERAGES

Everyday foods	Everyday caution with portion foods	Occasional foods	Save for a treat foods
Apple juice, cloudy, no added sugar 1 cup Ⓖ	Apple and Black-currant juice, pure 1 cup	Gatorade sports drink 1 cup	Nestlé's Quik in whole milk 1 cup Ⓖ
Carrot juice, freshly made 1 cup	Apple and Cherry; Apple and Man-darin; Apple and Mango; Apple juice, clear, no added sugar; Apple, Pineapple and Passionfruit juice 100% juice 1 cup		Malted Milk Powder, Nestlé, in whole milk 1 cup
Coffee, black, no milk or sugar 1 cup			
Diet soft drinks 1 cup			
Nestlé's Quik pow-der in skim or low-fat milk 1 cup Ⓖ			
Nestlé's Quik pow-der, Chocolate or Strawberry, in low-fat milk 1 cup	Apple juice, no added sugar 1 cup		
Soy Smoothie Drink, Banana low-fat 1 cup	Coca-Cola, soft drink 1 cup		
Tomato juice, no added sugar 1 cup	Cranberry Juice Cocktail, Ocean Spray 1 cup		
	Ensure, vanilla drink 1 cup		
	Fanta, orange soft drink 1 cup		
	Granny Smith apple juice, unsweet-ened, 1 cup		
	Grapefruit juice, unsweetened 1 cup		
	Malted powder in low-fat milk 1 cup		
	Malted powder in skim or low-fat milk 1 cup Ⓖ		
	Orange juice, unsweetened 1 cup		
	Orange juice, unsweetened, from concentrate, 1 cup		

Beverages, *continued*

Everyday foods	Everyday caution with portion foods	Occasional foods	Save for a treat foods
	Pineapple juice, unsweetened 1 cup		
	Prune juice, unsweetened 1 cup		
	Slim-Fast Drink, can, vanilla or chocolate 1⅓ cups		
	Slim-Fast Drink powder, all flavors, made with skim milk ¾ cup		

COOKIES AND CRACKERS

Everyday foods	Everyday caution with portion foods	Occasional foods	Save for a treat foods
Ryvita crispbread 1 ounce	Milk Arrowroot biscuits 1 ounce	Digestive cookies, plain 1 ounce	Breton wheat crackers 1 ounce
Ryvita Original Rye crispbread 1 ounce	Shredded whole wheat biscuits 1 ounce	Kavli Norwegian crispbread 1 ounce	Plain salted cracker 1 ounce
Ryvita Sesame Original Crispbread 1 ounce		Rice cakes, puffed, white, 1 ounce	Shortbread cookie 1 ounce
Whole-grain fruit bar, all flavors 1 ounce		Rich Tea biscuits 1 ounce	
Fruit Roll, Apple and Berry or Apple and Raisin 1¼ ounces		Plain crackers 1 ounce	
Stoned Wheat Thins, crackers 1 ounce		Wafer cookies, vanilla, plain 1 ounce	
		Water crackers, plain 1 ounce	

BREAD

Everyday foods	Everyday caution with portion foods	Occasional foods	Save for a treat foods
Cinnamon raisin bread, grainy, or whole grain 1 slice	Multigrain sandwich bread 1 slice	Black rye bread 1 slice	Bagel, white, small 2½ ounces
Dia-beat-it whole sprouted grain diabetic bread, Silver Hills Bakery 1 slice	Pita bread, white 1 4-inch pocket	Bun, hamburger, white 1¾ ounce	Baguette, white 1 ounce
Fruit & muesli bread 1 slice Ⓖ	Raisin toast 1 slice	Gluten-free multi-grain bread 1 slice	Lebanese bread, white 1 slice
Flaxseed and soy bread, 1 slice		Dark rye bread 1 slice	Light rye bread 1 slice
9-Grain bread 1 slice		White bread, regular sliced 1 slice	Melba toast, plain 1 slice
9-Grain muffins, small 2⅓ ounces		Stuffing, bread 1 ounce	
Pumpernickel bread 1 slice		Wonder white bread 1 slice	
Rye bread, whole grain 1 slice			
Sourdough bread, organic, stone-ground, whole wheat 1 slice			
Sourdough rye bread 1 slice			
Sourdough wheat bread 1 slice			
Spelt multigrain bread 1 slice			
Sunflower and Barley bread 1 slice			

BREAKFAST CEREALS

Everyday foods	Everyday caution with portion foods	Occasional foods	Save for a treat foods
All-Bran, Kellogg's ½ cup	Froot Loops, Kellogg's 1 cup	Bran Flakes, Kellogg's ¾ cup	Corn Pops, Kellogg's 1 cup
All-Bran Fruit 'n' Oats, Kellogg's ½ cup	Frosted Flakes, Kellogg's ¾ cup	Coco Pops, Kellogg's 1 cup	Crispix, Kellogg's 1 cup
Muesli, gluten-free 1½ cups	Mini Wheats, Whole Wheat, Kellogg's 2 biscuits	Corn Flakes, Kellogg's 1 cup	Rice Krispies, Kellogg's 1¼ cups
Oat bran, raw, unprocessed 2 tablespoons	Muesli, Natural ¼ cup	Honey Smacks, Kellogg's 1 cup	
Rolled Oats, raw ½ cup	Muesli, toasted ¼ cup	Oatmeal, instant, made with water ½ cup	
Oatmeal, made from steel-cut oats with water, raw ¼ cup	Muesli, Swiss formula, ¼ cup	Puffed Wheat ½ cup	
Oatmeal, multigrain, made with water, ¼ cup	Nutri-Grain, Kellogg's ¾ cup	Shredded Wheat 2 biscuits	
Oatmeal, old-fashioned, made from oats with water ½ cup	Special K, regular, Kellogg's 1 cup	Raisin Bran, Kellogg's ½ cup	
Puffed buckwheat cereal 1 cup			

CEREAL GRAINS

Everyday foods	Everyday caution with portion foods	Occasional foods	Save for a treat foods
Barley, pearl, boiled 1 cup	Barley, rolled, dry ¼ cup		Millet, boiled 1 cup
Semolina, cooked 1 cup	Buckwheat, boiled 1 cup		
	Cornmeal (polenta), boiled ⅔ cup		
	Couscous, boiled 5 mins 1 cup		
	Quinoa, organic, dry ¼ cup		
	Oatmeal, dry ½ cup		
	Rye, dry ¼ cup		
	Wheat, cracked, bulgur, ready to eat 1 cup		
	Whole wheat kernels, dry ¼ cup		

DAIRY PRODUCTS—
ICE CREAM, CUSTARD, AND DESSERTS

Everyday foods	Everyday caution with portion foods	Occasional foods	Save for a treat foods
Chocolate mousse, diet 2 ounces			Custard, home-made from milk, wheat starch, and sugar 3½ ounces
Custard, vanilla, reduced fat 3½ ounces			French Vanilla ice cream, full-fat 1¾ ounces
Ice Cream, Light and low-fat, choco-late or vanilla 1¾ ounces			Ice Cream, Regular, full-fat, average of several types 1¾ ounces
Vanilla custard, reduced fat, 3½ ounces			Pudding, chocolate, instant, made from packaged mix with whole milk 3½ ounces
			Pudding, vanilla, instant, made from packaged mix with whole milk 3½ ounces
			Chocolate ice cream, premium 1¾ ounces

DAIRY PRODUCTS—MILK
AND ALTERNATIVES

Everyday foods	Everyday caution with portion foods	Occasional foods	Save for a treat foods
Milk with omega-3 1 cup			Condensed milk, sweetened, full-fat 1¾ fluid ounces
Milk, low-fat, chocolate, with aspartame 1 cup			Rice milk, 1 cup
Milk, low-fat, chocolate, with sugar 1 cup			Whole milk 1 cup
Original soy milk, full fat 1 cup			
Skim, nonfat milk 1 cup			
Soy milk, reduced-fat, calcium-fortified 1 cup			
2%, low-fat milk 1 cup			
1% low-fat milk, 1 cup			

DAIRY PRODUCTS—YOGURT

Everyday foods	Everyday caution with portion foods	Occasional foods	Save for a treat foods
Diet yogurt, low-fat, no added sugar, vanilla or fruit 6 ounces	Soy yogurt, low-fat with sugar and fruit 7 ounces		
Drinkable yogurt, no fat with sugar, vanilla or fruit 5 fluid ounces			
Yogurt, all natural 99% fat free, plain natural, 6 ounces			
Yogurt, low-fat with sugar and fruit, all flavors 6 ounces			

FRUIT—CANNED

Everyday foods	Everyday caution with portion foods	Occasional foods	Keep for a treat foods
Fruit cocktail 4¼ ounces	Apricots, canned in light syrup 4¼ ounces		
Peaches, canned, in heavy syrup 4¼ ounces			
Peaches, canned, in light syrup 4¼ ounces			
Peaches, canned, in natural juice 4¼ ounces			
Pear halves, canned, in natural juice 4¼ ounces			
Pear halves, canned, in reduced-sugar syrup 4¼ ounces			

FRUIT—DRIED

Everyday foods	Everyday caution with portion foods	Occasional foods	Save for a treat foods
Apple, dried 2 ounces	Cranberries, dried, sweetened 1½ ounce		
Apricots, dried 2 ounces	Dates, Arabic, dried, vacuum-packed 2 ounces		
Prunes, pitted, Sunsweet 2 ounces	Figs, dried 2 ounces		
	Raisins 2 ounces		

FRUIT—FRESH

Everyday foods	Everyday caution with portion foods	Occasional foods	Keep for a treat foods
Apple, fresh 4¼ ounces	Banana, raw 4¼ ounces		
Apricots, fresh 6 ounces	Breadfruit 4¼ ounces		
Avocado 4¼ ounces	Watermelon, raw 4¼ ounces		
Cherries, dark, raw 4¼ ounces			
Montmorency frozen tart cherries, 2½ ounces			
Cherimoya, fresh, flesh only 4¼ ounces			
Figs 1¾ ounces			
Grapefruit, fresh 4¼ ounces			
Grapes, fresh 4¼ ounces			
Kiwi fruit, fresh 4¼ ounces			
Lemon 1½ ounces			
Lime 1½ ounces			
Mango, fresh 4¼ ounces			
Orange, fresh 4¼ ounces			
Papaya, fresh 4¼ ounces			
Peach, fresh 4¼ ounces			
Pear, fresh 4¼ ounces			
Pineapple, fresh 4¼ ounces			
Plum, raw 4¼ ounces			
Raspberries 2 ounces			
Cantaloupe, fresh 4¼ ounces			
Strawberries, fresh 4¼ ounces			

MISCELLANEOUS—FAST FOOD

Everyday foods	Everyday caution with portion foods	Occasional foods	Save for a treat foods
Consommé, clear, chicken or vegetable 8 fluid ounces	Black bean soup, canned 8 fluid ounces	Pumpkin soup, Creamy, Heinz 10 fluid ounces	Chicken nuggets, frozen reheated in microwave 5 mins 3½ ounces
Lentil soup, canned 8 fluid ounces	Green pea soup, canned 8 fluid ounces		Pizza, Super Supreme, thin and crispy, Pizza Hut 3½ ounces
Minestrone soup, Traditional, Campbell's 8 fluid ounces	Fish sticks 3½ ounces		Pizza, Vegetarian Supreme, thin and crispy, Pizza Hut 2½ ounces
Tomato soup, canned, reconstituted 8 fluid ounces	Lean Cuisine, French-style Chicken with Rice 14 ounces		Pizza, Super Supreme, pan, Pizza Hut 4½ ounces
	Macaroni and cheese, made from packaged mix, Kraft 6¾ ounces		
	Split pea soup, canned 8 fluid ounces		
	Sushi, salmon 3½ ounces		
	Veggie Burger, McDonald's 8 ounces		

PASTA

Everyday foods	Everyday caution with portion foods	Occasional foods	Keep for a treat foods
	Instant noodles, 99% fat free, 2¾ ounces		Instant noodles, regular, 2¾ ounces
	Capellini pasta, white, boiled 6½ ounces		Corn pasta, gluten-free, boiled 6½ ounces
	Fettuccine, egg, boiled 6½ ounces		Rice and corn pasta, gluten-free 6½ ounces
	Gnocchi, cooked, 6½ ounces		Rice pasta, brown, boiled 6½ ounces
	Linguine pasta, thick, durum wheat, boiled 6½ ounces		
	Linguine pasta, thin, durum wheat, boiled 6½ ounces		
	Macaroni, white, durum wheat, boiled 6½ ounces		
	Mung bean noodles (Lungkow bean thread), dried, boiled 6½ ounces		
	Pasta, protein-enriched, boiled 5¼ ounces		
	Ravioli, meat-filled, durum wheat flour, boiled 6½ ounces		
	Rice noodles, dried, boiled 6½ ounces		
	Rice noodles, fresh, boiled 6½ ounces		
	Rice vermicelli, dried, boiled, Chinese 6½ ounces		
	Soba noodles, instant, served in soup 6½ ounces		

Everyday foods	Everyday caution with portion foods	Occasional foods	Keep for a treat foods
	Spaghetti, gluten-free, canned in tomato sauce, 7¾ ounces		
	Spaghetti, gluten-free, rice and split pea, canned in tomato sauce 7¾ ounces		
	Spaghetti, protein-enriched, boiled 6½ ounces		
	Spaghetti, white, durum wheat 6½ ounces		
	Spaghetti, whole wheat, boiled 6½ ounces		
	Spirali pasta, white, durum wheat 6½ ounces		
	Star pastina, white, boiled 6½ ounces		
	Tortellini, cheese, boiled 6½ ounces		
	Udon noodles, plain 6½ ounces		
	Vermicelli, white, durum wheat, boiled 6½ ounces		

RICE

Everyday foods	Everyday caution with portion foods	Occasional foods	Save for a treat foods
Rice bran, extruded 2 tablespoons	Basmati rice, white, boiled, 1 cup		Broken rice, Thai, white, cooked in rice cooker 1 cup
	Rice, brown 1 cup		
	Rice, white, boiled 1 cup		Rice, brown, medium-grain, boiled 1 cup
	Long-grain rice, white, boiled 15 mins 1 cup		Rice, white, medium-grain, boiled 1 cup
	Wild rice, boiled 1 cup		Glutinous rice, white, cooked in rice cooker 1 cup
			Instant rice, white, cooked 6 mins with water 1 cup
			Jasmine rice, white, long-grain, cooked in rice cooker 1 cup
			Parboiled rice 1 cup
			Rice, brown, boiled 1 cup
			Risotto rice, Arborio, boiled 1 cup
			Quick rice, boiled 1 cup

SNACK FOODS

Everyday foods	Everyday caution with portion foods	Occasional foods	Save for a treat foods
Low-fat frozen fruit dessert, 3½ ounces	Apricot-filled fruit bar, whole wheat pastry, 1¾ ounces	M&M's, peanut 1 ounce	Cadbury's milk Chocolate, plain 1 ounce
Gelati, sugar-free, chocolate or vanilla, 3½ ounces	Cashew nuts, 1 ounce	Pretzels, oven-baked, traditional wheat flavor 1 ounce	Chocolate, milk, plain, Nestlé 1¾ ounces
Ironman PR bar, chocolate 2¼ ounces	Marshmallows, plain white ¾ ounce	Rice Krispie Treat bar, Kellogg's 1 ounce	Chocolate, milk, plain, reduced-sugar 1 ounce
Dried fruit snack ½ ounce Ⓖ	Muesli bar, chewy, with choc chips or fruit 1 ounce		Chocolate, milk, plain, regular 1¾ ounces
Chocolate Charger Nutrition Bar 1½ ounces	Muesli bar, crunchy, with dried fruit 1 ounce		Chocolate, milk, plain, with fructose instead of regular sugar 1 ounce
Berry Bliss Nutrition Bar 1½ ounces	Pancakes, prepared from package mix, 2½ ounces		Corn chips, plain, salted 1¾ ounces
Peanut Power Nutrition Bar 1½ ounces	Peanuts, roasted 1¾ ounces		Dark chocolate, plain, regular 1 ounce
Mint Mania Nutrition Bar 1½ ounces	Pecan nuts, raw 1¾ ounces		Dove, milk chocolate 1¾ ounces
	Popcorn, plain, cooked in micro-wave ¾ ounce		Gummi Bears, made with glucose syrup 1¾ ounces
	Power Bar, choco-late 2¼ ounces		Jelly beans 1 ounce
	Taco shells, corn-meal-based, baked 1½ ounces		Licorice, soft 2 ounces
	Nondairy, frozen fruit dessert 3½ ounces		Life Savers, pepper-mint 1 ounce
			Mars Bar, regular 2 ounces
			Plain white choco-late, Nestlé 1¾ ounce
			Chocolate bar, Nestlé 2 ounces

Snack Foods, *continued*

Everyday foods	Everyday caution with portion foods	Occasional foods	Save for a treat foods
			Pancakes, buck-wheat, gluten-free, made from packaged mix 2¾ ounces
			Pop-Tarts, Double Chocolate 1¾ ounces
			Fruit bar, strawberry 1 ounce
			Rice Krispie Treat bar, Kellogg's 1 ounce
			Roll-ups, processed fruit snack 1 ounce
			Skittles 1¾ ounces
			Snickers bar, regular 2 ounces
			Twix bar 2 ounces

SWEETENERS AND SPREADS

Everyday foods	Everyday caution with portion foods	Occasional foods	Save for a treat foods
100% Fruit jam, all flavors, 2 tablespoons ⓖ	Golden syrup 2 tablespoons		
Apricot fruit spread, reduced-sugar 2 tablespoons	Honey, commercially blended 2 tablespoons		
Fructose, pure 1 teaspoon	Maple flavored syrup 2 tablespoons		
Hummus, regular 2 tablespoons	Marmalade, orange 2 tablespoons		
Jam, strawberry, regular 2 tablespoons	Sugar 2 tablespoons		
Maple syrup, pure, Canadian 2 tablespoons			
Nutella, hazelnut spread 2 tablespoons ⓖ			

VEGETABLES

Everyday foods	Everyday caution with portion foods	Occasional foods	Save for a treat foods
Alfalfa sprouts ¼ ounce	New potato, canned 5¼ ounces	Potato, peeled, boiled 5¼ ounces	French fries, frozen, reheated in micro-wave 5¼ ounces
Artichokes, globe, fresh or canned in brine 2¾ ounces	Pumpkin 2¾ ounces	Instant mashed potato 5¼ ounces	
	Sweet potato, baked 5¼ ounces	New potato, unpeeled and boiled 5¼ ounces	
Asparagus 3½ ounces	Yam, peeled, boiled 5¼ ounces		
Bean sprouts, raw ½ ounce		Parsnips 2¾ ounces	
Beets, canned 2¾ ounces		Potato, peeled, microwaved 5¼ ounces	
Bok choy 3½ ounces		Potato, peeled, boiled, whole or mashed 5¼ ounces	
Broccoli 2 ounces			
Brussels sprouts 3½ ounces			
Cabbage 2½ ounces			
Pepper 2¾ ounces			
Carrots, peeled, boiled 2¾ ounces			
Cauliflower 2 ounces			
Celery 1½ ounces			
Cucumber 1½ ounces			
Eggplant 3½ ounces			
Endive 1 ounce			
Fennel 3 ounces			
Green beans 2½ ounces			
Leeks 2¾ ounces			
Lettuce 1¾ ounces			
Mushrooms 1¼ ounces			
Onions 1 ounce			
Peas, green, frozen, boiled 2¾ ounces			
Radishes ½ ounce			
Rhubarb 4½ ounces			

Everyday foods	Everyday caution with portion foods	Occasional foods	Save for a treat foods
Arugula 1 ounce			
Shallots ⅓ ounce			
Snowpea sprouts ½ ounce			
Spinach 2¾ ounces			
Squash, yellow 2½ ounces			
Sweet corn, on the cob, boiled 2¾ ounces			
Sweet corn, whole kernel, canned, drained 2¾ ounces			
Taro 5¼ ounces			
Tomato 5¼ ounces			
Turnip 4¼ ounces			
Watercress ¼ ounce			
Zucchini 3½ ounces			

Acknowledgments

*I*n thanking colleagues who have helped us with this book, we would like to single out Hachette Livre's publishing and production director, Fiona Hazard, for making it all "so easy," and our editor, Jacquie Brown, for her attention to detail and eye for consistency.

We wanted to create special Low-GI Eating Made Easy tables to make it really easy for readers to choose healthy low GI foods, and we could not have done so without the cheerful efforts and database wizardry of Associate Prof. Gareth Denyer at the University of Sydney.

We would also like to thank Johanna Burani, whose suggestions for the U.S. edition of The Top 100 Foods we have incorporated into this book; Gareth Hughes, who keeps us up to date with the GI Symbol Program; and Kate Marsh, who checked the information on PCOS for us.

Further Resources

FOR FURTHER INFORMATION ON GI

www.glycemicindex.com

This is the University of Sydney's glycemic index Web site, where you can learn about GI and access the GI database which includes the most up-to-date listing of the GI of foods that have been published in international scientific journals.

www.gisymbol.com.au

The Glycemic Index (GI) Symbol Program is a food labeling program with strict nutritional criteria that aims to help people make informed food choices. The site includes a complete list of foods carrying the GI symbol.

FOR INFORMATION ON

Food labeling and food additives
FDA's Office of Nutritional Products, Labeling, and Dietary Supplements (ONPLDS), part of the Center for Food Safety and Applied Nutrition
www.cfsan.fda.gov

Finding a dietitian
American Diabetes Association (ADA)
www.eatright.org

Diabetes
American Diabetes Association
www.diabetes.org

Heart health
American Heart Association
www.americanheart.org

Index

About the Authors

Kaye Foster-Powell is an accredited practicing dietitian with extensive experience in diabetes management. She provides consulting on all aspects of the glycemic index.

Jennie Brand-Miller is an internationally recognized authority on carbohydrates and health. She is Professor of Human Nutrition at the University of Sydney and president of the Nutrition Society of Australia.

Jennie and Kaye have coauthored 16 books in the worldwide bestselling New Glucose Revolution series, which has sold over three million copies and is changing the way the world views carbohydrates.

Philippa Sandall is an editor and writer who specializes in food, nutrition, health, and lifestyle. She was closely involved in creating the first New Glucose Revolution title with Jennie and Kaye in 1995, *The GI Factor,* and has played an integral role in developing and managing the series.